Anime Studies

Media-Specific Approaches to *Neon Genesis Evangelion*

Edited by José Andrés Santiago Iglesias & Ana Soler Baena

STOCKHOLM
UNIVERSITY PRESS

Published by
Stockholm University Press
Stockholm University
SE-106 91 Stockholm, Sweden
www.stockholmuniversitypress.se

Funding Institution: Spanish Ministry of Science and Innovation. This book was completed as part of the following project: *Exploring new graphic territories from a transdisciplinar perspective. Expanded-field comics, artist hyper-books and contemporary animetic theories* (ref. HAR2016-78215-P).

Supporting Agency: Universidade de Vigo

Note on Romanization

The romanization of Japanese words in this volume follows the modified Hepburn system, with macrons indicating prolonged vowels, except in citations where they appear in standard English, in globally established place names (such as Kyoto) and in proper names, for example, of major publishing houses (such as Kodansha). However, personal names are, without exception, indicated in the Western order, given name preceding surname.

First published 2021
Cover image credit: Tatiana Lameiro-González, José Andrés Santiago Iglesias
Cover designed by Stockholm University Press, Tatiana Lameiro-González and José Andrés Santiago Iglesias
Tables (contents): The author(s)
Tables (graphic design): Tatiana Lameiro-González

Stockholm Studies in Media Arts Japan (SMAJ), ISSN: 2004-1292

ISBN (Paperback): 978-91-7635-167-3
ISBN (PDF): 978-91-7635-164-2
ISBN (EPUB): 978-91-7635-165-9
ISBN (Mobi): 978-91-7635-166-6

DOI: https://doi.org/10.16993/bbp

Suggested citation:
Santiago Iglesias, J. A. and Soler Baena, A. (Eds.). 2021. *Anime Studies: Media-Specific Approaches to Neon Genesis Evangelion*. Stockholm: Stockholm University Press. DOI: https://doi.org/10.16993/bbp. License: CC-BY 4.0

To read the free, open access version of this book online, visit https://doi.org/10.16993/bbp or scan this QR code with your mobile device.

Stockholm Studies in Media Arts Japan

Stockholm Studies in Media Arts Japan (SMAJ, ISSN: 2004-1292) is a peer-reviewed series of monographs and edited volumes published by Stockholm University Press.

SMAJ strives to provide a multidisciplinary forum for research on media and arts associated with Japan, prioritizing investigations of forms, formats, materialities and creative practices. The scope of subjects is broad, including texts, performances and artefacts of various times and social position in a variety of local and transnational cultures.

It is the ambition of SMAJ to place equally high demands on the academic quality of the manuscripts it accepts as those applied by refereed international journals and academic publishers of a similar orientation. SMAJ accepts manuscripts in English.

Laura Moretti, Associate Professor, Japanese Studies, Cambridge University, United Kingdom

Sharalyn Orbaugh, Professor, Asian Studies, The University of British Columbia, Canada

Lukas R.A. Wilde, PostDoc Research Associate, Japanese Studies & Media Theory, Tübingen University, Germany

Titles in the series

1. Galbraith, P. W. (2021). *The Ethics of Affect: Lines and Life in a Tokyo Neighborhood*. Stockholm: Stockholm University Press. DOI: http://doi.org/10.16993/bbn. License: CC-BY 4.0

2. Santiago Iglesias, J. A. & Soler Baena, A. (Eds.). (2021). *Anime Studies–Media-Specific Approaches to Neon Genesis Evangelion*. Stockholm: Stockholm University Press. DOI: https://doi.org/10.16993/bbp. License: CC-BY 4.0

Peer Review Policies

Stockholm University Press ensures that all book publications are peer-reviewed. Each proposal submitted to the Press will be sent to a dedicated Editorial Board of experts in the subject area for evaluation. The full manuscript will be reviewed by chapter or as a whole by at least two external and independent experts.

A complete description of Stockholm University Press' peer-review policies can be found on the website: http://www.stockholmuniversity press.se/site/peer-review-policies/

The Editorial Board of *Stockholm Studies in Media Arts Japan* used an external double-blind peer-review procedure while evaluating this book proposal to maintain the integrity of the authors and the academic merit of the book. The book manuscript was assessed with a single-blind peer-review process. The Board expresses its sincere gratitude towards all researchers involved in this project. The author of the introductory chapter of this book stepped down momentarily from her role as Chair of the Editorial Board during the review process of the book to avoid a conflict of interest.

Recognition for reviewers

Stockholm University Press and the Editorial Board would like to extend a special thanks to the reviewers who contributed to the process of editing this book.

The manuscript was reviewed by the following experts:

Toshio Miyake, Associate Professor, Department of Asian and North African Studies, Ca' Foscari University of Venice, Italy
ORCiD 0000-0002-9078-4288

Joon Yang Kim, Associate Professor, Department of Interdisciplinary Economic Studies, Niigata University, Japan
ORCiD 0000-0003-4615-7073

Contents

List of Figures and Tables

Figures

Tables

Characters

Introduction

Jaqueline Berndt

To begin with a disclaimer, *Anime Studies: Media-Specific Approaches to Neon Genesis Evangelion* is not primarily dedicated to the famous franchise, which started as *Shinseiki Evangerion* directed by Hideaki Anno (b. 1960) on Tokyo TV in 1995–96 and has, over the course of the last 25 years, come to represent anime in the narrower sense against animated movies by 'auteurs' such as Hayao Miyazaki (b. 1941), Mamoru Oshii (b. 1951) and Satoshi Kon (1963–2010). In this volume, the initial TV series of *EVA* (as it is abbreviated hereafter) provides a case for the study of anime as distinct from, while connected to, Animation Studies, and as institutionalized within the humanities via academic societies and scholarly journals, among other things. The overall aim is not to make a claim that might help to establish new university programs, but rather to promote critical balance between the legitimization of studying anime through its service to authoritative disciplines or 'bigger issues,' and the consideration of forms, practices and institutions that have been associated specifically with anime and that have facilitated its global recognizability. Before surveying which aspects of Anime Studies are being foregrounded by each of the 10 chapters, it is first necessary to introduce the discourse on anime that forms the background to this volume. As several chapters touch upon notions of anime in a transcultural way, related specifically to *EVA*'s global spread (see, for example, the beginning of Chapter 6 by Manuel Hernández-Pérez), below the focus will be on the initial Japanese

How to cite this book chapter:
Berndt, J. 2021. Introduction. In: Santiago Iglesias, J. A. and Soler Baena, A. (Eds.). *Anime Studies: Media-Specific Approaches to Neon Genesis Evangelion*. Pp. 1–18. Stockholm: Stockholm University Press. DOI: https://doi.org /10.16993/bbp.a. License: CC-BY 4.0

context. Similar to Chapter 7 by Zoltan Kacsuk, which investigates the landmark role of *EVA* for *otaku* (geek) subculture as articulated by Japanese critics, the foregrounding of Japanese discourse is aimed not at generating Japanological expertise (i.e., using anime as a tool for knowledge about Japan), but complicating, or diversifying, the predominant English-language discourse on anime and illuminating a number of 'blind spots.' Consequently, this Introduction places an emphasis on the first two of the title's three components: the study of anime and the specificity of anime as media. Analytical and interpretative discussion of the third component, *EVA* itself, would go beyond the scope of an introduction and is therefore left to the individual chapters.[1] That said, a summary of the first TV series' plot as well as a list of the main characters and a chart of their interrelations are provided in the Appendix. Chapter 2 by Ida Kirkegaard highlights the contingency of the researcher's primary sources in the case of a globally circulating anime like *EVA*; Chapters 8 and 9 by Olga Kopylova and Selen Çalık Bedir, respectively, address the ensuing franchise with regard to some of its segments.

Popular and academic discourse shows an inclination to use the word *anime* in the sense of 'Japanese animation' (and, in Roman languages, it is often replaced by the latter term). Initially an abbreviation of the Anglicism *animēshon*, it entered Japanese industry jargon in the early 1960s, when programs that would later be identified as anime circulated under the name of TV manga (*terebi manga*). In the late 1970s, anime came to spread among wider audiences along with animated Science Fiction series for young adults, beginning with *Uchū senkan Yamato* (*Space Battleship Yamato* or *Star Blazers*, dir. Leiji Matsumoto and Noboru Ishiguro, 1974–75) (Nishimura 2018: 246). In Japanese today, the word may designate many different things, ranging from animation in a general, transmedial and transcultural sense, to a specific type of animation based on mangaesque drawings, whether manually produced or computer-generated.

1 See also Suvilay (2017) for an excellent textual analysis.

This volume seeks to advocate the study of anime as distinct from Animation Studies, but not in an attempt to privilege the 'Japan' component, which has admittedly played a significant role thus far with regard to both the global dissemination of anime and Japan Studies as its gateway into academia (cf. Napier 2001; Bolton 2002; Lamarre 2002; for an overview, Berndt 2018). Due to anime's turn into an easily recognizable transnational media form, its national specification as "TV animation mainly broadcast in Japan" (Nishimura 2018: 245)[2] or Japanimation (the label under which it was first promoted outside of Japan around 1990) has lost relevance, and so has anime's categorization as a 'genre,' of movies in general or animated movies in particular, something that harks back to non-Japanese distributors and critics (Sano 2011: 77; Clements 2013: 3). The fact that a Film-Studies volume like *The Japanese Cinema Book* (Fujiki & Phillips 2020) still posits anime as a genre (in line with horror, melodrama, yakuza film, etc.) is indicative of an approach from the outside of anime viewership and research. On the inside, anime is conceived rather as media and more closely related to televisual than cinematic culture, up to and including 'new television' (cf. Lamarre 2020).

The use of the term *media* below follows art historian W. J. T. Mitchell and media theoretician Mark B. N. Hansen, who deliberately employ it in the collective singular as a "term capable of bridging, or 'mediating,' the [traditional] binaries (empirical versus interpretive, form versus content, etc.)" (2010: location 41 of 5205), going beyond technical mediums and a prioritizing of single artifacts to include aesthetic forms and social contexts in equal measure and thereby mediations, that is, interrelations. Accordingly, this volume's focus on media specificity is broader than modernist aesthetic notions of medium specificity as associated with the work of Clement Greenberg (1940) or Noël Carroll (1985). Rather, this volume agrees with *Storytelling Industries: Narrative Production in the 21st Century* by Anthony N.

2. Translations from Japanese are all mine.

Smith, who employs the term *medium* in a similar sense as Mitchell and Hansen use *media*. Smith sees both the 'semiotic' and the 'technical' (but not the 'cultural') approach to a given medium undermined by digitization, and he does not play off economics, policies or society against aesthetics either:

> In the media convergence age, a given medium's distinct modes of production, circulation and reception, along with economic models, regulatory systems, and broader socio-cultural attitudes and practices underpinning these processes, can clearly set that medium apart in terms of its narrative constraints and affordances. (Smith 2018: 14)

Media scholar Lukas Wilde distinguishes, albeit for manga, but also applicable to anime, between three dimensions: semiotic-formal (i.e., artifact-oriented), material-technological (related to production, distribution and consumption in the narrow sense) and cultural-institutional dimensions, all with their respective actors and practices (2018: 133). Approaches like these also help to avoid generalizations that lead to simplified juxtapositions between anime and live-action movies, or manga and literature, highlighting instead differentiation within given media according to socio-cultural field and genre, for example.

As a matter of fact, not all animation made in Japan is subsumed under the heading of anime, at least not in Japanese discourse and among researchers like those who form the core of the Japan Society for Animation Studies (JSAS; founded in 1999): critics and historians who have been working outside of academic institutions, clinical psychologists and art-college professors of animation, as well as scholars in Media Studies. Strictly speaking, anime articulates TV and cel, or cel-look, animation in addition to 'Japan.' But, since the 1930s, cel animation has been employed in different ways and formats, with limited and full animation or TV series and movies for theatrical release being by far not the only ones. Pioneer Kenzō Masaoka (1898–1988), for example, used cels to emulate silhouette animation striving for smooth movement and illusion of depth, that is, creating a "cinematic impression" in his 5-minute sequence within *Momotarō: Umi no shinpei* (*Momotarō: Sacred Sailors*, dir. Mitsuyo Seo, 1945, 74 min.) (Sano 2019: 19). In contrast, by tendency, the following are not included in anime even if they are cel-animated: Japanese TV commercials of the 1950s, experimental films of the 1960s by the Animation Group of Three (*Animēshon sannin no kai*) (cf. Morishita 2018), award-winning shorts by independent animators such as Noburō Ōfuji (1900–61) and Kōji Yamamura (b. 1964), fan-cultural reworkings of commercial productions like Anime Music Videos (cf. Brousseau 2020) or animation in video games. 'Anime proper' prioritizes entertaining genre fiction, which is distinguished from *animēshon/animation* as being industrially motivated, highly formulaic and more committed to audience participation than authorial intent. For film scholar Mitsuyo Wada-Marciano, anime is "a commercial term invented and promoted with multiple marketing, targeting, and formatting strategies in Japan and subsequently adapted to a global cultural level" (2010: 244). Jonathan Clements, who authored the most comprehensive English-language history of anime to date, introduces it "as a particular *kind* of Japanese animation, that diverges in the 1970s by fastening itself to other objects and processes, including but not restricted to: foreign interest, transgression, visual cues, merchandising and integration into a media mix" (2013: 1, emphasis in the original). Obviously, anime's media specificity has always included a certain openness, that is, the inclination to go beyond Japan, TV and cel animation.

While Clements regards serial puppet animation on TV as a forerunner of anime due to format (2013: 140), popular discourse clings to cels and limited animation and traces the beginnings of anime back to *Tetsuwan Atomu* (*Astro Boy* or *Mighty Atom*, dir. Osamu Tezuka, 1963–66). Its format of 25-minute-long weekly episodes comprising less than 5,000 cuts formed the standard for animated TV series until the late 1990s and has been increasingly accompanied by feature-length franchise movies. With regard to media specificity as entwining textual with contextual characteristics, anime appears on the whole as an "assemblage of polarized tendencies" (Lamarre 2020: 317). In *The Anime Machine* (2009), Lamarre introduces several central terms related to production technology, most importantly *open compositing* (the variable layering of images enabled by the multiplane camera, which leads, among other things, to anime's characteristic placement of two-dimensional characters in front of apparently deep, three-dimensional backgrounds) and the *exploded view*, where the impression of depth appears from fragments spread across the picture plane instead of central perspective resting on a single vanishing point. This stylistic device was pushed forward by *EVA* and not limited to visuals: "In effect, the superplanar image—which brings multiple planes to the surface—unfolds as a superplanar narrative structure with multiple frames of reference . . ." (Lamarre 2009: 165).

Out of technical and economic constraints TV anime had to make do with immobility and discontinuity in several regards. This gave rise to an aesthetic of the *animetic interval*, as Lamarre calls it, where movement is rather suggested than represented (or fully animated), the visible is not necessarily in sync with the audible and, as seen in *EVA*, gaps and loose ends in narratives entice fan participation. Intervals induce *switching*. Recapitulating the lineage of anime-esque animation, Lamarre sees it arising "from transformations of an apparatus or social technology geared initially towards combining education and entertainment [in the case of *Momotarō: Sacred Sailors*], and then later towards code-switching, and finally towards media-switching" (Lamarre 2020: 322). Thus, compositing and switching connect characteristics of anime texts to exhibition formats and transmedia franchising.

Clearly, anime as media is not confined to the technical medium, or support, of cel animation. Before the introduction of cels in the 1930s, Japanese animation workshops were already engaged in the compositing of images, drawn on paper and held together with glass plates (Lamarre 2020: 314). *EVA* director Anno himself used drawings on paper when he began creating animation on 8-mm film as a student. His first attendance at PAF, the non-profit Private Animation Festival dedicated to amateur productions, in 1979 was crucial in that regard, as he encountered the work of Group Ebisen, to which today's art animator Yamamura and also animated-movie director Sunao Katabuchi (b. 1960) belonged back then. A year later, Anno showed his own animated metamorphoses drawn on paper at PAF, as part of Group Shado's program. It was in retrospect to this experience that he stated, "anime doesn't have to be cel" (Anno 1997: 32), when anime fans rejected the final *EVA* episodes 25 and 26 not only for the narrative turn from robot action to interiority, but likewise for its deviation in medium, using pencil drawings on paper, photos, storyboard pages and so on (Chapter 1 by José Andrés Santiago Iglesias and Chapter 2 by Ida Kirkegaard provide a closer examination of Anno's bold aesthetic choices). At a point in time when Fuji Film, which had supplied celluloid films to Japanese studios since 1934, discontinued its production in 1996, cels and mangaesque drawings were still regarded by fans as indispensable for anime proper. In addition to Anno's personal intention ("I drafted the final episode like that also because I was aiming at liberation from cel anime. Pigheaded anime fans maintain that it is not anime without cels, to my dislike," cited in Igarashi 1997: 45), it is interesting to note that in the pre-war period the medium (i.e., how an animated film was technically made) appeared less important to viewers than how it looked (Nishimura 2018: 59), namely, like a *manga film* (*manga eiga*) due to the entwinement of moving images (*dōga*) with humorous drawings (*manga*). Accordingly, Asia's first feature-length cel-animated movie, the Shanghai-made *Tiĕ shàn gōngzhŭ* (*Princess Iron Fan*, dir. Guchan and Laiming Wan, 1941, 103 min.) was marketed as 'long manga' (*chōhen manga*) upon its Japanese premiere in 1942 (Du 2019: 46–49). At that time, *manga* connoted primarily line drawings that served light-hearted educational stories for children (Nishimura 2018: 103). Animation historian Akiko Sano (2011: 74) describes the manga film as integrating flat, and as such mangaesque, character designs with spatial, by tendency, photorealist backgrounds.

Today, the term 'manga film' is mainly related to Hayao Miyazaki and his self-distancing from 'anime.' Remarkably, he has avoided the name 'animation,' which is favored in the field of art colleges and short-film festivals and is also attached to foreign animation auteurs like Jan Švankmajer and Yuri Norstein. With regard to these two artists, the pioneer of TV anime, Tezuka, reportedly introduced the term 'art animation' in the mid-1980s (Morishita 2018: 294) at around the same time when Miyazaki finished *Kaze no tani no Naushika* (*Nausicäa in the Valley of the Wind*, 1984, 117 min.) and began to label his works 'manga film.' In contrast to animation, 'manga film' suggests a commitment to feature-length narratives and stories which associate Japan. Such association is, however, not necessarily confined to setting and motifs, but it may also include the manga medium. As is well known, Miyazaki adapted Monkey Punch's *Lupin III* manga and furthermore serialized a graphic narrative of his own (*Kaze no tani no Naushika*, in *Animage*, 1982–94). As such, his animated movies already approximate anime, which is known for close ties to *story manga*, with its black-and-white sequences of still, paneled images on paper (cf. Steinberg 2012). But Miyazaki occasionally also employs anime-esque techniques and motifs, such as limited animation and cute 'anime smiles.' Traditional Film Studies publications tend to regard the relation of anime and manga film in Miyazaki's work as succession in a rather teleological way: turning away from TV and its manga-based series, and steering toward auteur movies instead (Greenberg 2018: 61). In actuality, Miyazaki's works occupy less an opposing than an intermediate position, as, for example, instances of collaboration with Anno indicate. Both directors have been acknowledged for their efforts in the mid-1990s to depart from the genealogy of industrial anime albeit with opposite vectors, namely, from without and from within (Igarashi 1997: 11–16). But Anno had also worked as an animator on the giant warriors in *Nausicäa*, and eventually he performed the voice of the protagonist in Miyazaki's *Kaze tachinu* (*The Wind Rises*, 2013, 126 min.). Furthermore, it is the reception of Miyazaki's works abroad that may suggest an intermediary position: "Just as the transnational reproduction, promotion and dissemination of Studio Ghibli's texts worked to spread Miyazaki's cinema as a new kind of art animation, fans have actively embraced that cinema for the resistant and ambiguous subcultural capital that it affords . . ." (Rendell & Denison 2018: 11).

The emphasis on 'animation' in the wider sense or even art animation, which is maintained in Japanese criticism against 'anime,' is primarily a matter of cultural field. But animosity against anime is not limited to Japanese discourse. In her monograph on 'Japanese animation,' film historian Maria Roberta Novielli uses the word anime once, in a footnote (2018: 58), concordant with her preference for experimental short films in the wake of Yamamura. In contradistinction, historians may apply the word anime retrospectively without considering discourse traditions, as is the case with Frederick S. Litten's investigation of early Japanese animation (2017). Much aware of such traditions are Japan Studies scholars Alistair Swale (2015) and Christopher Bolton (2018). But while they include the word anime in the title of their monographs, their actual discussion gives preference to animation auteurs and feature films that are not affiliated with franchises and as such not exposed to the distributive power of TV. Due to their bounded narrative structure and "their higher production standards" (Bolton 2018: 18), such movies appear to recommend themselves to critical intellectual readings, whereas TV anime series invite material (i.e., not ideology-focused) consumption, fan-cultural sharing and affective engagement. It is further noteworthy that recent media-theoretical approaches exercise restraint with regard to the term anime, but for different reasons. An emphasis is put on transnational networks in the age of digitization and "distributive experiences" that relate to "a different economy, a different temporality, a different phenomenology and a different memory structure in the social than the 'classic' model of cinematic spectacle" (Zahlten 2019: 314). Here, anime is conceived "less as a subgenre of animation but an organizing principle" (ibid.: 312). Media practices come to the fore, mediations and modi of "techno-social existence" (Lamarre 2018: 10), and the focus is less on anime than "animation produced via Japan" (Lamarre 2020: 322) in order to escape fixation on both national markets and media specificity. But the fact that the discursive 'nationalizing' of anime (i.e., its ascription to Japan) paradoxically increases in proportion to transnational distribution (Zahlten 2019: 313) may be taken up as a challenge to revisit the media-cultural identity of anime under transmedial and transcultural conditions. The anime-typical assemblage of polarized tendencies could also be discovered in the relation between dissolution and reinforcement of media specificity.

The chapters of this volume present 10 different aspects of Anime Studies, beginning with close attention to textual characteristics in the first half and broadening the scope to include subcultural discourse, genre categorizations, franchising and fandom in the second half. Chapter 1 by José Andrés Santiago Iglesias investigates anime as filmic media and pays special attention to forms of animating movement. Taking its departure from *EVA*'s famous long static shots and the definition of anime in general as limited animation, it demonstrates how immobility and mobility are actually interrelated, and it suggests not to conceptually juxtapose limited and full animation, but rather trace the variable ratio of almost motionless extended cuts and sequences of high-speed editing. In addition to this 'ratio dynamism,' two more aesthetic devices are analyzed: synecdoches that allow for indirect presentation of the main action; and line drawings, whose potential to interconnect without being fully animated is revealed with regard to comics, in particular the interrelation between panels. In Chapter 2 by Ida Kirkegaard, the anime-typical cel bank takes centre stage. Set up for each individual production, this pool of cuts intended for reuse had initially been deemed aesthetically unfavorable, a deficiency just like the immobility due to limited animation, but it developed into a style of its own, as evinced by *EVA*. While Chapter 1 argues against the simple binarism between stillness and movement, Chapter 2 employs bank cuts to question the opposition between repetition and originality, as well as that between fantasy narratives and realism in favor of an assemblage, so to speak, that takes the form of anime-specific realism and leans on viewers' familiarity with a whole set of visual and auditory conventions, intradiegetically as well as intramedially consistent narrative codes, and an audience engagement that oscillates between code recognition and affection. The chapter shows in particular how *EVA* first constructs anime-specific hyperrealism typical of the robot, or more precisely *mecha*, genre and eventually subverts it.

Chapters 3 and 4 explore anime with regard to sound, a dimension that has only recently begun to attract academic attention. In Chapter 3, Heike Hoffer provides a musicological analysis of the use of classical music in anime on the example of Beethoven's 9th and the "Ode to Joy," which plays a central role in *EVA*'s episode 24. Contributing a new aspect to the Anime Studies issue of repetition and 'recycling,' the chapter considers not only the deliberate use of the "Ode to Joy" in the *EVA* narrative (as anticipation of tragic events or dramatization), but also its connotations in contemporary Japan, resting on people's intimate relationship to it, for example, through amateur choirs. Thus, it becomes clear how anime conjoins traditional 'high culture' and contemporary subculture through emotional and social investment. While a discussion of anime music in general and *EVA*'s soundtrack in particular is not part of this volume, Minori Ishida addresses another crucial element of anime in Chapter 4: the voice actor. Her main focus is on gender, or more specifically anime's tradition of having women perform as boy protagonists, and how in the case of *EVA* the intra- and extratextual performance by Megumi Ogata attracted female viewers to robot anime. As distinct from contemporaneous South Korea, the anime media had already significantly matured in 1990s Japan, including a whole media environment that gave rise to voice-actor stardom. From an aesthetic point of view, it is noteworthy how the anime-typical discrepancy between the visible and the audible has changed since *EVA*. Ishida reminds us that precisely the visual dissimilarity between voice actor and anime character has been one of the main attractions for female audiences and an important resource of anime's aesthetic criticality.

Chapter 5 by Stevie Suan introduces anime as a performative media in a different way: It focuses on characters as actors or, more precisely, on how the way characters move creates different notions of selfhood. Whereas traditional *EVA* discourse has, for a large part, engaged in psychoanalytical readings of the characters and male otaku as their core target audience, Suan brings the perspective of environmental humanities into play and applies it to the two main types of character movement in anime, namely, embodied acting and figurative acting. He interprets the former as ultimately promoting an anthropocentric individualist subjectivity, and the latter as a kind of posthumanist objecthood that presents itself toward the end of the *EVA* series, among other things, in the form of characters assembled of parts of other characters.

Chapter 6 by Manuel Hernández-Pérez focuses on genre as a crucial part of Anime Studies. Recapitulating anime's global distribution since the mid-1990s, which has stretched from VHS and DVDs to TV channels and eventually streaming platforms, the chapter illuminates the contingency of genre categorizations, whether demographical (*EVA* as targeted to boys, i.e., *shōnen*) or thematic (*EVA* as Science Fiction, robot and/or *mecha* anime). At the same time, it demonstrates how useful the focus on genre still is, not only with regard to recent marketing tags outside of the domestic Japanese context, but also with regard to identifying differences within anime—instead of homogenizing anime and juxtaposing it, for example, to live-action cinema.

The last four chapters of this volume approach *EVA* and, through it, anime mainly from the perspective of users and their critical or affective engagement. Chapter 7 by Zoltan Kacsuk explains how closely the discursive construction of *EVA* as a landmark anime was tied to the subculture of otaku, introducing an enormous amount of representative Japanese voices and shedding light on a field of criticism located in between academia and fandom, that is typical of popular media in Japan, not only anime. While the chapter is informed more by Fandom Studies than anime research, it points to some important issues with regard to the latter. For example, it illuminates the segmentation of fandoms in the early 1980s, when separate communities emerged around Science Fiction literature, manga and anime and different modes of engagement evolved according to these different objects. It also historicizes the relation between otaku and anime, showing how anime occupied a privileged position especially for the second generation of otaku at a time when anime production, distribution and consumption was not yet extensively digitized. In this context, investigating media-specific approaches to anime on the example of *EVA* recommends itself precisely because *EVA* appealed to a core audience of viewers who were interested in anime's media specificity (and who were disappointed in view of their assumptions being subverted by the final episodes). Reversely, this fact may suggest that the focus on media specificity is outdated.

However, the *EVA* franchise continues unabated, and Chapter 8 by Olga Kopylova may stimulate a discussion of possible reasons for that insofar as it introduces in detail transmedial franchises of narrative texts in its first part, and modes of engagement with them in its second part, taking its departure from a critical discussion of Hiroki Azuma's theory of 'database consumption' (2009 [2001]).[3] Anime is addressed here as a narrative media, open to franchising and adaptation, for example, in manga and games. Differentiating between narrative-driven, (story)world-driven and 'database'-driven franchises on the one hand, and between encyclopedic, forensic and affective modes of fan engagement as ways to enjoy *EVA* as a transmedial franchise on the other, the chapter traces the changing significance of narrative and representational contents for active users through manga adaptations of *EVA*, which, again, are read as indicative of fannish modes of engagement: Apocalypse and trauma are met with striking indifference, while playful practices prevail. This links Chapter 8 to the subsequent Chapter 9, by Selen Çalık Bedir. Similarly interested in narratives, it focuses on anime as gamelike narratives, carving out their particularities in comparison to *EVA* video games. Rather than fannish engagement, it juxtaposes gameplay and narrative consumption, and it examines respective preferences induced from elements such as alternative scenarios and inconsistent causality.

The final chapter, Chapter 10, by Jessica Bauwens-Sugimoto, returns the focus to fans, but fans whose affective engagement with the characters and the textual openness of *EVA* leads to the production of fan fiction, which deserves conceptualization as a media in itself. With its focus on the mainly feminine boys-love fandom, the chapter connects to Ishida's study of voice actors as an attempt to feed gender-conscious perspectives into Anime Studies by paying tribute to other than male actors on the side of both production and consumption. It also connects to the above-mentioned fannish indifference toward *EVA*'s life-and-death issues that have been so prevalent in psychoanalytically informed feminist discussions and in broader otaku discourse. The playfulness of mainly female fans is interpreted

3. As one of the few media-theoretical texts available in English, Azuma features in many chapters of this volume, however, not necessarily in a canonical manner.

as a subversive revelation of the masculine anthropocentric overtone of the *mecha* genre, as well as the tradition of *EVA* reception.

All in all, the chapters of this volume share several concerns across their different emphases, which can be regarded as forms of assemblage: between aesthetic forms and economic constraints, media texts as artifacts and situated media experiences, anime's media-specific identity and media-ecological embeddedness, specific local situations and global flows. All contributions exercise restraint with regard to strictly representational readings of *EVA*, traditionally related to religion (touched upon briefly in Chapter 6), psychoanalysis or the 'lost decade' in Japanese society. As mentioned at the beginning of this Introduction, this volume does not claim to be a comprehensive or authoritative guide to *EVA*. Too many aspects are missing, among which two appear especially vital: the anime-specific economics of *EVA*, from funding to licensing,[4] and the distribution and reception of *EVA* in Asia, the Chinese-language markets to begin with. Yet, it is hoped that the contributions assembled here provide a first step to reconsider anime, media specificity and *EVA*, which may lead to a broader critical discussion.

References

Anno, H. (1997). *Anno Hideaki parano Evangerion* (ed. K. Takekuma). Tokyo: Ohta shuppan.

_____. (2019). "EVA" no na o akuyō shita GAINAX to hōdō ni tsuyoku ikidōru riyū. *Diamond online*, 30 December. Retrieved from: https://diamond.jp/articles/-/224881

Azuma, H. (2009) [2001]. *Otaku: Japan's Database Animals*. Minneapolis: University of Minnesota Press. (Introduction and translation by J. E. Abel & S. Kono).

Berndt, J. (2018). Anime in Academia: Representative Object, Media Form, and Japanese Studies. *Arts*, 7(4), 56. Retrieved from: DOI: https://doi.org/10.3390/arts7040056

4 See Denison 2018; Anno 2019; Denison 2020.

Bolton, C. (2002). From Wooden Cyborgs to Celluloid Souls: Mechanical Bodies in Anime and Japanese Puppet Theater. *positions*, 10(3), 729–771.

_____. (2018). *Interpreting Anime*. Minneapolis: University of Minnesota Press.

Brousseau, J. (2020). "SO MANY FEELS~!" Queering Male Shonen Characters in BL Anime Music. *Synoptique*, 9(1), 95–107.

Carroll, N. (1985). The Specificity of Media in the Arts. *The Journal of Aesthetic Education* 19(4), 5–20.

Clements, J. (2013). *Anime: A History*. London: Bloomsbury.

Denison, R. (2018). Anime's distribution worlds: Formal and information distribution in the analogue and digital eras. In F. Darling-Wolf (ed.), *Routledge Handbook of Japanese Media* (pp. 578–601). New York: Routledge.

_____. (2020). Transmedial relations—Manga at the movies: Adaptation and intertextuality. In H. Fujiki & A. Phillips (eds.), *The Japanese Cinema Book* (pp. 203–213). London: Bloomsbury.

Du, D. Y. (2019). *Animated Encounters: Transnational Movements of Chinese Animation, 1940s–1970s*. Honolulu: University of Hawai'i Press.

Fujiki, H. and Phillips, A. (eds.). (2020). *The Japanese Cinema Book*. London: Bloomsbury.

Greenberg, C. (1940). Towards a New Laocoön. *Partisan Review*, July–August, 296–310.

Greenberg, R. (2018). *Hayao Miyazaki: Exploring the Early Work of Japan's Greatest Animator*. London: Bloomsbury Academic.

Igarashi, T. (ed.). (1997). *Evangerion kairaku gensoku*. Tokyo: Daisan Shokan.

Lamarre, T. (ed.). (2002). Special issue "Between cinema and anime." *Japan Forum*, 14(2), 183–370.

_____. (2009). *The Anime Machine: A Media Theory of Animation*. Minneapolis: University of Minnesota Press.

_____. (2018). *The Anime Ecology: A Genealogy of Television, Animation, and Game Media*. Minneapolis: University of Minnesota Press.

_____. (2020). Anime. Compositing and switching: An intermedial history of Japanese anime. In H. Fujiki and A. Phillips (eds.), *The Japanese Cinema Book* (pp. 310–324). London: Bloomsbury.

Litten, F. S. (2017). *Animated Film in Japan until 1919: Western Animation and the Beginnings of Anime*. Norderstedt: BoD.

Mitchell, W. J. T. and Hansen, Mark B. N. (eds.). (2010). *Critical Terms for Media Studies*. Chicago and London: University of Chicago Press.

Morishita, T. (2018). Shōgyō to geijutsu no aida ni aru kojin seisaku animēshon no ba ni tsuite no kōsatsu: "Animēshon sannin no kai" o tegakari ni. *Nagoya geijutsu daigaku kenkyū kiyō* 39, 287–303. Retrieved from: http://www.nua.ac.jp/kiyou/kiyou2018_2.php?file=/0002%8C%A4%8B%86%8BI%97v%91%E639%8A%AA%81i%98_%95%B6%81j/0019%90X%89%BA%96L%94%FC.pdf&name=%90X%89%BA%96L%94%FC.pdf

Napier, S. (2001). *ANIME from Akira to Princess Mononoke*. New York: Palgrave.

Nishimura, T. (2018). *Nihon no animēshon wa ikani shite seiritsu shita no ka*. Tokyo: Shinwasha.

Novielli, M. R. (2018). *Floating Worlds: A Short History of Japanese Animation*. Boca Raton, FL: Taylor & Francis.

Rendell, J. and Denison, R. (2018). Special Edition Editorial: Introducing *Studio Ghibli*. *East Asian Journal of Popular Culture*, 4(1), 5–14.

Sano, A. (2011). "Animēshon" no meishō no hen'yō to "geijutsusei" nitsuite. *Bijutsu Forum 21*, #24, 73–78.

_____. (2019). Momotarō: Umi no shinpei-ron: Kokusaku animēshon no eizō jikken. *The Japanese Journal of Animation Studies*, 20(1), 17–29.

Smith, A. N. (2018). *Storytelling Industries: Narrative Production in the 21st Century*. Cham, Switzerland: Palgrave Macmillan.

Steinberg, M. (2012). *Anime's Media Mix: Franchising Toys and Characters in Japan*. Minneapolis, MN: University of Minnesota Press.

Suvilay, B. (2017). Neon Genesis Evangelion ou la déconstruction du robot anime, *ReS Futurae: Revue d'études sur la science-fiction*, September. Retrieved from: http://resf.revues.org/954

Swale, A. D. (2015). *Anime Aesthetics: Japanese Animation and the 'Post-Cinematic' Imagination*. New York: Palgrave Macmillian.

Wada-Marciano, M. (2010). Global and Local Materialities of Anime. In M. Yoshimoto et al. (eds.), *Television, Japan, and Globalization* (pp. 241–258). Ann Arbor, MI: Center for Japanese Studies.

Wilde, L. (2018) Character Street Signs (*hyōshiki*): "Mangaesque" Aesthetics as Intermedial Reference and Virtual Mediation. *Orientaliska Studier* #156, 130–150. Retrieved from: https://oriental iskastudier.se › uploads › 2019/01 › Lukas-R.A.-Wilde.pdf

Zahlten, A. (2019). *Doraemon* and *Your Name* in China: The complicated business of mediatized memory in East Asia. *Screen*, 60(2), 311–321.

1. Not Just Immobile
Moving Drawings and Visual Synecdoches in *Neon Genesis Evangelion*

José Andrés Santiago Iglesias

When thinking about anime, stillness is usually pointed out as one of the most defining traits. However, stillness can be used for different reasons (from budget restrictions to aesthetic choices) and in many different ways. *Neon Genesis Evangelion*[1] stands out as a paramount example of how anime employs stillness as a powerful aesthetic and visual narrative device.

First broadcast in Japan in 1995–96, *EVA* became an epoch-making series—and later franchise—with a deep impact on anime culture. Over the years, *EVA* has been praised for its visual innovations. Built upon aesthetic conventions, visual resources and narrative tropes that existed in action-oriented anime series (especially those from the *mecha*[2]—or giant-robot—genre), *EVA* subverted those conventions and rearranged them in a highly novel way. Thus, over the last 25 years, *EVA* has defined new standards for mecha anime in particular.

Many *EVA* viewers—both devoted fans and hardcore haters—immediately acknowledge iconic sequences in which stillness plays a paramount role, whether they opt to praise the director's bold artistic choices or to mock the technical making. The lift sequence, depicting Rei and Asuka, in episode 22; Shinji on the Eva-01, pondering whether or not he should kill Kaworu, in episode 24; and the especially thought-provoking final episodes 25 and 26, are all examples of masterful uses of stillness. Regardless of whether the viewer loves the series or not, these sequences are acknowledged as striking and utterly distinct, often triggering a response of discomfort and alienation,

[1] Henceforth abbreviated as *EVA*.

[2] Science Fiction narratives featuring battles with 'mechanical' devices, usually involving—although not exclusively—giant robots.

How to cite this book chapter:
Santiago Iglesias, J. A. 2021. Not Just Immobile: Moving Drawings and Visual Synecdoches in *Neon Genesis Evangelion*. In: Santiago Iglesias, J. A. and Soler Baena, A. (Eds.). *Anime Studies: Media-Specific Approaches to Neon Genesis Evangelion*. Pp. 19–48 Stockholm: Stockholm University Press. DOI: https://doi.org/10.16993/bbp.b. License: CC-BY 4.0

encouraging a need for resolve. From a visual standpoint, there is a sense of awkwardness in facing long static shots as characteristic of these iconic sequences, as cinema has accustomed the audience to increasingly accelerated montages, and even anime, though it still displays an abundance of static images, tends to compensate this immobility by means of dialogue and sound. Most visual and filmic characteristics of contemporary anime can be understood through *EVA*. In this chapter, I will pay attention to three features broadly used across the TV series which are defined by the dynamics between movement and stillness.

The first feature is what I will call, for the sake of argument, 'ratio dynamism.' As highlighted in the opening statement of this chapter, anime is usually defined in terms of immobility. This notion is connected to anime's origins in 'limited animation,' which has grown into an aesthetic device. From a technical perspective, animation criticism has foregrounded the dichotomy between full and limited animation. The first has been largely identified with Disney's long-feature films, their smooth and fluid motion accomplished through a large number of frames per second (fps) and multiple cels, while the latter has been traditionally singled out as one of the most distinctive features of Japanese anime. However, anime is not just about stillness. Instead, I would argue that anime is defined by the combination of sequences with a variable fps ratio, thus creating a certain sense of rhythm. The fact that anime juxtaposes still images that can last up to a minute, with sequences rendered in complex and smooth (i.e., full) animation, distinguishes it from both low-cost cartoons and Disney-style productions.

In *EVA*, stillness—in close interrelation with sound—is also used as visual trope in the form of synecdoche. Thus, the second feature I will discuss in this chapter is the use of visual and sound synecdoches as narrative devices, as well as the notion of *pars pro toto*, as manifested in some intriguing sequences. I am using 'synecdoche' (a type of metonym) not in the literal sense, as a literary figure of speech, but rather in regard to its underlying function: referring to one element (the part) to represent an entirety (the larger whole), or vice versa, to borrow from the Latin, *pars pro toto* and *totum pro parte*. This idea builds on the argument of non-linguistic metonyms by Roman Jakobson, who is known for the suggestion that "metonymy was the trope that stood at the basis of Realism, of Cubism, and of cinema" (Whitsitt 2013: 28). Moreover, synecdoches often develop as a type of personification by representing human aspects through non-human objects. In *EVA*, many emotionally intense situations actually take place off-screen, while some specific background objects—presented in still frames—relate what is actually happening in the scene.

The notion of visual synecdoches also allows the connection of the first feature of this chapter with the last one, under the heading of 'moving drawings.' The use of synecdoches and metonymic bodily representations (ultimately, metonymy can be understood as an umbrella term for this sort of indexical link) creates visual connections between anime and other media, for example, the pillow-shot in classic Japanese cinema (Burch 1979) and, most significantly, the decompression in comics (Cohn 2007: 15), closely related to McCloud's concept of panel transitions (1993: 72). Many sequences in *EVA* can be described in terms of McCloud's 'aspect-to-aspect' transition, as they let the viewer's eye wander around the scene of action.

Thus, by analyzing different sequences, this chapter will address the role stillness plays as a dramatic resource to build up tension. It will also highlight some of the bold aesthetic choices made in the last two episodes of the series, and demonstrate how motion can be achieved through stillness, relying on cels' displacement, rapid horizontal movement and frame speed. Moreover, I will attempt to explain how instrumental immobility is in *EVA*'s use of synecdoches, and how these visual tropes end up playing a key role in the way the narrative flows. However, in order to do so, it is important to address Marc Steinberg's concept of anime's "dynamic immobility of the image" (2012), as it allows the interconnection of anime and manga.

Stillness in *EVA*

Since his early works in the 1920s, Walt Disney pursued an animation style defined by 'realism,' bespoke technical advancement and refined craftsmanship. During the Golden Age of animation (1934–41), Disney pushed his cartoonists and engineers to reach even higher levels of sophistication, ultimately achieving what is usually regarded as the apex of cel animation, and setting the standards for any future feature-length productions. Disney cartoonists' pursuit of 'realism' is not the opposite to stylized character designs or non-accurate bodily proportions—which are quite usual in many of Disney's cel-animated feature-films—but rather movement: movement understood as the fluidity, smoothness and lifelikeness of motion, allowing drawn characters to drift naturally on screen and acquire a certain sense of weight and physicality. In order to accomplish this, animators used a large number of frames (18 to 30 fps), as well as techniques like rotoscoping, to accurately capture bodily movements. Smooth motion thanks to a high frame rate is the defining trait of 'full animation.' It goes without saying that full animation is not a style exclusive to Disney. Many studios and directors have embraced it. Studio Ghibli's films—and most notably Hayao Miyazaki's internationally acclaimed works—as well as Toei Animation productions, among many others, are examples of the fact that Japanese motion pictures are by no means strangers to full animation.

In its early stages, anime relied almost entirely on limited animation techniques such as the extensive use of still images and a low frame rate (8 to 12 fps), sometimes drawing just the keyframes while omitting the inbetweens (i.e., the intermediate positions). Thus, the combination of still images, in addition to the dynamics between motion and interrupted movement, is what has come to define anime. Characters' jerky movements have often been deprecated as poor and badly rendered, hindering physical mobility. However, according to Steinberg, it is precisely this motion that allows anime series to entice both affective investment and circuits of return (2012: 5).

The distinction between full and limited animation is a recurring topic in academic discussion. It helps to identify many of anime's defining traits. However, setting this distinction in dichotomous terms risks to polarize movement versus immobility. As a result of such polarization—and of McLaren and Disney's dominating assumptions regarding what 'good' animation should be—limited animation has been historically regarded as a lesser version of full animation or, at least, a version that does not meet the artistic expectations of the latter. Notwithstanding, Lamarre, Steinberg and Gan, among others, have promoted a simple, yet important notion: Anime's techniques of limited animation are different, not lesser.

EVA is full of examples of limited animation, from both formal and narrative standpoints. In episode 2, the clever visual juxtaposition between the two POV (point of view) shots of the ceiling—one of the hospital room where Shinji is confined after his first fight with an Angel, and one of his room at home when he recalls the battle of the previous day—consists of a series of still images, followed by a high-speed sequence of different still images played at a rate of one image per frame, to represent how Shinji's faded memories of the fight are quickly coming back (00:17:26). The conversation between Major Katsuragi and NERV Commander Gendō Ikari in episode 6 lasts 21 seconds (00:06:10–00:06:31), but it is entirely comprised of two static shots, and 'animated' by a variation on shot-reverse-shot and cross-dialogue techniques (Professor Fuyutsuki speaking while the screen shows a still image of Major Katsuragi). Shot-reverse-shot, subjective shots and cross-dialogues are well-known cinematic tools, which allow the presentation of a speaker's voice (off-screen) with the listener's emotional reaction (on-screen). Thus, characters are animated, despite the fact that the entire sequence is built on still images alone.

The above example helps in understanding Steinberg's *dynamic immobility of the image*. According to Steinberg, anime is no longer concerned with pursuing a smooth, naturalistic movement; instead, it has grown apart from the dominant cinematic style in animation into a form of its own, ruled by a unique set of rhythms of motion and stillness. In this sense, anime's traditional 'lack of motion' is not to be regarded as a limitation, but as a means to depart from filmic conventions. Steinberg connects anime's specificity to other media—*kamishibai*[3] and, most importantly, manga—which had provided early viewers with the necessary tools to understand that movement can be found in stillness. For Steinberg, this transmedia interrelation of still-but-dynamic images explains anime's potential for setting up connections across media forms as well as media networks (2012: 6–7). Furthermore, he understands the unique dynamism found in manga and *kamishibai* as follows:

> On one hand, this dynamically still image functioned as a kind of aesthetic precursor to anime, allowing spectators to feel the anime image moving and be moved by the image effectively—even if the image was formally immobile. On the other hand . . . manga's development of the techniques for the creation of this dynamically still image provided the toolbox for the development of devices and techniques essential to the production of anime's limited animation. (Steinberg 2012: 33)

Anime uses many techniques to produce movement from still images, like sectioning (animating only a part of the character, such as the mouth or eyes) and high-speed mosaics—in *EVA*, still frames from previous episodes are widely used, playing at 12 fps, very much like the opening of the series itself—but also background displacement and other cinematic effects, such as panning, tilting, traveling, zooming, and focus and out-of-focus sequences. The result is dynamic,

3. Jp. for 'paper theater.'

despite the fact that many episodes present many sequences comprised of long shots of still images. Steinberg highlights the idea that anime presents "unique rhythms of movement and immobility" (2012: 5). However, this notion is mostly focused on the still images themselves, and how they can be utterly dynamic despite their immobility (i.e., not being smoothly animated). In this regard, I would like to expand on the idea of "unique rhythms of movement and immobility," focusing on the alternating ratio of frames per second in contemporary anime.

Ratio Dynamism

In live-action cinema, a long static shot is often deemed as a classic yet risky move, not too closely connected to current filmic language and at times seen as too harsh, in visual terms, for the audience. It is well apparent that in a long static shot, if no striking action is taking place, a few seconds can trigger a sense of estrangement in the viewer, as if time were stretching out and lasting longer than it should. Therefore, a static shot of 5 or even 10 seconds has become quite unusual in today's mainstream cinema. But in any given static shot—be it of a landscape or an empty room—there is always a certain degree of movement, since the image is footage of a real scene: a blade of grass that moves, a change of light in the room, or small objects that drift in the background.

However, this is not the case in *EVA* or any other mainstream anime. Nowadays, anime's 'limited animation' no longer refers to a low number of frames per second, but rather to a variable ratio. Thus, it is not so much that anime is poor in movement, with an average of four or eight frames per second, but rather that it features a still image, sustained for several seconds, and then links it to an elaborate action scene, in which the animation is rendered with 18 or even 24 fps. Stillness is, indeed, one of anime's most defining traits, and these still images can appear very dynamic, but current anime is characterized by combining many different rates with filmic intention, leading to extremely sophisticated and complex animated sequences. This on-demand ratio of frames per second—which I call ratio dynamism—gives a new meaning to Steinberg's notion of movement and immobility, expanding the idea that anime has a unique rhythm. Animation researcher Antonio Horno highlights the involved aesthetic emphasis, as distinct from a more technical approach: "The evolution in anime in the past few years . . . harmonizes the movement of the drawings and balances the number of photograms, thus generating a new aesthetic . . ." (2014: 87). Ultimately, the frame-per-second ratio is nothing but a tool in the hands of the animator (one tool in a vast collection of animation techniques) related to the intended speed, smoothness and fluidity of the motion.

Consequently, anime shall be understood as "a style of animation based on the interruption of motion and the extensive use of still images" (Steinberg 2012: 3). The use of still images enables an impression of movement through a resourceful employment of filmic montage (shot-reverse-shot), dialogues, sound and other auditory elements, and a simplified parallax effect. Furthermore, ratio dynamism could be considered one of the most distinctive traits of contemporary anime. In *EVA*, the wide use of long static shots of one and the same still image answers (beyond production issues) to an aesthetic and narrative need.

Gan (2008) has proposed to speak of 'selective animation.' Her notion is concerned with the animator's choice and highlights the intentionality in choosing still images, 'jerky' movements and limited animation. Thus, 'selective' denotes not only the fact that the filmmaker decides on *what* to move, with techniques such as sectioning[4] or a variable image-per-second ratio, but also *when* to move, stressing the artistic choice, and foregrounding anime's unique rhythm between motion and stillness. However, Gan focuses on the voluntary introduction of stillness, rather than the way in which rhythm and pace

4. Sectioning usually refers to the fact that animators change just one element (like the eyes or the mouth of the character) rather than animating all the nuances of facial expression and other complex movements.

change, that is, technically and conceptually speaking, by means of ratio dynamism.

As jerky movements, stillness and ratio dynamism become some of anime's defining traits, their widespread use applies not only to TV series, but also to film productions (especially those based on franchises). In these latter productions, technical-stylistic features from the original show coexist with some high-budget features, such as the massive use of CGI to animate complex action sequences and elaborate backgrounds and settings. The 2007 theatrical reboot *Evangelion: 1.0 You Are (Not) Alone* mimics one of the original opening scenes from the initial *EVA* series—namely, when Shinji first arrives to Tokyo-3 and expects to meet Misato—matching perfectly almost every shot, but also the variable fps. The backgrounds are extremely detailed, revealing not only the higher budget invested in the movie (as expected in theatrical productions), but also the 12-year time gap between the two productions. However, the distinctive pace of the sequences remains the same, since the variable amount of fps in those scenes is the same.

From a purely technical perspective, the widespread use of ratio dynamism and the generalization of disruptive technologies such as CGI suggest that contemporary anime can be placed—in terms of smoothness and frame rate—halfway between limited and full animation. This hybridity has become common not only in theatrical anime films, OVA[5] and high-budget series for streaming platforms, but also mainstream TV anime series. Steinberg wrote: "Heterogeneity of image styles became the norm within television anime, rather than the exception. For this formal reason it is also not surprising to find that anime producers use 3-D animation in a patchwork style" (2012: 5). CGI allows the use of cinematic camera movements difficult to recreate with usual drawing techniques and rendered entirely 'on ones,'[6] but keeping the traditional cel-look style. Moreover, in contemporary TV anime series, it is not uncommon for

5. OVA, abbreviation of Original Video Animation; films and series to be released directly to home video.

6. A way to understand the fps ratio is to talk about animation 'on ones,' 'twos' or 'threes.' This denomination refers to the number of times a given image is repeated as a frame while creating the illusion of movement. The smoothest motion comes from animation made on ones, meaning that every single frame depicts a different image. Thus, in production with a speed of 24 fps, each second will be composed of 24 different images. 'On twos' means that every image is repeated twice, hence 12 different images per second. Finally, when images are repeated three times—or using a different image for every three frames—it is described as 'threes,' with a ratio of eight images per second. Of course, this ratio can climb as much as the animator wants, eventually arriving at completely still images.

two different speeds to coexist (a variable fps rate of sorts), relying on still images for narrative reasons and eye-catching sequences with a high fps ratio for spectacle, which results in a rich and extremely fluid animation.

In contemporary productions, animators are capable of rendering visually astonishing sequences with an incredible sense of speed and movement by means of 'trade-off.' This technique, as its name suggests, applies to a balance achieved between two desirable but incompatible aspects. In anime, this means a compromise whereby the drawn details (shading, clothing and accessories, and even characters' facial features) are sacrificed in exchange for a dramatic increase in the number of frames, resulting in an extremely smooth motion. Usually handled by the leading animators, these short pieces excel in *sakuga*—especially well-drawn and technically elaborate images—while the secondary team focuses on more mundane and generally less showy parts.

A variable fps rate means that, instead of animating all sequences in the same way with a fixed number of frames (in anime, usually 'on twos' and 'threes'), the amount of images per second is tailored to the narrative nature of the sequence and its specific aesthetic demands. Dialogues, landscapes, moments of reflection and observation by the characters or pillow-shots rely deeply on still images or partial movements (by means of sectioning). On the other hand, quick action sequences and naturalistic depictions of bodily movement usually involve a higher frame rate (18 to 24 pfs).

Anime's so-called limited animation is defined by the extensive use of immobility and decompression, but as a medium anime is also defined by a wide range of topics and complex story lines, the interplay between volume and flatness, complex-built and sophisticatedly rendered world-settings, engaging character designs and a unique drawing style. This style serves as a distinctive trademark, a part of anime's own identity, with a clear aesthetic and narrative purpose.

What was originally born from necessity (as a means of saving time and budget) has evolved into an aesthetically complex way of animating stories. Furthermore, ratio dynamism and stillness—or the tensions between motion and stillness—have become two of anime's major traits, creating movement though different resources, but also allowing for a deep emotional connection with the viewer. For Steinberg, as well as for Lamarre, anime's animation is not defined by immobility, but rather by a different kind of dynamism of the still image. *EVA* perfectly illustrates these tensions, as phenomenal animation sequences coexist with other rather poorly rendered ones. Yet, most importantly, *EVA* shows the aesthetic and narrative potential of the filmic resources in limited animation as only few anime series can, raising the use of stillness and a variable fps ratio to new stylistic heights.

Pars pro toto

At the beginning of this chapter, I presented synecdoche as a type of visual metonym used to refer to a part to represent the larger whole. Yet, I use the notion of synecdoche as a trope in a looser way than cognitive science and semiotics, namely, as a means to convey the idea that many sequences in *EVA*, comprised of still images, make sense despite their seeming limitations. Actually, synecdoches have been largely used in cinema as a narrative device. Chandler states how in filmic media a close-up can be simply considered as a synecdoche:

> Indeed, the formal frame of any visual image (painting, drawing, photograph, film or television frame) functions as a synecdoche in that it suggests that what is being offered is a 'slice-of-life', and that the world outside the frame is carrying on as in the same manner as the world depicted within it. This is perhaps particularly so when the frame cuts across some of the objects depicted within it rather than enclosing them as wholly discrete entities. (2002: 133)

Jakobson and Halle explained how metonymy and synecdoche are both based on contiguity (1956: 95). Synecdoche, as a trope, relies heavily on the audience's logical associations 'filling the gaps' (What is happening off-screen? What are these objects telling me about the ongoing action? What does that sound represent?). In *EVA*, those gaps are easily filled, allowing for a consistent flow of events. However, on closer inspection, the viewer will realize that many clips—lasting several minutes in each episode—are actually arranged as a series of still images, sometimes not even depicting the foreground action, but inferring what is actually happening by means of context and logical association. Sound effects, off-screen dialogues and crossed dialogues help to produce a passing-of-time effect in the face of still images. While the use of sound effects is broadly applicable to the entire audio-visual medium, the other two traits are cleverly used in anime, and quite specifically in *EVA*. For example, at the beginning of episode 24 (00.02.05), Asuka and Shinji have a bitter and quite heated off-screen argument about Kaji's disappearance and likely death. While both characters are screaming at each other, the clip—consisting of four different shots, the first three rendered as still frames and the last one partially animated—provides ambient information apart from the actual action, but sufficiently informative to infer the ongoing situation. The first shot is a wide-angle, still image of the dining room with the coffeemaker on the table; it is followed by a close-up of the very same coffeemaker, another still image of two empty cups on the table and a final shot of the coffee spilled all over the floor. The whole clip is resolved with a fifth shot of Asuka's face, barely animated by means of sectioning (Fig.1.1).

Interestingly, through an ellipsis, the next sequence returns to Asuka a few days later, naked and in a woeful physical and mental condition, having lost her ability to be an Eva pilot and hence her life meaning. Once again, the sequence combines several still images with a close-up of Asuka. As she speaks, her lips move to match with

her voice, but in a limited fashion, by means of repetition and sectioning. Instead of producing a realistic depiction of her mouth (via lip sync), the sequence is confined to three different instances in variation—lips fully opened, fully closed and an intermediate stage—allowing for minimum lip movement with a convincing impression of vocalization (Fig. 1.2).

Figure 1.1. Off-screen argument between Asuka and Shinji at the beginning of episode 24, consisting of four different shots. © khara, inc.

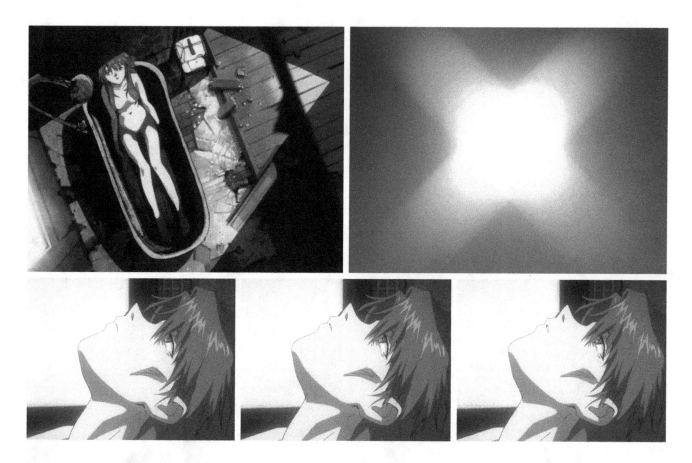

Figure 1.2. Asuka in episode 24, having lost her ability to pilot the Eva 02. As she speaks, the sequence is barely animated by means of sectioning. © khara, inc.

These are just a couple of humble examples of how synecdoche operates in *EVA*, often combined with ellipsis and other narrative tropes. Nevertheless, throughout the whole series, an array of synecdoches frequently appears, many of which allow the tracing of a visual connection from anime to other media.

EVA's episode 24 includes a scene celebrated as one of the most striking, iconic and powerful uses of a still image in anime, portraying Shinji and Kaworu's epic battle, which ends with the death of the latter. As Kaworu reveals himself to be Tabris—the 17th and final Angel—Shinji chases him on the Eva-01 to the Bottom of the Dogma Terminal. At some point, Shinji grabs Kaworu's fragile body—whose appearance is that of a teenager—with the massive fist of the Eva-01, and begins pondering whether he should accomplish his mission and eliminate the threat posed by Kaworu, or refuse to destroy his only friend. Lasting one minute and five seconds (00:21:55–00:23:00), the still image of the Eva-01 holding Kaworu in its hand (Fig.1.3) presents a really bold aesthetic choice. The only sign of the passing time is the soundtrack (analyzed in depth in Heike Hoffer's Chapter 3). In this scene, the still image has a narrative and aesthetic function, but it mostly helps to build momentum and suspense in an attempt to convey Shinji's psyche, the stalemate in which he has to choose between destroying what may be his only friend and saving humanity. Metonymically speaking, it could be argued that in this sequence, the Eva-01 is no longer a machine, but a visual representation of Shinji himself.

Interestingly, this scene is rendered in a simple way, with a quick fade-out to a black screen and a squishing sound, and then Kaworu's severed head falling into the fluid that floods the room. This visual expression responds to a narrative and aesthetic intention, but also to production issues, as it avoids having to draw in detail the beheading. In this regard, the long sequence can be understood as time in pause rather than a frozen image. In the same way that Groensteen (2007) affirms the 'iconic solidarity' between panels in comics (in which one panel modifies the next, and in turn is modified by the preceding one), the one-minute-long still image in episode 24 appears as passing time, because there is a sequence that precedes it and a resolution: the death of Kaworu.

In episode 22, there is another example, the lift scene (Fig.1.4) depicting Rei and Asuka, with no exchange of words. It has often been highlighted as one of *EVA*'s most prominent usages of stillness, but it has also been heavily parodied by fans as an unnaturally lengthy shot. Lasting 53 seconds (00:10:11–00:11:04), most of the time there is a still image with no movement at all, and the passing time is primarily defined by the ambient sound. The only movement that can be felt for almost a whole minute is an occasional blink of Asuka (which

Figure 1.3. In episode 24, the still image depicting the Eva-01 holding Kaworu lasts one minute and five seconds (1'05"). © khara, inc.

does not even involve a complete change of frame as the only animated object is Asuka's eye as it closes and opens again, by means of sectioning), as well as a twitch toward the end of the scene involving a simple modulation of four frames. Ultimately, director Anno's bet on immobility proves successful, as the sequence recreates the social awkwardness of being stuck in a lift with someone you simply don't want to share the room with.

Figure 1.4. The lift scene in episode 22. © khara, inc.

However, as in the previous example, tension created by the almost frozen image in that scene is achieved by means of synecdoche. After arguing, Asuka slaps Rei and leaves in a rush. In actuality, the viewer never gets to see how Asuka slaps Rei, but rather has to infer it from the black fade-off of the image and the sound, which is technically almost identical with the previous example from episode 24. In the next shot, as the tension is already solved, Asuka screams at a standing Rei and leaves in a rush. The invisibility of her action, the black fade and the use of a sound synecdoche again help to avoid drawing a complex scene with elaborate movements involving both characters.

Moving Drawings

Connections between manga and anime are well known to academics and enthusiasts alike. A large number of anime titles originate as adaptations of manga series. Nonetheless, it isn't unusual that a successful anime series leads to the publication of a derived manga work.[7] Such is the case of *EVA*. The original animated series paved the way for several manga spin-offs, as well as fan-created stories in peer-produced publications (*dōjinshi*). The connections between manga and anime pertaining to production, distribution and marketing aspects are obvious. On a formal and aesthetic level, there are many similarities that bind both media. The concept of database coined by Hiroki Azuma (2001), widely applied to anime for the construction of characters, can also easily be applied to the fictional imaginary of manga. Likewise, manga isotypes and morphemes (Cohn 2013), along with the super-deformed and *chibi*[8] versions of characters, have been adopted by anime. However, beyond these obvious similarities regarding conventionalized visual elements, there are abstract connections between manga and anime concerning issues such as rhythm, page layout and montage, some of which become quite clear in *EVA*.

7. Addressed in depth in Olga Kopylova's Chapter 8.

8. A style of caricature where characters are drawn in a comical and exaggerated way, usually depicted with small bodies, short and chubby limbs and oversized heads.

Shinji's shaking hand while he is talking with his father Gendō is a simple yet clever example of synecdoche different from the previous examples. The trembling hand shows his anxiety, but his face remains off-screen while he speaks, because the sequence is more invested in depicting Shinji's awkward relation with his father—and thus his problems with communicating—rather than what he is actually saying. In a similar way, Shinji or Asuka appear in extreme close-up—an odd and rather dramatic framing in cinematic terms—which draws attention to their mouths and leaves their eyes out of the frame. Ultimately, this has a double dramatic effect: on the one hand, highlighting the effort it takes for them to verbalize intimate and personal information; on the other, actively omitting their eyes serves an emotional intent. This form of close-up—choosing to highlight a secondary element, like a body part, rather than the face as a whole—is by no means unique to anime or *EVA*, but is used broadly in cinema. Indeed, as highlighted in the previous section, in filmic media a close-up is but a type of visual synecdoche. However, the abundance of these shots in anime in general and *EVA* in particular is truly noteworthy.

Shots of partially framed faces, feet, hands, legs or any other images of objects and places easily allow the identification of the character to which they refer. Misato and Kaji's sexual encounter in episode 20 (00:19:49) is yet another example of this type of synecdoche (Fig.1.5). The whole sequence consists of a simple array of shots, most of them still images of close-ups and off-action objects. It starts with Misato and Kaji's interlaced hands, followed then by a detail of one of the lights on the ceiling, a framed shot of Misato's legs, an extreme close-up of Kaji's face followed by another extreme close-up of Misato, and a still image—lasting 30 seconds—of the cabinet in the room, on top of which there are a glass of beer, a condom wrapper, a lighter and an ashtray, all shown while the two characters talk to each other. The whole sequence

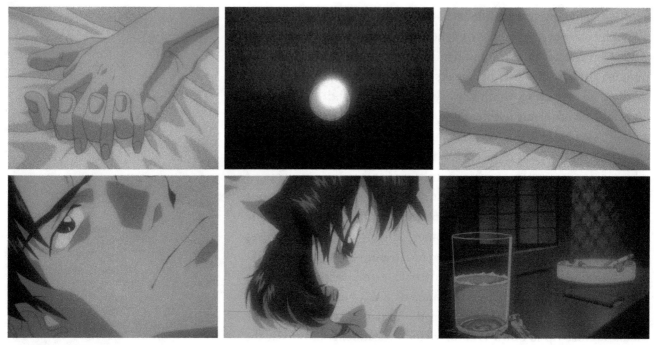

Figure 1.5. Six frames from Misato and Kaji's sexual encounter in episode 20. © khara, inc.

is rendered almost entirely in still images of secondary information combined with the ongoing off-camera dialogue, rather than the actual depiction of the characters. This peculiar interrelation of shots is actually reminiscent of panel transitions in manga, such as McCloud's 'aspect-to-aspect,' and the pillow-shots in Japanese classic cinema. First coined by Burch (1979), who borrowed the term from Japanese poetry, 'pillow-shots' refer to scenes composed of apparently random shots, depicting aspects secondary to the main action taking place. According to Burch, these shots "suspend the diegetic flow [. . .] while they never contribute to the progress of the narrative proper, they often refer to a character or a set, presenting or re-presenting it out of a narrative context. Pillow shots (the term is derived from Japanese poetry) most often achieve their uniquely de-centering effect by lingering unexpectedly on an inanimate object" (1979: 160).

This notion is close to McCloud's 'aspect-to-aspect' panel transition. According to McCloud, aspect-to-aspect transitions set a "wandering eye on different aspects of a place, idea or mood" (1993: 74) and are far more common in manga than in European or American comics. McCloud explains that such panel transitions are used to define the overall mood or a place in a given scene. The creation of the mood in the above-mentioned *EVA* sequence (the two lovers getting intimate) and the room is built on the described set of still images, which can be almost literally explained with McCloud's words: ". . . rather than acting as a bridge between separate moments, the reader [in *EVA*, the viewer] here must assemble a single moment using scattered fragments" (1993: 79). Ultimately, McCloud comes to the conclusion that this particularity of manga can be explained as an art of the interval, and that what is omitted is actually as important as what is depicted. This is exactly what happens with visual synecdoches in *EVA*.

The final two episodes (25 and 26) created great controversy upon their release and continue to raise heated debates among anime enthusiasts worldwide. Both episodes deviate from the previous storyline and present a puzzling introspection into the main characters. Moreover, they are almost entirely comprised of still images, connected by monologues and dialogues both in voice and script (white text on black ground), sound effects and the soundtrack.

Pioneering filmmaker and animator Norman McLaren wrote: "Animation is not the art of drawings that move but the art of movements that are drawn; what happens between each frame is much more important than what exists on each frame; animation is therefore the art of manipulating the invisible interstices that lie between frames."[9] This famous quotation is referenced by Lamarre in the early pages of *The Anime Machine* (2009), when he presents the key ideas to be developed in his seminal book. Lamarre argues that when it comes to anime, compositing—creating an image through layers

9. This quote has been consistently included in books on animation, often referencing a third-party source. *La capture de mouvement: Ou le modelage de l'invisible* (2014) by Marco Grosoli and Jean-Baptiste Massuet (Eds.) provides a very early reference to the quotation (p. 171), apparently written by McClaren himself at his work-desk, and spread by André Martin in the journal *Cinéma 57*, published by the Fédération Française des Ciné-clubs in 1957.

and invisible spaces between them—is more important than character animation. McLaren claimed that "how it moves is more important than what moves. Though what moves is important, in relative
order of importance, it's how it moves that's the important thing"
(McWilliams 1991: 105). However, McLaren's statement clashes
with anime's current dynamics. In anime, drawings are moved, rather
than movement being drawn. Or, as Lamarre points out, "this is precisely what happens in limited animation: you move layers rather
than animate characters" (2009: 66). *EVA*'s episodes 25 and 26 are
a testament to this.

At some level, episodes 25 and 26 show a joy of experimenting
with animation. Many of these resources are used by director Hideaki
Anno in order to meet schedule and economic constraints. However,
it is equally true that he employed many techniques typically used in
combination with still frames. Apart from the regular still images,
episodes 25 and 26 include text slides and the widespread use of
bank-images,[10] sequences and shots from previous episodes dubbed
with a new dialogue, or sometimes manipulated with filters to produce a surreal effect. In these two episodes, Anno also uses production
sketches and rough intermediate materials, collages (like Misato's
torn portrait fixed with actual sellotape, or text images composed
with newspapers fonts), seemingly random photographs (in a similar way to McCloud's 'non-sequitur' transitions, all of which provide
texture to the sequence, but are hardly related to the ongoing action
depicted in the sequence) and even abstract Rorschach test-like mirror paintings.

There are three sequences in episode 26 which, from a visual
standpoint, approximate abstract animation. Notwithstanding,
these sequences deserve deliberate analysis as they push the graphical
quality of the image further, accentuating the articulation between
movement and stillness. The first sequence is a colorful display of
over 300 still images—mostly recycled from previous episodes,

10. Addressed in depth in Ida
Kirkegaard's Chapter 2.

but also including photographs, random textures (like scanned bubble rapping) and intermediate materials (sketches, storyboards, script pages and so on)—superimposed like a 3D mapping projection onto Shinji's outlined face (Fig.1.6). At a rate of one image per frame, Shinji's masking-layer effect shows his traced silhouette on a neutral and undefined plain-colored background, while his face overlaps with background images in a pattern that appears abstract due to the speed at which the visuals are projected. This sequence—lasting over 40 seconds (00:06:48–00:07:30)—is a great example of how speed and change of images (despite their underlying flatness and stillness) create a sense of motion which does not necessarily involve drawing movement or dynamic immobility. As Steinberg states, anime is "a style that was free to emphasize graphism over volume, graphically immobile dynamism over smoothness of movement" (2012: 35).

Moreover, the whole sequence extends the conceptual notion of synecdoche. Ultimately, the flow of images—depicting Shinji's emotional journey through the events that have taken place throughout the whole series—materializes the very idea of *pars pro toto* (a part for the whole) when he is trying to answer his own question ("What am I?" [sic]), depicting different facets of his persona (his role as friend, son, high-school student, Eva pilot, etc.), and finally coming to terms with himself. Shinji, who has been struggling throughout the series to understand his place in the world, ends up realizing that "the whole is other than the sum of its parts"—citing Gestalt psychologist Kurt Koffka, who stressed that 'other' does not mean 'greater,' since it is not a matter of addition, but rather of the whole and the parts operating on indifferent planes—and that he is but himself, apart from the mental image of him others may hold.

The second sequence spans over five minutes of episode 26, and starts with Shinji's face fading into a sketched version of it (00:09:33,

Figure 1.6. Twelve frames of Shinji's face intertwined with other materials (from scanned textures to images from previous episodes) in episode 26. © khara, inc.

Fig.1.7), almost as if Anno had resorted to the intermediate materials, color drafts and storyboard images. From this point onwards, the whole sequence is rendered with sketch-style images, quite stylized, as if drawn by pencil and poorly colored with rough strokes of markers. However, these hand-drawn images act as a representation of Shinji's introspective journey. The deeper he dives into his psyche, the simpler the drawings become, reducing his body to a minimum (a trembling silhouette on a blank sheet of paper). Ultimately, this hand-drawn quality emphasizes the line in an almost meta-referential way: At some point (00:11:57), Shinji's outlined body is floating on a white canvas (lit., "a world where you can do whatever you want"), but suddenly he is given a "restriction" (sic), as explained by the

Figure 1.7. Scene from episode 26, as Shinji morphs into a sketched version of himself. © khara, inc.

voice-over that is leading the sequence, and a line is drawn under him—emphasized by the squeaky sound of a marker—a line that becomes the horizon (Fig.1.8), creates a sense of gravity and roots Shinji to the newly created ground.

For several decades, and until the generalization of contemporary CG animation techniques, animating anime has involved multiple overlapping celluloid layers combined into a single image or frame. Characters and objects are outlined, and together with the limited tone-shading provide a sense of flatness and a drawn quality. *EVA*'s episodes 25 and 26 push forward this drawn quality to an almost artistic and experimental facet, unexpected in mainstream anime. However, sometimes this hand-drawn finish is used for simple narrative purposes, to represent a flashback, or highlight an emotionally dramatic scene. Such is the case with *EVA*.

The third sequence adds an additional layer to the deconstruction process of the graphic image, abstracting the images—and therefore Shinji's psyche—to the very essence of animation. Paul Wells defined

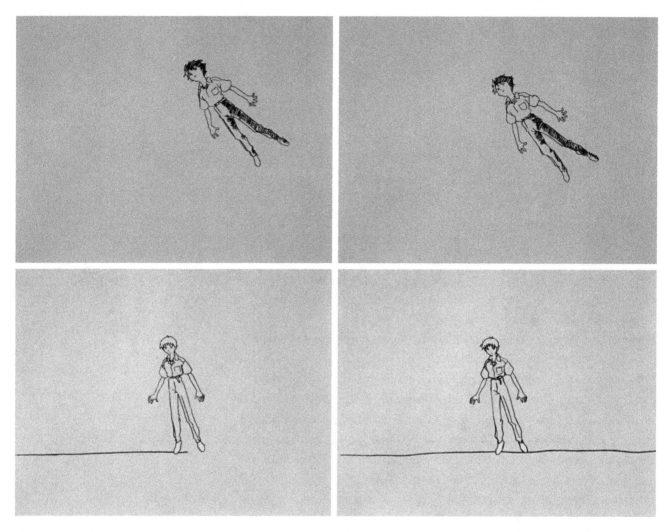

Figure 1.8. Shinji's sketched body is suddenly grounded by a drawn line (episode 26). © khara, inc.

animation as "the artificial creation of the illusion of movement in inanimate lines and forms" (1998: 10). As Shinji himself voices out, "I feel like I am disappearing," the image becomes a simple oscillating black line on a blank canvas (00:13:18) and a random doodle made up of lines with different thicknesses (Fig.1.9), without discernible meaning, which dance to the rhythm of the undergoing dialogue that dominates the scene. This naïf pattern keeps morphing into different

child-like drawings and finally becomes, once again, a sketch of Shinji himself as he begins to come to terms with his own dilemma.

Figure 1.9. Doodling drawings in episode 26. © khara, inc.

Groundworks of *EVA*

In a way, these three sequences work as a journey not only to the psyche of the protagonist, but also as an introduction to the groundworks of anime, emphasizing the role of stillness and the dynamic immobility of the image, the importance of line as opposed to volume, and the simple realization that anime is, essentially, drawings in movement.

Through *EVA*, anime is presented not as much as immobility, but as a significant amount of movement from different still elements. In a simple sense, this specific type of motion better refers to two or more still images (on two or more different planes) and how they move around, rather than drawing the different steps of a given movement (see Lamarre on "moving drawings" [2002: 359]). It is not all about stillness per se, but a different kind of movement that does not necessarily rely on smoothness and a naturalistic approach. In *EVA*, movement can be achieved through stillness, thanks to the parallax effect, background displacement of still images (pulling cels), and the potential that arises between frames, which Lamarre fully addressed when talking about the multi-planar space in *The Anime Machine*. In a similar fashion to speed-lines in comics, a single cel with an abstract patterned background moving in a direction opposite from the figure in the foreground can increase the sense of depth and motion, and achieve an emotional intensity.

However, at the beginning of this chapter, I argued that anime is not *just* immobility. If we look beyond stillness, anime is defined by what I called ratio dynamism, as a result of using a variable frame-per-second proportion which ultimately shapes the pace and rhythm of anime productions. Still images that can last one minute—building up tension and creating an atmosphere of strangeness—and large sections of different episodes which are almost entirely comprised of static frames are combined with sophisticated sequences, rendered in smooth animation. Moreover, I have presented *EVA* as a paramount example of the use of visual and sound synecdoches. Particular attention was paid to the role of close-ups as a significant type of visual synecdoche, and the large abundance of such devices in anime as a distinct trait from other filmic media—together with the prolonged still images consisting of a single frame, and the camera moving away from the human characters to highlight background unanimated objects as main descriptors of the ongoing action.[11] Ultimately, anime appears as something entirely different from other animation (neither Disney-style, high-end productions, nor low-cost, limited cartoons): a specific media form characterized by a series of narrative, aesthetic and filmic devices of its own.

References

Azuma, H. (2009). *Otaku: Japan's Database Animals*. Minneapolis, MN: University of Minnesota Press. (Introduction and translation by J. E. Abel and S. Kono)

Burch, N. (1979). *To the Distant Observer: Form and Meaning in Japanese Cinema*. Los Angeles, CA: University of California Press.

Chandler, D. (2002). *Semiotics: The Basics*. New York: Routledge.

Cohn, N. (2007). Japanese Visual Language the Structure of Manga. *Visual Language Lab*. Retrieved from: http://visuallanguagelab.com/P/japanese_vl.pdf

_____. (2013). *The Visual Language of Comics: Introduction to the Structure and Cognition of Sequential Images*. London: Bloomsbury.

Gan, S. H. (2008). The Newly Developed Form of Ganime and its Relation to Selective Animation for Adults in Japan. *Animation Studies*, 3, 6–17.

Groensteen, T. (2007). *The System of Comics*. Jackson, MS: University Press of Mississippi.

Grosoli, M. and Massuet, J.-B. (eds.) (2014). *La capture de mouvement: Ou le modelage de l'invisible*. Rennes: Presses Universitaires de Rennes.

Horno López, A. (2014) El arte de la animación selectiva en las series de anime contemporáneas. *Con A de Animación*. Valencia: Universidad Politécnica de Valencia, vol. 4, 84–97.

Jakobson, R. & Halle, M. (1956). *Fundamentals of language*. The Hague: Mouton.

11. Yet another way to create dynamism or, as Burch explains, "the tension between the suspension of human presence (of the diegesis) and its potential return" (1979: 161).

Lamarre, T. (2002). From Animation to Anime: Drawing Movements and Moving Drawings. *Japan Forum*, 14, 329–367.

_____. (2009). *The Anime Machine: A Media Theory of Animation.* Minneapolis, MN: University of Minnesota Press.

McCloud, S. (1993). *Understanding Comics: The Invisible Art.* New York: HarperCollins.

McWilliams, D. (ed.) (1991). *Norman McLaren: On the Creative Process.* Quebec: National Film Board of Canada.

Steinberg, M. (2012). Inventing Intervals: The Digital Image in *Metropolis* and *Gankutsuō*. *Mechademia*, 7, 3–22.

Steinberg, M. (2012). *Anime's Media Mix: Franchising Toys and Characters in Japan.* Minneapolis, MN: University of Minnesota Press.

Wells, P. (1998). *Understanding Animation.* Abingdon-on-Thames, UK: Routledge.

Whitsitt, S. P. (2013). *Metonymy, Synecdoche, and the Disorders of Contiguity.* Padova: libreriauniversitaria.it.

2. Play it Again, Hideaki
Using the Cel Bank in *Neon Genesis Evangelion*

Ida Kirkegaard

The control room shakes dramatically. Makoto Hyūga looks over his shoulder to relay the newest information to his superiors in a hurried voice. Data flashes on multiple screens in rapid succession. Shigeru Aoba turns around to yell that his systems can no longer monitor the situation. Captain Misato Katsuragi tenses her brow. More data flashes on a slanted screen, an all-caps LOST central to the image. Maya Ibuki looks down into a monitor and reads that the pilot can no longer be contacted. Misato's eyes narrow with determination, and the viewer may suspect that she is thinking about her last resort plan to blow up the facility, herself, and everyone in the room if this mission fails. In the background, a choir is belting out the climactic stanza of Beethoven's "Ode to Joy." It's an intense sequence, rapidly cut and suffused with dread. But it's also rather familiar. Indeed, the attentive viewer of *Neon Genesis Evangelion* might be experiencing a certain feeling of déjà vu right now. Because every single bit of animation in this sequence from episode 24 is a bank cut.

In anime, the term 'bank' is typically used to refer to cuts of animation that, once created, are used again and again in different contexts (Association of Japanese Animations 2019: 50). 'Cut' in an animation context refers to a continuous segment of animation where the 'camera' does not switch its viewpoint, analogous to a shot in live-action filmmaking (Cirugeda 2017). These cuts are determined and named in storyboards and generally handled by a single key animator. In other words, bank cuts are short sequences of animation that are made for and then routinely reused in a production, drawn from

How to cite this book chapter:
Kirkegaard, I. 2021. Play it Again, Hideaki: Using the Cel Bank in *Neon Genesis Evangelion*. In: Santiago Iglesias, J. A. and Soler Baena, A. (Eds.). *Anime Studies: Media-Specific Approaches to Neon Genesis Evangelion*. Pp. 49–83 Stockholm: Stockholm University Press. DOI: https://doi.org/10.16993/bbp.c. License: CC-BY 4.0

a virtual 'bank' or 'vault.' While the phenomenon is similar to what is commonly known as stock footage, the two terms in Japanese are not used synonymously, with bank being used primarily in animation contexts to describe cuts made for and used within a specific series, while stock footage describes 'canned' footage from a central archive that can be used in several different productions.

This chapter provides an in-depth, inductive reading of *Neon Genesis Evangelion* focused on the use of bank cuts. The analysis is based on both the 2019 Netflix release and the 2015 Japanese Blu-Ray release, as well as the official storyboard collections (*Evangerion ekonte shū*; GAINAX 1997a–e, 1998), and I will be referring to specific cuts by using their storyboard designations. For example, the oft-repeated shot of Misato drinking a beer discussed in a later section is denoted 2-c123, meaning cut 123 from episode 2 (its first appearance). While the foundation of this study is a formal analysis of the material, its goal is not to replicate the work of so-called *sakuga* fans. These are fans of animation as a craft who meticulously catalog cuts of anime that they find particularly well-animated, and identify specific key animators from the animation alone (Suan 2018). While such in-depth knowledge of anime production can help shed light on otherwise unnoticed aspects of a work, the accumulation of such knowledge for its own sake is not the goal of this chapter. Instead, minute observations and production literacy are employed here to understand the work and its reception, that is, the formal analysis is connected to decoding the narrative and meta-narrative meanings of the material.

This chapter is divided into six sections: first, an introduction to the concept of realism in animation and theories that are particularly relevant to the case of *EVA*. Second, a summary of these theories as they relate to *EVA*. Third follows a discussion of the concept of 'the original' when it comes to the material being used for this analysis. The fourth section is a short history of bank cuts in anime. The fifth section is the first half of an analysis of *EVA* focusing on bank cuts as a genre trope and production necessity. And, finally, the sixth section is the second half of the *EVA* analysis, a more in-depth treatment of a few selected sequences whose use of bank cuts particularly illuminates anime's media specificity through realism, followed by a discussion of how this use of the cel bank relates to the overall themes and significance of the work.

Anime's Realism

In academia, it can be hard to justify paying close attention to the texts of popular media culture, in particular when it comes to elements of these texts that are mostly the result of suboptimal circumstances. A phenomenon like bank cuts might appear to be simply an accident to be ignored, an unfortunate effect of the fact that anime production is, above all else, fast and cheap.[1] Indeed, the cheapness of anime in general can make it difficult to defend, characterized as it is by hurried, underfunded productions relying heavily on various forms of so-called limited animation.[2] This positions anime as outside the realm of what is often considered the pinnacle of animation within both popular and academic discourse, Walt Disney and his studio.

The overall trajectory of the Disney Studio in the 20th century was characterized by a move toward increasing sophistication with regard to embodied and character-specific movement. This new form of animation replaced the standardized and repetitive figurative movement of early animation, escalated the use of advanced mechanical tools such as the multi-plane camera to create movement into depth and, importantly, led to an ever-increasing adherence to a meticulous simulation of real-world physics (Crafton 2012). Driving this development was Walt Disney's own desire to simulate the realism of live-action film in animation, the end product of which has been called not realism, but hyper-realism, the reproduction not of physical reality

1. In the interest of clarity, it is important here to remember that the term 'anime' does not have one single definition. For the purposes of this chapter, I follow the definition laid out in Berndt 2018.

2. As for the latter, see Chapter 1 by José Andrés Santiago Iglesias.

precisely, but of the reality of cinema itself (Steinberg 2014: 288). In time, due to the commercial and critical success of Disney's productions and their central role to much writing on animation, cel animation in general came to be seen in part as either adhering to or diverging from a standard set by Disney, one that included the understanding that to make advancements in animation was to move toward detailed full movement and a Disney-style realism, inadvertently positioning stillness, stylization and reused assets as lesser in the minds of many critics and animators.

Here, it is crucial to discuss the topic of realism and to first emphasize that there is no one comprehensive realism, but rather several realisms. Even within the field of Cinema Studies, several mutually competing perspectives on the relationship between animation and realism exist (Rowley 2005: 67). While it is an oft-repeated truism that the classic Disney style represents a pinnacle of realism, this is simply the viewpoint of what Rowley (2005) calls the 'quest for realism' narrative. Here, the purpose of animation is seen as simulating cinematic realism as much as possible, developing toward a simulacrum of reality that may not be indexical, but is visually so close to photographic realism as to be indistinguishable from it. Indeed, developments in this direction are still being made in much three-dimensional computer-generated (3D CG) animation, driven in large part due to its foundation in engines and algorithms founded on meticulous reproduction of physics because they were originally developed to simulate a playable reality first for military training and then for video games (Bukatman 2014: 312).

While realism and drawings are not inherently opposed to each other—after all, pictorial realism has a long history in painting—the founding assumption of many traditional theories of realism in Cinema Studies is the idea that cinema is the photographic reproduction of a profilmic reality, something animation can by definition never be (Rowley 2005: 66). Indeed, one might characterize the drive toward visual realism in animation as an asymptotic trajectory that can approach the photographic image, but will never reach it. This thinking underlies what Rowley (2005) names the 'inversion narrative,' a medium-specific argument about what animation 'should do' that emphasizes its potential for the fantastic over its potential for simulation. In his famous essay fragments, Sergei Eisenstein (1986) criticized the Disney studio's development, insisting that their later films had lost the revolutionary plasmaticness that the earlier, more malleable form of animation had embodied. The fundamental idea at play in Eisenstein's critique is that animation possesses the potential for other forms of expression than live-action cinema does, and that this fact means that doing so is what animation *should* focus on. As Rowley puts it: "Realism is not what animation is best at, such a position holds, and therefore works that show freer invention and fantasy are privileged" (2005: 66).

While these perspectives on the relationship between animation and realism are opposite in their approach to what animation should strive for, they are not mutually exclusive, and are often found simultaneously in writing on animation (Rowley 2005: 67). This largely reflects how the concept of realism itself is particularly slippery when it comes to animation. Animation, after all, has no profilmic reality to refer back to, and so the question of what is or should be the referent for any attempt at realism is rather more open than it is for live-action films. Comparisons can be made between the animated image and both the real world itself and live-action film's depiction of that reality, and those two referents are far from always in alignment (Rowley 2005: 68). More than that, however, Rowley takes a third option when he argues that the hyperreal environment of Disney's films is not simply a reproduction of cinematic realism, but a realer-than-real environment that is entirely fake, yet is presented and experienced as real. This 'world' is created by exaggerating reality through, for example, squash and stretch animation and overdetermined movements. Eventually, these movements and other aspects of the consistent Disney style have solidified into a set of 'codified conventions that are understood by audiences to connote reality, even while they clearly are not literally realistic' (Rowley 2005: 69). That is, more than its relation to the real world or to live-action cinema, the realism of Disney is defined by a set of internally consistent conventions that are accepted by the audience as depictions of the real, regardless of their actual relationship with physical reality.

Even more than Disney-style animation, anime's claim to realism may be considered contentious at best. Compounding the lack of indexicality and removal from photorealism it shares with all animation, with its reliance on limited animation and tricks like bank cuts, anime can hardly be said to comply to the Disney ideal of exaggerated hyperrealism either. Instead, traditional cel anime relies on its own system of codified visual representation that invites the viewer to quickly scan the image instead of being drawn into it (Steinberg 2012a: 6). Critic Eiji Ōtsuka has identified three kinds of realism in anime and related media: scientific, biological and manga-anime realism (Ōtsuka 2003). Scientific realism refers to drawings of mechanical things striving for a simulation of photographic realism. In other words, it is a form of pictorial realism not dissimilar from (a) pictorial realism in painting and (b) filmic realism, or indeed from the way Disney-style animation attempts to reproduce the movements of living things, despite being instead focused on mechanics. In robot series like *EVA*, the usage of this type of realism is a well-established convention, and one that stands in noticeable contrast to the more stylized character designs. Indeed, it is those 'hieroglyphic' character designs that provide the spark of Ōtsuka's second realism, biological realism. This idea stems originally from the work of manga pioneer Osamu Tezuka, who claimed that his characters with their large eyes and cartoonesque forms were semiotic, abstract drawings, divorced from any real-world referent (cited in Berndt 2013: 366; originally in Tezuka 1979).

Despite this, Tezuka's characters were realistic in the sense that they possessed physical, vulnerable bodies that could bleed and die. The oft-cited first example of this form of realism is a character in Tezuka's 1945 short study manga *Until the Day of Victory* (Jp. *Shōri no hi made*) being shot and, rather than shrugging off the damage in a humorous way like the Looney Tunes characters he resembles, bleeding like a real person (Ōtsuka 2003: 217, cited in Steinberg 2014: 291). Biological realism is the antithesis of the archetypical immortal cartoon character, governed by the real-life physics of limited, vulnerable bodies rather than the limitless malleability of cartoon physics (Bukatman 2014: 302). It is a realism that does not depend on a particular type of visuals as scientific realism does, but instead on narrative, that is, visually non-realistic characters suffering, bleeding and dying as human beings. This form of realism is invoked in the very first episode of *EVA*, when the character Rei Ayanami is introduced covered in bandages that leave blood on protagonist Shinji Ikari's hands as he touches her (#1–290, GAINAX 1997a). Of course, by the time *EVA* aired in 1995, biological realism was a long-established part of anime and manga conventions and such a direct invocation would not have been strictly speaking necessary to make the audience expect that characters can bleed and die. Thus, its deliberate utilization here might be seen as a setting of expectations: not only *can* characters bleed and die in this series, they *will*.

Ōtsuka's third realism, coined in discussions of what are today known as light novels, but were then called character novels, is manga-anime realism. It is a realism which has as its referent not the real world, but the stylized yet internally consistent world of anime and manga, the environmental pervasiveness of which creates a sense of realness and plausibility for the viewer familiar with its conventions

(Ōtsuka 2003; Ōtsuka 2010). In that way, it can be said to be similar to Disney's hyperrealism, which also replicates not the real world, but the 'world' of Hollywood cinema. Ōtsuka compares the low culture light novel to the high literature form of the I-novel,[3] claiming that where the I-novel emulates the world of the 'author-as-I,' the light novel emulates the world of anime and manga in a similar way, in other words, while one draws from reality and the other from fiction, the two literary forms draw on their sources to construct their reality in the same way (according to Steinberg 2014: 293). While Ōtsuka's emphasis is on the role of manga-anime realism as an interface between anime and its related media, the fundamental idea that the conventions and codes of anime can constitute an alternative but no less valid referent for the story world resonates strongly with Rowley's idea of an animation realism founded on codified conventions, and it is a particular interesting form of realism to examine when engaging with *EVA*.

EVA's Realism

To discuss realism in the context of *EVA* means to lean on Ōtsuka's and Rowley's conceptions of realism. This is, after all, a series where impossible giants controlled by thoughts fight alien monsters over underground bases built from the shell of the egg that originated all life on earth. Rather, *EVA*'s baseline realism is very similar to the realism of Disney with its magical fairies, talking animals and wondrous transformations that nonetheless move and behave in ways that are so 'realistic' as to offend Eisenstein (Rowley 2005: 69). It is a realism that in Rowley's terms occupies positions on several different spectrums of realism—quite visually realist, but not particularly narratively realist, very character realist, but not very realist in terms of motion, at least not most of the time (Rowley 2005: 70). Importantly, the series' position on the spectrum of realism is mostly consistent, creating a believable, reliable portrayal of a particular story world,

3. The I-novel (*shishōsetsu*) is a Japanese literary genre that developed during the Meiji period (1868–1912) under the influence of Western naturalism. I-novels emphasize interiority and autobiographical themes and are typically written in the first person. See, for example, Suzuki (1996).

a diegetic realism the establishment of which is crucial for its later deconstruction. In Ōtsuka's terms, *EVA* strongly exhibits both scientific realism and biological realism. As mentioned above, *EVA* is full of characters who bleed, suffer and die as real people do, an aspect of the series' world established in episode 1 with the introduction of the injured, bleeding Rei Ayanami. Even the ostensible robots can and do bleed, and when characters die, they do not come back—or at least they should not, which makes it all the more jarring when Rei does come back from the dead in the later parts of the series. In terms of scientific realism, *EVA* sets up what appears to be a hard SF approach, constructing something that at least appears to be an internally consistent, scientifically plausible story world. Visually, vehicles, buildings, laboratories, computers, weaponry and giant robots are rendered in loving detail, reflecting the trivia-obsessed aesthetics of otaku culture and the historical conventions of the robot genre. Information about the ostensible science underlying the events of the series is given in rambling monologues by characters operating computers and carrying clipboards while data flashes on screens and hydraulic pumps push airlocks open. That none of this is based on actual science and draws more on esoteric kabbalah mysticism than anything truly scientific is in some ways beside the point: by presenting its made-up science in this way, *EVA* sets up the expectation that events will unfold according to, if not real science, then an internally consistent fantasy science. This is indeed the case when Rei Ayanami comes back from the dead–this break with biological realism is explained through the series' fantasy science, and there is a diegetic reason for her return to the land of the living.

When it comes to manga-anime realism, *EVA*'s relationship to the conventions of the robot genre becomes particularly important. And in many ways, *EVA* adheres closely to these conventions: it features color-coded robots operating out of a paramilitary base to fight monsters that are initially designed very similar to the monsters fought by Ultraman. Its characters are designed according to anime aesthetics and embody types that were popular with fans at the time, such as the *tsundere*[4] Asuka and the cool, reserved Rei. It employs a monster-of-the-week structure, meaning that a new enemy is introduced and defeated in (almost) every episode and the military action is juxtaposed with a relatable school dramedy set in the near future. *EVA*'s world is a collage of popular tropes and conventions from previous anime, manga and *tokusatsu*[5] productions, assembled with a nerdy fervor befitting the notoriously otaku-aligned director Hideaki Anno and Studio GAINAX. All of this intertextuality and adherence to convention establishes a strong manga-anime realism, an anime-style hyperrealism that is internally consistent and resonant with those familiar with the tropes it employs.

On the other hand, *EVA* is also a work that is commonly cited as transgressive of the conventions of anime, both in general and when it comes to the specific genre of robot anime. In particular, it is often described as a work that overcomes the perceived inherent childishness and immaturity of robot anime and uses the repetitive nature of the genre to subvert the expectations of the viewers, using formula and conventionality to "lull the audience into complacency" before undermining that complacency by breaking the formula (Bolton 2018: 224). *EVA* is often portrayed as being particularly ruthless in its critique of the otaku (hardcore fans) who formed the core of its most dedicated audience and indeed most of its creators (Shamoon 2015: 105).[6] Hiroki Azuma (2009) famously claimed that otaku consumed media in a new, postmodern way where detached 'database' analysis and emotional empathy were simultaneously possible due to the loss of the idea of a grand narrative behind the individual works consumed.[7] This approach to media also meant that otaku may be the people best able to truly accept manga-anime realism as a form of realism, engaging fully with the conventions and codes of anime as a valid referent for portrayals of character interiority. And while the characterizations of transgression tend to refer primarily to the

4. A *moe* character archetype originating in *otaku* subculture. *Tsundere* refers to a character, typically female, who initially appears harsh and cold (*tsuntsun*), but later acts warm and affectionate (*deredere*), especially toward the male protagonist.

5. Special Effects Films, specifically used to refer to Japanese live-action productions that rely heavily on suitmation and practical effects rather than stop-motion or CGI animation. The term is associated primarily with fantasy, Science Fiction and superhero works. Examples of *tokusatsu* are the *Godzilla* films, the *Kamen Rider* and *Super Sentai* TV series, and the *Ultra* series.

6. See also Chapter 7 by Zoltan Kacsuk.

7. See also Chapter 8 by Olga Kopylova.

structure of *EVA*, particularly the conventions of the robot genre that the series is famously said to subvert, *EVA* also plays with and subverts the series' own construction of realism throughout the series and particularly toward the end.

Defining the Materials

When analyzing a work based on something as relatively minute as bank cuts, minor differences between versions can dramatically alter the analysis and the ultimate understanding. Defining the 'definitive' source is crucial here, but when dealing with TV anime, that is not an easy task, and *EVA* is representative of that issue. On the most basic level, this chapter engages only with the 26-episode series, first broadcast 4 October 1995–27 March 1996 on TV Tokyo. It does not take into account the theatrically released recap film *Neon Genesis Evangelion: Death & Rebirth* (*Shin seiki Evangerion gekijōban: Shi to shinsei*, 1997), the newly animated alternative episodes 25 and 26 released theatrically as *End of Evangelion* (*Shin seiki Evangerion gekijōban: Ea/magokoro o, kimi ni*, 1997), nor the much later films in the *Rebuild of Evangelion* series: *Evangelion 1.0: You Are (Not) Alone* (*Evangerion shin gekijōban: Jo*, 2007), *Evangelion 2.0: You Can (Not) Advance* (*Evangerion shin gekijōban: Ha*, 2009), *Evangelion 3.0: You Can (Not) Redo* (*Evangerion shin gekijōban: Q*, 2012) and *Evangelion: 3.0+1.0* (*Shin Evangerion gekijōban: ‖*, 2021). There is doubtlessly much to be said about the way both *EoE* and in particular *Rebuild* meticulously recreate certain bank cuts from the series, but that is outside the scope of this chapter.

However, simply defining the TV series as material is easier said than done. When it comes to deciding what to highlight and what to exclude, particularly in the case of *EVA*, one must contend with the question of originality. Even the initial TV series is not one unchanging work. Rather, it has been edited, altered and re-edited over the last

25 years, ranging from edits for international distribution undertaken by third parties to deliberate re-cutting tackled by creators deeply involved in the original production. As an example of the former, the 2019 Netflix release of the series edits the ending song *Fly Me to the Moon* out of every episode, as well as two cases where it is used as background music within the series. This editing appears to have been done for licensing reasons, but only outside of Japan, meaning that the version a viewer will experience changes depending on ISP address. That this editing has taken place is not disclosed in any way by the platform, leaving viewers who have not seen the series previously unaware that they are watching an altered version. In fan discourse, such editing is typically seen as unwanted meddling by third parties, a relatively uncomplicated question of tainting the original. Unsurprisingly, the Netflix release was indeed met with fan outrage (Vilas-Boas 2019). In an age where streaming has become the primary way most people consume media, Netflix's alterations of *EVA* have consequences for the wider perception of the work, as it is the only version that has been made available to the general public outside Japan in almost 15 years, and the edits are not disclosed. This means that, for the average viewer, whatever Netflix presents *is EVA*, and they have no reason to question that it is the original, or at least the definitive version of the material.

The malleability of streaming media, where a video may change overnight without any easily discernible trace of alteration, complicates critical analysis. In the specific case of *EVA*, mass-market physical releases of the series featuring both original and re-edited versions of all episodes continue to be produced for the Japanese market, making the issue of version availability less of universal concern than one that waxes and wanes with the observer's access to Japanese releases of physical media.[8] Outside Japan, however, no physical release of the series exists except for long-out-of-print DVDs released in the mid-2000s (Vilas-Boas 2019). Thus, the Netflix release with its obscured

8. *EVA* was last released on Japanese Blu-Ray on 24 July 2019.

alterations is the only way the vast majority of the world's population can legally access *EVA*.

But even with knowledge of what cuts Netflix have and have not made to *EVA*, can we actually define what the original version of the series is? While one might assert that obviously, the version that was broadcast on TV Tokyo in 1995–96 is the original and everything else is an alteration, looking at *EVA*'s release history prior to the Netflix release reveals that when it comes to *EVA*, the question of what version is 'original' and 'definitive' is not entirely straightforward. The recap film *Death & Rebirth* is particularly relevant to that discussion, aside from being an interesting play with the conventions of TV anime in and of itself. The term 'recap' or 'compilation' film refers to theatrically released features created primarily or entirely from pre-existing cuts of a particular TV anime, recut so that, ideally, the film can function as an alternative, shorter version of the same story (Sevakis 2016). Recap films are a long-standing convention in TV anime production, and at least initially they served as a way to make an anime series available beyond its initial television run, aside from the obvious financial benefits of releasing a film without having to produce much, or any, new animation. Early examples of recap films include *Heidi, Girl of the Alps* (Nakao, 1979) and the very successful *Mobile Suit Gundam* film trilogy (Tomino, 1981–82). Despite the ubiquity of home video and streaming, recap films are still produced to this day (prominent examples from recent years include the 2012 *Madoka Magica* and 2018 *Made in Abyss* features) and their ubiquity seems to prove that they have come to occupy an established position as a convention of anime production. Recap films often, if not always, feature a few new cuts of animation alongside the recycled cuts from the TV series, as well as alterations to the music and compositing of the cuts, all serving to 'fix' perceived shortcomings of the TV version, whether those were the result of a rushed production or simply unpopular with fans. Rarer examples like *Macross: Do You Remember*

Love (Kawamori, 1984) even present the TV series' story through entirely new animation.

Death & Rebirth follows the recap film tradition by combining recycled cuts with new cuts, but rather than reassembling the material into a simple truncated version of the original storyline, the film also drastically reorganizes the material, presenting it in a thematic order. This shifts the emphasis from chronological storytelling (already jettisoned in the last two episodes of *EVA*) toward inward-facing character portraits. The events of the story are retold focusing not on when or how they occurred, but on how they affected the central characters. This renders *Death & Rebirth* nigh incomprehensible for an audience not already familiar with the series, thus deliberately failing the expected purpose of a recap film entirely. The nature of this recap film has interesting parallels with the use of bank cuts in the initial series, but more importantly for the immediate discussion is the fact that the new cuts created for *Death & Rebirth* were later edited into the TV series itself when it was released on laserdisc. This updated version of the TV series is often called the director's cut version, but only episodes 21–24 were altered in this way.[9] The cuts inserted in these episodes were subsequently removed from *Death & Rebirth* when that film was re-edited into the TV movie *Shin seiki Evangerion gekijōban: DEATH (TRUE)*[2] (Anno, 1998) and the freshly animated *EoE*. Subsequent releases of the series have largely preserved this division of the new material, rendering it part of the series proper and not the film. While in most countries Netflix presents episodes 21–24 in the director's cut rather than the broadcast version, they did not initially appear on Netflix when logged in from an ISP address in Japan, further muddling the question of what the 'original' version of this material is. To complicate the question more, the commercially released *Evangelion ekonte shū* storyboard collections also reproduce the storyboards for *DEATH (TRUE)*[2] rather than the original *Death & Rebirth*, suggesting that the former, not the latter, is considered the

9. The director's cut versions of these episodes are distinguished from the broadcast versions with an apostrophe, thus episode 21' is the director's cut version of episode 21.

definitive version of the material. Meanwhile, the same storyboard collections present the broadcast versions of episodes 21–24, not the director's cut versions of the same material, raising the question of where the cuts originally introduced in *Death & Rebirth* truly belong. Taking the storyboard collections as an authority, the answer to that question seems to be 'nowhere.' All of this suggests that, ultimately, there is no one true 'original' version of the material, and so it is all the more important that researchers name and define which version they are working with. As mentioned above, this study relies both on the Netflix release and the Japanese Blu-Ray release of *EVA*, and I have included the director's cut sequences into my definition of the TV series even if their intended place within the franchise ultimately remains muddled.

A Short History of the Bank System

While this chapter uses the name 'bank cuts,' there are several different terms for the same phenomenon, including 'image bank' and 'cel bank.' The latter term hints at the reason why bank cuts are and have been so ubiquitous in anime: using them in a production saves cels, the single frames painted on celluloid sheets that were photographed one by one to create pre-digital 2D animation (Clements 2013: 49). This is useful for TV productions operating under strict limitations of budget and production time, where reusing cels frees scarce resources to be used on other cuts. Even in today's digital age, reusing cuts saves time and work, as every second filled with bank cuts is a second of air time that does not need to be created anew and passed through the numerous complicated steps from storyboard to filming (Association of Japanese Animations 2019: 50). In the 1980s, when American TV stations routinely commissioned animation from Japan, a half-hour TV cartoon for the US market consisted of 12,000 cels per episode. Meanwhile, comparable anime productions made at the same studios for the domestic market were allowed 5,000 cels at best, going as low as 1,200 for certain productions (Watanabe 2019). This made cel-saving measures such as bank cuts particularly important for anime production compared to other forms of animation.

The effect of these limitations can be observed in the landscape of TV anime both old and new. Perhaps most striking is the ubiquitous use of bank cuts in magical girl series aimed at young girls, such as *Sailor Moon* (Satō, 1992). These series, almost to a fault, will include at least one elaborate transformation sequence that is repeated in every single episode, and often, in series featuring multiple heroines, up to five banked transformation sequences will be played in succession, taking up a significant amount of the episode's runtime. *Sailor Moon* in particular also relies on banked special attacks, speeches and even entire scenes repeated over and over again in its formulaic episodes. An example of this are the monster creation scenes, run at roughly the midpoint of every episode with only minor adjustments and often humorous changes to the dialogue, which mark each episode's transition from a school comedy to a superhero story. A similar if not as universal use of bank cuts is seen in anime aimed at young boys, where robots and monsters have equally long and elaborate transformation sequences, attacks and speeches. A recent example of this can be seen in the children's robot anime *Shinkansen Henkei Robo Shinkarion* (Ikezoe, 2018), where CGI bank cuts are extensively used to portray the robots launching and transforming. Indeed, bank cuts have come to be particularly associated with the robot genre as it has evolved through the years (Association of Japanese Animations 2019: 50).

It is interesting to note that this type of bank usage is often both conspicuous and elaborate, with bank cuts being assigned to senior key animators and paired with attention-grabbing theme songs and catchphrases for the audience to repeat at the playground. These are often gorgeous cuts, and their weekly repetition in already repetitive narratives aimed at children seem to take on a form of ritual quality. This is further suggested by the way anime aimed at a teenage or older audiences sometimes use similar bank scenes as a form of genre tribute. Examples of this can be seen in the transformation scenes of *Magical Girl Lyrical Nanoha* (Simbo, 2004). This series, drawing on magical girl genre conventions, but targeting an audience of adult men, includes elaborate transformation scenes in the style of those in *Sailor Moon*, but they are repeated only occasionally. Other genre pastiches, such as *Madoka Magica* (Simbo, 2011), do not repeat their transformation scenes at all, and as such they are not actually bank cuts, despite otherwise following the conventions of the format.

Beyond transformations and special attacks, bank cuts are still ubiquitous in anime, although their presence is less conspicuous. Studying production materials is often the most reliable way to identify bank cuts in these instances, as cuts may be drawn from disparate episodes and, especially in digital productions, obscured through digital filters or color changes. While they are common across all genres, the exact utility of bank cuts differs depending on the needs and format of a production. Due to their lack of identifying background details, emotional close-ups might be drawn from the bank, as is the case in *Candy Candy* (Imazawa, 1976), which otherwise contain very few bank cuts. Meanwhile, a series such as *Mobile Suit Zeta Gundam* (Tomino, 1985) relies on a small bank of standard robot action cuts to enhance its fight scenes (Watanabe, 2019). Bank cuts might also be used in marginal but still time-filling segments like the post-credits scene in *Card Captor Sakura* (Asaka, 1998–2000) which repeats the same few cuts of the character Kero talking to the audience in every episode.

Like so many other characteristic traits of TV anime, the ubiquity of bank cuts can be traced back to the Mushi Pro studio and the *Astro Boy* TV series (Tezuka, 1963). Even if it was not strictly invented for the series, Osamu Tezuka called it his 'bank system,' a term still commonly in use today, referencing the *star system* of reoccurring character designs he used in his manga (Clements 2013: 120). The bank system was just one of the many forms of limited animation the series relied on to meet its weekly schedule and keep somewhat within its very limited budget. Being a robot series, *Astro Boy* was also particularly suited to limited animation and bank cuts. As Marc Steinberg has pointed out, the main character's jet-propelled flying was convenient in its lack of need for any movement beyond a dynamic still image dragged across a background (Steinberg 2012b: 76). Flight as a form of locomotion detached from physical surroundings and the minimalist futurist backgrounds of *Astro Boy*'s world made it easier for the animators to insert the banked cuts into various episodes than if Astro Boy had, for example, commuted on a bicycle or swung through his city like Spider-Man. The strong connection between the highly influential robot anime *Astro Boy* and bank cuts can be seen as one plausible reason for the connection between genre and the ubiquity of bank cuts, which becomes particularly noticeable in the case of *EVA*.

Bank in *EVA*

As a TV anime, particularly one from the mid-1990s, *EVA* utilized bank cuts as a matter of production necessity. Their frequency increases over the course of the series' run until the final two episodes, which famously are comprised of little *but* bank cuts. Structurally, *EVA*'s form lends itself well to bank cuts, featuring as it does a small number of recurring locations and characters, as well as adopting, on the surface level, the repetitive monster-of-the-week structure typical to parts of the robot genre. One noticeable point about the use of bank cuts in *EVA* is that they are unevenly placed, that is, some types of sequences are much more likely to use bank cuts than others.

Combat sequences contain few to no bank cuts, even late in the series, and only rarely do sequences of character interaction contain anything but newly animated cuts (one rare exception can be seen in episode 21, where a situation recurring from episode 15 is highlighted through the use of bank cuts). Instead, bank cuts are primarily seen in two types of sequences: light, domestic and comedic sequences, and the conventional Science Fiction sequences taking place in the NERV control room and SEELE meeting chamber.

The domestic sequences that take place in Misato Katsuragi's apartment are particularly prone to containing bank cuts. This is a location introduced in the second episode and, with the exception of one sequence in episode 23, the only private home seen in the series. This location fills the role of 'home' in the series to such an extent that when Shinji imagines a family home, something he has never truly had, in episode 26, the exterior of Misato's house is explicitly used, cementing the symbolic meaning of this location (GAINAX 1997e: 528). The sequences in Misato's apartment use and reuse some very distinct bank cuts, often cued with the same musical theme, which serve to build a sense of familiarity that is similar to the role typically played by establishing shots. In several cases, for example, an instantly recognizable cut of Misato drinking a beer (Fig.2.1), first seen in episode 2 (2-c123 in the storyboard), is used to establish a sequence as taking part in her kitchen and set a mood that is, at least on the surface, one of sitcom-like light-heartedness and warmth (GAINAX 1997a: 186).

Even more conspicuous in their use of bank cuts than these domestic sequences, however, are the sequences taking place in the NERV control center. Here, often intercut with moments of high action, commanders and technicians bark orders, react in shock and recite largely meaningless pseudoscientific data about the Angels, the Evas or the situation at hand, while graphic user interfaces signal synch rates, alerts and critical emergencies. These sequences use a small

Figure 2.1. The cut of Misato Katsuragi drinking a beer appears for the first time in episode 2. © khara, inc.

number of shots over and over again, mostly sourced from episodes 2 (the first time a battle is shown in the series) and 14 (an episode set entirely within this location). Particularly noticeable as bank cuts are a group of shots showing the command technicians turning around and talking (Fig.2.2), while other shots are subtler and only stand out as repeated if the viewer pays closer attention. These shots are

reused again and again with only the dialogue replaced, creating a strong sense of continuity between the different Angel attacks, no matter their precise form or severity. In fact, as the production progresses, the volume of bank cuts used in these sequences grows until the final battle sequence, which contains just two new cuts taking place in the control room (24-c234 and 24-c262), out of about 60 cuts (GAINAX 1997e). True to form, however, even in this late and presumably resource-strapped episode, the action taking place outside the control room is comprised almost entirely of newly animated cuts. This kind of resource distribution falls in line with the philosophy of Mushi Pro-style limited animation, ebbing and flowing between high and low energy rather than spreading limited resources evenly over the running time (Steinberg 2012b: 34).

What types of sequences are comprised of bank cuts also determines which are not, and in *EVA*'s case those are the earlier mentioned action sequences and the sequences of emotional, non-comedic interaction between characters. While that might seem obvious at first glance—what else would an ostensible robot action series allocate its animation resources to if not the battle sequences—this spread is by no means universal. As mentioned above, anime such as *Sailor Moon* (Satō, 1992) and *Mobile Suit Zeta Gundam* (Tomino, 1985) repeatedly rely on bank cuts in action scenes.

Figure 2.2. The cuts of the NERV technicians turning around are first seen in episode 2. © khara, inc.

EVA's action sequences, meanwhile, are high quality set-pieces, a showcase for the skill of the animators and a key selling point of the series itself.

The control room sequences with their high number of bank cuts seem to largely be an artifact of the conventions of the robot genre. Control room sequences are an established and expected trope in this genre, often recurring in every episode alongside the fight of the week as part of the rhythm of the series. They enhance the tension of the fight and provide commentary for the audience, but they are not part of the main action itself and do not need as much unique animation to do their job. They also tend to feature the same characters, wearing the same uniforms in the same location, over and over again. For all of these reasons, control room sequences lend themselves especially well to bank cuts. And while their recurrence is not quite as schematic as in children's robot anime such as *The King of Braves GaoGaiGar* (Yonetani, 1997), where certain bank cuts repeat almost on the same minute each week, *EVA*'s control room sequences and their reoccurring rhythm still constitute an important aspect of the series' relationship with robot anime genre conventions.

Interestingly, *EVA* seems to approach the recurring nature of these sequences somewhat ironically. Throughout the storyline, Angel attacks disable the headquarters in various ways, but each time, the characters manage to carry on to the extent that the same bank cuts can be employed. In a striking move toward the end of the series, when the control center itself is destroyed, the characters relocate to a henceforth unmentioned secondary control center that just so happens to be identical to the original—and the same bank cuts are reused again. The recurring nature of the control room sequences forms an interesting contrast to the increasingly horrifying occurrences in the Angel fights themselves: no matter what is happening, the control room is almost eerily unchanging, the cuts are the same, in *EoE* even when approaching the end of the world. That is to say, even as the narrative heads into territory far away from the then typical themes of robot anime, the control room sequences continue unabated, emphasizing the tie between the unfamiliar ground the story is treading and its genre roots. The use of bank cuts in this case ends up being a reinforcement of this effect: as characters, stakes and environments change drastically, the control room stays the same, literally, because it is depicted through the same exact cuts of animation as it was back in episode 2.

Bank and Anime-Specific Realism

As mentioned earlier, *EVA* is a work that repeatedly undermines and calls into question its own constructed realism. This is most noticeable toward the end of the series, where characters start entering into close contact with the Angels and the series' mostly consistent use of scientific and biological realism in its portrayal of the characters and their surroundings gives way to highly abstract, expressive portrayals of their mental landscapes. In these episodes, long sequences depict the minds of the characters being probed, presented largely through monologues in a dark featureless space, dialogues superimposed over still images, abstract lines and plain text taking the place of figurative drawings of characters. In the final two episodes, as everyone worldwide comes into contact with one another and the Angels through the Third Impact, this break from *EVA*'s particular brand of scientific realism is supplemented with others, such as photographic still images, rough pencil sketches and a sequence that eventually breaks down into loose production materials, culminating in pans over a script accompanied by voiced lines. In another sequence, the main character is given freedom over the shape of his own body and surroundings, morphing into all sorts of different forms without suffering any harm, reduced in a way to a more primal, plasmatic state

 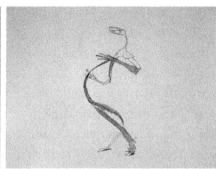 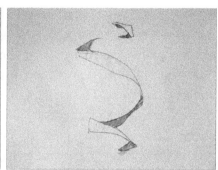

Figure 2.3. Shinji Ikari's form morphs plasmatically in episode 25. © khara, inc.

(Fig.2.3). These sequences stretch the credibility of the series' own claim to biological realism to its breaking point by highlighting the non-indexical nature of the characters and removing their physical bodies, either by distortion or by simply taking them away and leaving only the script.

A very similar, albeit less spectacular, effect is achieved even earlier in the series through two distinct usages of bank cuts. The first of these, by far the most frequent, is the way very conspicuous bank cuts are reused with new dialogue in introspective sequences, crucially and unlike the control room sequences discussed earlier, with no serious attempt being made to hide the fact that these cuts are indeed bank and do not combine into a realistic diegetic whole.

Two examples of this, sharing a very noticeable number of bank cuts, can be seen in episodes 16 and 25. Here, a cut of Asuka wearing a towel (#16-c11, GAINAX 1997d), originally used in one of the previously mentioned sequences in Misato's kitchen, is repurposed and twisted in introspective sequences as the dialogue associated with the footage changes (Fig.2.4a). In the cut's original context, a relatively mundane sequence in Misato's kitchen, Asuka is talking to Misato, scolding her for being 'too soft' on Shinji, and for getting together with her ex-boyfriend, Kaji, whom Asuka herself has been dating previously, albeit unsuccessfully. This follows immediately after a sequence of cuts where Asuka berates Shinji for apologizing too

much, and one where she simply complains about the temperature of the bath water. In the wider context of the series, this is a cut that is about Asuka herself and her need to take out her own frustrations on other people, particularly in this part of the narrative, where her confidence has been eroded after a series of setbacks. But as the cut is recontextualized, its meaning shifts subtly from being about Asuka to being about Shinji's impression of her. When the same cut reappears later in the same episode, Shinji has been swallowed by an Angel during battle and is speaking with a disembodied voice (that calls itself the Shinji that exists within his mind) about his guilt and self-blame. Then, two blatantly unrelated bank cuts of Asuka—one wearing a T-shirt, the other the above-mentioned #16-c11—appear, overdubbed with new dialogue of Asuka blaming Shinji for his self-deprecation. When the cut reappears in episode 25, it is in the narrative context of Instrumentality, a process that removes all barriers between people. Shinji is sitting alone in a black room, talking to a vision of Asuka who appears in several different bank cuts that seem to have been reassembled with no intention of creating a believable

Figure 2.4. The same cut of animation is repurposed in different contexts and with altered dialogue in episode 16. © khara, inc.

continuity between them, her outfit changing with every cut back to Shinji. This time, Asuka scolds Shinji for his loneliness and dependency on others, and it is worth noting that, unlike in the previous example, the background from Misato's apartment has now been replaced with the same black nothingness in front of which Shinji is depicted (Fig.2.4b).

Importantly, and unlike the control room bank sequences, these examples all come from sequences where a character is conversing not with another character, but with their own impression of that other person, something that is explicitly spelled out in the series (during the previously mentioned sequence in episode 16) as 'the me in your mind.' Shinji, the viewpoint character in these examples, is not talking to Asuka, but to a memory of his own impressions of her. Here, the very conspicuous use of bank cuts works to emphasize this effect. The reuse of the same section of animation makes it very clear that the 'Asuka' appearing in the sequence is not supposed to be read as an autonomous character or individual, but an assemblage of impressions of that person. The use of new dialogue, however, also distinguishes this use of bank cuts from the tried-and-true trick of replaying cuts to signify a memory. While these cuts may seem like memories, the dialogue is new and unique to this sequence, not a replay of anything said earlier. Likewise, the selection of cuts to create these dialogues with what is ostensibly a character through bank cuts highlights that Asuka is not supposed to actually be there—her outfit, and sometimes her location, as signified by the background, changes with every cut, breaking the illusion of realism. In the episode 25 sequence, all cuts of Asuka are bank (except for #25-c93 and #25-c105, which show her in the same frame as Shinji), while every shot of Shinji except one (#25-c104, recycled from #2-c-321) is newly drawn, strongly suggesting that the effect is intentional. There is an uncanny, malleable quality to these repeated cuts that works to show the treacherous quality of memories and impressions of others. It is a memory of Asuka, speaking in Asuka's voice—but it is not Asuka.

Bank cuts are used in this way several times throughout the series, most prominently in episode 25, where not only Shinji but several other characters are subjected to similar 'interrogations' by their own impressions of other characters, all rendered through recombined bank cuts. It is perhaps worth noting that the narrative context of these sequences is also similar—unlike the conventional use of bank cuts in the control room sequences noted above, where cuts are assembled to support the illusion of a coherent world, these fluttering, reassembled characters appear in sequences where the series is depicting an inner, psychological world rather than a physical one.

One particular sequence, one of the above-mentioned director's cut additions originally part of the *Death & Rebirth* film, provides a unique use of bank cuts that perhaps more than any other highlights their potential as a tool to play with the construction of reality in anime. In this sequence from the extended cut of episode 22, Asuka is fighting the 15th Angel, Arael, a floating creature in low Earth orbit. The Angel's psychic attack hits her and she is thrown into an abstract interrogation where her mind and memories are probed by the Angel, breaking down her sense of self and will to fight. Visually, the sequence is similar to the previous interrogation of Shinji, taking place in a black void, but how the bank cuts are used is significantly different. Following a flashback related to her past, a voice we are meant to assume belongs to Asuka's mother (who in her childhood rejected her in favor of a doll) asks her the question "Who are you?" Immediately, a sequence of four bank clips of Asuka are played, the original backgrounds replaced with alternating solid black and red: her self-introduction to her new classmates (Fig.2.5a, from episode 8), an angry glare at Shinji (Fig.2.5b), a smug expression (Fig.2.5c, also from episode 8) and a desperate, sexual plea to be noticed by Kaji (Fig.2.5d, from the extended version of episode 22). The sequence

I'm Asuka Langley Soryu. Nice to meet you!

Are you an idiot or something?

Here's my chance!

So please look at me!

Figure 2.5. Four bank cuts are recycled multiple times with different voice actors reading the same lines in episode 22. © khara, inc.

ends with a new cut of Asuka screaming "No! That's not me!", and immediately starts over. This sequence of cuts is replayed five times. Unlike in the previous example, the lines of dialogue are unaltered. However, in these five repetitions of the same few cuts, the role of Asuka is played not by her usual voice actress Yūko Miyamura, but by the five actresses who play the other main female characters in

EVA: Mitsuishi Kotono (Misato Katsuragi), Megumi Hayashibara (Rei Ayanami), Miki Nagasawa (Maya Ibuki), Yuriko Amaguchi (Ritsuko Akagi) and Junko Iwao (Hikari Horari). It is interesting to note that Megumi Ogata, the woman who plays the male main character Shinji, is noticeably absent among these alternate Asukas, suggesting that it is the characters, not the actresses, who are taking over Asuka's identity in this sequence.[10]

While in terms of narrative and tone this sequence and the ones mentioned earlier have little in common with the *Tom and Jerry* cartoon used by Bukatman (2014) as an example, the sudden break from an otherwise mostly realist form is similarly jarring in these late-series sequences. But where in *Tom and Jerry* the result of the striking break with realism is comedy, in *EVA* it is something quite different. Instead, the shock to *EVA*'s realism created by repeated cuts paired with unexpected vocals creates a sense of wrongness and unease that reinforces the narrative events. The on-the-surface unspectacular replacement of Asuka's voice with that of another actress highlights the artificiality of her identity as a character. This can be read both in connection to the narrative, where Asuka is fighting an assault on her personal barriers, and as a deliberate questioning of the construction of reality within the series itself.

In the sequence under scrutiny here, the division between visuals and voice in animation, and specifically in anime, is employed in tandem with bank cuts to question the claim to realism of the cuts. In anime specifically, the illusion of a natural connection between sound and image is potentially even more tenuous than in other forms of animation, as sound is recorded after the animation is finished. This means that unlike in classic American animation, where sound is recorded first and lip movement is painstakingly animated to create an illusion of a natural connection, in anime lip flaps are highly abstract. Because of this gap, we really have no evidence to suggest that any of these 'other Asukas' are 'not me' beyond the voice of Yūko Miyamura

10. See also Chapter 4 by Minori Ishida.

screaming that they are, and as such, this use of bank cuts, instead of being simply a cheap trick, serves to call into question Asuka's personal identity and depict what is happening narratively through the form of the animation itself.

It would be easy to analyze this sequence, and indeed many sequences in the last quarter of *EVA*, as the animation revealing its own trick, drawing our attention to the artificial nature of everything happening on screen and the fact that Asuka is, in fact, not a person, but simply an assemblage of painted celluloid and film trickery, voiced by an interchangeable actress. One could even point to the readings of *EVA* that emphasize its challenge to the otaku audience and claim that the point of this sequence is to show them that the world of anime they are so invested in is nothing but an illusion. However, I argue that the series is doing the very opposite. After all, otaku are fully aware of the reassembled, constructed nature of the anime they love, and no less able to feel strong emotions for its characters regardless (Azuma 2009). This is not a sequence where the veil is pulled back and whatever empathy the viewer might have felt for the character is revealed as a misdirected, sad obsession with an unfeeling construct of which the viewer is instructed to let go. Rather, through the narrative and voice performance, the viewer is asked to *further* empathize with Asuka as her reality is unraveled, and the visual unraveling presented through the use of bank cuts enhances that feeling as not only Asuka's identity, but the viewer's perception of the indexical connection between her component parts, sound and vision, is distorted. If we accept that anime conventions can be used as a referent for realism, as Ōtsuka's concept of manga-anime realism postulates, the distortion of this realism here portrays not simply a construction being torn down, but *reality itself* being destabilized. The viewer is expected to accept manga-anime realism *as realism* and react to the unraveling of this realism as one would react to the real world coming undone; in other words, feeling what the characters are feeling in an empathetic, inward-facing way that would not be easy, or perhaps possible, to replicate through even the most impressive CGI effects. Rather than detachment, in other words, this break from the baseline realism of *EVA* through the simple use of bank cuts creates empathy, and showcases through the form of the animation itself what the narrative is about in these sequences, namely, the deconstruction of reality, identity and certainty as humans meet Angels and all personal boundaries are broken down in Instrumentality.

Conclusion

For reasons that are mostly connected to the economic realities of anime production, *EVA* is a series that relies heavily on labor-saving forms of limited animation typical to anime. These include the focus of this chapter, bank cuts, that is, cuts of animation recycled in various new contexts often paired with new dialogue. The series uses these in both genre-typical ways and as a deliberate tool during certain sequences in the latter half of the narrative where they are employed as part of a collection of breaks from the reality the series has been constructing.

While *EVA*'s stylized character designs and limited movement may be seen as less realist than photorealist CGI imagery or the embodied acting of a Disney film, the series adheres to all three of Ōtsuka's anime-typical realisms. Through the employment of scientific, biological and manga-anime realism, *EVA* constructs an internally consistent alternative reality that the otaku spectator is prone to accept as real. In specific sequences in the second half of the series, however, the use of bank cuts highlights the constructed nature of this alternate world by breaking the rules of realism that were used to construct it. In this way, *EVA* is able to depict the breaking down of reality itself in a particularly visceral way that echoes and emphasizes the events of the narrative—and of the outside, social world.

References

Association of Japanese Animation [Nihon dōga kyōkai] (ed.). (2019). *Animēshon yōgo jiten*. Tokyo: Rittorsha.

Azuma, H. (2009). *Otaku: Japan's Database Animals*. Minneapolis, MN: University of Minnesota Press. (Introduction and translation by J. E. Abel and S. Kono).

Berndt, J. (2013). Ghostly: 'Asian Graphic Narratives,' *Nonnonba*, and Manga. In D. Stein and J.-N. Thon (eds.), *From Comic Strips to Graphic Novels: Contributions to the Theory and History of Graphic Narrative* (pp. 363–384). Berlin: deGruyter.

_____. (2018). Anime in Academia: Representative Object, Media Form, and Japanese Studies. *Arts*, 7(4), 56. Retrieved from: DOI: https://doi.org/10.3390/arts7040056

Bolton, C. (2018). *Interpreting Anime*. Minneapolis, MN: University of Minnesota Press.

Bukatman, S. (2014). Some Observations Pertaining to Cartoon Physics; or, the Cartoon Cat in the Machine. In K. Beckman (ed.), *Animating Film Theory* (pp. 301–316). Durham, NC: Duke University Press.

Cirugeda, K. (2017, 11 January). *SakuQ&A: Anime Industry and Production Questions #1*. [web log]. Retrieved from: https://blog.sakugabooru.com/2017/01/11/sakuqa-anime-industry-and-production-questions-1/

Clements, J. (2013). *Anime: A History*. London: Palgrave Macmillan.

Crafton, D. (2012). *Shadow of a Mouse*. Berkeley, CA: University of California Press.

Eisenstein, S. (1986). *Eisenstein on Disney*. Ed. Jay Leyda. Kolkata: Seagull Books.

GAINAX. (1997a). *Shin Seiki Evangerion ekonte shū 1*. Tokyo: Fujimi Shobō.

_____. (1997b). *Shin Seiki Evangerion ekonte shū 2*. Tokyo: Fujimi Shobō.

_____. (1997c). *Shin Seiki Evangerion ekonte shū 3*. Tokyo: Fujimi Shobō.

_____. (1997d). *Shin Seiki Evangerion ekonte shū 4*. Tokyo: Fujimi Shobō.

_____. (1997e). *Shin Seiki Evangerion ekonte shū 5*. Tokyo: Fujimi Shobō.

_____. (1998). *Shin Seiki Evangerion gekijōban ekonte shū*. Tokyo: Fujimi Shobō.

Ōtsuka, E. (2003). *Atomu no meidai: Tezuka Osamu to sengo manga no shudai*. Tokyo: Tokuma Shoten.

_____. (2010). World and Variation: The Reproduction and Consumption of Narrative. (Introduction and translation by Marc Steinberg). *Mechademia*, 5, 99–116.

Rowley, S. (2005). Life Reproduced in Drawings: Preliminary Comments upon Realism in Animation. *Animation Journal*, 13, 65–85.

Sevakis, J. (2016) Answerman: Why Are Compilation Films Made? *Anime News Network*. Retrieved from: https://www.animenewsnetwork.com /answerman/2016-12-02/.109367

Shamoon, D. (2015). The Superflat Space of Japanese Anime. In E. Lim and L. Chee (eds.), *Asian Cinema and the Use of Space: Interdisciplinary Perspectives* (pp. 93–108). London: Routledge.

Shin Seiki Evangerion Blu-ray BOX STANDARD EDITION. (n.d.). Retrieved from: https://www.evangelion.co.jp/ng.html

Steinberg, M. (2012a). Inventing Intervals: The Digital Image in *Metropolis* and *Gankutsuō*. *Mechademia*, 7, 3–22. DOI: https://doi.org/10.1353 /mec.2012.0003.

_____. (2012b). *Anime's Media Mix: Franchising Toys and Characters in Japan*. Minneapolis, MN: University of Minnesota Press.

_____. (2014). Realism in the Animation Media Environment: Animation Theory from Japan. In K. Beckman (ed.), *Animating Film Theory* (pp. 287–300). Durham, NC: Duke University Press.

Suan, S. (2018). Consuming Production: Anime's Layers of Transnationality and Dispersal of Agency as Seen in Shirobako and Sakuga-Fan Practices. *Arts*, 7(3), 27. Retrieved from: DOI: https://doi.org/10.3390 /arts7030027.

Suzuki, T. (1996). *Narrating the Self: Fictions of Japanese Modernity*. Stanford, CA: Stanford University Press.

Vilas-Boas, E. (2019). Anime Classic Neon Genesis Evangelion Is Finally on Netflix. So Why Are Some Fans Upset? *Vulture*. Retrieved from: https://www.vulture.com/2019/06/neon-genesis-evangelion-netflix -controversy-explained-guide.html

Watanabe, H. (2019). Interview with the author.

Films and Series

Bishōjo senshi Sailor Moon. Directed by Jun'ichi Satō and Kunihiko Ikuhara. Toei Animation, 1992–97.

Card Captor Sakura. Direkted by Morio Asaka. Madhouse, 1998–2000.

Chōjikū yōsai Macross: Ai, oboete imasu ka. Directed by Shōji Kawamori. Tatsunoko, 1984.

Evangerion shin gekijōban: Jo. Directed by Hideaki Anno. Khara, 2007.

Evangerion shin gekijōban: Ha. Directed by Hideaki Anno. Khara, 2009.

Evangerion shin gekijōban: Q. Directed by Hideaki Anno. Khara, 2012.

Gekijō-ban alps no shōjo Heidi. Directed by Sumiko Nakao and Isao Takahata. Zuiyo Eizo, 1979.

Kidō senshi Gundam I. Directed by Yoshiyuki Tomino. Sunrise, 1981.

Kidō senshi Gundam II: Ai senshi. Directed by Yoshiyuki Tomino. Sunrise, 1981.

Kidō senshi Gundam III: Meguriai sora. Directed by Yoshiyuki Tomino. Sunrise, 1982.

Kidō senshi zeta Gundam. Directed by Yoshiyuki Tomino. Sunrise, 1985–86.

Kyandi Kyandi. Directed by Tetsuo Imazawa. Toei Animation, 1976–79.

Mahō shōjo Madoka Magika. Directed by Akiyuki Simbo. Shaft, 2011.

Mahō shōjo ririkaru Nanoha. Directed by Akiyuki Simbo. Seven Arcs, 2004.

Shin Evangerion gekijōban: ‖. Directed by Hideaki Anno. Khara, 2021.

Shin seiki Evangerion. Directed by Hideaki Anno. GAINAX, 1995–96.

Shin seiki Evangerion gekijōban: DEATH (TRUE)². Directed by Hideaki Anno. GAINAX / Production I.G, 1998.

Shin seiki Evangerion gekijōban: Ea/magokoro wo, kimi ni. Directed by Hideaki Anno. GAINAX / Production I.G, 1997.

Shin seiki Evangerion gekijōban: Shi to shinsei. Directed by Hideaki Anno. GAINAX / Production I.G, 1997.

Shinkansen henkei robo Shinkarion THE ANIMATION. Directed by Takahiro Ikezoe. OLM, Inc., 2018–19.

Tetsuwan Atom. Directed by Osamu Tezuka. Mushi Production, 1963–66.

Yūsha Ō Gaogaigā. Directed by Yoshitomo Yonetani. Sunrise, 1997–98.

3. Beethoven, the Ninth Symphony and *Neon Genesis Evangelion*
Using Pre-existing Music in Anime

Heike Hoffer

In present-day Japan, the music from the seminal television anime *Neon Genesis Evangelion* (*EVA*), which aired in 26 episodes between 1995 and 1996, is just as recognizable and easily encountered in daily life as images from the anime itself. The catchy melodies of the score by Shirō Sagisu are found in unexpected places, heard as background music in furniture stores, as punctuation for Japanese comedy and news broadcasts and spilling out of pachinko parlors to herald the arrival of the latest game machines featuring the anime's characters. Similar to many TV anime today, the budget for *EVA* was tight, and the application of Sagisu's score reflects a certain economy of means where pieces of music are repeated and recycled from episode to episode, getting the maximum practical use out of each track and allowing for less time in the recording studio. This reuse of musical material is valuable because it creates a sense of continuity for the viewer as the series progresses through its weekly episodes. Some characters, primarily women, have musical themes that represent them—think of Misato's jazzy, laid-back flute melody, the Debussy-esque harmonic planing of Rei's pensive theme or the rootin'-tootin' country-western music that accompanies Asuka—and battle scenes or scenes of daily life are colored by a handful of specially crafted tracks that capture the essence of those moments.

Given the amount of musical repetition found in *EVA*, scenes where the music deviates from what the viewer expects serve to fore-ground the music's relationship to the images and the narrative, drawing

How to cite this book chapter:
Hoffer, H. 2021. Beethoven, the Ninth Symphony and *Neon Genesis Evangelion*: Using Pre-existing Music in Anime. In: Santiago Iglesias, J. A. and Soler Baena, A. (Eds.). *Anime Studies: Media-Specific Approaches to Neon Genesis Evangelion*. Pp. 85–109 Stockholm: Stockholm University Press. DOI: https://doi.org/10.16993/bbp.d. License: CC-BY 4.0

attention to these new connections. This process is what makes the 24th episode of *EVA* so remarkable in its use of only a single musical idea in the entire episode, the fourth movement from Ludwig van Beethoven's Ninth Symphony, colloquially referred to as the "Ode to Joy" after the name of Friedrich Schiller's poem that serves as the textual basis for the movement. *EVA* director Hideaki Anno's choice to select a mode of presentation that would highlight one of the most well-known pieces in the repertoire of Western classical music raises many questions: Why did Anno choose a piece of pre-existing music rather than having his staff composer Shirō Sagisu write something new for that episode? Why did Anno choose Beethoven's Ninth Symphony rather than the Third or the Fifth or a symphony by a different composer? Is there a connection between the Ninth Symphony and the Japanese audience for whom *EVA* was originally intended? How can this meaning-laden combination of music and images be interpreted from an audience-oriented perspective? Before attempting an analysis of the musical, cultural and cinematic elements found in the 24th episode of *EVA*, two levels of groundwork need to be laid: the first placing Beethoven and the Ninth Symphony in the context of modern Japan; and the second defining the interpretive and expressive issues that a director must consider when using a piece of pre-existing music in anime.

Beethoven in Context

Since Beethoven's death in 1827, most people in Europe and North America have possessed a basic familiarity with the composer's primary traits, having learned about him through school music classes, youth orchestra programs, television shows or even feature-length films (Yang 2014). Beethoven's well-known portrait, painted by Joseph Karl Stieler in 1820, captures his demeanor perfectly, depicting a scowling man with unkempt hair wearing a dark suit coat, a crisp white shirt and a red scarf, balancing a writing pen in his hand poised over the manuscript score of his *Missa Solemnis*. This portrait was Beethoven's personal favorite of the many likenesses produced in his lifetime, and he regularly had prints of it made to distribute to his admirers. Most notable in Stieler's portrayal is the composer's wild hair, which he refused to cover with the tightly curled wigs that were part of formal attire in 18th-century Vienna. This rebellious spirit, found both in his tumultuous life and in his adventurous music, was one of the composer's most admired traits and became the subject of many apocryphal tales. His lack of a wife or children, his failed romance with the mysterious Immortal Beloved and his struggles to conceal his deafness all contributed to Beethoven's image as a suffering artist, a mindset of self-sacrifice reinforced by his famous words from the *Heiligenstadt Testament* of 1802, in which he wrote:

> But what a humiliation for me when someone standing next to me heard a flute in the distance and I heard nothing, or someone standing next to me heard a shepherd singing and again I heard nothing. Such incidents drove me almost to despair; a little more of that and I would have ended my life – it was only my art that held me back. Ah, it seemed to me impossible to leave the world until I had brought forth all that I felt was within me. So I endured this wretched existence . . .
> (cited in Fisk & Nichols 1997: 59)

The premiere of the Ninth Symphony on 7 May 1824 in Vienna marked the pinnacle of Beethoven's compositional achievements, containing a utopian vision of hope for mankind. The high point of the symphony was the fourth movement, a massive setting of Schiller's popular ode *An die Freude*—with a few textual additions by Beethoven himself—composed for an expanded orchestra with a full chorus and four vocal soloists. Adding words to the instrumental genre of the symphony was a new idea that came as a revelation to audiences at the premiere, and Schiller's text about brotherhood and human achievement was an ideal choice that resonated strongly with the citizens of Vienna in the decade following the Napoleonic Wars.

Beethoven's legacy was transformed during the Romantic era, elevating him to the position of the ultimate creative master whose utter devotion to his art was to be emulated by anyone claiming to be an artist themselves. His superhuman persona was furthered by numerous biographical recountings of his life—some more reliable than others—that appealed to a broad general public, most notably Alexander Wheelock Thayer's *Life of Beethoven*, a multi-volume set written in the 1860s and 1870s, and later Romain Rolland's *Beethoven the Creator* from 1903. This god-like image of Beethoven was introduced to Japan during the period of rapid modernization that characterized the early Meiji era, when Japanese leaders invited European and American experts into the country to overhaul many aspects of Japanese life and society (Wade 2014). As part of this push to modernize, prominent German music professors were installed in newly founded music universities, where they imparted an immense respect for German music to their Japanese students—a respect that remains today (Galliano 2002: 40–42). At the primary level, Japanese compulsory education for children was modified to mirror Western pedagogical models. Music became a required subject nationwide and didactic school singing books were created that included pieces drawn from a variety of sources, containing mostly European and American traditional music and themes from masterpieces of Western classical music that were fitted with newly written Japanese lyrics, as well as a handful of Japanese folk melodies set to a tonal harmonic accompaniment, all designed to expose Japanese children to the sound of Western classical music from an early age (Eppstein 1994). Modern versions of these singing books continue to form the cornerstone of Japanese musical education today, with the "Ode to Joy" still featuring prominently among the hand-picked repertoire.

Of all the Western classical composers, Beethoven is treated with a special reverence in Japan, largely due to the national phenomenon of listening to and performing the Ninth Symphony (Jp. *Daiku*) as part of the celebratory period leading up to the New Year. This music, especially the "Ode to Joy" movement, has become deeply intertwined with notions of self-betterment connected to the New Year, which in Japan is traditionally considered to be an important time of rebirth and renewal spent with close family and friends. Speaking to the *New York Times*, Naoyuki Miura, long-time Artistic Director of the New York-based association Music from Japan, explained: "For Japanese, listening to Beethoven's Ninth at the end of the year is a semi-religious experience. People feel they have not completed the year spiritually until they hear it" (cited in Weisman 1990: 13). Miura is definitely excessive in his description, but it is true that the "Ode to Joy" serves as an important aural marker of the holiday season, similar to the role of Christmas songs heard in many Western countries. The *Daiku* is broadcast on television and radio shows, while the "Ode to Joy" accompanies commercials, sounds through the speaker systems in public areas, and plays in shopping malls, convenience stores and supermarkets, making for a pervasive presentation that continually reminds listeners of the imminent arrival of the New Year, with its themes of rejuvenation and personal transformation.

One particularly unique feature of Japan's New Year season is the tradition of amateur choirs giving performances of the *Daiku* during the month of December, a group activity that has been well documented in the works of Kerry Candaele (2013), Eddie Chang (2007, 2009) and Michel Wasserman (2006). Although concerts featuring the Ninth Symphony can be confirmed as having been held in Japan as far back as World War I, its current form as an end-of-year staple originated primarily in the 1980s, a time of affluence in Japan due to the bubble economy when many professional orchestras, community music groups and state-of-the-art concert halls were founded. The *Daiku* can be performed year round, but the vast majority of concerts occur during the last two weeks of December, with the frequency of performances numbering well into the hundreds across the country. Concert halls nationwide are booked solid for these events, and venues in large cities may host as many as four per day, each given by a different ensemble. Certain *Daiku* concerts are especially famous for their larger-than-life presentation, particularly the Suntory *Daiku* in Osaka, which boasts a chorus of a staggering 10,000 members, and the slightly smaller Sumida Ward *Daiku* in Tokyo, with an impressive 5,000 singers. *Daiku* concerts are usually spectacular affairs organized by large corporations, local governments or amateur choral groups, who frequently join forces to share the expenses of renting a hall and hiring a professional orchestra and soloists. Choir members are predominantly non-professional volunteers who come from a wide range of ages and socio-economic backgrounds, making the complement of the Japanese *Daiku* quite different from the Ninth Symphony, which is a piece reserved for professionals in the Western performance context. Choristers choose to participate in *Daiku* concerts for many different reasons, but there are two overarching ideas that serve as their primary motivation. First, singers perceive a close connection between Schiller's jubilant lyrics and the festive celebrations of the approaching holiday, heightening the joyful atmosphere of the New Year season. Second, chorus members feel that singing Beethoven, who overcame substantial personal struggles to write enduring masterpieces, will give them the inner strength to overcome their own troubles in the coming year. Learning the difficult music and memorizing the complicated German text is seen as a short-term challenge that the choristers conquer together by encouraging and supporting one another, believing that withstanding these difficulties and working as a team will be a catalyst for success in their future goals. As choir director Yutaka Tomizawa told *The Japan Times*:

> Of course there are many choral works we could do . . . But there's nothing like the Ninth. It seems impossible for amateurs to sing, but Beethoven casts a spell on you. Many start off thinking, 'I can't do this,' but then other members urge them to try harder, and working together they get it done. The feeling of accomplishment is sublime. (cited in Brasor 2010: n.p.)

It is this fighting spirit that *Daiku* singers want to channel into their own activities, drawing on Beethoven's example to overcome hardships in both the musical arena and in their personal lives.

In Japan, the "Ode to Joy" carries a strong aural reminder of the festive end-of-year celebrations, but also evokes themes of personal rejuvenation connected to the New Year and serves as an anthem to hard work, dedication to self-betterment and achieving success by relying on the mutual support of others who are also struggling in their own way. Modern Japanese are definitely familiar with the formidable image of Beethoven and the Ninth Symphony present in the Western historical context, but they also think of Beethoven in a more personal, intimate way as a composer whose music they sang from their school songbooks with their classmates and whose admirable ability to surmount his individual hardships can provide inspiration for overcoming the trials of daily life.

The Strengths and Weaknesses of Pre-existing Music

There is no doubt that the musical score of an anime exerts a powerful influence on the images and narrative, forming an integral part of the viewer's experience. This impression is heightened when directors choose to include a piece of pre-existing music as part of the score, creating a wide variety of interpretive and expressive perspectives that must be considered carefully in relation to how the music is understood by the viewer. Claudia Gorbman describes the use of pre-existing music in Western film as the director's attempt to create "a point of experience for the spectator" (1987: 2), a cinematic moment that is memorable, unique and imbued with powerful expressive meaning. The ways in which pre-existing music can influence a scene are greatly dependent on factors stemming from the viewpoint of both the director and the viewer, inspiring many possible interpretations in the complex counterpoint between music and image. Gorbman has outlined three distinct ways in which music functions to create meaning in film, methods that can also be applied to anime (1987: 13). First, meaning is generated through purely musical codes, the vocabulary and syntax of musical discourse. These include tonality, tempo, key, meter, structure, form, orchestration and other elements. At the risk of oversimplifying, is the music fast or slow, loud or soft, happy or sad, elaborate or simple, and how do these elements interact with what appears on the screen? These components can be observed and analyzed directly from the printed score, but are most often acquired through direct listening in the case of anime because the original scores are not available in archives or commercially. Second, meaning can come from recognizing cultural musical codes, which stem from the viewer's reactions to the music based on their own particular cultural conventions (Anderson 2016). Viewers understand what types of music are appropriate or inappropriate for certain settings, know which music represents high-class or low-class values, can identify music that represents other time periods or a stereotyped view of another culture or social group and so on. Third, meaning comes from cinematic musical codes that govern the interaction between music and image based on the conventions of visual media. For example, music is impacted by techniques of sound editing and image editing, the necessity to prioritize the dialogue, the manner in which the position of the sound source is understood spatially and many other factors. These three forms of meaning-making work together to influence the viewer's interpretation of anime's music, images and narrative.

When pre-existing music appears in anime, it almost always exists alongside the images as an equal, not as a subordinate in the manner of the original score. This comment is not meant to belittle the role of the original score in the experience of watching anime, but to convey that original scores are often treated as a secondary form of expression working in the background to support the images, what Gorbman refers to as the "bath of affect" that "lessens the awareness of the frame; it relaxes the censor, drawing the spectator further into the fantasy-illusion suggested by filmic narration . . . a catalyst in the suspension of judgement" (1987: 6). In contrast, using pre-existing music is a way of foregrounding a particular piece and its contribution to the narrative, giving both pre-existing music and the original score important, but different, roles in anime. These roles are distinct from music's position as diegetic or non-diegetic sound, offering the director a wide variety of ways to position music in relation to the images to create many types of expressive meaning. Pre-existing music functions actively as part of the storytelling mechanism, rather than as an inconspicuous assistant, because every piece carries a host of extramusical associations from the life, history and culture of the piece outside the anime that impose a meaning on the images. These extramusical associations are inescapable, but also imperative to the director's artistic vision. As Royal S. Brown wrote:

> . . . [T]he excerpts of classical music compositions that replace the original film score no longer function purely as a backing for key emotional situations, but rather exist as a kind of parallel emotional/aesthetic universe . . . [T]he affect . . . tends to remain within the music itself, which sheds its traditional invisibility rather than being transferred onto a given diegetic situation to which it is subordinated. Put another way, the music, rather than supporting and/or coloring the visual images and narrative situations, stands as an image in its own right, helping the audience read the film's other images as such rather than as a replacement for or imitation of objective reality. (1994: 239–240)

Here, Brown is writing specifically about the use of Western classical music in Western film, but his ideas can easily be applied to all genres of music in any visual media, anime included. Using a pre-existing piece puts the music in the expressive foreground, showing off the referential aspects of the piece and allowing viewers to compare the life of the music from outside the anime with its role inside the anime, hopefully leading the viewer to understand why the director chose that particular piece in the first place. Adding to the opinions of Brown, Jonathan Godsall wrote:

> By comparing (our conception of) what the quoted text [pre-existing music] *is*, and what it *means*, *outside* of the film, with the form and placement of the quotation *within* the film, we can come to an understanding of the latter's purpose and effect . . . the *referentiality* of the music within the film is central to the deployment and interpretation of pre-existing music in the cinema. (2019: 92; emphasis in the original)

There are many reasons an anime director might choose to use pre-existing music in an anime. To give a few examples: if the piece is in the public domain in Japan, then it might be inexpensive or even free to use; the music can evoke ideas of culture or class that give a sense of authenticity to the anime world; the music can give an impression of a character's personality; or perhaps the director feels that pre-existing music is less risky because it is a fixed entity that he or she can control rather than depending on the whims of a composer who may not 'get' the director's artistic vision. A director also chooses pre-existing music based on the way the piece conveys meaning when removed from its original musical context and is given a new context in the anime. For example, in the concert setting, the "Ode to Joy" movement of Beethoven's Ninth Symphony is understood in the context of the musical material that came before it as the culmination of the three preceding movements. But when the "Ode to Joy" is excerpted from the symphony and placed into an anime, it now stands alone and works as a discrete entity. Again, turning to Claudia Gorbman:

> What all these set-pieces have in common is not any one function of music, or its narrative status as diegetic or nondiegetic, or its historical provenance or form. Rather, once heard they are all choices that seem ineluctable, at once wittily detached and emotionally appropriate and poignant. Welding themselves to visual rhythms onscreen, they become the music of the specific movie scene rather than the piece one may have known before. (2006: 4)

Every viewer carries with them a unique, highly personal set of extramusical associations about pieces of pre-existing music that are expanded when the viewer experiences that music in the new context of the anime, adding to their overall image of the piece itself. The director takes on a substantial responsibility when using these works because the piece will be changed forever in the mind of the viewer through these new associations. For example, the 15th episode of *EVA* includes a scene where the main character Shinji Ikari plays the cello, performing the opening of the "Prelude" movement from J. S. Bach's *Cello Suite #1 in G major*, BWV 1007. Some Japanese viewers reported that they had been unfamiliar with the First Cello Suite and had heard it for the first time in that particular scene, inspiring them to find out more about Bach's music based on their positive impressions of the piece. For those viewers, Bach's First Cello Suite became indelibly linked to *EVA* as its primary context and the piece's role in music history was secondary, whereas the interpretation would be the opposite for a musician who was already familiar with the First Cello Suite and its existing 300-year history.

The various levels of knowledge brought by the viewer to the experience of hearing a piece of pre-existing music in an anime creates an artistic risk a director must face, since there is no guarantee that the viewer's interpretation will be the same from person to person given the wide range of historical and cultural associations available. Technically, it is not necessary for the viewer to recognize the piece at all, since they can still enjoy the music under the assumption that it is part of the original score, but this situation is clearly not what the director desires. Most risky for the director's artistic vision are personal associations. Perhaps this particular piece of pre-existing music played when the viewer walked down the aisle on their wedding day or was on the radio when their boyfriend broke up with them, coloring their viewpoint in a way the director could not have imagined or controlled. Conversely, the viewer recognizes that a film is not made by chance, but through intentional acts, meaning that they are also guessing about the director's intent (Godsall 2019: 70–82). Foregrounding the music by using a pre-existing piece signals to the viewer that the director is trying to communicate a meaningful relationship between the music and images, but the message itself may seem ambiguous unless the director has provided an interpretation publicly, which they rarely do.

Including pre-existing music in an anime can be a blessing and a curse given the many factors influencing the viewer's interpretation. This inherent unpredictability makes *EVA* director Hideaki Anno's use of the "Ode to Joy" especially notable because he was able to assume that Japanese viewers would possess a fairly similar set of historical, cultural and personal associations for this particular piece, an uncommon situation when interacting with a wide range of audience members possessing many different life experiences. By using such ubiquitously understood music, Anno could be reasonably confident that viewers would recognize the artistic message he was trying to convey, taking advantage of a clear line of musical communication that is rare in anime or any type of visual media.

Scene Analyses

As mentioned previously, the musical underscore for the 24th episode of *EVA* is made up entirely of portions of the fourth movement from Beethoven's Ninth Symphony. Long segments of the episode contain no music at all, drawing attention to three specific scenes where the "Ode to Joy" is heard, and the episode contains none of Sagisu's original score, temporarily abandoning the music to which the viewer has become accustomed and highlighting the "Ode to Joy" as a key component of interpreting the visual and narrative events. The "Ode to Joy" theme is used to represent the character Kaworu Nagisa, who makes his first appearance in this episode, and to signal his great importance to the story. It is extremely uncommon for a major character to be introduced at the very end of an anime series, but the utopian vision of the "Ode to Joy" combined with Japan's seasonal ideas of personal renewal and the collaborative tradition of the *Daiku*, communicate to the viewer that Kaworu will have substantial impact on the world of *EVA* despite his last-minute arrival. This momentous relationship between character and music necessitates a close reading of each scene with its musical context in mind.

Encounter at the Crater Lake

Kaworu is introduced in this scene, which opens with the main character Shinji standing at the edge of a huge lake formed in a bomb crater. Shinji gazes over the lake with his back to the viewer as we hear a voice-over of his thoughts in which he expresses his anguish that there is no one in his life that he can consider a friend. The burning light of the setting sun directly behind his head emphasizes the intensity of his mental pain. His anxiety rises, but the sound of someone humming the "Ode to Joy" theme breaks his train of thought. The melody sneaks into the scene so that the beginning of the tune is not audible, giving the impression that Shinji was so wrapped up in his self-torment that he did not immediately notice when his unknown companion started humming. Since the tune is so well-known, viewers can recognize it easily even though they are not hearing it from the beginning. Following the tradition of *Daiku* singing where the "Ode to Joy" is an uplifting collaborative music meant to be performed with the help of others, used in combination with this aural reminder of Schiller's text concerning brotherhood and mutual support, this theme provides a clue that the unidentified singer might be the solution to Shinji's loneliness and be able to renew his spirit. Shinji and Kaworu are the only two characters shown making music in *EVA*, so this special skill immediately forges a unique connection between them in the mind of the viewer and suggests that they would be a good match as friends.

Shinji looks to his left to find the source of the sound and sees Kaworu seated on a tall piece of concrete rubble staring out over the water. He finishes humming the first part of the "Ode to Joy" theme before acknowledging Shinji, establishing a firm link between the character and Beethoven's famous tune. Kaworu finally speaks while continuing to look out over the lake. "Singing is good," he says, "It brings joy and revitalizes the soul. I think that song is the greatest achievement of Lilim [human] culture." This statement shows Kaworu's recognition of the prominent position of the "Ode to Joy" worldwide as a message of brotherhood and compassion, as well as calling on the seasonally inspired idea that performances of this piece serve to promote personal rejuvenation. Kaworu, who is actually an enemy creature called an Angel created to mimic humans, seeks to experience feelings of intimacy that he has never encountered among his own species by using the "Ode to Joy" to communicate his wish for meaningful companionship.

Suddenly, the image shifts to Shinji's viewpoint as Kaworu turns toward the camera, showing his face for the first time, and asks, "Don't you agree, Ikari Shinji?" Kaworu is waiting for Shinji's opinion on his assessment of the "Ode to Joy" as the greatest human achievement, but as Kaworu stares into the camera, he seems to be speaking to the viewer. This is the first of a number of examples in this episode in which Kaworu appears to recognize the world outside the anime, as if he is asking the viewers themselves, not just Shinji, whether the act of singing or the music known as the "Ode to Joy" are powerful forces in their own lives.

Kaworu and Shinji continue to talk as the camera pulls back to show the entire setting, with Kaworu perched on the tall concrete block on the left-hand side of the screen, towering over Shinji on the right-hand side, and the reflection of the red setting sun in the lake making a sort of visual barrier between them. Kaworu's physical position above Shinji, the fact that he knew Shinji's name when Shinji did not know his and Kaworu's easy confidence in the face of Shinji's crippling self-doubt puts Kaworu in a position of superiority. Musically, this superiority had already been established from the opening of the scene based on the type of music associated with each of the two boys. Although Shinji has been presented as weak and lacking confidence, his ability to play the cello as demonstrated in the 15th episode endears him to the viewer by revealing that he is capable of feeling personal satisfaction and emotional depth. On the other hand, by selecting the "Prelude" from Bach's First Cello Suite, an unaccompanied solo piece for a single player, Shinji can make music while avoiding any interaction with other musicians, embracing a kind of self-imposed isolation that is inclined to be viewed as suspect in Japan, where joining in group activities has long been thought of as necessary for good mental health and social acceptance. Conversely, Kaworu has opted for the "Ode to Joy," the performance of which requires a large chorus and orchestra to perform and which promotes collaboration and a sense of community, traits that draw attention to Kaworu's seemingly better-adjusted worldview. Bach and Beethoven are both composers who are strongly connected to the idea of the power of the human spirit: Bach as a man working in the service of God who accepted that his music had to conform to certain artistic parameters to fulfill his role as a musical servant—much like Shinji obediently following the orders of the adults to save humanity; and Beethoven as a man working in the service of his own artistic ideals who refused to accept the limitations of the musical status quo—similar to Kaworu's decision to reject his destiny as humanity's destroyer later in the episode. In today's world, a genius rebel is generally preferred to a brilliant conformist, elevating the independent, confident Kaworu with his Beethovenian spirit over the compliant, Bachian Shinji.

Waiting in the Wings

Shinji's next encounter with Kaworu and the "Ode to Joy" comes later in the episode as he waits for Kaworu to finish his Eva robot pilot training at the NERV military headquarters. The first shot in the scene is an extreme close-up of Shinji's left ear with a small, black earbud headphone inside. Although Shinji's face is not visible, he has been shown using his black headphones to listen to music on his SDAT cassette player frequently throughout the series, making him easy to recognize here. The close-up image of his ear and headphone emphasizes the act of listening, encouraging the viewer to take notice of the music. In earlier episodes, Shinji's choice of listening material has been barely audible to the viewer, consisting of peppy, upbeat Japanese pop songs engineered to sound thin and dull as if his headphones were the sound source and the viewer is hearing the music from the outside. Since Shinji's preference for popular music has been established in numerous scenes, this moment in the 24th episode comes as a surprise because the sound coming from his headphones is not pop music, but a recording of an orchestra performing the fourth movement of Beethoven's Ninth Symphony. The sound is only audible for about one and a half seconds, just long enough for the violins to play a mere seven notes of the "Ode to Joy" theme, but the excerpt is perfectly cut to include a portion of the theme that the viewer can recognize immediately even in the incredibly short time frame. Shinji opting to replace his usual Japanese pop tunes with the "Ode to Joy" is significant because it is a clear sign of Kaworu's developing influence over him. It is the first time in the anime that Shinji has taken an active interest in getting to know another person and he has sought out a cassette recording of the Ninth Symphony as a way of learning more about Kaworu, showing that Shinji is not as closed off to the possibility of human relationships as he may claim. Following the ideas of collaborative *Daiku* singing and seasonal rebirth, this scene contains the second musical suggestion that these two boys might be able to sustain and encourage each other as friends.

Kaworu emerges from behind a set of formidable-looking steel doors and enters the long, grey corridor where Shinji is waiting. Shinji was listening to "Ode to Joy" with his head down, as if concentrating carefully on the music, but now he looks up and removes the headphones from his ears, blushing as Kaworu greets him. The camera momentarily adopts Shinji's point of view, again giving the impression that Kaworu is speaking directly to the viewer, as he asks if Shinji was waiting for him. As Kaworu and Shinji chat, the "Ode to Joy" continues to stream unobtrusively out of Shinji's headphones, accompanying their awkward conversation with music representing personal renewal and the power of working together for mutual support. Initially, this musical passage, which is excerpted from the opening orchestral material of the fourth movement, is played only by the strings with the "Ode to Joy" theme in the violins, making for a purposefully understated section that remains quietly under the dialogue and hints at their budding friendship. But when Kaworu suggests that they go to the facility's large communal bath together so that they can continue talking, the wind and brass sections join the strings, taking over the "Ode to Joy" theme with a triumphal, soaring quality that reveals Shinji's sense of elation that Kaworu wants to spend time with him. Even though the music is limited in volume and emotional impact by being restricted to Shinji's headphones as the sound source, hearing the instruments of the orchestra come together in the "Ode to Joy" theme offers up a genuine hope that Kaworu and Shinji can come together as companions.

The Final Battle

Ultimately, Kaworu reveals his true identity as the enemy Angel that Shinji will have to destroy to save humanity, crushing any hope of their developing friendship. The entire final battle scene between the two boys is accompanied by the fourth movement of the Ninth Symphony in the role of the non-diegetic underscore, serving as the climax of an orchestrational crescendo that has mirrored the narrative pacing of the episode: Kaworu's simple diegetic solo humming of the "Ode to Joy" marked his first meeting with Shinji, after which the piece grew within the diegetic realm to include an orchestra emanating from Shinji's headphones, and finally moved into the non-diegetic realm, using a full recording of the symphony with both orchestra and chorus in the final battle to save humanity. The events of the battle are not specifically timed to match the music, nor has the music endured any substantial cuts or adjustments to fit the images, but there are certain points where the two elements are carefully synchronized to great narrative effect.

The full orchestra sounds the "Ode to Joy" theme as Kaworu lowers his mental protective shield and allows the humans' defensive sensors to identify him as an enemy, triggering an extended series of quick cuts showing the flurry of intense activity in the NERV military headquarters as the humans rush to protect themselves. This musical statement is harmonically stable, a somewhat strange match for the chaotic images, but the tension of the scene aligns with the music as the piece begins to modulate to other keys, creating a sense of harmonic instability. The moment when Kaworu passes through an important defensive checkpoint has been timed to correspond with a highly dissonant chord that represents artistic chaos, displaying the true horror of his seemingly effortless progress through the supposedly impenetrable military structure.

Thus far, the underscore has only included instruments, but Shinji's arrival on the scene in his Eva robot is accompanied by the singers, marking Shinji as the spokesman for humanity. The solo baritone, singing alone, sounds his declamatory lines "O Freunde, nicht diese Töne! Sondern lasst uns angenehmere anstimmen und freudenvollere" (Oh friends, not these tones! Rather let us sing more cheerful and more joyful ones), as we see Kaworu descending through the NERV military headquarters and witness Shinji, alone inside his Eva robot, screaming angrily at Kaworu, "You betrayed me and hurt my feelings . . . just like my father did!" Both the solo baritone and Shinji are attempting to cope with the musical and emotional uncertainty they are experiencing, but the baritone will be able to rely on the help of the orchestra, chorus and other soloists, while Shinji has no one to aid him during his struggle and is forced to endure his internal turmoil alone.

The baritone sings the lyrical "Ode to Joy" theme and its famous text "Freude, schöner Götterfunken, Tochter aus Elysium . . ." (Joy, beautiful divine spark, Daughter of Elysium . . .) as Shinji and Kaworu come face to face and engage in combat, recalling moments from earlier in the episode when this melody was a symbol of their developing friendship. Various scenes unfold during which the humans plan to self-destruct the NERV military headquarters and Kaworu rhapsodizes about fate, all taking place as the "Ode to Joy" theme continues to develop in the orchestra and chorus with a text about brotherhood and utopian ideals. There is another convergence of music and image as Kaworu unlocks the final defense system to open "Heaven's Door" and enters the underground chamber where he can destroy humanity. The timing of this event coincides with the chorus and orchestra as they rise to a fever pitch for a huge fortissimo arrival on a massive fermata with the text "vor Gott!" (before God!), a fitting prelude to Kaworu's encounter with the Angel Lilith in the underground chamber, a godlike creature that will determine humanity's final judgement.

Beethoven's score has remained intact so far, but now a large cut skips over the stylized Turkish march to a choral statement of the "Ode to Joy" found later in the movement accompanied by regal triplet figures in the strings. This triumphant music accompanies the progression of the next scene as Shinji intensifies his attacks and Kaworu questions the Angel Lilith about the future of humanity. The musical arrival at Beethoven's ponderous *Andante maestoso* section—scored for men's voices, trombones and low strings—corresponds with Shinji using his Eva robot to smash his way into the underground chamber, after which he approaches Kaworu menacingly and grabs him with the robot's massive armored hand. Trombones were an uncommon instrument for use in the symphony in Beethoven's era, but they were a mainstay of the opera world as the harbingers of the underworld and the presence of death, a role Beethoven calls on here. The text concerns "Diesen Kuss der ganzen Welt" (This kiss for the whole world), the idea that a loving God will provide salvation to all mankind, but the sound of the trombones serves as a reminder that a cold death awaits anyone who does not receive this blessing. The trombones and their ominous underworld sounds pervade this entire scene, during which Kaworu rejects his destiny and begs Shinji to kill him to save humanity, making Kaworu's death an event that is foretold in the orchestra long before it takes place on screen.

Finally, this extended battle scene reaches one of the most exceptional moments in anime history, a still shot lasting an entire minute in duration that pauses the images at the most climactic point in the action. We see a single shot of Shinji's Eva robot clutching the tiny body of Kaworu in its hand as the *Andante maestoso* section continues to play, forcing the viewer to focus their full attention on what they are hearing and engage with this musical commentary on the events of the narrative. This particular moment in the *Andante maestoso* contains a textual assurance of the existence of a kind, forgiving God, with choral passages that are hymn-like and reflective sung in stately dotted rhythms over insistent, shimmering figures in the strings in their upper register, reminiscent of the glimmering canopy of stars mentioned in Schiller's poem. It is a spellbinding moment in the symphony, with rich harmonies and brilliant orchestration that comprises some of Beethoven's most beautiful music. But this passage is not the most famous music from the Ninth Symphony and is likely not a section that most viewers recognize, so why is it used to underscore this pivotal scene?

Imagine how this scene might be interpreted if it was instead underscored by the bombastic finale section from the end of the movement, where Beethoven pounds away enthusiastically on the tonic chord for an unmistakably jubilant finish. By the final measures of the symphony, everything has reached its logical conclusion musically: all the themes have been developed properly, dissonances are revolved, harmonies are stabilized and returned to the tonic key and everything is predictably orderly. This well-ordered closing material makes a wonderfully satisfying end to the musical journey of the Ninth Symphony, but highlighting such tidied-up music during the still shot would shift the focus away from the psychology of the main character to the abstract idea of 'winning,' retreating into the anime genre's well-worn story of an insecure boy who pilots his giant robot to victory with the help of some cute girls and crazy classmates. These types of conventional anime tropes are what the *EVA* series has actively tried to subvert, meaning that such an ending would go against the overall thrust of the series and render the controversial 25th and 26th episodes, during which Shinji finds forgiveness and accepts the love and support of his friends and family, completely unnecessary.

Instead, the viewer is presented with Beethoven's deeply introspective, religious-sounding music to foster a meditation on the profound events that have taken place in the series. The focus is on the internal: loss, acceptance, grief, forgiveness and all of the other complex emotions *EVA* has explored. The viewer is asked to consider what is tragic and personally life-changing for Shinji and the other characters, who have endured very real struggles in their lives, much like Beethoven did. We share the full depth of Shinji's last private, intimate moment with his first true friend and realize how hard-earned mankind's salvation from the Angels really is in terms of the personal costs to the survivors. Beethoven's *Andante maestoso* is a glorious requiem to the living and dead that offers the viewer the opportunity to contemplate the many emotions generated in this series by means of the powerful musical underscore, an experience that is far more meaningful to the human spirit than reveling in a clichéd act of winning.

Conclusion

Kaworu's connection to the "Ode to Joy" from Beethoven's Ninth Symphony clearly has a substantial impact on the scope and interpretation of *EVA*. Of course, the profound music of the *Andante maestoso* that accompanies the culminating still-shot scene also serves as a requiem for Kaworu, honoring his choice to sacrifice his life for humanity in Beethovenian defiance of his destiny to be mankind's destroyer. At the moment Shinji makes the choice to kill his friend, the still shot suddenly cuts to a black screen and the music stops jarringly mid-measure, revealing Kaworu's fate to the viewer before witnessing his decapitated head splashing into the liquid covering the floor of the underground chamber where the final battle took place.

To return briefly to an idea mentioned earlier, Kaworu often seems to be aware of the viewer, and his manipulation of the "Ode to Joy" is part of this perception. As a music maker, Kaworu has the ability to communicate ideas and emotions that cannot be expressed in words or images, allowing him to transcend the borders of the narrative and reach the viewer in a uniquely powerful way. When Kaworu is introduced in the crater lake scene, he manipulates the division between the viewer's world and the narrative world by addressing the camera directly when it assumes Shinji's point of view, appearing to ask the viewer if they agree that the "Ode to Joy" is the greatest human creation. Later in the NERV military headquarters, Kaworu appears to address the viewer again when asking if Shinji was waiting for him and does the same a third time in the final battle scene, looking directly into the camera to make important philosophical statements about the nature of human life and to tell Shinji that knowing him has made his life meaningful.

Kaworu has been given the privilege of speaking directly to the viewer and, in doing so, has been granted a seemingly directorial power to manipulate the border between the narrative world and the viewer's world. He can also traverse the diegetic and non-diegetic musical realms, enacting a process of musical replacement to express the intensity of his search for companionship. When Shinji is shown listening to the "Ode to Joy" on his headphones, it is possible to interpret this act as something willed by Kaworu, who has used his directorial ability to control the music to which Shinji listens. Kaworu does not comment on hearing his favorite piece streaming out of

Shinji's headphones, as if he already knew what Shinji was listening to because he had chosen the music himself.

A similar form of musical replacement occurs in the final battle, where Sagisu's original score, with its tried-and-true battle music heard in almost every previous episode, is completely absent because Kaworu has crossed the boundary between musical realms and replaced the non-diegetic music of the viewer with his beloved "Ode to Joy," essentially dictating his own requiem. The *Andante maestoso* takes on a fascinating character when understood as the music selected by Kaworu for his own death, resulting in a quiet, reflective end, rather than a heroic finale. Finally, connecting Kaworu to the "Ode to Joy" allows him to spread his Beethovenian spirit widely inside and outside the *EVA* world. Like Beethoven himself, whose life and death empowered the next generation of composers to write music inspired by their personal convictions rather than societal expectations, Kaworu's death passes the Beethovenian torch to Shinji and to the viewer, asserting the seasonally driven, *Daiku*-inspired message to stay true to your beliefs and find people to support you in your struggles on your path to rejuvenation.

The decision to accompany the 24th episode of *EVA* with a single piece of music is certainly a unique, one-of-a-kind phenomenon in anime, but the use of Western classical music itself is a common technique employed regularly by anime directors. A wide range of Western classical pieces appear in anime, spanning a range of almost 300 years from the Baroque masters Antonio Vivaldi and J. S. Bach, to the stark modernism of Dmitri Shostakovich in the 20th century. Naturally, the viewer expects to hear a wide variety of music drawn from this repertoire in anime about music schools and conservatories—*Nodame Cantabile, Hibike!Euphonium, Your Lie in April, Kids on the Slope*—or in anime concerning ballet or ice skating—*Princess Tutu, Yuri on Ice*—where the presence of Western classical music forms are an important part of authenticating the diegetic soundworld of the narrative, but this music is also heard in many genres of anime (even pornographic anime!) that are not related specifically to music in any way. The "Ode to Joy," for instance, features prominently as an important expressive element in *Psycho-Pass*, *Tokyo Godfathers* and *Gunslinger Girls*, to name a few of the more notable anime from the many available examples. Anime directors often elect to use pieces of pre-existing music in their works, drawing from Western classical music, jazz, pop, rock, religious pieces and folk music just as often as they choose pieces from Japanese folk, traditional and popular music sources. The decision to use pre-existing music in anime is a meaningful act that necessitates special attention to the director's artistic intent. By making use of the extramusical associations connected to the life, history and culture of the piece outside of the anime, the director can impose a multilayered meaning rich with complexity on the images and the narrative that adds powerfully to the viewer's experience, enriching the art that is anime and the viewer's interpretation of it.

References

Anderson, L. (2016). Beyond Figures of the Audience: Towards a Cultural Understanding of the Film Music Audience. *Music, Sound, and the Moving Image*, 10(1), 25–51.

Brasor, P. (2010, 24 December). Japan Makes Beethoven's Ninth No. 1 for the Holidays. *The Japan Times Online*. Retrieved from: https://www.japantimes.co.jp/culture/2010/12/24/music/japan-makes-beethovens-ninth-no-1-for-the-holidays/

Brown, R. S. (1994). *Overtones and Undertones: Reading Film Music*. Berkeley, CA: University of California Press.

Candaele, K. (Producer and Director). (2013). *Following the Ninth: In the Footsteps of Beethoven's Final Symphony* [Motion Picture]. Venice, CA: Battle Hymns Productions, LLC.

_____ & Mitchell, G. (2012). *Journeys with Beethoven: Following the Ninth, and Beyond*. New York: Sinclair Books.

Chang, E. Y. L. (2007). The Daiku Phenomenon: Social and Cultural Influences of Beethoven's Ninth Symphony in Japan. *Asia Europe Journal*, 5(1), 93–114.

_____. (2009). Ode to 'Personal Challenge': Reconsidering Japanese Groupism and the Role of Beethoven's *Ninth* in Catering to Socio–Cultural Needs. In E. Kolig, V. S. M. Angeles and S. Wong (eds.), *Identity in Crossroad Civilisations: Ethnicity, Nationalism and Globalism in Asia* (pp. 147–171). Amsterdam: Amsterdam University Press.

Eppstein, U. (1994). *The Beginnings of Western Music in Meiji Era Japan*. Lewiston, NY: E. Mellen Press.

Fisk, J. and Nichols, J. (1997). *Composers on Music: Eight Centuries of Writings*. Boston, MA: Northeastern University Press.

Galliano, L. (2002). *Yōgaku: Japanese Music in the Twentieth Century*. Lanham, MD: Scarecrow Press. (Translated by M. Mayes)

Godsall, J. (2019). *Reeled in: Pre-Existing Music in Narrative Film*. New York: Routledge.

Gorbman, C. (1987). *Unheard Melodies: Narrative Film Music*. Bloomington, IN: Indiana University Press.

_____. (2006). Ears Wide Open: Kubrick's Music. In P. Powrie and R. J. Stilwell (eds.), *Changing Tunes: The Use of Pre-Existing Music in Film* (pp. 3–18). Burlington, VT: Ashgate Publishing.

Wade, B. C. (2014). *Composing Japanese Musical Modernity*. Chicago: University of Chicago Press.

Wasserman, M. (2006). *Le Sacre de l'hiver—La Neuvième Symphonie de Beethoven, un mythe de la modernité japonaise*. Paris: Indes savantes.

Weisman, S. R. (1990, 29 December). Japan Sings along with Beethoven. *New York Times*, 13, 16.

Yang, M. (2014). *Planet Beethoven: Classical Music at the Turn of the Millennium*. Middletown, CT: Wesleyan University Press.

4. Voice Actresses Rising
The Multilayered Stardom of Megumi Ogata in the 1990s

Minori Ishida

In Japanese discourse, the year 1995 is considered the beginning of the third anime boom, as it has come to be referred to in Japanese discourse,[1] and this boom took its departure from *Neon Genesis Evangelion* (*EVA*). Many critics have attempted to explain what was so innovative about *EVA*, and as this volume also evinces, the issue is still under discussion. But most studies have analyzed *EVA*'s visuals and not paid sufficient attention to its acoustic side. *EVA*'s 'voices' remain underdiscussed, although they have played a crucial role in creating the series' psychologically substantiated characters. In one of the few exceptions, Fang Jin Lee (2010: 241–244) points out that it is the voices that warrant narrative coherence in the 26th episode of the first anime series. This episode surprised viewers by its unconventional collage of different visual materials, ranging from rough sketches to live-action footage. But even if the visuals appeared chaotic at times, the characters conveyed their thoughts and feelings clearly—by voice. Thanks to the voice acting, even the unusual visuals made sense.

As the 26th episode of *EVA* demonstrates, the functions of voice should not be underestimated at all; rather, they are necessary factors to establish anime as an audio-visual medium. The voice works on several levels of anime. First, it represents the characters' acoustic appearance. At the same time, the voice helps to create the narrative. In addition, the voice belongs to voice actors and mediates between them and the audience. Voice actors establish their own persona by performing different characters throughout their career. Thus, audiences come to receive a specific voice as connected not only to a character,

1. See Tsugata (2011: 30), Hikawa (2000: 104-105) and Masuda (2007: 119), as well as Kacsuk's chapter in this volume for a survey of the three anime booms.

How to cite this book chapter:
Ishida, M. 2021. Voice Actresses Rising: The Multilayered Stardom of Megumi Ogata in the 1990s. In: Santiago Iglesias, J. A. and Soler Baena, A. (Eds.). *Anime Studies: Media-Specific Approaches to Neon Genesis Evangelion*. Pp. 111–133 Stockholm: Stockholm University Press. DOI: https://doi.org/10.16993/bbp.e. License: CC-BY 4.0

but also to a specific actor. Furthermore, the voice is not limited to a certain character within a certain work.

Pre-existing research on the voice in live-action cinema is helpful for investigating the way in which the voice works in anime, from production to reception. Discussing the talkies, film scholar Mary Ann Doane defined "the body reconstituted by the technology and practices of the cinema" as "a *fantasmatic* body, which offers a support as well as a point of identification for the subject addressed by the film" (1985: 162; emphasis in the original). According to Doane, "the voice serves as a support for the spectator's recognition and his/her identification of, as well as with, the star" (1985: 164). The voice in anime shares many functions with the one in the talkies. However, because the audience does not see the face and body of the voice actors performing the characters, the characters in anime have more "fantasmatic" bodies compared to live-action cinema, and the voice actors reconstitute them in more complicated and innovative ways.

This chapter aims to reconsider the way in which voice and voice acting developed in *EVA*, focusing on Megumi Ogata, who performed Shinji Ikari, the 14-year-old boy protagonist of the 1995 anime series. Shinji is one of the most fantasmatic bodies among the characters in *EVA*, because he is performed by a voice actress. However, employing a female performer for the voice of a boy character in anime was not innovative in itself, as there was already such a tradition in place. In the first TV anime series of the 30-minute weekly format, *Tetsuwan Atomu* (Astro Boy, 1963–66), a 26-year-old theater actress, Mari Shimizu, played the eponymous robot. Thereafter, many boy characters performed by voice actresses appeared both in anime for the whole family and in anime specifically targeted to otaku fans. To name just a few, they included Nobita in *Doraemon*, voiced by Yoshiko Ōta in 1973, Noriko Ohara from 1979 to 2005 and Megumi Ōhara since 2005; Son Gokū voiced by Masako Nozawa in the *Dragon Ball* series (1986–2018); Luffy by Mayumi Tanaka in *One Piece* (since 1999); and Loran by Romi Park in *Turn a Gundam* (1999–2000).

Interestingly, this casting convention was a by-product of the Japanese Child Welfare Act and Labor Standards Act, both enacted in 1947. In line with Japan's democratization after World War II, these acts were aimed at securing children's rights and protecting them from labor exploitation, with strict regulations for minors (i.e., persons under the age of 18), which included the prohibition of children from working past 8pm. Hence, child actors were not allowed to participate in night-time recordings or film shootings,[2] and when going through compulsory education, school days were to be avoided whenever possible. Thus, in the late 1940s, adult voice actresses came to play child characters in radio dramas and TV puppet plays produced by NHK (Nippon Hosō Kyōkai, the Japan Broadcasting Corporation), as well as TV animation and live-action TV dramas imported from the United States. From 1953, when TV broadcasting began, until the mid-1960s, the broadcasting was live.[3] Because of both the children's labor regulation and the technological limit of live broadcasting, actresses were employed for child characters of both sexes. One of them was Masako Nozawa, who began to voice boy roles in the 1950s (Nozawa & Hirano 2016). Voice actresses can easily pass as boys, unless they show their faces and bodies to the audience. Anime, that is, animated TV series produced in Japan starting with *Astro Boy* in 1963, inherited the discrepancy between voice and character in terms of age and sex from previous radio drama and developed it into one of its outstanding characteristics. In the United States, especially in Disney's feature-length animations, boy characters have been performed by boy actors such as young Bambi by 6-year-old Donnie Dunagan in *Bambi* (1942). This fact shows that the US casting of voice actors has been based on similarities of sex and age.

2. Kikuko Kinoshita, who began to play child roles of both sexes in 1948 as a member of the voice actors' section of TV station NHK (Tokyo Hosō Gekidan), stated in an interview with the author on 7 December 2016 that the officers of the CIE (Civil Information and Educational Section), a section of the General Headquarters for the Allied Powers, ensured that there were no child actors on the set after 8pm.

3. The four-head video-tape recorder for TV broadcasting was invented by Ampex in the United States in 1956; in 1959, Japanese companies succeeded in its domestic production. By the mid-1960s, it had spread to all Japanese TV broadcast stations as standard equipment (Kawamura 2001: 8–9).

Recently, there is an increasing critical interest in voice acting and voice actors in Japanese-language Anime Studies. Shō Kobayashi (2015) and Ryōta Fujitsu (2018) provide general histories of voice actors, pointing out how they differ from performers on radio and TV, as well as in cinema. However, their investigations do not focus on the convention of casting voice actresses as boy characters, and neither does Jin's analysis (2010).[4] The issue of those voice actresses is closely related to the social and cultural history by which anime has been shaped. Moreover, taking the issue seriously leads us to rethink anime as an audio-visual medium and focus on its specificity in comparison to other similar media. This is why I am discussing the acoustic achievements of *EVA* on the example of Ogata performing the role of Shinji. As mentioned above, casting Ogata for that role was part of anime conventions. But her actual performance was qualitatively unprecedented in anime history, in particular within the context of the 1990s, when it became usual for voice performers to gain stardom by disclosing their face and body.

My discussion below foregrounds performers and paratextual materials: it considers Shinji's voice in dubbed versions of *EVA*, Ogata's performance of characters in other anime series and articles on Ogata in magazines specializing in anime. This approach will serve to analyze voices objectively in view of the methodological issue that sound in non-visual narratives such as radio drama shows "the heavy reliance on the cultural connotation" (Hill 2001: 109) and the interpretation of voices is inclined to be highly subjective. First, I analyze how Ogata's performance as Shinji was received by the South Korean audience in comparison of the Japanese original to the Korean-dubbed counterpart. Although both voiced by actresses, the performances were significantly different due to the status of anime and of voice actors in both Japan and South Korea in the 1990s. Second, I investigate the representation of Ogata's body in an anime magazine, *Animage*, focusing on the interrelationship between Ogata and her

4. In English language anime studies, Rayna Denison discusses voice actresses performing boy characters, focusing on Romi Park and Rie Kugimiya in the *Fullmetal Alchemist* series (2003–11) (2017: 101–117).

audience pertaining to the two characters she played before Shinji. Correlated with the characters she performed, her visual appearance changed considerably between 1992 and 1995. Third, I show how Ogata's performance as Shinji extended the convention of casting voice actresses to perform boys' voices in anime, and I illuminate this extension in detail on the example of Ogata's voice performance in the animated feature film *The End of Evangelion* (1997).

The Sombre and Sexy Voice of Shinji: Differences from the Korean-Dubbed Version

Shinji, the protagonist in *EVA*, is a troubled boy. He has been abandoned by his father for many years, but he is then suddenly called in by him to pilot the Eva unit. Shinji is forced to fight with enigmatic enemies called Angels to save the world without even knowing what he is doing. Throughout the narrative, he is troubled by his relationship with the people surrounding him, including his father, Gendō, and his peer pilots Rei, Asuka and Kaworu. Moreover, he is repeatedly injured in battle. In short, Shinji is far from the heroes of generic robot anime; rather, he is a miserable child, neglected by his father and sometimes even abused. Ogata expresses the vulnerability of his body and soul using a sombre voice, which made Shinji stand out among other boy characters played by voice actresses up until that point.

For an analysis of Ogata's performance, the Korean-dubbed version of *EVA* provides some interesting insights. In 1996, Champ, a label run by the South Korean animation production company and distributor Daewon Media, launched *EVA* on VHS. In this localized version, South Korean performers voiced the characters, and the Korean casting shared the Japanese convention of voice actresses playing the roles of boys, by employing Gyeong Jin An to perform Shinji. In contrast, in the North American, South American and European dubbed versions, Shinji's voice was performed by male voice actors:

Shinji was dubbed by Spike Spencer in the English version, Albert Trifol Segarra in the European-Spanish version, Victor Ugarte in the Mexican-Spanish version, Donald Reginoux in the French version, Hannes Mauver in the German version and Fábio Lucindo in the Brazilian-Portuguese version. Interestingly, only Lucindo was 15 years old, while the others were adults. In 2019, Netflix launched a new English-dubbed version, and Casey Mongillo, a transgender voice actor, performed Shinji.[5] Both the Japanese and the Korean dubbing leaned on actresses, but the two versions of Shinji differed significantly. Ogata's pitch is lower and huskier in tone than An's. As a result, An's Shinji sounds more childlike and innocent. A South Korean female viewer evaluated the two performances as follows:

> Shinji's voice performed by Ogata is a thousand times sexier than An's. I was especially stunned by the screams when he was wounded. Ogata's shouts seemed to stem from deep agony and grief, not simply from physical injury.[6]

The viewer also considered reasons for the difference between the two versions of Shinji:

> Undoubtedly, An is an equally talented and skillful voice actress. So, I believe that the Japanese and the Korean versions differed not merely due to technical matters. Rather, An's performance of innocence may have been influenced by the understanding of anime in South Korean society, which was different from that in Japan. South Korean society was not familiar with the concept of a young-adult audience taking anime seriously and thinking deeply about characters and stories.[7]

To understand her comments more precisely, it is useful to consider how the opening song of *EVA* was modified in the localization process. Although the 1996 Korean version adopted the Japanese song, *Zankoku na tenshi no tēze* (A Cruel Angel's Thesis), the lyrics and the visuals were changed completely. The Japanese version starts with the line "Zankoku na tenshi no yō ni, shōnen yo, shinwa ni nare," which

5. Regarding the information on Mongillo and Lucindo, see https://www.huffpost.com/entry/shes-changing-the-game-ca_b_8193014 and https://tvtropes.org/pmwiki/pmwiki.php/Trivia/NeonGenesisEvangelion.

6. Personal interview with the author on 25 November 2018.

7. Ibid.

translates into English as "Young boy, like a cruel angel's thesis, live up to be a legend" (A.D. Vision, 1997), or "Like a cruel angel, become a legend, young boy" (Netflix, 2019). However, in Korean, "cruel" was replaced by "brave," and words that manifest a clear dichotomy between good and evil, such as "justice" and "hero," were added, words that can be traced back to the opening songs of classic robot anime series of the 1960s and the 1970s: *Tetsujin 28-gō* (Iron Man No. 28, or Gigantor, 1963), *Majingā Zetto* (Mazinger Z, 1972) and *Gettā Robo* (Getter Robo, 1974). And it is precisely this connotation that reveals the Korean distributor's marketing strategy, namely, to categorize *EVA* as a title aimed at children. The re-edited visuals of the opening reinforce that orientation: Shots from the Japanese opening and from some of the episodes were conjoined and female nudes removed (which in the Japanese version appear only as a silhouette, but with an emphasized outline of the bust).

In contrast to South Korea, anime audiences in 1990s Japan included a considerable number of young adults. The coming of age of anime as a young-adult media was epitomized by *Uchū senkan Yamato* (Space Battleship Yamato). In March 1975, the TV series which had started the previous year was cancelled due to low audience ratings, but dedicated viewers in their late teens to early 20s achieved a re-broadcast by sending letters to the production company and TV stations. And when an animated feature film of *Space Battleship Yamato* was produced in 1977, it became a huge box office hit. Thus, *Space Battleship Yamato* made visible young adult audiences' serious and strong interest in anime.[8] From then on, they became a constant factor for anime productions to reckon with, and they led to intricate narratives with detailed settings and psychologically substantiated characters. This was the context in which *EVA* and, with it, Shinji emerged. I now proceed to analyze in detail how voice actors accommodated young adult viewers' expectations, and how they refined their craft.

8. On the campaigns by the young adult audience, see Nakatani (1982), as well as Nakatani and Kushino (1982).

Voice Actors as Stars and the Impact of Anime Magazines

In cinema, TV drama and theater, the term *star* is used to indicate a privileged actor or actress who has a personality that extends beyond the characters he or she plays. I call this personality "star persona."[9] The visibility of a star's face and body is vital for their star persona in cinema, TV drama and theater. In contrast to those media forms, the faces and bodies of voice actors remain invisible when performing characters in anime. More importantly, the criteria for casting them are not necessarily based on their visual similarity with the characters they play, since in the process of anime production, the visual and aural tracks of a character are separately created: voice actors bring characters to life with their voices, whereas animators do the same thing with a succession of drawings that are to appear moving when screened. Consequently, anime characters are located in between audio and visual tracks, being split into the two mediums. In the case of a voice actress playing the role of a boy, this splitting becomes quite clear. When Mari Shimizu performed Astro Boy in the early 1960s, she was even asked to erase her visual presence in public for maintaining the plausibility of the anime character. When she got pregnant, the discrepancy was heightened, and she tried not to appear in public at all (Shimizu 2015: 90). However, in due course, anime matured as entertainment for young adults, and the audience soon became interested in the characters' voices and the voice actors themselves, which again gave rise to a new generation of voice actors. For example, Yōko Asagami, who played Yuki Mori, the heroine in *Space Battleship Yamato*, had been a big fan of anime and eager to become a voice actress before she actually became one (Kobayashi 2015: 10–11). This contrasts with the voice actors of previous generations, who began their careers as stage actors in theater. Asagami's case also shows how the cultivation of voice actors in anime became self-sufficient and autonomous.

9. Richard Dyer names it "star image," as a set of effects produced by the media including magazines, advertisements and so on (1998: 60–63).

In correspondence with the voice actors' new position in the reception of anime, the opportunities to show themselves to the audience increased. Anime magazines played a crucial role in this process. The late 1970s, when the popularity of *Space Battleship Yamato* peaked, saw the launch of the magazines *OUT* (1977–95), *Animec* (1978–87) and *Animage* (since 1978). While editing the first issue of *Animage*, Toshio Suzuki, the future producer at Studio Ghibli, lent his ear to the potential readership of late-teen anime fans. Suzuki realized that the anime characters were stars or idols for them, and that they wanted to know the creators behind them (Ōtsuka 2016: 143). Hence, staff interviews became feature articles. Voice actors were no exception, and many articles about them were accompanied by portrait photographs. Due to continued interest, a magazine exclusively on anime voice actors was launched in 1994: *Voice Animage*, a subsidiary of *Animage*. Thus, specialized anime magazines made voice actors' visual presence and self-presentation an essential part of the reception of both voice actors themselves and anime as a media form. Audiences began to share performers' star persona and participate in their stardom, going beyond the visual difference between them and their roles. Consequently, stardom shifted from characters to performers.

Ambitious Casting: Ogata as Kurama in *Yū Yū Hakusho*

In 1992, Ogata debuted in the role of Kurama, a 15-year-old boy, in *Yū Yū Hakusho* (1992–95), a TV anime series based on the manga of the same name by Yoshihiro Togashi. At the time, the media facilitating voice actors' stardom were already in place—magazines to begin with. However, for a voice actress playing boy roles, one issue remained, namely, how she could possibly fill the gap between the boy character and herself in terms of visual or bodily appearance. Casting Ogata as Kurama raised many controversies. Ken Hagino, the producer of the anime version of *Yū Yū Hakusho*, said that the production crew had a long discussion on that issue. According to Hagino, the fans of the original manga expressed their discontent over the choice of Ogata (2011: 308) because Kurama was much older than any other boy character played by a voice actress up until that point. Moreover, Kurama had a delicate and complicated personality with a dark and tragic background, a fox monster in the past and now reborn as a human. His appearance, with long red hair and deep green eyes, was elaborately designed. In the battle scenes, he fights elegantly using even roses as his weapon, and he is often injured and bleeds. In other words, he is mysterious, fragile and sensual.

In retrospect, Ogata herself described the strong pressure she felt. Before she played Kurama, it was rare for a voice actress to play the role of a high-school boy; this happened only once in a special case when Masako Nozawa played Gokū from his childhood to his youth in *Dragon Ball*. Besides, Kurama is a reserved character and not pushy. Hence, Ogata had to develop a new sensibility for him, which she explained as follows:

> I had to give to Kurama as real a presence as the boy characters voiced by male actors. Kurama is not a boy who is surrounded by girls. He always stays behind and pacifies the other boy characters' anger and anxiety. So, if my voice sounded lighter than those of the boy characters played by male actors, Kurama's presence would have been diminished. Performing in a low and suppressed tone requires higher skills than just shouting. I was not sure if I could do this. Fortunately, my vocal cords are tough. But they are completely different from those of male actors. I was suffering. (Ogata 1997: 51; translation by the author)

Clearly, Ogata was in a quandary regarding her ability to perform the part of Kurama. But she succeeded by opting for a lower pitch with a mellow tone in accordance with Kurama's psychological depth and visual appearance. As a result, she was hailed by the audience, especially

female viewers. In a fan voting for characters by *Animage*, the anime version of Kurama was rated one of the most popular characters in the 1990s (Fig.4.1).[10]

This led to Ogata acquiring star status. Certainly, having Ogata play the role of Kurama followed a convention of anime casting that began with Astro Boy. But, at the same time, Ogata subverted the convention by giving rise to a way of voicing boy characters

10. According to the monthly character ranking in *Animage*, Kurama remained in the top 20 throughout the 1990s.

that differed from previous male performances. Not unlike the stylized masculinity invoked by female impersonators on the Takarazuka stage (which comes to the fore in the following section), Ogata's masculine voice appealed to female audiences, and to male viewers, too.

Not Just Anime: Ogata's Visual Presence in Anime Magazines

Interestingly, Ogata changed the way in which voice actresses were accepted by the audience, ultimately assuming a star persona. Anime magazines played an important part in this process. In *Animage*, Ogata first appeared in issue 178 published in April 1993. The article introduced her as a voice actress playing the role of Kurama, and it was accompanied by her picture, as well as a comment that she was training her abdominal muscles for acting in a lower voice. At that time, long-haired, she looked very feminine (*Animage* 1993a: 119). Shortly after that, issue 186 featured an interview with her. Although again accompanied by a photograph of her with long hair, the headline read "Ogata-san wa seiyūkai no Takarajenne?" (Is Ms. Ogata a *Takarasienne* among the voice actors)? (*Animage* 1993b: 138), alluding to her performance of Kurama's gender (Fig.4.2).

This headline by an editor was not just a figure of speech, because from then on, the topos of the Takarasienne provided the platform on which Ogata and her fans communicated with one another.

The word Takarasienne refers to a member of the all-female Takarazuka Revue Company which has existed since 1914. Among these performers, those who play male parts, so-called *otokoyaku*, are usually most popular with the mainly female fans. Similarly, Ogata playing Kurama gained huge support from female viewers. According to an article in *Animage* (1993b: 138), 99 percent of her fans were female. The female audience accepted her unhesitatingly, including the difference between female voice actress and male anime character.

The fans' reception of Ogata as Kurama did not depend on a simple realism that lays emphasis on matching actors and characters in terms of sex and age.

Sociologist Sonoko Azuma's analysis of the relationship between Takarazuka performers and their fans can be helpful in understanding Ogata's reception by female viewers. In the Takarazuka context, fans support male impersonators (*otokoyaku*) and enjoy their performance of male roles knowingly. Azuma points out that four

Figure 4.2. *Animage* (#186). © Tokuma Shoten.

layers construct the figure of a Takarasienne for the fans: her role-name existence, her stage-name existence, her nickname existence and her real-name existence:

> To the audience, the role-name existence is connected to the tale being performed on stage. Similarly, each member of the audience has, to a greater or lesser extent, an image and some kind of story for each of the Takarasienne's four layers in mind. The stage-name existence connotes the performer's special qualities and past roles, as well as the general images of *otokoyaku* and *musumeyaku*.[11] The nickname existence is associated with the character as introduced by the media and other offstage information. Should an audience member imagine a Takarasienne's struggle, such thoughts would concern the real-name existence. (Azuma 2019: 272–273)

Azuma describes how Takarazuka stardom and fandom are created by utilizing these four layers. Each layer is classified according to whether it is internal or external to the play, enacted onstage or offstage, made public to the fans or not. And these layers are interconnected in a multilayered way (Azuma 2019: 272). In the case of a male impersonator, the role-name existence on stage becomes a component of the stage-name existence, reinforcing fans' reception of her as male. At the same time, the nickname existence indicates that she does not deny her offstage gender. Fans participate in this seamless overlapping of the layers, and the fact that the *otokoyaku* actors do not have male bodies beneath their costumes becomes insignificant. Instead, the central issue is whether they "create their own unique *otokoyaku* persona" (Azuma 2019: 268).

This analysis of the reception of *otokoyaku* in the Takarazuka Revue can be applied to understanding the reception of Ogata by the female audience. Moreover, even though Azuma does not refer to stardom itself, her discussion can be stretched to the process in which an actor or actress is received as a star, because the stardom requires the audience to participate in the network of the four layers highlighted by Azuma. namely that is, a star persona. She neither denied nor erased

11. *Musumeyaku*: female parts and their performer.

the gap between the two, but utilized it to construct her star image as an effect of interweaving the four layers.

In March 1994, Ogata released her first CD with songs and narration, entitled *Half Moon*. The CD includes a boy-meets-girl story in which Ogata plays both roles. She had already become adept in playing both girl and boy roles, for example, in *Yū Yū Hakusho*, where she also voiced several minor girl characters. In October 1994, Ogata revealed that she wanted to express the two sides of her mind: masculine and feminine (*Animage* 1994: 64). Her portrait on the CD cover was likely to help fans understand. In her paratextual relation to her audience, she did not hide being female; rather, she deliberately foregrounded it. Apparently, for her, the image of the Takarasienne proved useful as a performative model.

Character Reinforcing the Star Persona: Tenoh Haruka/Sailor Uranus in *Sailor Moon S*

Soon after the release of *Half Moon*, Ogata began to play another role that was to become important for her career, that of Haruka Tenoh, or Sailor Uranus, in *Sailor Moon S* (1994–95). It brought her an enthusiastic admiration by female fans.[12] Haruka questions gender and sexuality further: the narrative of the anime defines Haruka's sex as female, and she also self-identifies as female, but she wears male attire and always refers to herself with the male first-person pronoun, *boku*. Furthermore, she is in a romantic relationship with her female partner, Michiru, or Sailor Neptune. In contrast to the anime, the manga version by Naoko Takeuchi, on which it was based, depicted Haruka/Sailor Uranus as androgynous. There, masculine-clad Haruka uses an even stronger male pronoun, *ore* (Takeuchi 1994a), while Sailor Uranus in her feminine costume uses the female variant *atashi* (Takeuchi 1994b). In the manga, the correspondence between speech and costume stays static, tying the masculine verbal expression with the male costume and vice versa.

12. In 1996, Haruka was seventh in the annual *Animage* voting by female readers (issue 212), and 93rd in the annual character ranking (*Animage*, 1996). Her popularity was supported by female fans with a deep affection for the character (i.e., *moe*), which indicates that, in the 1990s, *moe* was not exclusively male.

Therefore, Haruka never actually disturbs the gender boundary (Ishida 2019: 30–33). In contrast, the anime version of Haruka/Uranus is much more provocative, and Ogata's performance accentuated this. Her voice is lower and huskier than the one she used for Kurama and, in battle scenes, when she shouts, it is much stronger. When Haruka transforms into Uranus, her male attire turns into the sailor warrior's costume. As a result, Ogata's powerful masculine voice becomes incongruous with the sailor warrior's feminine costume, the discrepancy between the visual appearance and the voice being much more prominent.

This playful representation of Haruka in the anime attests to the maturation of anime voice acting in the 1990s, or to put it another way, the fact that mature audiences were to be addressed, which included an erotic dimension. The role of Haruka also contributed to the development of Ogata's own star persona. Ogata adopted Haruka's features: she cut her hair short and began to wear suits when making public appearances in magazines and at fan meetings and concerts. The new look complied with the stage-names and nicknames of Takarazuka's male impersonators who also keep their hair rather short and wear pants in a masculine style. The most significant among the articles about Ogata is "Ogata to deito" (Going on a date with Ogata), a serial published in *Animage* in 1995–96 (Animage 1996a: 106–107; Animage 1996b) (Fig.4.3).

Ogata entertained one or two female fans on a date, and the magazine reported on this in detail. Ogata herself was always in masculine attire, while the female fans wore dresses, the former and the latter respectively emulating the masculine Haruka and the feminine Michiru in *Sailor Moon S*. Adopting a behavior that corresponds to Haruka's sexuality, Ogata could make gender/sex fluidity a component of her star persona.

Magazines serve special interests and communities, while newspapers are to provide coverage and primary information to civil society at large. Unlike radio and television, magazines target "small

readerships establishing a strong and deep connection" (Yoshida 2017: 12). Anime magazines were particularly specific since they addressed a youth subculture, and precisely the limitedness of their subject incited readers' active participation. It was this participation by female magazine readers that helped construct Ogata's star persona in correspondence with the characters she voiced. Her fans realized that she and her characters were different. However, as implied by the critical keyword Takarasienne in Ogata's first

Figure 4.3. *Animage* (#211). © Tokuma Shoten.

interview in *Animage*, fans willingly participated in constructing her star persona, picking up the characters' features ranging from visual appearance to personality and projecting them onto Ogata's body. As "Going on a date with Ogata" suggests, female fans saw her like an *otokoyaku* in the Takarazuka Revue. Thanks to the interaction with female fans via the anime magazine, Ogata's persona assumed fluidity with regard to gender and sex. Thus, her own sexuality and that of her characters coexisted successfully, along with her own star persona. In summary, the voice actress with the stage-name Megumi Ogata is a construct that emerged from multilayered stardom.

Innovative Performance in *The End of Evangelion* (1997)

After establishing her star persona as one of gender/sex fluidity in the performance of Haruka, Ogata returned to a boy role, Shinji. At first glance, Shinji seems to be more conventional than Kurama and Haruka, very much in line with the genre of robot anime. However, he is neither cheerful nor straightforward. On the contrary, he is in conflict with the people around him, including his father, his commander Misato, his companions Rei and Asuka, and hence, the narrative revolves around his suffering and agony. With regard to psychological depth, Shinji belongs to the same category as Kurama and Haruka, and Ogata's performance of him reveals this continuity in terms of tone and pitch.

The second animated feature film, *The End of Evangelion*, released in the summer of 1997, is especially significant. This film elaborates on the last two episodes of the initial TV series that went on air without having been completed. Produced to provide a definitive ending, the film addresses sexual issues in an extremely overt way. Ogata strived to act a scene that depicts Shinji's sexual arousal, too. At the beginning, Shinji visits Asuka in hospital. He confesses his fear of Misato and Rei, and he repeatedly asks Asuka to help him. However, she is in a coma and cannot respond. Driven by anxiety, he grabs her shoulder. The sheet turns over, and her naked breasts are revealed. This is followed by shots of the electric light on the ceiling, the monitor screen showing the cardiac rate, a droplet pouch, and the locked door knob, and it is accompanied by the sound of repeated shallow and brief breaths. When the breaths stop, there is a sharp groaning sound, and Shinji's palm is covered with white cum. This act of masturbation is one of the most critical scenes in voice acting history because of the challenge it posed to an actress voicing boys. Ogata controlled her breath skillfully and conveyed the physical immediacy of adolescent Shinji. One Japanese female viewer commented:

> First, I was astonished by Shinji's masturbation, it was too realistic. But later, I understood this scene was necessary to depict his vulnerability. Driven by fear and cowardly as he is, he implored Asuka for help.[13]

This indicates the degree to which Ogata embodied Shinji, namely, up to his sexual arousal. With her performance of the angst-filled adolescent boy, she innovatively expanded the scope of voice acting in boy roles. This gave rise to a whole new trend, represented, for example, by Mitsuki Saiga, who debuted as a voice actress in 1998. She has performed late-teen boys in dark, sexual and violent stories like Kyōsuke Date in *The Soul Taker* (2001) and appeared also in a game with sexual scenes and an NC-17 rating aimed at male players, *Ko ko ro . . . voice ban* (2001). Paratextually, she has presented herself in the media as a tall, thin person with short hair, always wearing masculine attire. Saiga utilizes her visual masculine appearance to reinforce the effect of cross-gender acting. Eventually, her stardom depends on the support from female fans who participate in playful communication with her. This case demonstrates that other voice actresses have followed the path trailblazed by Ogata in the 1990s.

13. Personal interview with the author on 20 July 2019.

Conclusion

Ogata's performance in *EVA* was groundbreaking, but there were more factors involved than just talent. First, anime had matured as a young-adult media with an increasing interest in voice actors. Second, this interest was boosted by newly launched anime magazines, where the voice actors' bodies became visible in photos. Third, voice actors responded proactively to fans' demands, expectations and engagement, gaining star personae that went beyond characters of their own performance and construction. In an environment where these factors met, Ogata articulated the discrepancy between her characters and herself to the audience, and she embodied it as her star persona with the support of her fans. Consequently, she was able to endow a tangible, even sexual, presence to the anime characters. As such, she subverted long-standing conventions of voice acting in anime to create a new form. Her performance and multilayered stardom based on the interaction with her fans deserves to be counted as one of the acoustic achievements of *EVA* in the 1990s.

Twenty-five years have passed since Ogata gained fame and popularity. Today, the popularity of voice actresses is utilized differently in idol-themed anime, works that narrate the life and dreams of idol protagonists and generate profits by means of live shows that display voice actors' visual similarity with their young and beautiful characters.[14] Under these conditions that require visual coincidence between the voice actresses and the characters, *EVA* assumes a new critical meaning, because Ogata's stardom went in the opposite direction, that is, beyond visual similarity. Her innovation still calls for exploring the unexhausted possibilities of voice acting and anime expression, which can be found in the deliberate discrepancy between the visual and the acoustic.

14. The huge commercial success of *Love Live!* (since 2010) demonstrates that live shows by voice actresses in the role of characters is beneficial for the anime industry. The market for live entertainment including concerts by voice actors has purportedly expanded 2.5 times from 2013 to 2017 (Association of Japanese Animation 2018: 4).

References

Animage. (1993a). On Air. *Animage*, 178, 119.

_____. (1993b). Aoyama nichōme monogatari: Ogata-san wa seiyūkai no Takarasienne? *Animage*, 186, 138–139.

_____. (1994). Aoyama nichōme monogatari, vol.12: Ogata-san to futatsu no kokoro. *Animage*, 196, 64.

_____. (1996a). Ogata to deito. *Animage*, 211, 106–107.

_____. (1996b). Tokubetsu kikaku: Akemashite Best 100. *Animage*, 212, 1–2.

Anonymous. (2018). Personal Interview by the author, 25 November.

_____. (2019). Personal Interview by the author, 20 July.

Association of Japanese Animation. (2018). *Anime sangyō repōto 2018 samari ban*. Retrieved from: https://aja.gr.jp/jigyou/chousa/sangyo_toukei

Azuma, S. (2019). Multilayered Performers: The Takarazuka Revue as Media. In J. Berndt, K. Nagaike and F. Ogi (eds.), *Shōjo across Media: Exploring "Girl" Practice in Contemporary in Japan* (pp. 261–281). Cham: Palgrave Macmillan.

Denison, R. (2017). Anime's Star Voices: Voice Actor (*Seiyū*) Performance and Stardom in Japan. In T. Whittaker & S. Wright (Eds.), *Locating the Voice in Film: Critical Approaches and Global Practices* (pp. 101–117). New York: Oxford University Press.

Doane, M. A. (1985). The Voice in the Cinema: The Articulation of Body and Space. In E. Weis & J. Belton (Eds.), *Film Sound: Theory and Practice* (pp. 162–176). New York: Columbia University Press.

Dyer, R. (1998). *Stars*. London: British Film Institute.

Fujitsu, R. (2018). Seiyū ron: tsūshiteki, jisshōteki ichi kōsatsu. In M. Koyama & A. Sugawa (Eds.), *Anime kenkyū nyūmon ōyōhen: Anime o kiwameru 11 no kotsu* (pp. 93–117). Tokyo: Gendai shokan.

Hagino, K. (2011). Interview. *Yū Yū Hakusho* 4 (pp. 305–310). Tokyo: Shueisha.

Hikawa, R. (2000). *Seikimatsu anime netsuron*. Tokyo: Kinema Junpō-sha.

Hikawa, R. (ed.) (2013). *Japanese Animation Guide: The History of Robot Anime*. Tokyo: Mori Building Company, Ltd. https://mediag.bunka.go.jp/projects/project/images/JapaneseAnimationGuide.pdf

Hill, M. L. (2001). Developing *A Blind Understanding*: A Feminist Revision of Radio Semiotics. In A. S. Weiss (Ed.), *Experimental Sound & Radio* (pp. 107–115). Cambridge, MA: The MIT Press.

Ishida, M. (2019). Deviating Voices: Representation of Female Characters and Feminist Readings in 1990s Anime. *IMAGE: Journal of Interdisciplinary Image Science* (29), 22–37. Retrieved from: http://www.gib.uni-tuebingen.de/own/journal/upload/22f86d56124584c64 6c53e8211ae9898.pdf

Jin, L. F. (2010). Nihon no animation ni okeru onsei no kinō: *Ghost in the Shell/Kōkaku kidōtai, Shinseiki Evangelion, Sokyū no Fafner* o chūshin ni. *Hokkaidō daigaku daigakuin bungaku kenkyūka kenkyūronshū* (10), 235–251.

Kawamura, T. (2001). VTR sangyō shi no kōsatsu to genzon shiryō no jōkyō. In Kokuritsu kagaku hakubutsukan (Ed.), *Gijutsu no keitōteki chōsa hōkoku dai 1 shū*. Tokyo: Kokuritsu kagaku hakubutsukan.

Kinoshita, K. (2016). Personal Interview, 7 December.

Kobayashi, S. (2015). Seiyū shiron: "Anime Boom" ni miru shokugyō seiyū no tenkanten. *Animēshon kenkyū*, 16(2), 3–14.

Masuda, H. (2007). *Anime Bujinesu ga wakaru*. Tokyo: NTT Shippan.

Nakatani, T. (1982). Yamato fivā, yomigaeru Uchūsenkan Yamato. In K. Ikeda (Ed.), *Anime daisuki Yamato kara Gundam e* (pp. 87–117). Tokyo: Tokuma Shoten.

_____ & Kushino, A. (1982). Uchūsenkan Yamato Hasshinsu!. In K. Ikeda (Ed.), *Anime daisuki Yamato kara Gundam e* (pp.23–50). Tokyo: Tokuma Shoten.

Nozawa, M., & Hirano, F. (2016). Lejendo seiyū interview: Nozawa Masako × Hirano Fumi, Kōhen. *Otocoto*. Retrieved from: https://otocoto.jp/interview/nozawa002/

Ogata, M. (1997). SAY YOU HISTORY. *Animage*, 223, 50–52.

Ōtsuka, E. (2016). *Nikai no jūnin to sono jidai: Tenkeiki no sabukaruchā shihi*. Tokyo: Seikaisha shinsho.

Shimizu, M. (2015). *Tetsuwan Atomu to ikite: Seiyū ga kataru anime no sekai*. Saitama: Saitama shuppankai.

Takeuchi, N. (1994a). *Bishōjo senshi Sailor Moon 7*. Tokyo: Kodansha.

_____. (1994b). *Bishōjo senshi Sailor Moon 8*. Tokyo: Kodansha.

Tsugata, N. (2011). Anime no rekishi. In M. Takahashi and N. Tsugata (eds.), *Anime gaku* (pp. 24–44). Tokyo: NTT Shuppan.

Tvtropes (2019). Children Voicing Children in Triva/Neon Genesis Evangelion. Retrieved from: https://tvtropes.org/pmwiki/pmwiki.php /Trivia/NeonGenesisEvangelion

Yoshida, N. (2017). Zasshi bunka to sengo nihon shakai. In Noriaki Yoshida (ed.), *Zasshi media no bunkashi: Henbō suru sengo para-daimu, zōhoban* (pp. 10–38). Tokyo: Shinwasha.

5. Objecthood at the End of the World

Anime's Acting and its Ecological Stakes in *Neon Genesis Evangelion*

Stevie Suan

Performing Selfhood

Neon Genesis Evangelion (*EVA*) appears to have an obsession with selfhood. Such a concentrated focus on selfhood is made explicit, for example, in the TV series' enigmatic, but optimistic, final episodes 25 and 26. This emphasis is also evident in how the anime's narrative directly connects the protagonist's examination of his selfhood, something that would initially appear intimate and localized, to the results of global destruction. While the direct linkage between personal introspection and large-scale catastrophe is taken up throughout the TV series, it is perhaps the clearest in the ending of the feature film *The End of Evangelion* (below, *EoE*). Much darker in tone, it lacks the positivity of the TV series ending. Despite their overlap with regard to depicting an introspection of selfhood, on closer inspection, these two endings present differing concepts of selfhood and relations to the world.

Often, discussions on *EVA*'s approach to selfhood focus on the human subject. Frequently explored through an explicitly psychoanalytical framework, there is a general tendency to provide readings of the protagonist Shinji's (among other characters') psychological journey. Indeed, *EVA* features overtly Oedipal themes (Shinji's relationship with his father, and his mother's clone, Rei) and an abundance of visual imagery that reflects 'the act of seeing' (an emphasis on globular and eyeball imagery), which readily lends itself to such

How to cite this book chapter:
Suan, S. 2021. Objecthood at the End of the World: Anime's Acting and its Ecological Stakes in *Neon Genesis Evangelion*. In: Santiago Iglesias, J. A. and Soler Baena, A. (Eds.). *Anime Studies: Media-Specific Approaches to Neon Genesis Evangelion*. Pp. 135–180 Stockholm: Stockholm University Press. DOI: https://doi.org/10.16993/bbp.f. License: CC-BY 4.0

interpretations (cf. Endō 1997; Kotani 1997). To cite one such reading by Tōru Endō, the general thrust of the narrative into the psyche—both into the mysterious architecture of the headquarters of NERV (the organization building the Eva units), and Shinji's mind—readily invites the consideration of larger, philosophical questions that deal with pressing issues of selfhood (1997: 83). This movement inwards becomes central to *EVA*'s association with the *hikikomori* phenomenon, where people shut themselves off from the world by never leaving their homes. One standard reading is to see the 'pulling into oneself' as indicative of *hikikomori* and otaku practices, and the *EVA* endings as directly attacking these by viciously exposing their psychology.[1] So great is this approach toward psychoanalytically analyzing *EVA* that Tsunehiro Uno critiques it, regarding the "pulling into oneself/psychological" (*hikikomori/shinrishugi*) tendency in readings of *EVA* as emblematic of a general mode of intellectual thought at the time (Uno 2008: 69–71).

However, many such readings tend to elide a focus on anime's performance as a media-form. In particular, it is important to consider that in animation there may be different ways of performing selfhood. It is not simply that someone (or something) exists and acts as their selves naturally, but *how* they act (or not) can be regarded as the attestation of their selfhood (or denial of it), all expressed through their movement. That is to say, the performance of movement in animation constitutes the moving object as an actor. Indeed, this capacity of animation, according to Ursula Heise, enables animation to depict a world where human subjects and non-human objects are all seen as active agents with agency and selfhood, allowing us to "inquire into their 'objecthood'" (2014: 303). Although Heise notes that anthropocentric views of selfhood can be mapped onto the active object, animation still allows an exploration of alternative modes of existence through the direct visualization of objects moving as actors.

1. Takashi Murakami features *EVA* prominently in his essay in the catalogue for his *Little Boy* exhibit (2005). It should be noted that *hikikomori* and otaku may overlap, but they are also distinct from each other.

With this in mind, the performance of movement by objects in animation can be seen as a site for the analysis of the selfhood enacted by the actor (the active object), whether human or non-human. This can be conceptualized through notions of performance from the theater, where certain types of acting presuppose certain types of performance of the self: for someone to act as someone or something else, we have to presume there is a type of self that the actor can act as, and consider the means by which to present that type of self. As such, there are various modes of existence which are brought into being through certain modes of performance, ultimately enacting a type of selfhood in the process. Similarly, in animation, there are different ways of performing movement and, consequently, the actors become constituted in a manner afforded by the tendencies of the mode of performance utilized. In other words, *how* an object (human or non-human) performs constitutes the acting object as a specific type of actor based on the movement they enact, and thus realizes a tendency toward a certain type of selfhood—the types of which under consideration here are labeled 'individualism' and 'objecthood' (see Suan 2017).

Taking this as a point of departure, a very prominent mode of performance that deserves consideration is what Donald Crafton calls *embodied acting* (2013). Built from classically modern notions of human stage acting, embodied performance enacts characters not just through the sequence of actions that they perform, but through the subtle gestures and looks they make, movements which seem to originate from inside them, defining them as a person. Dramatic criticism traditionally involves this type of performance, judging characters on their being 'round' and having an interior that holds their depth of personality. On stage and in film, actors are usually expected to play a very different character than themselves, to present a new self through acting whose interiority is indicated through subtle motions of the eyes, minor gestures and bodily gesticulations, as if that character were really performing those actions (and not an actor playing another self). The process gives rise to highly individualized movements that differentiate one character from another, locking it to that body to enforce its uniqueness, and presenting a discrete inside/outside boundary for that self.

However, such embodied acting tends to build an anthropocentric view of selfhood through those actors' performances. This is what happens in films like *Beauty and the Beast*, where not all the objects in the film are active, but only a select few, such as the candlestick Lumière and the clock Cogsworth. Each object has their own peculiar types of movements that are specific to their character and body shape; each is individualized in the process. But, in terms of the narrative, these objects are actually humans that were turned into those objects and later return to being human, providing a succinct example of how the above noted type of embodied acting actually enacts human-like sensibilities in something that is non-human, through the mode of performance in/of animation. Put bluntly, embodied acting as commonly performed in animation tends to hone in on the specific type of selfhood that is human individualism, even if performed through non-human characters, for better or for worse.

There is another important type of performance of/in animation which Crafton labels *figurative acting*. In this mode of performance, codes and patterns are utilized to produce a self; conventionalized gestures that pre-exist and are external to each specific character are employed. In anime, these codes include facial expressions like arched eyes for happiness or glimmering eyes for overflowing emotions, all cited from prior instantiations of those codes by other characters. Consequently, performances of selfhood via figurative acting do not evince the same inside/outside boundaries for expression as individualism. Such dynamics are supported by anime's own media-form: figurative acting is sustained by anime's conventionality itself, extending beyond *EVA* to a variety of different anime productions from which these very same codes are cited. It is these operations of figurative acting that are called into focus in the TV series ending, as if examining the very idea of performing selfhood through figurative acting in anime's media-form. This effectively visualizes anime's tendency to embrace a type of selfhood that might be called 'objecthood,' a tentative term for a mode of existence that builds on Heise's view of active objects and Timothy Morton's conception of 'objects.'[2] Objecthood can be considered as a type of selfhood (or rather, a mode of existence enacted as a type of selfhood) that is non-human (but does not exclude humans), whereby one is constituted as an object made up of other objects and in relation to other objects—in this case, a character constituted by figurative acting codes from other characters.

It should be noted that there may be other ways of performing selfhood than figurative and embodied acting, but both are prominently featured in *EVA*. Moreover, though these modes of performing selfhood are usually enacted in their extremes; they are not found in complete isolation, but rather in a tense relationship with each other—one always implicated in the other, even if just barely: embodied performance usually employs movements that are individualized, but must retain something recognizable (and thus repeated/repeatable) for the gesture to be legible (e.g., a smile, tears); otherwise it is so 'individual' it is overly abstract, isolated and unintelligible. Not all figurative codes are performed exactly the same, making them specific to their instance of enactment. This mutual implication is evident in *EVA*, where we do not find a strict division of types of selfhood, but a general retention of their mutual implication, keeping taut the tensions of these modes of performance in/of animation for humans and non-humans.

Throughout the *EVA* series, modernity's assumptions are turned on their head, as objects of human creation, the Eva units, boldly display their agency: they exhibit performances of embodied acting, appearing with the same autonomy as human individuals. At the same time, humans are broken into fragments, their psyche examined in parts as

2. This also includes reference to the ideas of Bruno Latour.

they delve into their interiors to find only more parts of other characters, interrogating the constitutive codes of figurative acting. These two modes of acting are mutually implicated throughout the *EVA* series, favoring one extreme or the other in different sequences as the anime probes their respective tendencies toward each type of selfhood (individualism and objecthood), even though one tendency is never completely subsumed by the other.

As if a culmination of exploring the extreme ends of these tendencies in the performance of selfhood, the TV series and film endings can be read as inverse images of each other. The former lands on the examination and embrace of objecthood via the operations of figurative acting, whereas the latter depicts the dynamics of the extreme tendency of embodied acting, focusing on human individualism, and directly tying such a selfhood to the ecological catastrophe of the end of the world. Leaning heavily toward the tendencies of the extreme of figurative acting, the TV series ending presents a sense of selfhood that resembles the operations of a more ecological mode of existence close to Morton's conception of objects. For Morton, this is needed to counteract the modern, human-focused autonomous individualism which carries with it disastrous ecological consequences: maintaining a strict sense of inside 'human me' and outside 'environment' (composed of non-human objects), the human individual subject is seen as in control of non-active objects; consequently, pollution or global warming do not actually affect humans, as they are simply external objects that cannot act.

Instead, Morton sees humans and non-humans both as active objects, each consisting of "a potentially infinite regress of other entities" (2017: 105). Here, inside and outside are thoroughly blurred, because 'I' am both inside the 'environment' and the 'environment' is inside 'me.' This means that the pollution is not 'out there,' it is in the air I breathe in my lungs; it is me, in some sense, just as the biosphere is what I depend on to exist. In such a configuration, global warming can now be seen as acting upon me as it too is an active object, deeply affecting myself and my life. As the final episode presents a sense of selfhood that distinctly leans toward the operations of figurative acting, where the self is made up of various different codes (something like an active object made of other objects, where the classically conceived borders of inside/outside of individualism do not operate quite the same way), it appears more in line with Morton's ecological mode of existence, one which the optimistic tone of the finale seems to endorse: the final image of the series depicting Shinji performing a figurative acting code for smiling.

While ecological readings of *EVA* may initially seem out of step for the anime, it is important to consider that *EVA* is clearly set during the Anthropocene (the geological era where humans are the greatest influencer of climate and environmental change), constantly addressing the issue of humanity's devastating impact on the world: the Second Impact, the cause of the disaster that reshaped the world of the series, was in fact induced by humans. Furthermore, the collapse of the environment is consistently mentioned throughout the series, as by the elderly school teacher droning on in front of the class, or the mention of the strange seasons here and there, the reason why there are the iconic cicadas, a sign of summer, constantly ringing all-year-round. It is also a part of the surrounding media discourses and events around the time of production and release, in particular the Kyoto Protocol in 1997, which extends the 1992 UN Framework from the Convention on Climate Change. Ecological concerns are even overtly shown in the megahit anime *Princess Mononoke*, which was also released in 1997.

Released the same year, the film *EoE* reveals a startlingly different view of the ecological stakes of performing selfhood compared to the TV series ending, with depictions of environmental disaster that are more overt and bleak. Indeed, *EoE* features scenes of lush forests (filled with a concealed military) early on in the film, and ends with scenes of a dead landscape made desolate by humans. Since the entire film's conclusion turns on the destruction or salvation of the world as decided by one individual (Shinji), *EoE* can be read as exploring how selfhood and global devastation are linked. While the optimistic TV ending leans toward the tendencies of figurative acting and its operations of interrelated objecthood, in contrast, the filmic ending is far more pessimistic, moving toward the dynamics of individualism in the extreme of embodied performance, displaying the ecological destruction of this type of selfhood. The filmic ending takes the ideals of modern individual agency and its discrete inside/outside divide to its logical conclusions, but simultaneously undercuts it, as the individual decisions of Shinji inside of himself lead to the external destruction of Earth (for which he is not the catalyst), even as he reaffirms the barriers between people to uphold individualism, evincing an ambivalence of individual agency. The resulting destruction of the world is subsequently presented as linked to the operations and agential assumptions of the performance of anthropocentric individualism, exposing the impasses of its ability to attend to ecological catastrophe.

Embodied Acting and Human Control of Objects

While examples of embodied performance are scattered throughout the series, episode 19 contains one of the most memorable sequences in the TV anime: when Eva-01 goes 'berserk' beyond Shinji's control, viciously destroying the Angel, miraculously operating without a power source (Fig. 5.1: 20:20–21:25). Performed by key animator Mitsuo Iso, in place of the movements commonly seen in fight sequences of robots piloted by humans (often mimicking human combat, with sword slashes and gun blasts), Eva-01 executes a wild and brutal beating on its Angel opponent. Once thought to be a giant robot piloted by a human, Eva-01 shatters this concept by scuttling on all-fours and devouring an

Figure 5.1. Eva-01 going berserk in episode 19, presenting a savage autonomy through embodied acting. © khara, inc.

Angel like a carnivorous mammal in a humanoid figure. Much of the savagery of the Eva unit is articulated through the bestial movements performed, making it a prime example of embodied acting.

In this mode of performance in/of animation, "animators perform movement to perform emotion," effectively giving the impression that the animated bodies are expressing themselves through their specific gestures and actions (Crafton 2013: 44). Embodied acting is thus 'introverted,' and tends toward the constitution of modern individuals that appear to provide a sense of depth in their enactment of emotional movement (2013: 36). Such a performance is partly afforded by full animation, which, according to Thomas Lamarre, employs "closed compositing," hiding the gap between the layers of the celluloid images, a tendency toward the movement-into-depth of cinematism and, in character animation, a heightened sense of sentiment in character acting (2009: 200). Historically, it is through Disney's innovations in the 1930s that embodied acting is developed, whereby the 'fullness' of the animated movement is used to give the impression that it is an individualized actor whose inner emotions and drives command the movement that is expressed externally.

This is heavily indebted to Konstantin Stanislavski's acting method, where an actor internalizes a character and expresses their personality not just in words, but in the manner in which they execute actions and gestures. Disney in fact had his animators take acting lessons and observe human actors trained in this mode of acting (Crafton 2013: 37–41). What occurs in embodied performance is a manner of controlling the body to operate through the insertion of individualism by creating interiority. The emphasis on control is similar for both human and animated actors. Embodied performance gives the impression of naturalness, a sense of internal motivation that appears to organically originate from inside the character expressed in its movement, and consequently hides how trained and constructed the production of that movement is (by actor or animator). This applies even if that character is controlled by someone else, even if the movement will emphasize that their 'original self' is somehow under another's control due to the discrepancy between the 'original' and 'controlled' movements of the character.

All in all, the effect of embodied acting is one of a character with a sense of emotional depth, that is, emoting from the interior, but expressed externally in the movement. The point to stress is that embodied performance tends to be associated with depth, and in the case of its execution in animation, a spatial dynamic whereby there is a discrete inside and outside to the character, isolating it from the external world as it operates with full autonomy. This emphasis on autonomy links to a modern idea of 'realism' in this type of acting. As Crafton notes, a sense of scientific realism underpins the development of embodied acting developed by Disney in the 1930s (2013: 41–42). Depth is once more foregrounded here: Disney seeks to produce interiority as expressed through the individualized movement of the characters—their exterior movements providing a way for viewers to grasp the depth of the character's uniquely emotive personality to make them seem 'realistic.' Although this deviates from Crafton's conceptualization, it is important to stress the connection of this type of realism to anthropocentric individualism. Indeed, it often appears as if embodied performance in animation imitates the emotive movements of people in the real world, even if the animated objects are non-humans. Simply put, embodied acting produces humanistic individualism, with all its depth and personality, in the performing objects.

But this might be a double-edged sword. On the one hand, it does allow the easy acceptance of a world of moving non-humans, providing a simple means to display how, through the animation and its subtle movements, it is not just humans that have complex depth and agency, as Heise contends (2014: 309–310). On the other hand, it is a thoroughly anthropocentric selfhood performed by the non-humans. *EVA* seems to bring this tension into focus, succinctly encapsulated in the bodily movements of the Eva units, supposedly non-human objects that turn out to be close to humans, which display a depth that (from a modern perspective) should not be there.

Indeed, although one of the central themes of the *EVA* TV series is the mastery of the world through human scientific control, the series displays not just the immense prowess of the modern scientific human, but their fragility, their gaps in understanding and their lack of control of the non-human, even those of their own creation: the Eva units. There are multiple instances referencing the hubris of humanity, obliquely asserting the role of anthropocentrism, of the human at the top, distant and distinctive from all other life. In some sense, the dream of modernity, of the human subject controlling the object, is encapsulated in NERV and SEELE (the enigmatic parent organization of NERV) which create the Eva units, objects which are supposed to be simple tools to defeat the Angels. NERV (and SEELE) tend to follow a modern approach to science, of subjects who calculate to control and manipulate non-human objects.[3]

However, while the Eva units initially evince the human prowess for control of the object, right from the beginning the Eva units themselves defy this simplistic view: episode 2 shows Eva-01 going berserk, beyond Shinji's control as it defeats the Angel, and later episodes show the cracks in understanding of their operations for the lead scientist Ritsuko Akagi. Eventually, the attacking Angels and the Eva units themselves are revealed to be somehow close to human. But this is not just in the dialogue. The Eva units are portrayed as having their own agency through their animation via embodied acting. It is important to repeat that in *EVA* embodied acting tends to be seen not in the human characters, but in the actions of the Eva unit's themselves, carefully animated in a manner not employed by the human characters. In fact, most of the Eva unit battle animations are not reused bank footage (which are frequently utilized for human characters),[4] further attesting to how much emphasis went into producing unique, individualized movements for each combat sequence.

With that in mind, returning to Eva-01's bestial actions in episode 19, this embodied performance provides a vivid display of agency (in this case, to literally be active and enact effects on its own, even without a source of power), a sense of a primal, savage character.

3. Much of the conception of the modern divide between human subject controlling non-human object is drawn from Bruno Latour (1993).

4. See Ida Kirkegaard's Chapter 2 on 'bank cuts.'

Importantly, this sequence reveals both the isolation and agential capacity of individualism, so distinct it is difficult to relate to, so autonomous it cannot be controlled. Because it is an Eva unit, such a performance reveals the actual agency of the non-human, dispelling the divisions between humans and non-humans, reversing modern conceptions of inanimate object (one that humans can control) and active (human) subject. Yet, as if insisting on resistance to any strict divisions, in the narrative, Eva-01 is an object of human construction operating on its own; at the same time, Eva-01 maintains at least a tinge of humanity as it is, in fact, the remnants of the soul of Shinji's mother (Yui Ikari), which are somewhere inside it.

Objecthood and Figurative Acting

It is not just objects that blur the divisions between human and non-human through their performance in/of animation in *EVA*. Contrary to the Eva units, the humans stay within anime's recognizable brand of figurative acting, which is in part supported by the prevalence of limited animation in anime. Although the figurative codes used in anime are not usually critiqued, limited animation's prevalent display of jerkier movements is often scorned. The long-standing valorization of the movement of full animation as *the* standard for animation (even in Japan) might also be connected to the valorization of embodied performance as *the* measure of quality character acting in/of animation.

However, limited animation has its own dynamics of movement. At times, holding still images for nearly a minute, as Lamarre notes, *EVA* optimizes limited animation's techniques of working with layers and using stills to produce, what he calls, "hyperlimited animation," highlighting the flatness of the image, presenting its own manner of compositing, editing and producing motion in animation (2009: 202). Investigating the type of limited-animation compositing employed by

EVA's central production studio, GAINAX, Lamarre theorizes the "exploded view," a quasi-orthogonal perspective, where the parts (or layers) are separate, but also assembled, a tension of unity and multiplicity in this alternative structure of depth. This is not the movement-into-depth of cinematism, but the impression of depth spread across the surface in a sequence of images. We can see this in the commonly used trope of a character or vehicle avoiding a barrage of missiles, as demonstrated by Asuka in her Eva-02 in the *EoE* film (25:04–25:07). Such sequences tend to "flatten the hierarchical ordering of the image. It is impossible to say whether any one element in the perceptual field is intrinsically more important" (Lamarre 2009: 136). For Lamarre, "instead of one-point structuration to produce depth with distinct positioning, the structure of exploded projection generates fields of potential depth traversed by lines of sight . . . the result is very close to a logistics of information retrieval," whereby viewers are "asked to skim and scan fields, and to discern degrees of separation or connection in the manner of a network" (2009: 136).

Such limited animation dynamics, where potential depth rises to the surface providing a different mode of perception, can be seen as overlapping with figurative acting. Operating differently than embodied acting, figurative performance utilizes a combination of familiar expressions. In its extreme, it is only predicated on the repetition of codes, in the process producing a sense of surface as the codes sometimes appear at the same time, or in varying frequencies in the same scene—that is, *on* the characters, not necessarily *in* them. This emphasis on surface even appears in character designs. In fact, *EVA*'s characters are seen by Lamarre as emblematic of what he describes as "soulful bodies," where personalities (as potential depth) are inscribed on their surfaces (2009: 201). Yet it is not just their physical designs that display their character, but also the types of movements these soulful bodies perform. In anime, the prevalence of limited animation affords the regular switching between these codified gestures and expressions, often facilitating sudden shifts between emotional registers (e.g., characters going from sad to happy to angry very quickly). Indeed, the 'jerkiness' of limited animation's dynamics allows for the rapid deployment of different types of expressions, often with very little physical movement of the character's body until the next expression is employed in the following frame.

Figurative acting is in this sense closer to contemporary, digitally informed perception: reading, scanning, connecting, jumping between parts and whole. This does not mean that figurative acting is somehow simpler or lacking in skill. It is quite the opposite, as performing figurative acting is incredibly difficult to achieve. Here, the sense of control is measured by the capacity to adhere to the set of codes, which if performed within the appropriate range can be quickly identified and read. Proficiency with these codes, as well as their enactment in combination in a manner that makes the character appear cohesive and not just a dull, incongruous collection of traits is a very particular way of building characters. That one may confuse the collection to be the character is evidence of the prowess in subtlety of figurative acting. In the process, agency and autonomy in the modern sense are muddled: does a human perform the codes, or do they force the human to act a certain way as the codes exist outside the human who must enact them within a specific register to be recognizable; are characters producing the codes or are the codes producing the characters?

All in all, because figurative acting relies on its relation to prior codes, its operations resemble Hiroki Azuma's notion of the database of character parts (what he calls *moe*-elements, Azuma 2009), where otaku consume (and create) characters by dividing them up into their various (conventional) parts. However, here the elements are the figurative codified expressions; and they do not operate by precise replication, but rather by the act of citation, that is, repeated in different contexts (also implying a sense of change and variation rather than exact duplication). Moreover, each character is enacted through the accumulative combination of cited codes, making the frequency and grouping of those codes produce that particular character, which serves to differentiate actors from one another in a manner that is distinct from their visual design.

This process also genders characters, and although the operations of gender via figurative acting in anime are outside of the aims of this chapter, it is worth touching on the topic as an illustration of how figurative codes work in general. To give one example of how gendered codes operate, in episode 12, each character is piloting their respective Eva units, but each Eva unit runs differently (18:28–19:00), with Rei's Eva-00 running in a manner that is codified as feminine in anime. Such a gendering is most apparent in the position of Rei's arms and hands (arms spread out to the side), with a slight bounce in her gait, rather than the closed fists of Shinji's Eva-01 in his forward-leaning sprint. This is not to say that all codes are gendered, nor that these hand gestures and ways of running fully determine gender. Rather, these codified gestures are often performed by female characters and, following Judith Butler's conception of gender performativity, become associated with femininity, giving them the impression of naturalness when performed by female characters due to a sedimentary effect (1988; 1993; 1997). Further drawing on Butler, these codes operate as cited instances where each iteration itself becomes a site for further citation, thus sustaining the illusion of 'naturalized gender.' Such an illusion is both sustained by and its operations exposed in the performance of these gendered codes by the Eva units: these movements differentiate each pilot's operations from one another, the female-piloted robots running with the feminine code; but it also displays how gendering can operate as the performance of codes, as the bodies of the Eva units are not overtly gendered male or female revealing their performativity and the external source of such gendered codes as they express the pilot's mannerisms in the way they are made to run.

This is also where a little of the embodied acting tendency shines through, as it differentiates each character from one another in an almost individualizing way, especially with regard to Asuka and Rei, who are both running differently, with Rei's movements employing more overtly 'femininely' coded running gestures than Asuka's. It should also be noted that such gendered codes are used in anime to facilitate the common trope of cross-gendering through body swapping (e.g., a female character inhabiting a male body, but performing feminine codes in the male body—utilized in the film *Your Name*), which is similar to this dynamic of piloting a robot, revealing how important citation is to gender performativity.

In any case, the operations of citation, whereby each instantiation is both a re-enactment of prior instances and a 'source' for further iterations, is fundamental to the performative constitution of the selfhood of characters via figurative acting. Furthermore, as noted above, the frequency of codes performed by actors is important for differentiating characters. There will be characters that smile less frequently or those that are cheerful all the time, which is displayed through the frequency of sterner or more bubbly expressions. This does not mean, however, that characters will not change over time. In fact, an actor's character is produced through a cumulative compounding of the various codes they perform over time. Accordingly, different expressions are added onto that actor's grouping of codified expressions, for instance, when a usually serious character may execute the occasional smile, the rarity of the expression making it all the more meaningful (and thus implying character growth). Furthermore, sudden bursts of expression (such as anger or fear) are not uncommon, making their enactment often comedic or endearing, adding another codified expression onto the compound that is that actor's character.

The result is a character who enacts codes that are specific to that instantiation, but also extending outside of the current citation to the earlier performances of that code. As such, figurative performance operates by linking different iterations of those codes despite their distance spatially (they are separate characters) and temporally (enacted at different times). Instead of the anthropocentric individuality of embodied acting, figurative performance enacts 'particularity,' whereby a character is specific, but only as it is made up of iterations in a certain series of codes. Furthermore, when constituting characters through that precise collection of codes, they extend beyond that character outwards to other codes. Indeed, the very capacity to produce a character via figurative acting is premised on prior iterations of those codes in other places and other times on other characters.

With this in mind, it is worthwhile considering what type of selfhood is afforded by figurative acting. Although Crafton does not go so far as to consider this, figurative acting in the performance in/of anime's animation could be seen as constituting 'objecthood' (for lack of a better term): a self that is operating as an object, which is made of, interacting with and dependent on other objects. Here, Timothy Morton's conception of 'objects' and how to think them is instructive, as it greatly differs from the modern view. Instead of autonomous human subjects that act on the passive non-human objects, for Morton, humans and non-humans both exist as objects, here seen as entities that contain "a potentially infinite regress of other entities" (2017: 105). In other words, each object, under closer inspection, might be seen as having other parts, which could also be seen as objects; these object-parts themselves are made up of parts, and so the process continues. Morton sees this as a way to include even humans as "a partial object in a set of partial objects, such that it comprises an implosive whole that is less than the sum of its parts"—that is, if each object has many object-parts, then to consider the object is to also consider the object-parts, which outnumber the singular object itself (2017: 104).

This produces what Morton describes as "a whole that subscends into its parts," various parts that are both somehow external and internal (from the modern perspective) to the object, each always haunted by other objects. At the same time, one object is specific, while still retaining the necessity of all the other objects that constitute it. In Morton's model, even if a person were to dig down deep, they might find something that is not themselves, not theirs, and even non-human, because they are entirely comprised of objects, all the way up and down—a self that is constituted of object-parts, making them quite distinct from the sharp inside/outside boundaries of the anthropocentric individual. Figurative acting executes this in a somewhat literal way: the external object-parts of the figurative codes (or in Azuma's terminology, *moe*-elements) are *on* the characters; they are 'shared' by many characters, making each character somehow part of the others, but also distinct. For instance, each character has a particular 'personality' because of their codified gestures and expressions, which are cited from other characters who enacted them in prior instances.

An example of objecthood can be found in the human-looking character of Rei Ayanami, often treated in the narrative as an object in the modern sense: without agency and to be acted upon—scientifically produced by humans, even replaceable, as she is one of a series of clones of Shinji's mother.[5] In this sense, she is an emblem of objecthood and figurative acting: a copy, somehow not human, and built through the repetition of codes to constitute a reserved personality. In terms of selfhood, she would then have the most overtly complex problem: how does she differentiate herself from the other clones of her? Rei even addresses this issue in a monologue on her existence in episode 14 (12:01–14:07), where she first mentions multiple random objects (mountains, skies, flowers, people, Eva units, blood, etc.), then questions what humanity is, and eventually states that she is an object ("*kono buttai wa jibun*"—"this object is me")[6] (Fig. 5.2).

Toward the end of this sequence, when Rei is supposedly delving into herself, she says that she feels someone else is there, and then names a number of the other characters accompanied by their images. This can be read as a very literal examination of how figurative

5. For the most extensive feminist reading of *EVA*, see Kotani (1997).

6. All translations from the ADV release of the *EVA* DVDs.

Who am I? What am I? What am I? What am I? What am I?

This object is me.

I feel the presence of someone who is not me.

Is someone there, beyond this?

Figure 5.2. Rei's monologue about her selfhood in episode 14. Her characteristic (lack of) expression shown on the top left. © khara, inc.

acting works, as there are always elements of other characters in/on the character. In a way, her declaration that she is "a vessel for a soul" is somewhat accurate: her body contains (or rather, has on its surface) the codes of others. Interestingly, Rei's reliance on relations and linkages is directly expressed, as when she is asked in episode 6 why she pilots the Eva unit, and she responds by saying "*kizuna*," or "bonds." The word *kizuna* contains elements of emotional ties, of relationship and connection and linkage, which is precisely how figurative acting must operate: it fundamentally cannot function without those linkages to others.

For Rei, these linkages can even be considered as going beyond the *EVA* series. Crucially, this is due to Rei's particularity, which has made her, perhaps more than any other character, a fan favorite that is repeated not just in merchandise, but in variations of characters like her in other anime. She even spawned an entire character type (sometimes labelled as *kūdere* by fans) that is extremely reserved, sometimes cold and often not technically human, such as the robot Yuki Nagato from *The Melancholy of Haruhi Suzumiya*. What marks Rei's character in *EVA* is not necessarily her particular expressions, but actually her *lack* of a variety of expressions. It is as if she does not perform many figurative codes at all, in stark contrast to the hot-headed Asuka and the boisterous but concerned Misato. This absence of expressive variety goes hand in hand with the 'hyperlimited animation' of *EVA*: Rei hardly switches codes, barely moving at all.

Such operations further evince the dynamics of figurative acting: the absence of expressions itself actually developing into a type of expression (especially as it is repeated in other characters). Performing objecthood through figurative acting can be seen as working similarly: Rei is both highly specific and yet herself becoming another object for other objects. Yet such an interrelation does not mean she has no capacity to act and induce effects. In fact, Rei regularly operates according to her own volition in the series, even against her orders, including when she sacrifices herself in episode 19, disobeying Gendō in *EoE* or any number of times she aides Shinji in his introspective moments. Additionally, her character patterns become the template that restricts later character repetitions into Rei's range (or lack) of expressions. Rei also exemplifies the more radical possibilities of objecthood, which becomes especially apparent in the finale of the TV series, episode 26. For there is no other episode in which Rei's particularity and its limits are brought to the fore in such a stark manner.

Moving into Objecthood

Before directly addressing the TV series ending, it is important to reiterate that embodied acting and figurative acting are involved with each other; similar to the human-like non-humans (Eva-01, moving through embodied acting as an active object) and the non-human-like humans (Rei, a figurative actor who is both a copy of and made of others). Like depth and surface, the two can appear separate, but are actually interrelated. At their absolute extreme—that is, impossible in actual enactment as there will always be something of the embodied in the figurative and the figurative in the embodied—embodied acting is so interiorized it is all depth, so singular it is isolated; figurative acting is so externalized it is all surface, so codependent it is rigidly repetitive. Figurative acting is restrictive as it is reliant on repeated codes and must stringently reinforce them in relation to earlier instances; the individualism of embodied acting can bring with it a liberation from such restriction, but it can also be isolating and walls off the boundaries of the self with a strict separation.

As *EVA* explores the extremes of these performances in non-human and human objects, it exposes their interrelation by inverting the modern dynamic. In some sense (as already mentioned above), it is as if the series attempts to flesh out interiority in the characters of figurative acting. However, humans become objects, and Eva units are somehow haunted by humans, as Eva-01 is with Yui Ikari. *EVA* pulls on both threads to show how they loop into each other. The tension between interiority (indicative of embodied individualism) and figurative acting (where each character is composed through the relations to other characters on their surface) is further revealed through the incursion of other characters in their minds: there is almost always another character there, either speaking or acting or viewing, even if the other character is another version of the character whose interiority is shown as they break one layer of surface to move into another surface layer.

This dynamic of interrelation is grappled with in the final episodes as they move through the most focused and explicit examination of selfhood in the TV series, delving into the interior of the main characters. For example, episode 26 shifts rapidly between abstract, metamorphic images and partialized elements of Shinji (his voice, his facial expression). This covers the extreme tendencies of both modes of acting: on the extreme of embodied acting, the bodies swerve and morph into different shapes, as if enduring meaningless transformations that are so individualized, they cannot be understood; for figurative acting there are abstract symbols that are not repeated (like the outline of fish), making them singular symbols that are unintelligible in this context.

Throughout this sequence, in the voice-over dialogue, the characters seem to guide Shinji toward an understanding of the necessity of others for the formation of self. Occasionally, Shinji follows, seeing the faults in individualism, at one point even claiming in exasperation: "If I'm alone, I'll always be alone, no matter how far I go with it! The whole world is just me!" In these sequences, there is a display of both abstract embodied acting and figurative acting, as if Shinji's turmoil is explicated in the rapid switching between the extremes of the two modes of acting: extreme metamorphosis that displays unreadable emotion due to hyper-individuality; and disparate parts that constitute a self completely divorced from the body. The latter tendency (that of figurative performance) is exemplified in the moments when Shinji transforms into only his facial expression, which takes over the whole screen. In this display, it becomes obvious that facial codes are themselves able to function as objects, as Shinji has now become the code, just as the codes had constituted him. Such a sequence seems to directly visualize what Morton describes as a "whole that is less than the sum of its parts," "'a whole that subscends into its parts," extending outwards and inwards at once. But this is not necessarily a smooth or easy process of realization, especially coming from the position of a modern human individual:

As one becomes aware of more dimensions of oneself, that one is not in fact one nor dissolved into multiplicity, but haunted by spectral parts of oneself that are also not parts, that subscendently wiggle around all by themselves, one might go crazy. (2017: 160)

Indeed, the fear of the self completely disaggregating into parts lies at the edge of figurative acting, and the brink of madness is always threatening to seep through in these scenes, as it does throughout the series and films.

Ultimately, the torrent of imagery and Shinji's dialogue seem to move to the side of figurative acting, toward objecthood. But in a strange way, this recognition and acceptance of an object-oriented selfhood occurs through engagement with embodied acting and the individual's insistence on depth, only to realize that the depth returns us to the surface: Shinji's insistence on his individuality is accompanied by the crude image of a human that seems to be endlessly repeated as it zooms in on itself, like a fractal, before Shinji morphs into the parts of his face, followed by the other characters refuting his claims regarding individualism (Fig.5.3). It is as if, in an effort to reconcile the tensions between surface and depth, figurative and embodied, there was a brief attempt to think of a different kind of depth, a fractal type of depth that seems to constantly rise up into itself even as we descend downwards.

It is important to note the dialogue at this moment, spoken by different female characters: "By recognizing the differences between yourself and others, you shape who you are. The very first other person is your mother. Your mother is a person separate from you." Significantly, this segment raises the point of a person's relationship to their mother, a topic often ignored by (sexist) conceptions of individualism because it radically undermines the strict inside/outside and self/other divisions presupposed by individualism (see Morton 2017: 2). Instead, one person is born from another person, literally originating from inside another, dependent on the (female) other, yet somehow distinct. This is reflected in the next lines, where Shinji states, "Right, I'm me. But it's also certain that the other people shape my mind

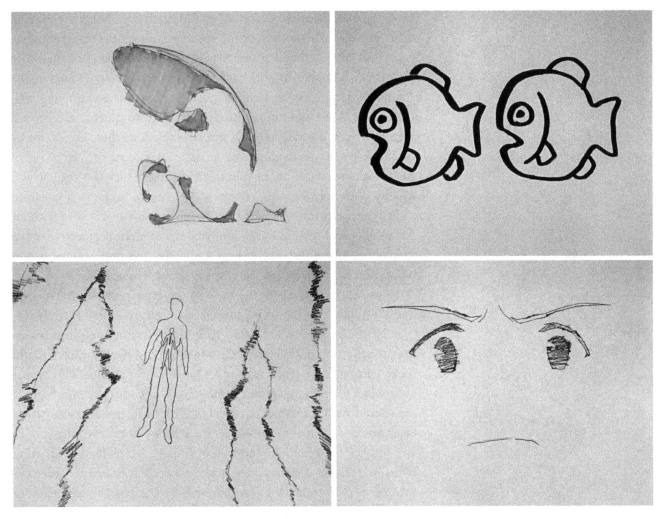

(*kokoro*) as well." What finally results from these exchanges is a sense of figurative acting which affords an organization of a selfhood that is constituted by its connection to others, but one which does not deny itself its particularity: Shinji is a character who is distinct from the others, even as those others are also part of what constitutes him.

After this sequence, Asuka exclaims that Shinji finally understands, and the scene suddenly switches back to fully colored animated imagery,

Figure 5.3. Shinji's movement through abstract embodied acting (top left), strange symbols (top right), moving through a fractal image of the human (bottom left) and his subsequent subsendence into parts (bottom right). © khara, inc.

entering an 'alternative everyday' world, with the characters playing different roles. This section of the episode explores the transformative capacities of a selfhood where Shinji, along with many of the other characters, are slightly different in their personality. However, the standout example is Rei, here imagined as a completely different character type (loud and unorganized as opposed to quiet and reserved) (Fig. 5.4). Such a version should not be a shock as there are examples of multiple Rei's throughout the series, even a scene of a large vat of Rei clones in episode 23, each of them smiling (which the 'regular' Rei usually does not). Yet this version of Rei can be taken as a violation of her character (even in merchandise, she is only rarely seen without her somber and forlorn look), implying the modern perspective of the individual, where she is closed-off and defined in that original personality, making such a contrast a betrayal to her 'true self.'

However, read through the tone of the later parts of the episode and the silliness of the scene, this can be interpreted as playfully displaying the radical lack of closure in figurative acting—and subsequently for selfhood as objecthood—whereby the character is not locked into place, but always has the potential for change. This occurs even when we think a certain combination of codes becomes heavily associated with a character, repeated with such frequency (or their clear absence) that they appear as their personality, as in the case of Rei and her somber look (and lack of smiles). But as figurative acting is maintained by certain codes, and each code is linked to other iterations of that code, it is also haunted by the possibilities of other codes. Each code thus subscends into other codes. As Morton notes, subscendence would actually allow for emotional registers to have, on some level, elements of emotions that are traditionally not supposed to be there. In anger, we may see elements of hesitation, grief or even humor (Morton 2017: 104). In this sense, there will always be the potential for a radical shift in character through the execution of figurative codes, something which is constantly enacted in anime as characters switch between emotional registers rapidly.

Figure 5.4. Rei's display of uncharacteristic figurative acting codes for her character in episode 26. © khara, inc.

Rei as a character produced by such codes is emphasized here in the 'alternative everyday' by the fact that her general design is the same (although, significantly her costume is different, with an added vest on her uniform), but she performs certain figurative codes that are, for lack of a better phrase, uncharacteristic of her previous character: specifically the running with bread in her mouth (a common code for lateness and sloppiness), arched-eyes and cheery smile during her introduction to the class and an explosively angry face when she accuses Shinji at the end of the sequence. These produce a different character by their combination, emphasizing that the design can remain the same, but the specific aggregation of codes marks a shift. As such, a starkly different particularity is created for the 'alternative everyday' version of Rei's character, highlighting one of the ambiguities at the heart of figurative acting: Is the character producing the expressions, or are the codes producing the character? Furthermore, why should this version not be considered as another addition to Rei's cumulative combination of codes?

While the change is sudden, rapid switches to different emotional registers are featured constantly in anime (even in *EVA*, as in Misato switching from joyful to scolding in episode 1). Yet, in the case of Rei, there is no narrative justification, where different emotional codes are slowly accumulated to prepare for a shift in character. Moreover, the change is not just one or two different expressions, but appears comprehensive, a complete transformation in character type, jarring in comparison to the earlier version of Rei (who exhibited her normal register just moments before in the episode), as if it were an all-too-abrupt violation of her perceived totality as an individual character. In consideration of this, Rei's stark change can be seen as approaching a limit of particularity, and exposing a continued reliance on the framework of individualized characters, even in anime. The performance of Rei, then, might not be so much a betrayal or violation, but rather an example of the potential for both particularity and radical change, even in a mode of performance that relies on repetition; at the same time, it displays the limits of a self that is constituted by figurative acting, which cannot completely subsume any individualizing tendencies.

After these scenes with Rei, Shinji reflects on the events and says, "This is also a possible world. One possibility that's in me. The me right now is not exactly who I am. All sorts of me's are possible." This leads to Shinji's revelation of a greater acceptance of himself, and in the last moments of the episode, Shinji makes a literal breakthrough: He shatters the world around him, which is whirled away for him to be greeted by the entire central cast congratulating him, the last image of the series featuring Shinji performing the widely used figurative code for smiling with arched eyes. There is an optimism in these final segments and a sense of solidarity among those shown as they congratulate Shinji, to which he responds with thanks. Shinji's revelation can be interpreted as an alignment with the tendency toward objecthood (even for humans), a particularity of self that is gained through the specific combination of other codes (or objects) that exist both outside and inside him. This is directly revealed in Shinji's acceptance of his own selfhood and the congratulations of the others that surround him, somehow, in terms of the diegesis, existing both on the inside of Shinji and, visually, on the outside of him.

In this sense, the final sequences land closer to the operations of figurative acting, embracing a sense of interrelated selfhood, where Shinji is, like Rei, something like an active object made of other objects, where the classically conceived borders of inside and outside of individualism do not operate quite the same way. As such, the TV series ending concludes with an optimistic affirmation of objecthood that reveals the potentials of the performance of anime's media-form: anime broadly and *EVA* in particular invoke a general tendency toward (inclusive) objecthood that had been obscured by modern individualism, a blurring of the line between internal and external, human and non-human entities (objects), a mode of existence which may hold ecologically positive potentials.

Styling Selfhood with Objects

Historically, *EVA* overlaps with the general sense of crisis that is often attributed to the 'lost decade' for Japan in the 1990s, when the economic bubble burst, leading to the restructuring of society, the Aum Shinrikyō terrorist attack and the Kobe earthquake, among other events (Maejima 2010: 31–33; Uno 2008: 17–21). However, one might also see this as a more general crisis of the modern human in post-modernity, which extends beyond Japan to a more global reach (which *EVA* itself did, even during its initial release), one which is most prominently apparent in consumer practices in varying ways.

Among the explosions of niche consumer products and their corresponding consumer categories that (continued to) take hold in the 1990s are late-night (*shinya*) anime, their surrounding media mix products and the visibility of the otaku who consume them. *EVA* is noted by commentators such as Satoshi Maejima as integral to the popularizing of anime for that late-night time-slot, and it is these late-night anime that are correlated with otaku fans who admit strong feelings for anime (and other media and merchandise) objects. Such objects are often anime characters of a certain type that are materialized in various media, whether it be an anime, manga, game and/or figurine. But what links these different products, despite their differences in material and medium, are often character designs and figurative acting codes that help animate the inert materials through the codified poses, each imbued with what Marc Steinberg calls "dynamic immobility" (Steinberg 2012: 6).

It is important to stress that these various figurative acting codes (or object-parts) are also utilized in fan production and imply a dispersal of agency that is seen throughout figurative acting: while the otaku can direct a character in different directions than the source works by introducing new codes, the codes must be enacted by the otaku, meaning that the otaku must ultimately work within a certain register to maintain recognizability. Moreover, though there is some tendency to maintain a certain degree of similarity to the character in the source works, deviations like the 'alternative everyday' Rei version are also very common, performed by utilizing various other figurative acting codes; subsequently, it becomes unclear if it is actually the human actor or the object-parts of figurative codes or the character itself which become the central locus of agency—that is to say, there is a distribution of agency in the production of derivative works by otaku.

In consideration of this, what Azuma calls database consumption of *moe*-elements (which can be extended to figurative acting codes and other object-parts) might be reimagined as otaku overtly engaging with the various object-parts that constitute the objecthood of a specific character; characters can not only be broken down into parts, but are constituted from them—they are wholes less than the sum of their parts, they subscend themselves, and otaku openly engage with this in their cultural activities. This type of database consumption-production evinces an overt engagement with objects, especially as anime characters themselves are sold as physical merchandise.

Consequently, otaku consumption often appears as a type of literalized commodity fetishism that is derided. Indeed, otaku are generally regarded as 'strange' because they let these anime objects affect them so much, let themselves engage with them in a manner deemed excessive. Perhaps it is the characters' human-like figure which makes it too obvious that there is activity, if not an agency, of objects involved here, in part causing a negative reaction by non-otaku as it violates the modern order of human subjects controlling passive objects. In some senses, this violation might be seen as the focus of much of the literature on otaku around the turn of the 21st century, which seemed to hone in on otaku as the new vanguard of the post-modern subject (e.g., Azuma 2009). Indeed, the type of otaku consumption-production involving moe-elements can be seen as an emblem of a contemporary (post-modern) mode of existence, one where objects are increasingly relied upon in practices of fashioning selfhood for humans.

This includes the concurrent performances of a 'lifestyle' that increases in visibility during *EVA*'s initial broadcast in the mid-1990s and continues to be a globally dominant mode of expressing selfhood. Beyond otaku practice (which may itself be conceived of as a type of 'lifestyle'), this is perhaps most visible in the realm of fashion, where certain clothes, housewares, architecture, restaurants and cafes, and music, among other objects, establish a certain 'style' of living. Gabriella Lukács (2010) sees lifestyle as coming into prominence in Japan in the 1990s as neoliberalism continued to widen its spread, and is evident in the shifts in the era's media. In particular, Lukács points to the rising number of live-action 'trendy dramas' that depict certain lifestyles and their connection to the growth of niche consumer marketing. Lukács notes that lifestyle is premised on the idea of choice, of personal, individual selection, which plays out the neoliberal fantasy of a discrete self, disconnected from the external social world, who acts freely in the market—you express your individualism through the purchase and usage of certain products (if you can afford them), employed in your personal combination of such commodities, regardless of economic station (i.e., social class). In some senses, this may appear empowering and liberating, enabling someone to break constraining, even oppressive cultural categories in the effort to reinvent a selfhood that feels comfortable and appropriate for them as an individual.

At the same time, this endorsement of constant flux overlaps with an idea of autonomy premised on selection of consumer goods, which works well for sustaining a constant flow of new products to consume as trends ebb and flow. People are regularly incited to (re)define themselves, finding 'who they truly are' by exercising their self-determination through consumption of these new (and ultimately disposable) commodities—they are always in the process of becoming their self through styling their life with the most recently trending objects. These objects are mass-produced commodities, connected to a large array of branding techniques and images, all of which are carried with the objects as they become included in the person's selfhood.

Explicitly external to the human person, they are somehow meant to be expressions of our internal individuality.

In this sense, there is a similarity to the operations of figurative acting in the performance of lifestyle: using external objects to constitute a sense of self. In addition, just as each performance of a figurative code becomes the site of citation for further iterations, a person may even begin to embody a certain type of lifestyle that becomes the model for others to style their own lives on, and the cycle continues as a new trend catches on. Here, we find a strange double-bind for performing selfhood under neoliberalism: while styling the self appears to activate a type of individualized agency as one chooses their products, that person also becomes an object of consumption, creating not just products for consumption, but a selfhood that is consumable as recognizably in (or against) trend. Ultimately, there is a tension between these two dynamics: individualism in expression, only to be turned into an object in the process (Diederichsen 2012).

Although lifestyle performance is *not* an explicit endorsement of neoliberalism and more an example of how integrated into daily life neoliberalism has become, it is important to note the underlying political underpinnings of performances of selfhood. More to the point, this politics of performing selfhood has gained a new layer of relevance as taken up in contemporary ecological theory. In fact, Morton sees the neoliberal sense of individualism as inherently destructive (for humans and non-humans), but sees ecological potential in the relationship to consumer objects (2017). The latter mode (lifestyle performance of selfhood via consumer objects) is ecological in the sense that the lifestyle performer implicitly acknowledges their relationship to non-human objects, their interdependence on them.

For Morton (although he does not name it precisely), lifestyle performance can also be seen as a 'chasing of the self' to find that there is something else there, the non-human objects with which you define your selfhood: "As we style ourselves according to our products and our thingies, something else is happening. We are being styled by them" (2017: 138). This is "an aesthetic mode of relation. And it's about allowing that thing to relate to us" (ibid.). Morton cautiously sees consumer fetishism and lifestyle performance as something that might be moved into (or in his terms, "underneath") as it is "a distorted actuality," and one of the few places in our contemporary culture where objects are included in social space, and thus in some senses ecological because we acknowledge and accept their inclusion (2017: 69).

This is crucial for Morton because this type of selfhood not only allows for a very different sense of conceiving of the human self, but of the idea of groups, of inside and outside borders, and of relating to the (hyper)object of global warming (2013). According to Morton, if we think of humans as the only agential actors, then the changing climate and the pollution cannot appear to affect us, because they are seen as non-active objects. However, if objects are not just part of us, but necessary for our production of selfhood, then we are more open to recognizing that 'I' am not an isolated human individual, but rather am made up of a plethora of other human and non-human objects, from bacteria to language, from evolutionary products from other creatures (human lungs having evolved from fish) to clothes. When considering this, one can also understand how these non-human objects *are* part of that person, affecting them in fundamental ways, just as global warming is active upon us. This destructive (hyper)object is not something out there, but inside people (in the lungs that breathe in pollution; the food we eat), on and around people (as in clothing, which can link to environmentally destructive production processes), with people at all times. Moreover, this is not only a personal or even local problem, but also concurrently a global one. According to Morton, the next step is "acknowledging this always-already quality of nonhuman impingement, and bringing that awareness, which is not the opposite of action but rather a quantum of action . . . into actions at other scales" (2017: 139).

Yet, despite this potential, the movement toward acknowledgment of the non-human brought into action at larger scales is no easy or simple task—although there are some 'ecologically oriented lifestyles,' indications that lifestyle performance is directly relating to any large-scale shifts in tackling global warming, pollution and environmental destruction is minimal. Perhaps the difficulty of moving to a larger scale is due to how lifestyle, despite operating in a similar manner to figurative acting with regard to objects, is marred by a strong tendency toward (neoliberal) individualism and its affinity for endless, disposable consumption, which has clear, damaging ecological effects especially as it scales up. But engagement with the scales necessary for ecological action is obstructed by the central unit of neoliberalism: the individual. Significantly, it is precisely an examination of individualism and scale that is central to *EVA*'s narrative of a chosen child-pilot who must save the world. It is this connection of the individual to the global that becomes the focus of the filmic ending of *EoE*, where the examination of selfhood shifts toward exploring the destructive tendencies of individualism and its direct relation to planetary scale devastation.

Ecologically Destructive Individualism

As episode 26 presents a literal exposition of the 'chasing of the self' and lands with a heavy lean toward objecthood and a subscendence into parts, the TV ending can be read as embracing a more ecologically oriented mode of existence. However, the joyous optimism of the TV anime's ending was rejected by many viewers of the show all over the world. Despite the wide involvement of objects in lifestyles, even otaku, who can be seen as openly engaging with objects, were upset by the TV anime's ending, ironically admitting to how much an object (in this case the anime series) can affect them, but also revealing how ingrained and resilient modern, anthropocentric thought is, even in such communities.

In the aftermath of such reactions, instead of re-emphasizing the objecthood embraced in episode 26, the final film *EoE* presents a radical break from the TV ending, especially as regards the type of selfhood that is enacted and explored. Interestingly, this break is revealed through the impression of a continuity of narrative (which takes place after TV episode 24, skipping over episodes 25 and 26) and of the character of Shinji: unlike the jarring shift of somber Rei to an unorganized, loud character in episode 26, Shinji is supposedly the same as he was in the TV series, as if a 'rounded' (though disturbed and depressed) character. However, the ecologically oriented objecthood potentials of the TV ending are eschewed in favor of pursuing Shinji's selfhood as an individual. The result is not the movement from individualism into objecthood as in the TV ending, but rather a staging of the choice between two different types of individualism in *EoE*. Moreover, what can be read in this division is an ecological politics about the stakes of embracing the tendencies of (neoliberal) individualism when performing selfhood.

Regarding the reasons for the divergence between the two endings, it is difficult to provide a definitive answer. In some ways, the filmic ending of *EVA* can be seen as a direct response to the negative reception of the TV series ending (and subsequent rejection of the objecthood episode 26 lands on) in *EoE*'s stark difference in tone and content, literally ending the world. Apocalyptic scenarios (from global warming to various doomsday cults) were prevalent in Japan and around the world at the time, but the large-scale extinction of life in the finale also recalls that of the much earlier anime *Space Runaway Ideon*. A concrete answer is difficult to provide from the staff as well, as anime production is incredibly complex, with multiple layers of decision-making that are beyond the singular vision of a director, writer or producer, even occurring across national boundaries (parts of *EVA* even involved Korean and Chinese animators and cel-painters).[7] However, irrespective of the reason, the sharp shift in tone—from

7. For a more detailed breakdown of anime production and its dispersal of agency, see Suan (2018).

playfulness and optimism to grotesque visions of catastrophe—does allow for a comparative interpretation where the two endings each provide differing views on the respective tendencies of performing selfhood they explore.

Thus, read in relief of each other as an examination of the two extremes of performing selfhood (i.e., objecthood and individualism), the two endings reveal what is at stake, ecologically, in each type of selfhood. The TV series ending might be able to sustain an interpretation as ecologically oriented in its embrace of the inclusion of other objects (especially with regard to Morton's views on a potential for scaling up a 'quantum of action'); but, as noted above, under neoliberalism even some of the more object-accepting performances of selfhood in lifestyle contain a latent tendency of anthropocentric individualism that reaches an impasse for acting ecologically. This is what the filmic ending brings to the fore as it reveals the ecological dangers of the other extreme of selfhood performance: exposing the explosive, planetary-scale destructiveness of (neoliberal) individualism.

To begin, it is worthwhile comparing the type of acting in the filmic ending to the TV series. As anime characters—in terms of their 'soulful body' design and enactment of figurative acting codes—every (human) actor in (TV and filmic) *EVA* is constituted through the tendencies of figurative acting. But instead of moving through individualism into objecthood (or embodied performance into figurative performance) as in the TV ending, *EoE* moves away from the figurative acting tendency toward interrelated objects, to the individualism in the extreme of embodied performance. Indeed, the film concludes in a spectacle-oriented fashion, including phenomenal embodied performances of/in animation. For example, there is the fight sequence between Asuka and the mass production Eva units, by key animators Mitsuo Iso and Yoshinari Yoh (Fig. 5.5). Asuka's Eva unit in particular is important, because it operates with such lucidity that it seems almost human, intentional in its operations. The movements feel hefty, bodies

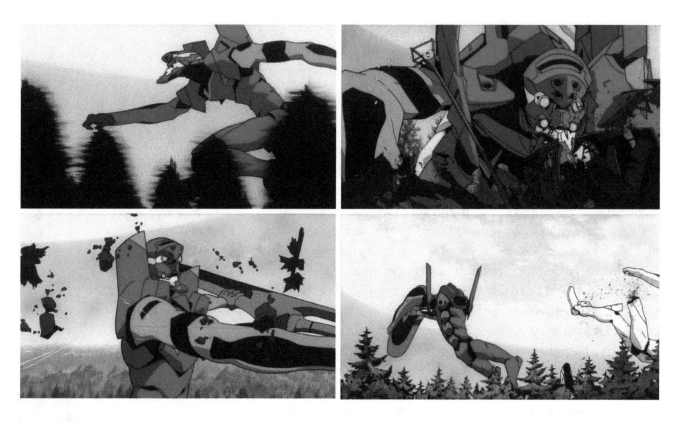

Figure 5.5. Asuka's adept piloting of her Eva-unit in *End of EVA*, displaying weighty movements through embodied acting. © khara, inc.

clashing as they wield heavy objects. Each action evinces the weight of the swings, of their blowbacks, a sloppiness to the grappling that results in broken and severed limbs; a viciously efficient dance of executions as Asuka struggles against the other Eva units while she runs out the clock on her Eva unit's on-board energy. But unlike the scene in episode 19 where Eva-01 goes berserk, here her unit stops when it runs out of energy, and the embodied performance evinces Asuka's deftness in operating (controlling) the non-human Eva-02 unit (albeit only after she accepts its idiosyncrasies as an object with some connection to her mother—another instance of the human haunting the non-human Eva unit).

The above-described embodied performance is one of the stand-out scenes of the film, and a preview of the focus on human individualism that defines the filmic ending. As distinct from the TV ending, instead of the helpful guidance of others in Shinji's mind, in *EoE* when we delve into the depths of Shinji's interior to find others, the potential horror (from the perspective of individualism) of figurative acting in the idea of other things inside of an individual is exposed, and in the process, moves toward the tendencies of individualism. This is succinctly displayed in the sequences of Asuka and Shinji in Misato's apartment, images which are part of Shinji's psyche visualized. In contrast to the lighter domestic scenes of the TV series ending, Asuka is aggressive, berating Shinji. Such hostility elicits a violent response from Shinji, who chokes Asuka, and spirals into his expression of feelings of complete isolation. Images of the other characters flash across the screen at dizzying speeds, accompanied by a torrent of many random, sometimes abstract, images. In addition, many of the scenes of lush, complex animation feature grotesque, confusing imagery, such as the mutating Eva units. The attempt to produce individualism despite anime's reliance on codified expressions seems to slip into the extreme separation of individualism on the one hand, or resort to codes that no one will understand on the other. This illegibility in some senses applies to the entire film itself, which features so much surreal imagery that it is almost impossible to decipher through traditional techniques.

In some ways, this does resemble the strategies and imagery of the TV ending, but in *EoE* a different spatial organization arises: the division between internal and external. This inside/outside separation is not present in the TV series ending, where the diegesis stays resolutely inside of Shinji to have him subscend into various parts and then get reconstituted, in the process disclosing and emphasizing the interrelated operations of figurative acting. In contrast, in the sequences of *EoE* where we delve into Shinji's psyche, the separation between internal mental state and external world operates closer to the spatial dynamics of embodied acting's individualism: the interior is the source of actions that have effects on the external world.

We frequently switch between Shinji's interior state and the exterior events, with constant reference to Shinji's internal decisions affecting the rest of the world. Although Shinji did not instigate these events directly (Gendō and/or SEELE appear to orchestrate and/or intervene behind the scenes), the fate of the world seems to fall on Shinji's shoulders. At one point, Gendō's confidant Kōzō Fuyutsuki even states, "the future is up to Ikari's son [Shinji]," emphasizing the internal struggle of Shinji and its effects on the external world, but also the thematic of personal, individualized responsibility. Shinji is literally closed off from the world, the fate of which rests on his mental state and his subsequent decisions based on that. Eventually, Shinji's feelings of isolation and unhappiness transition into scenes of the literal dissolution of all the other characters into liquid, the result of Gendō and/or SEELE's initiation of the Human Instrumentality Project. All of humanity is merged in this liquid state, which is presented as the final goal of the Human Instrumentality Project, seen by SEELE as the final configuration of humanity, worth all the destruction to initiate. Shinji is shown interconnected with Rei in this amber 'soup of life' (the 'sea of LCL') to quell Shinji's fears of rejection and emotional pain, and here Shinji is given the chance to stay in this state or not. What is featured, then, is a similar crisis of self as in the TV series ending, but here Shinji is presented with a distinctive set of choices to make on his own: to maintain the complete breakdown of barriers where all people are merged into one, or to raise those barriers completely.

Such a selection between these two poles might be described, in the words of Christophe Thouny (albeit with different concerns and not in reference to this particular sequence), as "the two sides of a modern social structure that relies on the production of individual subjects forced to occupy an agonistic position: that of having to navigate between the two dangers of a complete isolation of the self from the social collectivity in a movement of infinite fragmentation and of both the fusion and dissolution of the self" (Thouny 2009: 114–115). This latter option (fusion and dissolution of the self) becomes literal for Shinji in 'the sea of LCL' where all barriers between people are erased, and the former (isolation) can be seen in the reinstatement of boundaries between people. Moreover, Thouny's description draws attention to how, despite the apparent visualization of a fully merged and dissolved self, the choice with which Shinji is faced can be read as still operating within the bounds of modern, individualistic selfhood—that is, Shinji must actually choose between two different types of individualism: an individualism of isolation or an individualism of a singular (but merged) whole.

Such a choice between individualisms also recalls Morton's conceptions of contrasting ideas of holism and their relationships to individuals. What was discussed above as objecthood would correlate with what Morton calls "implosive holism" (the whole subscends into its parts; the whole is less than the sum of its parts). But this is only one version of holism. According to Morton, individualisms can be conceived as different types of "explosive holism," whereby the whole is seen as greater and/or more real than the sum of its parts. Morton further explains that there are variances to explosive holism, describing them in three positions: (1) "the whole is more real than the parts"; (2) "the whole is greater than the parts"; and (3) "the whole is less real than the parts."

For Morton, the first and second explosive holisms can easily slip into each other and indeed, this is evident in the result of the Human Instrumental Project in *EoE* (the completely dissolved selves in the 'sea of LCL'): the first position—the whole is more real than its parts (the final configuration of humanity)—easily extends into the second position—the whole is greater than its parts (it is most important that all humanity merge into this final configuration). The third position (the whole is less real than the parts) Morton connects to neoliberalism, its valorization of the individual at the expense of the whole: "There is no such thing as society [only individuals]," as Margaret Thatcher, proponent

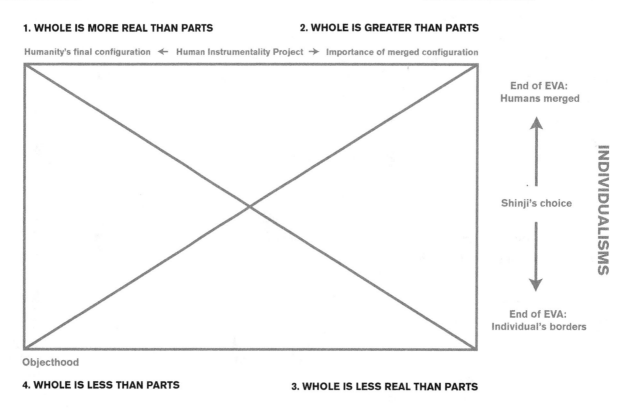

EXPLOSIVE WHOLISM   EXPLOSIVE WHOLISM

1. WHOLE IS MORE REAL THAN PARTS   **2. WHOLE IS GREATER THAN PARTS**

Humanity's final configuration ← Human Instrumentality Project → Importance of merged configuration

End of EVA:
Humans merged

Shinji's choice

INDIVIDUALISMS

End of EVA:
Individual's borders

Objecthood

4. WHOLE IS LESS THAN PARTS   **3. WHOLE IS LESS REAL THAN PARTS**

IMPLOSIVE WHOLISM   EXPLOSIVE WHOLISM

Figure 5.6. An adapted version of Morton's logic square of explosive and implosive holism, depicting the choice between individualisms that Shinji must make in *End of EVA*: either choose between the first and second positions' merging of humanity or the third position's individual borders (Morton 2017: 107). License: CC BY 4.0.

of neoliberalism, famously said (2017: 107). This is the direction that Shinji moves toward in the *EoE*, choosing to maintain individuality, to prop up borders around people (the third position), instead of dissolving one another into a soupy mass of humanity's merging (the slippage between the first and second positions) (Fig. 5.6).

Thus, in *EoE*, there are only the varying options of explosive holism from which Shinji must choose. Gone is the subscendence into various parts. Instead, there is an attempt at working through individualism, specifically at keeping up the borders between people. For Morton, these explosive holisms are dangerous and ecologically destructive.

They allow for either the replacement of some cog in a larger machine ("let that species die, another will take its place"), because the whole (the ecosystem) is greater or more real than the parts (positions 1 and 2); or it draws lines around things in advance (the human individual and its inside/outside borders) and actively operates on the non-human outside that border, ignoring the larger effects because the whole is less real (position 3). These are ecologically devastating concepts and, indeed, the former (positions 1 and 2: the whole is greater than and/or more real than its parts) in *EVA* (SEELE) end up with complete evisceration of the Earth. Even Shinji's choice to seemingly end or 'reverse' the end of the world by choosing individualism still leaves us on a dead Earth. In this way, *EoE* literally enforces the spatial dimensions of embodied acting, the inside/outside divide, the reproduction of borders, and ties this to the fate of all humanity and planetary destruction in general.

In this sense, then, the film reveals the shortcomings of modern, anthropocentric individualism, exposing its inability to address ecological devastation by making an overt connection to the conception of a strictly discrete self, individual decision and external global destruction, while simultaneously displaying the ineffectiveness of such agential assumptions of individualistic selfhood to enact macro scale change. For instance, the moments when Shinji chooses to reinstate the barriers between people are presented with a somewhat positive inflection; it seems Shinji has saved his individual selfhood and humanity by extension, but this is only to unveil the twist: Shinji floats to the surface of an already dead world, where humanity has caused the end of life on a planetary scale. The film thus takes the logic of the autonomous individual, fully responsible for his (or her) actions on the world to its logical extreme and yet undermines it completely: on the one hand, it is a personal decision that leads to a massive, global disruption ("just one person can change the world"); on the other, Shinji's decisions do little to change the actual outcome as he is alone with only Asuka at the end of the world. While we may feel that Shinji made the right choice in selecting individualism, seemingly averting global disaster, the world has still ended, even though Shinji did not necessarily start it (with Gendō and/or SEELE as the actual catalyst).

Ultimately, despite its emphasis on a single individual's choice, the film is ambivalent with regard to an individual's agency in its finale, taking its agential assumptions to task: individuals' decisions are both ineffective and grandiose on a global scale. As Morton asserts, this is the strange problematic we humans must contend with in the Anthropocene, where individual output of pollution is in some ways statistically meaningless, but also clearly a part of the massive ecological catastrophe underway (2018: xxvii). Such a dynamic of scale underpins the harrowing ecological vision provided by *EoE*: that despite Shinji's decision to reinstate human individualism, we are still left on a dead Earth, his individual actions only one part of the larger environmental destruction already underway. Instead of showing the strange fantasy of 'last man' narratives (surviving in a world after the fall of humanity) (Morton 2018), *EoE* depicts the ecologically devasting catastrophe, directly tying it to explosive holisms and human individualism, exposing their inadequacy to act against the end of the world.

References

Azuma, H. (2009). *Otaku: Japan's Database Animals*. Minneapolis, MN: University of Minnesota Press. (Introduction and translation by J. E. Abel and S. Kono).

Butler, J. (1988). Performative Acts and Gender Constitution: An Essay in Phenomenonology and Feminist Theory. *Theatre Journal*, 40, 519–531.

_____. (1993). *Bodies that Matter: On the Discursive Limits of "Sex."* London: Routledge.

_____. (1997). *Excitable Speech: A Politics of the Performative*. New York: Routledge.

Crafton, D. (2013). *Shadow of a Mouse: Performance, Belief and World-Making in Animation*. Berkeley, CA: University of California Press.

Diederichsen, D. (2012). Animation, De-Reification, and the New Charm of the Inanimate. *E-Flux Animism*, Special Issue, 1–11.

Endō, T. (1997). Konna kitanai kirei na hi ni wa. In *EVA no nokoseshi mono* (ed. T. Shimotsuki) (pp. 80–93). *Poppu karuchā kuritīku*. Tokyo: Seikyūsha.

Heise, U. (2014). Plasmatic Nature: Environmentalism and Animated Film. *Public Culture*, 26, 301–318.

Kotani, M. (1997). *Seibo Evangerion*. Tokyo: Magazine House.

Lamarre, T. (2009). *The Anime Machine: A Media Theory of Animation*. Minneapolis, MN: University of Minnesota Press.

Latour, B. (1993). *We Have Never Been Modern*. Cambridge, Massachusetts: Harvard University Press.

Lukács, G. (2010). *Scripted Affects, Branded Selves: Television, Subjectivity, and Capitalism in 1990s Japan*. Durham, NC and London: Duke University Press.

Maejima, S. (2010). *Sekaikei to wa nani ka: posuto EVA no otakushi*. Tokyo: Soft Bank Creative.

Morton, T. (2013). *Hyperobjects: Philosophy and Ecology after the End of the World*. Minneapolis, MN: University of Minnesota Press.

———. (2017). *Humankind: Solidarity with Nonhuman People*. London and New York: Verso.

———. (2018). *Being Ecological*. Cambridge, MA: MIT Press.

Murakami, T. (2005). Earth in My Window. In *Little Boy: The Arts of Japan's Exploding Subculture* (pp. 98–149). New York and New Haven, CT: The Japan Society and Yale University Press. (Translated by L. Hoaglund)

Steinberg, M. (2012). *Anime's Media Mix: Franchising Toys and Characters in Japan*. Minneapolis, MN: University of Minnesota Press.

Suan, S. (2017). Anime no 'kōisha': Animēshon ni okeru taigenteki/shūjiteki pafōmansu ni yoru 'jiko.' *Animēshon kenkyū*, 19(1), 3–15.

_____. (2018). Consuming Production: Anime's Layers of Transnationality and Dispersal of Agency as Seen in *Shirobako* and *Sakuga*-Fan Practices. *Arts*, 7(3), 27. Retrieved from: DOI: https://doi.org/10.3390/arts7030027

Thouny, C. (2009). Waiting for the Messiah: The Becoming-Myth of Evangelion and Densha Otoko. *Mechademia*, 4, 111–129.

Uno, T. (2008). *Zeronendai no sōzōryoku*. Tokyo: Hayakawa Shobō.

6. Discussing 'Genre' in Anime through *Neon Genesis Evangelion*

Manuel Hernández-Pérez

Introduction: Authorship and Genre as Foci of Approach

The worldwide distribution of *Neon Genesis Evangelion* (1995–96) had a significant impact on the audiences for anime markets. However, unlike previous TV anime megahits, such as *Dragon Ball* (1985), *EVA* distribution in Western countries started in domestic and young adult markets. The series gained its reputation in a period of transition between VHS and DVD formats and even managed to be successful on a new route for anime: from *niche* video markets to thematic TV channels through small broadcasters and cable stations.

That was the case of *EVA* distribution across the United States, at that time already one of the main markets for anime overseas. The series began to be distributed in June 1998 for the VHS market (A.D. Video), although it wouldn't be broadcasted on TV until 2002 (KQEH), being later offered by other theme-specialized channels such as Cartoon Network (through the special event 'Toonami's Giant's Robot week' broadcasted in February 2003) and Adult Swim (October 2005). *EVA* distribution in France (1996), Italy (1997) and Spain (1997) followed a similar strategy, as it was distributed first as a video product rather than being broadcast to general audiences. Most of the time, the series was dubbed to the domestic language, except for France, where it was distributed in Japanese with subtitles. This was due, perhaps, to its early release (1996). The distribution in Australia (1998) and Southeast Asian markets such as the Philippines was different as ADVision didn't manage the copyrights for these markets. The main agent of distribution was the main national broadcasters instead. The franchise would arrive

How to cite this book chapter:
Hernández-Pérez, M. 2021. Discussing 'Genre' in Anime through *Neon Genesis Evangelion*. In: Santiago Iglesias, J. A. and Soler Baena, A. (Eds.). *Anime Studies: Media-Specific Approaches to Neon Genesis Evangelion*. Pp. 181–214 Stockholm: Stockholm University Press. DOI: https://doi.org/10.16993/bbp.g. License: CC-BY 4.0

in Central and South America some years later, only for cable and satellite thematic channels (Canal 22 Mexico, 2007; Animax for Latin America, 2008).

At the end of the 2010s, the initial *EVA* series had apparently achieved the status of a cult product. Internet streaming services made possible its access to a much wider and, arguably, global audience. The worldwide release of *EVA* on Netflix (2019) has introduced this series to new international audiences for the first time. Netflix's global broadcasting has also highlighted the historical significance of this series in national markets already familiar with the franchise. The response of these markets, influenced by nostalgia, has not always been positive though. There have been many examples of controversy, including complaints about how new translations of the script and subtitles hide key plot elements, such as the homoerotic subtext of the story.[1] Besides, the redubbing of the series in several countries, casting different actors, has been read as pure 'betrayal' by fan audiences. Also, limitations of copyrights have contributed to this disappointment and resulted in a modified version of the ending without the different covers of the well-known 1954 song *Fly Me to the Moon*. While it is not always easy to identify the voices behind social media, primarily fan audiences seem to be suspicious about the new Netflix version, due to their long-term emotional investment.

Discourses on *EVA* have extensively highlighted its uniqueness when comparing the series to other anime series from the same period. One of the factors behind this is the complexity of its plot and certain lack of closure, due to its open ending (or even 'endings' if we take into consideration other paratexts). Social media is full of reviews and deconstructions of the series, performed by fans.[2] While these discourses may involve different communities, *EVA*'s uniqueness is usually constructed through comparison with other examples, that is, similarity among a group of texts, which share a common

1. See Chapter 10 by Jessica Bauwens-Sugimoto.

2. See Chapter 8 by Olga Kopylova on types of fan readings.

property based on material, rhetorical or semantic properties. In a later step, the similarity among the members of this category allows the differentiation from members outside the definition criteria.

Therefore, readings of *EVA* and its uniqueness usually fall into highlighting the belonging to these categories, a conceptual strategy also known as 'genre classification.' An alternative reading is authorship, which is a common construct to attribute the unique style of a product to the personality of its main creator(s). Readings of *EVA* have often been oriented at the personality of Hideaki Anno, the filmmaker responsible for the series' script and direction. However, collaboration played an equally important role during the production and pre-production processes:

> The impression of 'Live' concert that gives me the birth of Eva, was the team joining me in developing it, in the manner of an improvisation: someone plays the guitar and, in response, the drums and bass are added. The performance ended with the TV broadcasting end. We only started working on the next script once the previous one was done. (Anno 1996b: 12)

Anno's strong personality has been emphasized by many as the main reason for the series' singular style and narrative (Azuma 2016; Watanabe 2001: 148). But, as in other cases of authorship in the world of Japanese anime, personality as an author takes the form of 'persona,' a mask (Hernández-Pérez 2016), and this can easily shadow other readings of anime as a collaborative medium. Anno himself has contributed to the construction of this mask through numerous paratexts, such as biographical and autobiographical notes, interviews and media reviews. Probably, the most obvious example of cultural criticism inspired by biographical paratext can be found in psychoanalytical readings of *EVA*'s plot:

> On its deepest level, Evangelion has become inseparable from the life of its creator, Hideaki Anno—and from the arc of coming to terms with his (and the audience's own) lifelong struggles with depression and

alienation, and how they often lead us to seek refuge and withdraw into inner landscapes of the imagination. But this pillar of culture all starts with a few nerds in one small room, and Anno, a brilliant prodigy among them. (Stewart-Ahn 2019: para. 5)

Anno himself may have contributed to this mystification by statements such as the following:

> Evangelion is like a puzzle, you know. Any person can see it and give his/her own answer. In other words, we're offering viewers to think by themselves, so that each person can imagine his/her own world. We will never offer the answers, even in the theatrical version. As for many Evangelion viewers, they may expect us to provide the 'all-about *EVA*' manuals, but there is no such thing. Don't expect to get answers from someone. Don't expect to be catered to all the time. We all have to find our own answers. (Anno 1996a: 20)

Reading media texts through authorship is a common strategy shared by general audiences, fan communities and professionals. However, in Media Studies, and especially in Film Studies, the term has a particular history of debate and confrontation. Authorship implies that audiences can identify a signature, corresponding to an individual or group of individuals, behind a media product. It has been noted that in media industries it is possible to identify different kinds of authorships, either multiple, collective or even corporative (Dyer 1998: 151). While the work of the professionals involved in a production is always necessarily collaborative, 'multiple authorship' differs from 'collective' understood as the identification of different works rather than a single complex artistic piece. In manga, collective authorship (if acknowledged at all) applies to the artist, or mangaka, and the editor, while in anime adaptations of manga, authorship and copyright tend to be distributed between the mangaka and the production committee.[3] In the case of *EVA*, it is not difficult to consider multiple authorships. In that sense, the series proposal, written in 1993 and employed with promotional purposes, identifies Hideaki

3. Production Committees are subsidiary companies created to produce and distribute a particular anime. They may include copyright holders, TV broadcasters, anime producers and toy manufacturers. Usually, both manga creator and production committee are identified as co-owners of these copyrights.

Anno as director and writer, Yoshiyuki Sadamoto as character designer and Ikuto Yamashita as mechanical or *mecha*[4] designer, which are all common and main roles within anime productions (GAINAX 1997: 86). Arguably, corporative authorship also played a significant role in the international distribution of both *EVA* and post-*EVA* products. Studio GAINAX, famously created by a group of enthusiasts, had been a well-known brand, but it didn't start recovering from its initial debts and gaining nationwide fame until the *EVA* success (Takeda 2005: 132). Anno left GAINAX in 2006, with the goal of releasing the tetralogy of *NGE Rebuild* films with his new Studio Khara (Studio Khara 2006).

While authorship has been related to the uniqueness of a media text, the designation of a genre tends to be associated with the limits of authorial creativity. Criticism addresses this constraint when defining the prescriptive use of genres, the so-called producer's game (Altman 1999: 38), which devalues the work of creators to identify successful formulas. In the case of *EVA*, it is the similarity to other productions in the Super Robot, or Mecha Genre, whose conventions are usually employed as criteria to measure its originality. However, while authorship and genre seem to be opposing terms, in fact, many authors find their stylistic and thematic approaches to be linked to a particular genre (Feuer 1992: 143), as identifying their work with a particular genre could be a creative choice in itself. That is the case of Anno and *EVA*, a work that is defined by its uniqueness but that still employs genre in constructing a framework to interact successfully with producers, distributors, and global audiences.

In this chapter, I will focus on how the *EVA* anime and franchise can be categorized with regard to genre. I will start with a focus on narrative contents, primarily, the main tropes of *mecha* anime. However, this may not be enough to define and identify genre categories properly. As I will demonstrate, *EVA* feeds on multiple genres, including traditions of Science Fiction (SF), the Japanese Special Effects

4. Mechanical Designers are artists specialized in the illustration of technologies and are usually associated with the Super Robot Genre, also known as *mecha*. Due to the well-known synergies between the toy industry and anime, this figure became essential in the design of mechanical characters that can be adapted to toys, plastic model kits and other forms of merchandise. The first artist signing as *mecha* designer was Kunio Okawara (b. 1947), who was responsible for *Mobile Suit Gundam* (*Kidō Senshi Gandamu*, 1979).

TV shows (*tokusatsu*) and the Monster Films (*kaijū eiga*), as well as other Japanese TV anime. Actually, the different ways of addressing the relationship between *EVA* and the concept of genre, including authorship readings of anime, are at the heart of this chapter. It sets out to demonstrate the role that Genre Studies can play in Anime Studies and the challenges behind the cross-media and transmedia conceptualizations of genre. Eventually, it is expected that these strategies can facilitate Anime Studies through the lens of Cultural Studies and Media Studies.

Discussing *EVA* from the Perspective of Genre

The term 'genre' refers to the creation of categories and groups of texts. Genre theory had a long tradition in literary studies before it started to be employed in the context of Media Studies. There's a considerable corpus of work about genre in Film Studies (Altman 1999; Wood 1998) and TV Studies (Feuer 1992; Mittell 2001). This chapter leans mainly on TV Studies, assuming some material and structural features in anime to be similar to other broadcasted serial products.

Genre categorization implies the differentiation of a whole set of elements combining various historical and also textual approaches. In Media Studies, for example, genre is employed when the production of a specific period or by specific creators is identified with regard to the recurrent use of archetypal characters, a particular set-up, iconography, narrative content or style and the casting of screen celebrities. It is easy to see the fallacious logic of genres. Once the labels are established, they will define the product and all of its 'family' due to resemblance. But discovering new exemplars will defy the integrity and identity of this group. Jacques Derrida responded to this dilemma and denied the need for any text to belong exclusively to a category, a prerogative coined as the 'principle of contamination':

With the inevitable dividing of the trait that marks membership, the boundary of the set comes to form, by invagination, an internal pocket larger than the whole; and the outcome of this division, and this abounding remains as singular as it is limitless. (Derrida & Ronnel 1980: 59)

Derrida's ideas point to a new, more complex conception of textuality and the singularity of artistic production. However, this singularity can be read not only as an exclusively textual property of each work of art, but also as a property that emerges from the dynamics of a particular set of texts or discourse. Genres are embodied in texts and discursive practices. Mittell reminds us that "there is a crucial difference between conceiving of the genre as a textual category and treating it as a component of a text, a distinction most genre studies elude" (2001: 5). His cultural definition of TV genres is articulated through several paratexts and discursive practices involving industry and audiences.

Following these ideas, many authors disengage from a strict vision about texts belonging to a particular genre. They assume that films are, first and foremost, hybrid or transgeneric products, as they always combine elements from different genres (Altman 1999: 53). Therefore, genres are constructs that designate not only a set of texts, but the properties of a given text. They can change and mix. Adopting a strategy of hybridization is a common feature in all media products.

While there's a wide range of genre theories, scholars have questioned the utility of genre as an evaluation method, regarding its problematic reflexivity. Genre is usually employed to select a group of texts. However, the main interest of the researcher would be, precisely, to prove that certain texts belong to the predefined group. Since, as noted by Feuer (1992: 108), the formation of categories responds to arbitrary decisions, rather than induction or data collection, research methodology is compromised.

Anime Studies require defining genres from historical, cultural, discursive and even ideological perspectives. As I will demonstrate, cultural criticism and academia link the *EVA* TV series to the tradition of mecha anime, while *EVA* authors, including Anno, usually refer to the influence of other genres, for example, Speculative Fiction. Defining the textual properties of a genre would be the first step, while identifying the interrelation of *EVA* with other generic forms is also necessary.

Historical and Cultural Approaches to Anime Genres

Genres are constructed by the images that audiences and creators have about large groups of texts. Film genres have been traditionally defined through a process of authoritative deduction, resulting from the work undertaken by the community of cultural critics curating films from a specific period, and this classification becoming eventually accepted by audiences and producers.

Anime industries, on the other hand, have been defined in terms different from cinema and animation. Publishers' definition of demographic sectors was employed as the main classification for manga and later extended to anime products. Taxonomies traditionally correspond to the potential readership of manga magazines, defined by age and gender. Thus, the Japanese publishing market distinguishes between four categories: *kodomo* (children), *shōnen* (adolescent boys) and *shōjo* (girls), *seinen* (initially aimed at young male adults) and *josei* (women). This classification only refers to the potential audience of the product. It says little about textual or material properties. As a matter of fact, there is a mismatch between demographic genre labels and actual audiences. These taxonomies become arguable when thematic labels such as sports (*supōtsu*) or communicational purposes such as educational (*gakushū*) are also employed as subgenres. There is significant criticism toward the idea of assimilating such different conceptualizations of genre at the same time. For example, it has been pointed out that there is a historical trend to hybridization not only among the products originally addressed to demographic sectors, but also in the diversification of thematic labels (Yamaguchi 2004: 104–106).

At first glance, *EVA* may appear as a text belonging to the demographic genre of *shōnen*. This applies, for example, to features of its narrative setting, such as the school life subplot, the use of teenagers as main characters or the considerable amount of battle scenes involving monsters and piloted robots (*mecha*). However, Anno declared to have had an adult demographic target in mind (over 30 years of age), while acknowledging that some concessions were made, such as the introduction of female characters, to make the product more accessible to (male) fan audiences:

> You need to understand that Japanese animation is an industry that is, for the most part, male, and as is quite evident, everything is made for their gratification. Further, it is more gratifying for us to draw this sort of character, rather than old grandmothers. (Anno as quoted in Giner 1997: 19)

Furthermore, some manga adaptations of the original TV anime notably shifted with regard to target audiences. Sadamoto's *Shin Seiki Evangelion* (NGE) was originally serialized in a *shōnen* magazine (*Monthly Shōnen Ace*, 1994–2008), but continued in a *seinen* publication by the same publisher (*Young Ace*, 2009–2014). This appears exceptional, as anime-to-manga adaptations usually hold on to the initial demographic target, which applies also to the aesthetics of the source text, its main plot and its premises. On the other hand, despite the existence of several paratexts such as interviews, making-of and talks recorded at comic conventions, there are no statements by the *EVA* creators that point out any generic definition of the franchise. This contrasts with the references by Anno and other initial GAINAX members to anime titles and novels in the SF genre tradition.

Historical, cultural and even ideological approaches to genre categorization should be understood as part of shared constructions among professionals and creators. A necessary condition for this is the self-acknowledgment of genre elements and formulas that starts with their informal analysis, or mere consumption. The creators learn these formulas and incorporate them into their own practice, as implied by

Thomas Schatz when he describes the transformation "from straight-forward storytelling to self-conscious formalism" (Schatz 1981: 38). Thus, genre must necessarily be discussed with regard to textual properties and be differentiated concerning stylistic and narrative elements that may indicate affiliation, in the case of *EVA*, *shōnen*, *mecha* and SF.

Textual Approaches to Anime Genres

So far, I have discussed approaches to anime genres as historical or cultural categories. However, while considering genres as categories, they are still texts or, more specifically, a group of texts, and their textual features are almost inseparable from those aforementioned classification practices.

At this point, it may be necessary to clarify that anime is not a genre. Many scholars consider anime a medium (Hu 2010; Napier 2001) that is defined by its own language. Genres constitute a set of media texts based on familiarity or resemblance with a particular tradition. Some scholars try to define anime with transformations of the term *genre*, such as a transnational meta-genre (Denison 2015: 24). While there's goodwill in defending the diversity of anime acknowledging, at the same time, its identity as a common set of narrative, cultural and stylistic conventions, this categorization seems unnecessary. For anime is rather a medium, as stated above. And medium is a valid category to define the embedded physical, cultural and historical properties (Ryan 2004: 16).

Traditionally, textual definitions of genre differentiate between semantic and syntactic elements in reference to Altman (1999: 89) and his dual conceptualization of genre. Semantic approaches refer to those elements that are most noticeable. This idea is extended by iconographic approaches to genre (Buscombe 1970; Grant 2007) which maintain that even isolated elements can be associated with a particular genre. Syntactic definitions of genre refer to the meaning emerging from the relationships between these elements. Syntactic approaches have found that the extensive use of particular plots and subplots, or 'formulas,' is enough to identify genres such as Film Noir or Adventure Movies (Cawelti 1976). In addition, style can contribute to the identification of genres, but it is not addressed specifically by Altman (1999), who seems to consider it to be part of the iconography and, therefore, of semantic reading.

Audiences may identify a particular form or language resource and, subsequently, realize the meanings that emerge from the associations between the codes employed (Altman 1999: 38). Anime formulas or clichés, for example, do exist and are usually associated with particular demographic genres. Semantic approaches to manga and anime have reduced genres to narrative contents. Regarding this, *mecha* is one of the most distinctive genres within manga and anime (Bryce & Davis 2010: 17; Drazen 2003: 240). Therefore, it could be a categorization similar to that of *shōnen*, designating a tradition with well-identified semantic and syntactic features.

Of Mechas and Monsters: *EVA* within Genres

The *mecha* genre's central trope was introduced by Gō Nagai's *Mazinger Z* (1972), which arguably featured the first piloted robot in manga. *Mecha* designers and *mecha* animators are established professions in the industry and, arguably, highly influential in the success of any franchised intellectual property, as their design may inspire different kinds of toys. Anime in particular and Japanese popular culture in general show a fascination of writers and designers with humanoid robots. Robots are usually linked to other anthropomorphic representations of technology or mechanics whose presence in popular culture dates back to *kamishibai*. Within the industry, creators use 'robot' as an umbrella term for all kinds of artificial bodies, while others within SF communities tend to differentiate between cyborgs, androids, (real) robots and piloted vehicles (aka *mecha*).

It seems somehow inappropriate to regard *mecha* as a subgenre of *shōnen*. While both can easily be traced in terms of authors, stylistic conventions and traditions, *shōnen* is a demographic classification and *mecha* a mere thematic one. Connections between *shōnen* and *mecha* themes are usually expressed with the 'boy and robot' label (Poitras 2001). This is a dual form that, in fact, reflects the animist motivation behind *mecha* narratives. *Mecha* characters facilitate safe drama, providing these narratives with a character that can be repaired at the end of each episode or season. In this sense, the *mecha* genre accommodates sacrificial heroes who aren't really alive, but are still able to reflect the audience's and their pilot's emotional states. Many media texts for adult audiences incorporate such projection of human emotions onto real robots and *mechas*, for example, anime inspired by the work of Masamune Shirow, such as *Patlabor: The Movie (1989)* and *Appleseed (2004)*.

While *mecha* is assumed to be a quintessential Japanese genre (Wong 2010: 332), the idea of using piloted robots for military purposes was already a common topic in Western SF. Robert Anson Heinlein introduced in his *Starship Troopers* (1959) the concept of the exoskeleton or mobile suit, a robotic armor that allows the increase of the pilot's combat skills. Although far from being as influential as Osamu Tezuka and Mitsuteru Yokoyama's robots in Japan, the work of Heinlein had a considerable impact after its translation in 1967. The similarity of the Japanese illustrations from the 1977 edition with Kunio Okawara's *mecha* designs for *Mobile Suit Gundam* (1979) has attracted attention (Tatsumi & Bolton 2008: 192). Other Western influences, mainly *Thunderbirds* (1965–66), have been emphasized by cultural criticism and academia. In this TV series, as in many other works by producer Gerry Anderson, technological and futuristic designs play a crucial role. However, Anderson's SF productions, addressed to young audiences, may have had more influence in terms of style than characters. While *Thunderbirds* does not feature robots, it introduced the 'transforming/combining' features so characteristic of robot anime (Hikawa 2013: 10), popular transformation scenes common in both *Tokusatsu* TV shows and *Magical Girl* anime.

The main narrative of the *EVA* TV anime is articulated through episodes featuring spectacular battles among monsters and giant robots. Purportedly, Anno's only interest was the renewal of *mecha* genre, despite some statements that have linked *EVA* to the *Tokusatsu* tradition (particularly how *Ultraman* (1966) may have inspired the Eva units). Producers pitched *EVA* as a Super Robot anime:

> The protagonist is but an ordinary boy one could find just about anywhere. Until now, the pilots of giant robot animation have all had natural ability and talent from the start. That unique hero is one children aspire to be, and is someone they relate to. (*NGE Proposal*, extracted from GAINAX 1997: 85, translated by EvaWiki)

Interestingly, the Eva units do not faithfully reference the *mecha* genre, but rather divert from this tradition. They seem to have their very own emotions.[5] They are living beings, creatures cloned from relatives of the protagonists themselves, a narrative turn that justifies the intimate bond which, at the subconscious level, seems to exist between pilots and Eva units. In fact, regarding the tradition of SF literature, Eva units would be cyborgs or modified humans instead of robots. Ikuto Yamashita was the *mecha* designer for *EVA* and responsible also for the visual development of previous GAINAX works such as *Gunbuster* (*Aim for the Top!*, 1988) and *Nadia: The Secret of Blue Water* (*Fushigi no umi no Nadia*, 1990). Yamashita's design has been described as more organic and curvier than the typical linear forms and metallic textures used in traditional *mecha* anime (Cavallaro 2009: 66). As remembered by Yasuhiro Takeda, GAINAX's General Manager of Animation Production (1984–2016), Yamashita's organic designs challenged the *mecha* genre conventions since the early stages of the project's development:

5. See Chapters 2 and 5 by Ida Kirkegaard and Stevie Suan, respectively.

(Toshimichi) Ōtsuki brought the proposal to a certain unnamed toy company, the guy there told him a robot with a design like that would never sell. He said the legs were too skinny, and then proceeded to give Ōtsuki a lecture on the principles of robot design. (Takeda 2005: 167)

Mecha designs in *EVA* work at a semantic level, but also ignite syntactic readings that ultimately connect with meanings usually related to other narratives. Anno highlights the influence of Nagai's work, particularly his manga *Devilman* (1972), as inspiration for the Eva units. We should remember that, regarding the main storyline, the Eva units are clones of the first Angel, Adam. Their designs are, therefore, an alternative version of what humanity (also Adam's children) could be. This is acknowledged by Anno himself:

There is a monster in Japan called the *oni*, which has two horns sticking out of its head, and the overall image of the *EVA* is based on that. I wanted also to have an image that beneath the image of that robot monster is a human. It's not really a robot, but a giant human, so it's different from other robot *mecha* such as those in *Gundam*. (Animerica 1996: para. 3).

On the other hand, it is a known fact that the *EVA* creators were avid consumers of SF products. Anno is a big *tokusatsu* (special-effects cinema) and SF consumer. In 1983, still a student, he and other members of Daicon Film, the seeds of the future GAINAX, created a fan film by the name *Return of Ultraman*. In recent years, it has been common to find Anno participating in specialized forums, such as conventions, special screenings or live talks (Chapman 2017: para. 3). In his role as an expert, he has even directed the Media Bunka report focused on the history of the *tokusatsu* genre (Anno & Higuchi 2013).

There are semantic and syntactic relationships between *tokusatsu*, its monster *imaginary* and the *mecha* tradition that can be directly observed in *EVA*. After all, one of the first *mecha* series, *Mazinger Z* (1972), follows the formulaic journey of fighting a monster every week. This connection is also reflected in the idiosyncratic manufacture of these television shows and their 'texture' (Anno & Higuchi 2013: 11), a syntactic element that is arguably transferred to *EVA*. Despite being live-action shows, *tokusatsu* products are, in fact, all about their monsters. The main difference between *tokusatsu* and stop-motion is purely performative, since most Japanese shows tend to use masks, costumes and make-up (a set of tools described as 'suite motion') instead of stop-motion techniques. In this sense, the *EVA* franchise creators have pointed out how the original premise was to create a remediation of a *tokusatsu* and *mecha* serial with a twist based on subjectivity:

> Up until that time, there had never been an anime about gigantic robots battling these mysterious monsters invading the planet, while at the same time focusing on what was going on in the minds of the main characters. (Watanabe & Otsuki 2006: para. 12)

EVA receives influences of all these genre traditions, borrowing characters and even plots from *tokusatsu* or *kaijū* cinema[6] and *mecha* narratives. However, the relationship of *EVA* to these genres is one of hybridization. Those narrative tropes have migrated across genres and media. Since one of the main notions of the genre is aesthetic (Feuer 1992: 109), the interrelation between *EVA* and these influences can no longer be intertextual, but it is necessarily intermedial or transmedia. The aforementioned hybridization of *mecha* and *tokusatsu* traditions within *EVA* is a result of a transmedia adaptation of iconography. Anno went on to pursue these interconnections in the live-action film *Shin Godzilla* (2016), a remake of the classic *kaijū* movie, co-directed with Shinji Higuchi.

Exercises in Intertextuality and their Semantic Readings on Genre: Is *EVA* an SF Anime?

Some genres are easier to define from a semantic perspective than others due to their most identifiable spatial and temporal settings. That is

6. *Kaijū* (monster beast) *eiga* refers to a group of serial nature movies starring giant monsters. Inaugurated by the iconic *Godzilla* (1954), its homogenous style and narratives, combining spectacular visual effects, the destruction of urban environments and its effects on the characters all have their legacy in the later Disaster Films of the 1970s and 1990s (Napier 1993: 328).

the case with SF stories, which many audiences associate with a set of particular iconographic elements (spaceships, aliens, etc.), narrative formulas (time travels, man-made creatures, etc.) or the creation of idiosyncratic images that work as focal points of their narratives (distant uninhabited planets, monumental star ships, lonely laboratories). However, after the recognition of semantic and syntactic elements of a genre, there is yet another level of decoding for the audience: the recognition of intertextual relationships among products in terms of family resemblance, a process that structural narratology denominated *architextuality* (Genette 1992: 83).

SF forms a group of texts with a long tradition in Literary and Media Studies and, yet, it is still often subjected to the controversy concerning its definition as a genre. SF involves the creation of fictional worlds that are perceived as plausible. Some authors have discussed the potential semantic mechanism that identifies these parallel worlds in contrast with other fictional stories. SF narratives, for example, introduce a bridge to avoid 'cognitive estrangement' in the reader's mind, a so-called *novum* that is accepted implicitly by the audience (Suvin 1972: 373). The *novum* usually takes the form of technological innovation, but, in the logic of SF, this innovation creates a chain of technological, cultural and, ultimately, social consequences that shape the new world and characters' psychology. The *novum* is exclusive to SF, while the fantasy genre lacks this element and, even more importantly, dispenses with the construction of a chain of consequences. In contrast with SF, speculative genres such as fantasy or horror may also create coherent worlds, but their narratives are not intended to explain those rules. SF is based on the dialectics of these 'estrangements' and the appeal to the reader's 'cognition' (Suvin 1979: 7).

Referring to SF as a 'genre' is rather conservative, as distinct from regarding this corpus of texts as a tradition. SF responds more to the idea of a set of genres, or a genre colony, a term originally coined to describe the interaction between different genres that are serving the same communicative goal (Bhatia 1999: 29). There is a SF colony, which through its many different genres across media (novel, TV series and so on) shows formulas and tropes of great persistence.

This has contributed to its capacity for transmedia expansion (Jenkins 1992). And all these SF narratives would have in common the presence of a *novum*, although some other genres, even those developed in different media, could be part of what has been called 'family' due to their resemblance (e.g., the television space opera, the 'soft' SF novel or the superhero narratives in comic-books).

SF has been frequently employed as a framework to read Japanese popular culture as a whole. The fact that a generation of Japanese authors experienced the consequences of war has led to a large number of readings of Japanese SF as post-World War II narratives (Orbaugh 2009: 112; Watanabe 2001: 120). However, those narratives have been, at the same time, linked to the Japanese predilection for 'disaster' narratives and dystopia (Napier 1993: 329).

As often happens with explorations on genre, semantic accounts are easier to perform. Studies have pointed out a relevant number of anime framed as SF narratives, especially in relation to artificial bodies, including robots and *mecha* (Bolton & Csicsery-Ronay 2007; Orbaugh 2009: 119). There are, however, also reasons to assume syntactic relationships between anime and SF, which are a consequence of this medium's specificity. Anime is different from other media such as animation or live-action film, as scholar Toshiya Ueno states:

> In contrast, the technology and visual detail of animation in Japan is unusually sophisticated. With the exception of the gold or green color of characters' hair and the exaggerated shapes of their mouths and eyes, animation in Japan simulates reality to an excessive degree. (This is especially striking in reflections of light and water or the depiction of details in vehicles and *mecha*). It does not aim for the simple reproduction of reality but the hyperreality of things with no referent, things that are "more realistic than reality." (Ueno 2006: 112–113).

With this statement, Ueno doesn't deny other visual styles within anime, such as exaggeration, but emphasizes hyperreality and thereby suggests the pedagogical value of anime. And what is SF but a pedagogy of alternate world's scenarios?

In the light of such considerations, is *EVA* an SF narrative? The *EVA* franchise's discourse collects references to the SF tradition or 'SF colony of genres,' and this manifests in two complementary facts. First, Western audiences tend to consider *EVA* as SF, in part, due to the characteristics of the spatial and temporal settings of the fictional world, like the plot set in a dystopian future. It is not easy, however, to identify the *novum* within *EVA*'s narrative. Perhaps, the AT (Absolute Terror) Field, or shield that Evas and Apostles share, or the obscure technology of cloning behind the Evas could be the most likely match. There are, however, some examples of SF rhetoric in the construction of *EVA*'s world. The technical requirements and infrastructures needed to move Eva units, for example, might have been the cause for the rigid militarization of Japanese society as depicted in *EVA*, as well as the compliance of its citizens who accept to live in an ongoing state of alert. It is technology behind the Eva units that vests an incontestable power to the government and makes the temporal and spatial settings adapt logically to the resolution of this dystopian alternate world scenario.

In summary, shared iconography through SF genres can be found in *EVA*, and there are elements of both estrangement and appeal to readers' cognition. However, other iconographies that populate the series connect with religious and, specifically, apocalyptic narratives. Perhaps those intersections can give us a better cue of genre hybridization in *EVA*.

SF Meets Apocalypticism: The Nihilist Message of *EVA*

EVA has been frequently described as a post-apocalyptic (Thomas 2012: 71) or apocalyptic narrative (Napier 2001: 29). The Apocalypse or Book of Revelations written by St John is a Christian canonical text that relates in future voice (prophecy) to the end of God's creation. As we know, *EVA*'s narrative is the realization of an announced tragedy that will end, unless NERV can avoid this, in the Third Impact. The references to Judeo-Christian iconography may suggest that the *EVA* subtexts are readings of other Christian narratives (Ortega 2007). An author interested in millenarist readings of popular culture, however, denied that *EVA*'s story was a genuine portrait of apocalypticism and described it as "scarcely more than *mecha* anime in apocalyptic dress" (DiTommaso 2014: 484).

The rupture of *EVA*'s linearity (especially in the last two episodes) can disorient audiences in a way similar to prophetic texts. Do *EVA* fans need to be initiated in their hermeneutics? Napier (2001: 193) designates the series as paradigm of what she defines as apocalyptic narrative mode, which she describes as one of the main narrative directions within anime. *EVA* may not be an apocalyptic text, but there is a clear apocalyptic mood behind *EVA*'s plot. First, this is because of the historical relationship of apocalyptic or pseudo-apocalyptic narratives with the genre of SF. Classifying *EVA* as an apocalyptic narrative would strengthen its participation in the SF colony of genres. Second, it can help to discuss whether the definition of a clear theme associated with a recognizable iconography can be the basis for a generic definition of texts, a strategy that we have identified as the semantic approach to genre.

Apocalyptic scenarios are quite common among SF. In the heart of its narratives, 'catastrophe' can be found, which is a mirror concept of the utopia projected by technological development (Mousoutzanis 2009: 458). The depiction of catastrophe can point to a moral message when SF narratives refer to the negative consequences of technologies. But apocalypse in SF usually lets the story begin after the catastrophe. In *EVA*, we have two scenarios. First, using Christian terminology, the story speaks of a 'Second Impact' which, like the 'Second Coming of Jesus,' presents the beginning of the End of Times.

This event places the story in a catastrophic scenario: the arctic poles have melted, the temperature of the planet is increasing and the international relations among the economic powers have changed. Second, this catastrophe determines the narrative as it is followed by creatures called Angels. The rest of the story features efforts of the humans to stop world destruction, but they fail.

EVA's distribution overseas tried to create stronger links to SF through the translation. In the second episode, the 'Human Complementation Project' is translated as 'Human Instrumentality Project.' This incorporated a reference to the work of Cordwainer Smith (1993), an American SF writer and author of *Instrumentality of Mankind*, a collection of short stories originally published in 1979. In Smith's fictional universe, this term is referring to his story-world, but it is also the name of the organization which controls different species derived from human beings across the galaxy. As such, his narrative shares some of the post-humanist subtext of the *EVA* anime, but it is difficult to find more similarities.

EVA constantly refers to Christian mythology, particularly the so-called eschatology or tales about 'last things.' However, such religious and spiritual aspects arise from its relationship with different traditions within SF rather than an explicit reference to the Christian tradition. Apparently, in Japan, the franchise has elicited some interest in cultural artifacts related to Christianity (Thomas 2012: 71); however, this seems to have resulted more from the story setting and its inherent exoticism for non-Christian audiences. Kazuya Tsurumaki, assistant director of the series, distanced himself from any Christian reading of *EVA*:

> There are a lot of giant robot shows in Japan, and we did want our story to have a religious theme to help distinguish us. Because Christianity is an uncommon religion in Japan we thought it would be mysterious. None of the staff who worked on Eva are Christians. There is no actual Christian meaning to the show, we just thought the visual symbols of Christianity look cool. (Tsurumaki interviewed by Thomas 2001: para. 23)

EVA adapted Christian myths into familiar forms through a process of domestication. Drazen (2003: 360) pointed out, as an example, that the Spear of Longinous seems to reproduce the narrative of Izanagi and Izanami's Spear of Heaven. This domestication of narratives is also evident in the lack of linearity of the *EVA* story. While the Christian apocalypse corresponds to a linear conception of time, *EVA*, like many other anime, transforms apocalyptic tales and their inherent linearity into eternal cycles of reincarnation. These cycles of death and rebirth have been called 'apocalyptic' (Napier 2001: 193), but this may not be the right term. In *EVA*, the battle between good and evil is less important than Shinji's mental battle with his own anxieties. The anime series' ending that presents Shinji and Asuka is not so much a happy closure as a bitter new beginning without God and, in that sense, it breaks the expected linearity of apocalyptic narratives. *EVA* speaks to viewers about the end of the world. However, in the anime, the apocalypse stands in not only for social anxieties, but also existential concerns. The end of life and, therefore, of subjective experience manifests in an obsession with the transience of life, which ultimately creates nihilistic visions of existence which appear as criticism of technology (Napier 1993: 330).

Within the series' storyline, there is no direct reference to the Gospels or the prophecies. Perhaps this is unnecessary. The symbiosis of SF and apocalypticism finds its justification in the fear of technology and human solitude, which are outcomes of a post-secular world. *EVA* more closely resembles an eschatological narrative, as it describes the end of things, an afterlife story. In that sense, *EVA* can be considered a text of spiritual nature, but it can hardly be regarded as religious as it doesn't establish an intertextual reference to religious texts, either by quotation, discussion, parody or adaptation. After all, *EVA*'s lack of closure has always been part of the image that its creators sought to project.

Discursive Practices on *EVA* Distribution and Consumption

So far, I have explained the ways in which semantic (mainly iconography) and syntactic (intertextuality and the peculiarities of anime's visual language) elements of *EVA* may allow for a discussion of this series in terms of genre. However, both vocabulary and syntax would be only one, though significant, part of the genre equation. The consideration of common narrative tropes, settings or plot formulas, for example, could help, but genre is necessarily a result of a whole conversation between audiences and producers as well. This conversation will take place only when audiences identify codes as part of each genre's inner rules. Definitions of genre that put the focus on cultural consumption (Mittell 2001) have to be linked to practices of genre consumption, conceptualized as 'an exchange between industry and audience, an exchange through which a culture speaks to itself' (Feuer 1992: 109).

Anime audiences have been studied in relation to fan audiences or those with a higher level of engagement with their narratives. In this sense, *EVA* is closely connected to the otaku culture.[7] The creators of the *EVA* TV anime have been linked to this movement by their first works, which came into being before their professionalization. That is the case of *Otaku no Video* (1991), which has been frequently read in a biographical key as a portrait of the initial GAINAX members and even as a manifesto or 'discourse' representing otaku culture and even anime (Lamarre 2004 156). However, while Hideaki Anno and Toshio Okada self-identify as otaku (Horn 1996: para. 8), other members of the initial Studio GAINAX tend to distance themselves from that identity label (Manry & Yamaga 2010: para. 56). Actually, some scholars also deny the otaku element in GAINAX products. What *Otaku no Video* shows is the need for challenging the fictional identities of otaku 'fabricated by media' (Shen 2015: 83).

At the time of *EVA*'s first broadcast, the availability of anime titles overseas was determined by the different circumstances of each

7. See Chapter 7 by Zoltan Kacsuk.

national market. *EVA* found its public among adolescents and fans of SF, but since then it has been presented as the flagship of anime culture. At that moment, the market was still dominated by OVAs, or limited series and movies distributed in domestic video formats, before the companies began to work with longer series. Even after the international success of products such as *EVA*, the anime production committees were promoting their products adopting a low-risk approach. These strategies were intended to build an image that would eventually help the successful sale of the rest of the product cohort. Anime historian Jonathan Clements points out how festival advertising tended to homogenize manga and anime audiences:

> I still fondly remember how Evangelion and Escaflowne, in their original PR, were made to sound exactly the same. If left to their own devices, many marketers will be happy with 'Boy gets Robot in a heart-warming masterpiece with several girls who are demure and nice and childhood sweetheart who is a mysterious girl'. (Clements 2010: 66)

When the catalogue of TV series increased, satellite and cable-based broadcasters started to include this offer in the form of thematic channels. In response to new audiences, keen on all forms of Japanese visual culture, specialized magazines appeared (*AnimeLand*, *Newtype USA*, *Otaku US*, etc.). In many cases, manga and anime were at first only an extra, introduced in magazines dedicated to comics or video games, that is, markets expected to share audiences with anime. A transition can be seen in the video market just like in the publishing market, whereby anime moves away from using generic labels derived from Western cinema and literature to develop its own vocabulary. In the beginning, manga was considered a genre by the publishing market, due to the small number of titles and the limited diversity of their catalogue. The same applied to the anime market. The local video market was monopolized by a small number of distributors employing 'manga' and 'anime' stamps for a heterogeneous collection of titles that prioritized contents perceived as subversive for non-Japanese audiences (Hernández-Pérez, Corstorphine & Stephens 2017).

At that time, many scholarly sources disregarded demographic labels in their discussion of genre (Bryce & Davis 2010: 34; Drazen 2003; Poitras 2001; Richmond 2009). Thematic categories derived from cinema or literature such as drama, noir, SF and comedy predominated, attending to iconographic elements, such as *mecha* in anime.

As we have seen through different approaches to genre, objects or motifs represented within narratives (i.e., the most evident or iconographic elements) are perhaps the most intuitive way of establishing classifications. We tend to complement those casual categories with the similarity to other texts. When working on iconography, those references are linked in terms of architextuality, a common term for previous sets of text or traditions (mecha anime, SF). Another way would be to employ natural language which ultimately can describe not only feelings and emotional assessments of the experience with the product, but also motivations behind its consumption (a 'casual' *shōnen*, a reference in this genre, etc.).

In the last 30 years, media classification has become increasingly sophisticated with the development of the so-called social web and the integration of folksonomies, or collaborative classifications, in the construction of databases and recommendation systems. In the context of web 2.0, users are both the main resource and mechanism for content classification and indexing. Part of this evolution has been reflected in media platforms such as Netflix or, the most anime-specific streaming service, Crunchyroll, which include these tag-based recommendation systems.

Although these classification systems share architectures, they differ in their resulting lists of tags or terms, due to the different roles that communities have in their construction and maintenance. Interestingly, virtual communities with a large fanbase, and also some streaming platforms, seem to share a predilection for the demographic labels used in the Japanese market. On Crunchyroll, for example, we find the use of *shonen* [sic] and *shojo* [sic], along with definitions related to other media (romance, SF, thriller, mystery, etc.) or fandom-derived definitions (like *ecchi*[8]). The recommendation systems, on the other hand, function as more inclusive information structures, employing terms provided by users, practically inseparable from tagging behavior. Members of a virtual community often recycle categories proposed by digital curators and even create their own descriptions of a cultural artifact when submitting information to the system, such as 'Japanese animated series' or 'Japanese animated films.'

Platforms such as Netflix or Crunchyroll present closed systems that do not allow for user curation, directing consumption through the algorithms responsible for their own recommendations systems, as well as their own indexing systems. This selection of categories responds to editorial decisions. Therefore, political discourse uses ideology (Altman 1999) in the very same way that genres are curated. When referring to the *EVA* anime series and movies, Netflix labels them under the categories 'Anime Action,' 'Sci-Fi & Fantasy Anime' and 'Japanese TV Programmes,' but it also uses other tags such as 'cyberpunk' and 'exciting.'

Previous studies have resorted to content analysis to understand how audiences conceptualize anime. A study of the recommendations on Anime News Network (Cho et al. 2018) noted 19 features commonly used in the recommendation system, including Work, Theme, Genre, (Target) Audience and Mood, while other features such as Artwork/Visual Style, Audio Style and Language were found to be used less often. Genre categorizations in these databases are usually employed in combination with a list of similar products obtained from the platform's catalogue metadata. Thus, this suggests that the similarities among products (same director, same production/release date, same mood, etc.) may be regarded as a better predictor of user behavior than shared conceptualizations of a particular genre and/or artistic tradition.

8. *Ecchi*—derived from erotic (*ero-chikku*)—can be translated as sexy, naughty or dirty. It is a common label used to describe light and playful sexual plots within anime or manga.

This fact may explain the popularity of online repositories such as TVtropes.org, a site that collects a large myriad of definitions and includes thousands of categories for stylistic, narrative and even authorial classifications of anime. In the *EVA* entry at TVtropes, the available information is presented in a similar way to any Wiki site or collaborative encyclopedia, where the anime series page links to another one containing information about the franchise as a whole. Therefore, these pages provide a good example of aggregation. While tags like 'anime' or 'franchise' could be part of other ontological representations such as library databases, the same metadata structure also includes appreciations (awesome, HoYay, 'TearJerke,' 'Nightmare Fuel,'[9] 'YMMV,'[10] etc.), or other related information ('Quotes,' 'AwesomeMusic,' 'FanWorks,' 'Videos,' 'Trivia,' 'WMG,'[11] 'Pantheon' or character's genealogy). Moreover, when the provided material links to other pages—such as those with the characters from the expanded world-setting—the categorization of such information may include many other intertextualities that combine commentaries with actual facts. For example, the 'ideal casting' for a live-action production based on the series may include actual actors who had been considered for the same role in the past.

Cultural databases are a common construct to articulate the idea that meanings within narrative do not need to be presented in the form of cohesive structures, but are rather acquired in interaction with audiences. When it comes to anime, post-structuralist theoreticians like Azuma (2009) have proposed the use of these cultural databases to explain the disappearance of 'grand narratives,' a figure that works as synonymous of the more usual discourses in the context of post-structuralist and post-modernist philosophies. They also claim that databases or small narratives not only explain the cultural success of *moe* consumption, but are also the way in which modern 'readers' will engage with texts. *EVA*'s case is particularly relevant for Azuma's cultural theory. The author examines the use of *EVA*

9. Referring to aspects of the product that can be frightening or disturbing for some audiences.

10. Short for 'Your Mileage May Vary.' These sections collect information about those aspects in which fan audiences may differ in their appreciation of the product.

11. This stands for 'Wild Mass Guess,' or speculations about the meaning of a given aspect of the narrative.

as a grand narrative, accepting classical readings in relation to genre in terms of dystopian narrative or environmentalist rhetoric (Azuma 2009: 30–33). Otherwise, he uses the character of Rei Ayanami as a prototype of the small narratives in its *moe*[12] consumption (ibid.: 37) when it is presented de-contextualised in other parallel narratives such as video games or even non-narrative media, including merchandising. Azuma's otaku database (2009) reflects a process of structured induction based on the familiarity within exemplars (i.e., characters with a shy behavior, blue hair, an eye patch, etc.).

On the contrary, databases such as TVtropes are not articulated to any research narrative. Those are constructed as an effect of social interaction that shadows the need for intellectual definition, and subsequently (re)model after many subjectivities from fan community members. These databases are, perhaps, useful as a repository of unstructured collective data, but not in order to construct articulated thought.

We employ genres in our daily life and communication, but we also rely on other ways to classify and recommend products. Can those be non-curated databases of interest for the study of anime? All the communities I have examined—including curated databases, recommendation systems, streaming platforms and folksonomies—differ in the way in which they establish anime genres, as a consequence of the use of different terminologies. Although genres are supposed to be shared constructions, it is also argued that ordinary language and community participation can offer insights to guide genre classification (Swales 1990: 220). Folksonomies can therefore help the definition of texts, as well as modes of consumption, since their formulation can also be the answer to a common intellectual problem. In fact, this seems to be the case with Wikipedia, as the global site has proven to be quite efficient in terms of construction and maintenance costs, as well as impervious to fake information (McDowell & Vetter 2020).

12. Moe refers to the affective relation between fan audiences and anime objects.

Conclusions: The Shifting Nature of Genres in *EVA*

The problem behind soft approaches to genre is that the concept is used just as a descriptor without any critical thought about its actual implications, ultimately undermining the concept of genre itself. Genre becomes an introductory framework, challenged by case studies. In this chapter, I discussed previous approaches to genre—including the role that audiences, textual properties and media have in the construction of genre concept—in order to address *EVA*'s case.

Nowadays, anime tends to be considered not as a genre, but as a medium defined by its material traits, rather than focusing on its content or target audience. However, this is but one way of considering genre categories. Instead, it would be fitting to think of anime narratives as a genre colony (or a family of genres) that can still be defined as a medium. Consequently, genre becomes a way to define qualities within the anime medium.

Such an approach to Anime Studies would allow the inclusion of an iconographic perspective, in which an indeterminate number of identifiable objects represents a genre, and eventually enable multiple undefined hybridizations. Ultimately, this provides a transmedia perspective of 'genre,' in which two or more media share aesthetic or material qualities, and where the genre becomes an intermedial exchange space.

It has been noted that Film (Wood 2008: 46) and Media Studies tend to assume an opposite approach: genre vs. authorship. In the case of *EVA*, the discussion of genre is defined by its textual characteristics (syntactic and semantic), but also by the author, as he is responsible for the main creative choices. Tropes and formulas may establish a relationship between *EVA* and various genres, including SF and dystopian/post-apocalyptic narratives. However, the identification of *semata* (or meaningful units) is not enough for a genre definition. In this regard, it is worth mentioning how through both semantic and syntactic approaches, *EVA* can be related to exotic influences, such as the Judeo-Christian iconography or the conventions in apocalyptic narratives, but also to established traditions within anime, including *mecha* and *tokatsu* genres.

References

Altman, R. (1999). *Film/genre*. London: BFI Publishing.

Animerica (1996). Hideaki Anno's Roundtable Discussion. Excerpts from a Roundtable Disccussion with Hideaki Anno at the Anime Expo '96 Convention, *Animerica*, 4(9), 27. Retrieved from: http://web.archive.org/web/20021208123622/http://masterwork.animemedia.com/Evangelion/anno.html

Anno, H. (1996a). About Neon Genesis Evangelion. *Newtype*, November, 20–23. Retrieved from: https://www.gwern.net/otaku (translated by Miyako Graham/Protoculture Addicts)

_____. (1996b). Interview with Hideaki Anno. *Newtype*, June. Retrieved from: https://www.gwern.net/docs/eva/1996-newtype-anno-interview (translated by Gwern Branwen)

_____ & Higuchi, S. (2013). *Nihon tokusatsu no kako, genzai, soshite mirai o fukan shite*. Commissioned by Japan's Agency for Cultural Affairs Manga, Animation, Games, and Media Art Information Bureau. Tokyo: Mori Building Co., Ltd. Retrieved from: https://mediag.bunka.go.jp/projects/project/images/tokusatsu-2013.pdf

Azuma, H. (2009). *Otaku: Japan's Database Animals*. Minneapolis, MN: University of Minnesota Press. (Introduction and translation by J. E. Abel and S. Kono)

_____. (2016). Anime or Something Like it: Neon Genesis Evangelion. *Intercommunication*, 18. Retrieved from: https://www.ntticc.or.jp/pub/ic_mag/ico18/intercity/higashi_E.html

Bhatia, V. K. (1999). Integrating Products, Processes, Purposes and Participants in Professional Writing. In C. N. Candlin and K. Hyland (eds.), *Writing: Texts, Processes and Practices* (pp. 21–39). London: Routledge.

Bolton, C. & Csicsery-Ronay Jr, I. (2007). *Robot Ghosts and Wired Dreams: Japanese Science Fiction from Origins to Anime*. Minneapolis, MN: University of Minnesota Press.

Bryce, M. & Davis, J. (2010). An Overview of Manga Genres. In
T. Johnson-Woods (ed.), *Manga: An Anthology of Global and Cultural
Perspectives* (pp. 17–33). New York: Continuum International.

Buscombe, E. (1970). The Idea of Genre in the American Cinema. *Screen*,
11(2), 33–45.

Cavallaro, D. (2009). *The Art of Studio Gainax: Experimentation, Style
and Innovation at the Leading Edge of Anime*. Jefferson, NC: McFarland.

Cawelti, J. G. (1976). *Adventure, Mystery, and Romance: Formula Stories
as Art and Popular Culture*. Chicago, IL: University of Chicago Press.

Chapman, P. (2017). Hideaki Anno Hosts Tokusatsu History Panel in
Shinjuku in March. *Crunchyroll*. Retrieved from: https://www.crunch
yroll.com/en-gb/anime-news/2017/02/25-1/hideaki-anno-hosts-toku
satsu-history-panel-in-shinjuku-in-march

Cho, H., Schmalz, M. L., Keating, S. A. & Lee, J. H. (2018). Analyzing
Anime Users' Online Forum Queries for Recommendation Using
Content Analysis. *Journal of Documentation*, 2. DOI: https://doi.org
/10.1108/jd-08-2017-0122

Clements, J. (2010). *Schoolgirl Milky Crisis: Adventures in the Anime
and MangaTtrade*. London: Titan Books.

Denison, R. (2015). *Anime: A Critical Introduction*. London: Bloomsbury
Academic.

Derrida, J. & Ronnell, A. (1980). The Law of Genre. *Critical Inquiry*,
7(1), 55–81.

DiTommaso, L. (2014). Apocalypticism and Popular Culture. In
J. J. Collins (ed.), *The Oxford Handbook of Apocalyptic Literature*
(pp. 473–510). Oxford: Oxford University Press.

Drazen, P. (2003). *Anime Explosion! The What? Why? & Wow! of
Japanese Animation*. Berkeley, CA: Stone Bridge Press.

Dyer, R. (1998). *Stars*. London: BFI.

Feuer, J. (1992). Genre Study and Television. In R. C. Allen (ed.),
Channels of Discourse, Reassembled (pp. 138–160). Chapel Hill,
NC: University of North Carolina Press.

GAINAX (1997). Neon Genesis Evangelion Move!! In *Neon Genesis Evangelion Newtype 100% Collection* (pp. 85–89). Tokyo: Kadokawa Shoten. In EvaWiki (2020), Neon Genesis Evangelion Proposal. Retrieved from: https://wiki.evageeks.org/Neon_Genesis_Evangelion _Proposal

Genette, G. (1992). *The Architext: An Introduction*. Berkeley, CA: University of California Press.

Giner, P. (1997). Interview Hideaki Anno. *AnimeLand*, 32, 19–21. Retrieved from: https://www.gwern.net/docs/eva/1997-animeland-may -hideakianno-interview.pdf

Grant, B. K. (2007). *Film Genre: From Iconography to Ideology*. London: Wallflower.

Hernández-Pérez, M. (2016). Animation, Branding and Authorship in the Construction of the 'Anti-Disney' Ethos: Hayao Miyazaki's Works and Persona through Disney Film Criticism. *animation. an interdisciplinary journal*, 11(3), 297–313. DOI: https://doi.org/10.1177/17468 47716660684

_____., Corstorphine, K. & Stephens, D. (2017). Cartoons vs. Manga Movies: A Brief History of Anime in the UK. *Mutual Images*, 2(1), 1–39. Retrieved from: DOI: https://doi.org/10.32926/2017.2.HER.carto

Hikawa, R. (ed.) (2013). *Japanese Animation Guide: The History of Robot Anime*. Tokyo: Mori Building Company, Ltd. https://mediag .bunka.go.jp/projects/project/images/JapaneseAnimationGuide.pdf

Horn, C. (1996). "Return of the Otaking." *Toshio Okada at Anime America 1996 (*Written Statements*).* Retrieved from: https://web .archive.org/web/20000305012502/http://www.j-pop.com/anime /archive/feature/04_gal_999/otaking2.html

Hu, T. Y. G. (2010). *Frames of Anime: Culture and Image-Building*. Hong Kong: Hong Kong University Press.

Jenkins, H. (1992). "Strangers No More, We Sing": Filking and the Social Construction of the SF Fan Community. In L. A. Lewis (ed.), *The Adoring Audience: Fan Culture and Popular Media* (pp. 208–236). London: Routledge.

Khara, Studio (2006) Kabushikigaisha karā [Studio Khara History]. Retrieved from: http://www.khara.co.jp/history/

Lamarre, T. (2004). An Introduction to Otaku Movement. *EnterText*, 4(1), 151–187.

Manry, G. & Yamaga, H. (2010). Interview: Gainax's Hiroyuki Yamaga. *Anime News Network*. Retrieved from: https://www.animenewsnet work.com/interview/2010-06-03/interview-gainax-hiroyuki-yamaga

McDowell, Z. J. & Vetter, M. A. (2020). It Takes a Village to Combat a Fake News Army: Wikipedia's Community and Policies for Information Literacy. *Social Media + Society*, July–September, 1–13. Retrieved from: DOI: https://doi.org/10.1177/20563051209 37309

Mittell, J. (2001). A Cultural Approach to Television Genre Theory. *Cinema Journal*, 40(3), 3–24. DOI: https://doi.org/10.2307/1350192

Mousoutzanis, A. (2009). Apocalyptic SF. In M. Bould, A. Butler, A. Roberts and S. Vint (eds.), *The Routledge Companion to Science Fiction* (pp. 458–462). London: Routledge.

Nagai, G. and Dynamic Productions (1999). Extracts from *Devilman Tabulae Anatomicae Kaitai Shinsho* Art Book. In Gwern Branwen (ed.) (2010), *Neon Genesis Evangelion Source Anthology*. Retrieved from: https://www.gwern.net/otaku

Napier, S. J. (1993). Panic Sites: The Japanese Imagination of Disaster from Godzilla to Akira. *Journal of Japanese Studies*, 19(2), 327–351.

_____. (2001). *Anime from Akira to Princess Mononoke: Experiencing Contemporary Japanese Animation*. New York: Palgrave Macmillan.

Orbaugh, S. (2009). Manga and Anime. In M. Bould, A. Butler, A. Roberts and S. Vint (eds.), *The Routledge Companion to Science Fiction* (pp. 112–122). London: Routledge.

Ortega, M. (2007). My Father, He Killed Me; My Mother, She Ate Me: Self, Desire, Engendering, and the Mother in *Neon Genesis Evangelion*. *Mechademia*, 2(1), 216–232.

Poitras, G. (2001). *Anime Essentials: Everything a Fan Needs to Know*. Berkeley, CA: Stone Bridge Press.

Richmond, S. (2009). *The Rough Guide to Anime: Japan's Finest from Ghibli to Gankutsuō*. London: Rough Guides.

Ryan, M.-L. (2004). Introduction. In M.-L. Ryan (ed.), *Narrative across Media: The Languages of Storytelling* (pp. 1–40). Lincoln, NE: University of Nebraska Press.

Schatz, T. (1981). *Hollywood Genres: Formula, Filmmaking, and the Studio System*. New York: Random House.

Shen, L. F. (2015). Traversing Otaku Fantasy: Representation of the Otaku Subject, Gaze and Fantasy in Otaku no Video. In P. W. Galbraith, T. H. Kam and B.-O. Kamm (eds.), *Debating Otaku in Contemporary Japan: Historical Perspectives and New Horizons* (pp. 73–88). London: Bloomsbury Academic.

Smith, C. (1993). *The Rediscovery of Man: The Complete Short Science Fiction of Cordwainer Smith*. Framingham, MA: NESFA Press.

Stewart-Ahn, A. (2019). Neverending Evangelion. How Hideaki Anno Turned Obsessions and Depression into an Anime Phenomenon. *Polygon*. Retrieved from: https://www.polygon.com/2019/6/19/18883634/neon-genesis-evangelion-hideaki-anno-depression-shinji-anime-characters-movies

Suvin, D. (1972). On the Poetics of the SF Genre. *College English*, 34(3), 372–382.

_____. (1979). *Metamorphoses of Science Fiction: On the Poetics and History of a Literary Genre*. London: Yale University Press.

Swales, J. (1990). *Genre Analysis: English in Academic and Research Settings*. Cambridge: Cambridge University Press.

Takeda, Y. (2005). *The Notenki Memoirs. Studio GAINAX and the Men Who Created Evangelion*. Tokyo: Wani Books. (Translated by ADV Manga)

Tatsumi, T. & Bolton, C. (2008). Gundam and the Future of Japanoid Art. *Mechademia*, 3, 191–198.

Thomas, J. B. (2012). *Drawing on Tradition: Manga, Anime, and Religion in Contemporary Japan*. Honolulu, HI: University of Hawaii Press.

Tsurumaki, K. & Thomas, O. (2001). Amusing Himself to Death (Interview with Kazuya Tsurumaki). *Akadot*. Retrieved from: https://web.archive.org/web/20070806063455/http://www.akadot.com/article.php?a=182

Ueno, T. (2006). Kurenai no metalsuits, "Anime to wa nani ka/What is animation." *Mechademia*, 1, 111–118. DOI: https://doi.org/10.1353/mec.0.0055. (Translated by M. Arnold)

Watanabe, K. & Otsuki, T. (2006), Interview with Toshmichi Otsuki, Mainichi Manga Town. Retrieved from: https://wiki.evageeks.org/Statements_by_Evangelion_Staff

Watanabe, M. (2001). Imagery and War in Japan: 1995. In T. Fujitani, G. M. White and L. Yoneyama (eds.), *Perilous Memories: The Asia–Pacific War(s)* (pp. 120–151). Durham, NC and London: Duke University Press. doi:10.2307/j.ctv1131czf

Wong, W. S. (2010). Globalizing Manga: From Japan to Hong Kong and Beyond. In T. Johnson-Woods (ed.), *Manga: An Anthology of Global and Cultural Perspectives* (pp. 332–350). New York: Continuum International.

Wood, R. (2008). Ideology, Genre, Auteur. In *Auteurs and Authorship: A Film Reader* (pp. 84–92). Maldwell: Blackwell Publishing.

Yamaguchi, Y. (2004). *Nihon no anime zenshi*. Tokyo: Ten Books.

7. The Making of an Epoch-Making Anime
Understanding the Landmark Status of *Neon Genesis Evangelion* in Otaku Culture

Zoltan Kacsuk

1995 was a year of shocks for Japan. The Great Hanshin earthquake destroyed and damaged large portions of Kobe and its surroundings in January, resulting in the largest-scale destruction by an earthquake in Japan since the Great Kantō earthquake in 1923. Next, the Aum Shinrikyō sect committed an unprecedented act of terrorism, an orchestrated sarin gas attack in the Tokyo subway system in March. The general mood engendered by these events was further exacerbated by the growing sense of realization that the boom of the bubble economy that had burst at the end of the 1980s was not returning, and the economic stagnation that followed in its wake was the new norm (Maejima 2010; Uno 2008). The uneasiness felt at the time contributed to pop psychology and words like 'trauma' and 'adult children' becoming prevalent in popular discourse, leading to an increased interest in the inner-self and self-reflection (Maejima 2010: 32).

It was with this general social backdrop that *Neon Genesis Evangelion* (*EVA*) started airing in the fall of 1995. After a low-key reception with a small core audience on its initial broadcast, the series grew exponentially into what is commonly referred to as a social phenomenon (or *EVA* shock) during its first re-airing in 1997 and then leading into the theatrical release of both *Neon Genesis Evangelion: Death & Rebirth* and *The End of Evangelion* in the same year. This phenomenal popularity seems to indicate that *EVA* did indeed manage to capture the zeitgeist in a unique way (cf. Uno 2008), and resonated

How to cite this book chapter:
Kacsuk, Z. 2021. The Making of an Epoch-Making Anime: Understanding the Landmark Status of *Neon Genesis Evangelion* in Otaku Culture. In: Santiago Iglesias, J. A. and Soler Baena, A. (Eds.). *Anime Studies: Media-Specific Approaches to Neon Genesis Evangelion.* Pp. 215–246 Stockholm: Stockholm University Press. DOI: https://doi.org /10.16993/bbp.h. License: CC-BY 4.0

1. The closest translation of otaku would be geek in English. For a discussion of the meaning of the term, see the next section. In Japanese, otaku is written in various forms (hiragana, katakana and Latin script) to connote different positions regarding its implied meanings. For my present analysis, these nuances are secondary and I therefore quote all instances of otaku in this single, simple form. For a discussion of the connotations of the various forms in Japanese, see, for example, Galbraith, Kam & Kamm (2015) or Yoshimoto (2009).

2. Although Morikawa does not directly attribute the transformation of Akihabara from electric town—with a large concentration of shops dealing in electronic devices—to otaku town to the success of *EVA*, he does list a number of pieces of evidence that seem to suggest a strong link, and he offers a detailed interview excerpt as an illustration of this being the actual case for at least one of the pioneering shops to make the move (2003: 56–62). Before, *EVA* figurine shops were mostly located in Tokyo neighborhoods where young people would gather, such as Kichijōji or Shibuya. But the capital injection provided by the sudden increase in demand—engendered by the *EVA* boom—for custom hobby model kits led to said shop relocating to Akihabara, purely based on the notion that most of their clientele would go there for electronics supplies anyway. The success enjoyed by the first pioneers quickly led to an exodus of small and larger retailers all relocating to or opening branches in Akihabara. This account of Akihabara's transformation from Morikawa's book is also available in English (2012 [2003]).

with an audience beyond its original target audience of otaku.[1] This widespread success led to a re-evaluation of the then denigrated figure of the otaku, and the sheer commercial force of the otaku market could no longer be ignored (Lamarre 2009: 153), as also evidenced by the rapid transformation of Tokyo's Akihabara, with an unprecedented concentration of shops catering to otaku interests, which opened up in the neighborhood within the span of a couple of years after the *EVA* boom (Morikawa 2003).[2] The anime industry was also changed by the series' and the subsequent movies' impact, leading to what is commonly understood to be the third anime boom, "facilitating the creation of the new time-slot and category of 'late-night anime'" and "propagating the production committee model of anime production due to its successes" (Suan 2018: 204).

It is easy to assume that the above-outlined economic impact of the series and its influence on anime production and distribution practices is responsible for how it has come to be considered an epoch-making anime. Although these facets of its impact are undeniably a part of the equation, I would like to suggest that there is a more fundamental level on which *EVA* has proven to be epoch-making, and it is this deeper level that is in part responsible for the perceived naturalization of the economic and business arguments. The reason I refer to the economic and business arguments as less fundamental is because the significance of these types of changes can be reinterpreted according to the relative symbolic weight carried by the works under discussion, as we will see in the case of anime booms below. Few are the cases like that of *Astro Boy*, where a given work is undeniably the source of the economic and business effects associated with it. Thus, examining the arguments and positions in relation to this more fundamental level will be the focus of the present chapter.

From a perspective informed by the sociology of art, great works of art—or in our case epoch-making ones—are created neither by a genius author nor by a team, but rather, as Becker (1982), Bourdieu (1996

[1992]) and Williams (1980 [1961]) all point out with differing voca-
bularies, they are the products of much larger systems of production
and dissemination, of popular and critical reception, of consecrating
institutions, of scholarly and archival work, and of latter works that
consciously or unknowingly engage with them. The way in which
great works are selected and consecrated operates along very similar
logics in the subfields of cultural production further away from the
already legitimized arts—to use Bourdieu's vocabulary—as Beaty and
Woo (2016) demonstrate in relation to comic books.

It is in this vein that I turn to the Japanese critical discourse to
make sense of how *EVA* has come to be constructed as an epoch-
making great work of anime there. Although this is not the only arena
in which such construction takes place, it is definitely an important
one. By critical discourse, I refer to a particular domain of mostly
written intellectual exchange in Japanese, which comprises a range
of publications that are not necessarily rigorously academic: Indeed,
they are often written with a more general audience in mind, but they
are nevertheless invested in moving forward the discussion around
their topics of interest as opposed to a simple popularization of works
or concepts. This discursive space borders on and overlaps with the
domain of academic research in one direction, on art/literary/cultural
criticism in another, and finally on popular science and public intellectual discourse along a third angle. Its contributors thus come
from various backgrounds ranging from the humanities (e.g., Hiroki
Azuma), psychology (e.g., Tamaki Saitō) and social sciences (e.g.,
Kaichirō Morikawa), to critics writing on popular media (e.g., Gō Itō,[3]
Satoshi Maejima, Tsunehiro Uno, Taimatsu Yoshimoto), journalists,
editors and even creators themselves (e.g., Eiji Ōtsuka, Toshio Okada).
Despite its breadth and variety in positions, the discourse nevertheless provides a semi-coherent space, which is not only evidenced by
the way these authors build on one another's ideas, but also in the
way they are regularly featured in conversation with or alongside one

3. See especially Itō 2005.

another in publications. This unique space of intellectual exchange has been highly productive in relation to new approaches and concepts for engaging with anime, manga, light novels, video games, otaku and related domains, some of which will be discussed in the following; and which, in general, as I have argued elsewhere, can significantly further the theoretical work being undertaken, for example, in Anglophone Fan Studies, Comics Studies and beyond (Kacsuk 2016a).

The status of *EVA* as a landmark work in the Japanese critical discourse is aptly demonstrated by the way it is either seen as (1) a culmination or end point, (2) an origin point or (3) as the single best representative of a larger phenomenon or paradigm shift. For example, in relation to (1), Ōtsuka (2004) concludes that *EVA* is the ultimate attempt at addressing "Astro Boy's dilemma" (*Atomu no meidai*), and for Uno (2018) it is the "final accounts" of the robot anime genre. As (2) an origin point, for instance, *EVA* is not only the fountainhead of a major anime boom and potentially responsible for sparking the transformation of Akihabara, but is also understood to be one of the major inspirations for the *sekaikei*[4] mode/genre, and the source of its original conceptualization (Maejima 2010). Finally, with reference to (3), for Uno (2008), *EVA* embodies the imagination of mid-1990s Japanese popular culture, and for Azuma (2009 [first edition: 2001]) and Maejima (2010), *EVA* marks a number of important shifts in otaku culture, discussed in detail later.

Tracing the various arguments in the Japanese critical discourse that position *EVA* as a landmark work, two things become very obvious straightaway. First, it is an unquestionable consensus that *EVA* was a watershed phenomenon. Even authors like Ōtsuka (2004), who vocally disliked the series initially, or Uno (2018), who has been one of the strongest voices in providing a counter-reading to the significance of post-*EVA* works and thereby to the significance of *EVA* itself (2008), have found approaches to re-evaluate it in a way that conforms to this idea, as explained later. Second, although there are

4. See below for a detailed discussion of the term's meaning.

arguments that underline the impact of *EVA* in relation to anime or Japanese society at large, the majority of the points raised center on the series' relationship with otaku culture. This points toward another, more fundamental aspect of *EVA*'s position in the Japanese critical discourse, one that only becomes apparent when considering the shifts in this discursive space over time. As a result of *EVA*'s impact on it, *EVA*'s landmark status and the meaning of otaku culture have inextricably become constituted together.

The way otaku culture and the significance of *EVA* are constituted together is precisely why *EVA* can be considered an epoch-making work: it has engendered an intervention in the discourse around otaku culture that has effected lasting discursive changes. The very content of the term otaku has been warped by *EVA*, or more precisely, the changes in the meaning of the term have been determined by the position of *EVA* in the critical discourse. It is not just one term, however, it is a host of terms and concepts that have been mobilized and reconfigured, most notably 'anime boom,' 'otaku generations' and '*sekaikei*.'[5]

In order to demonstrate this interrelation between the meaning of otaku culture and *EVA*'s consistent positioning as a landmark work within the Japanese critical discourse, I will proceed by first providing a short introduction to the complexity of defining otaku culture, followed by a look at the significance of anime for otaku culture. I will then turn to discussing the concepts of anime boom, otaku generation and *sekaikei* and how they attest to *EVA*'s impact on conceptualizing otaku culture. Finally, in the last two sections of this chapter I will, on the one hand, offer further potential ways to see the interrelation between the significance of *EVA* and the meaning of otaku culture; and, on the other, I will highlight the force exerted by the consensus regarding *EVA*'s landmark position even on authors who have demonstrated a critical stance in relation to the show and its reception.

5. These interlinked shifts in meaning are not unlike the ones highlighted in Williams (1979 [1976]), albeit on a far more compact timeline and a much smaller scale.

Otaku and Otaku Culture

Otaku culture, like any (sub)cultural formation, is very tricky to pin down. On the one hand, otaku culture only exists on the level of discourse, be it theoretical or popular.[6] It is a concept created to refer to a set of phenomena, far from being cohesive and well-delineated. Indeed, if we were to shift our emphases and groupings along different lines, we would end up with a very different version of what otaku culture means. This, in fact, is one crucial topic of this chapter. As Aida notes, 'discourses on "otaku" . . . and "actual otaku" must be strictly distinguished' (2015: 105). On the other hand, however, as this distinction itself implies, there are people who explicitly or implicitly identify with the term (however varying the meaning); there are shops, products and media that supposedly cater to an otaku clientele, and there are conventions and other types of meetings where people come together to engage in activities commonly associated with otaku. This, then, is the double bind of discussing social and cultural formations: there are categories that exist on the level of theory and discourse, and then there are myriad forms of action, tastes, artifacts, modes of engagement and belonging, which do seem to demonstrate patterns of affinity, but never equal the concept. As Alfred Korzybski put it so well, the "map *is not* the territory it represents, but, if correct, it has a *similar structure* to the territory' (1996 [1933]: 58, emphases in the original). Various solutions to this problem have been put forward, for example, by Azuma (2009 [2001]), Morikawa (2003), Yoshimoto (2009), Galbraith, Kam and Kamm (2015) and Kacsuk (2016b). In this chapter, however, I only highlight two aspects of the discussions on otaku culture. First, in relation to the popular discourse, I will offer an ever-so-brief history of the term itself in Japan. Second, to reference the just as complicated level of actual social interactions and tastes, I will highlight the way in which otaku practices and interests are addressed in the Japanese critical discourse.

6. For a very thorough summary of the various approaches to otaku and otaku culture in the Japanese scholarly and critical discourse, see Aida (2015).

The term *otaku* was supposedly first used by SF fans from Keiō University Tokyo, some of whom went on to create the TV anime *Super Dimension Fortress Macross* (1982–83), which featured the term in dialogue. It was then appropriated by a wider strata of fans and taken up as a derogatory term within the fandom itself (Okada 1996: 8–9). This phase of the term's history is followed by its endlessly retold appearance in the magazine *Manga Burikko* in the provocative four-part series *Otaku no kenkyū* (Otaku research) written by Akio Nakamori (with the last piece authored by Sonta Eji) and starting in 1983 (for discussions of the series see, e.g., Ōtsuka 2004; Yamanaka 2015; Yoshimoto 2009). Precisely because *Manga Burikko* was a niche medium (cf. Thornton 1996 [1995]) of the culture itself, this exposure had an effect within the concerned fandoms, that is, an internal debate about the ethics of using the term to denigrate others. Yamanaka points out how the debate surrounding the article series led people to re-adopt the term otaku in self-mocking fashion (2015: 46–47), which is often the first step toward the reclamation of an identity. The next stage in the evolution of the term was the infamous Tsutomu Miyazaki serial murder case, which brought about both mainstream exposure of otaku and a moral panic (Ito 2012: xxi; see also Kamm 2015). The negative image was further reinforced by the March 1995 Sarin gas attack committed by members of Aum Shinrikyō in the Tokyo subway system, and the discussions that followed regarding whether Aum Shinrikyō had been an otaku sect.[7] Finally, after a series of events, such as the publication of Okada's *Otakugaku nyūmon* (Introduction to Otakuology, 1996) and his public appearances and lecture series on otaku culture at the University of Tokyo, the generational mainstream success of *EVA*, and then almost a decade later the society-wide popularity of the media franchise *Densha Otoko* (*Train Man*), the term otaku came to be rehabilitated to mean people deeply engaged in very specific non-mainstream interests (see Kikuchi 2015; Ito 2012).

7. Both Morikawa (2003) and Uno (2018) discuss the obvious anime influences on Aum Shinrikyō's propaganda and teachings.

Turning to the level of practice, the emergence of otaku culture can be seen as a result of the expansion and diffusion of SF culture around the late 1970s and early 1980s (Okada 2008; Yoshimoto 2009). Most of the implicit and explicit definitions of otaku culture in the Japanese critical discourse center on one or more of the following: (1) the level of content and media, or in other words, genres and formats characteristic of otaku culture; (2) the different interest communities or fandoms; and (3) the specific mode of engagement.

There is a further group of definitions, which I deliberately omitted from this list and which will not be discussed here, as they are more focused on otaku personality traits—often framed as pathologies—rather than otaku culture as a cultural formation, such as Saitō's famous characterization that otaku are distinguished by their sexual interest being focused on two dimensional characters (2011 [2000]).[8]

Enumerations of the interests within otaku culture (e.g., Azuma 2009 [2001]; Morikawa 2003; Okada 2008; Yoshimoto 2009) are strikingly similar, with SF, fantasy, games, manga, anime and idol culture acting as central nodes for most of them. For Morikawa, the "structure of interest"—the affinity between technology such as personal computers and laser discs on the one hand, and anime, video games, fan-made manga, custom hobby model kits, etc. on the other (2003: 63)—ultimately defines what otaku are (2003: 268). In a similar fashion, Yoshimoto's "otaku genre" is characterized by the presence of "bishōjo[9], mecha[10] and further SF elements, magic and other fantasy elements, sexual and romantic elements," and otaku are defined as males who enjoy works that belong to the "otaku genre" and who self-identify as otaku (2009: 8). Although the elements of these two enumerations are different insofar as Morikawa focuses on various media and product types,[11] whereas Yoshimoto concentrates on various traits of genre fiction, they actually complement each other to provide a general picture of the range of otaku interests.

8. See Aida (2015) for an overview of a number of such definitions.

9. Meaning beautiful young girl, bishōjo is often used as an umbrella term for a family of character types heavily featured in many Japanese anime, manga and video games.

10. Large (fighting) machines, often resembling a humanoid or bipedal form, commonly operated by a single pilot from a cockpit inside the mecha itself. See Chapter 6 by Manuel Hernández-Pérez.

11. Namely "doujinshi, cosplay materials, trading cards, dolls, anime character goods, products related to manga-anime-games" (Morikawa 2003: 47).

Okada (2008) and Yoshimoto (2009) also enumerate a series of interrelated fandoms that belong to (the larger) otaku culture, such as military fans, railway fans, SF fans, anime fans, manga fans, special effects fans, *kaijū* fans,[12] etc. Again, some of these fandoms seem to be defined along the lines of media form, while others are organized around content and genre. For Okada, however, otaku culture differs from specific fandoms such as those invested in SF, anime, *kaijū* or manga, in the way in which it operates on a level that requires a nuanced understanding of the canons and conventions of all these areas (1996: 28).[13] There is a sense of the coming together of elements from various genres and media in all of these definitions. But while Okada locates otaku culture in the mode of engagement, Yoshimoto assumes the crystallization of a whole new genre on the level of works.[14] This is probably the reason why Yoshimoto sees a direct continuity with the emergence of *moe*[15] works, whereas Okada positions moe-focused consumption in opposition to the "true mode of otaku appreciation," a point to which I will return later.

The Significance of Anime for Otaku Culture

For overseas fans of otaku culture, the primacy of anime is an unquestionable fact, especially from a historical perspective, with anime having been the most important entry point and catalyst for the growth of anime-manga fandom in many countries (see, e.g., Eng 2012; Kacsuk 2016b; Leonard 2005; Malone 2010; Pellitteri 2010). Anime, however, is just as central to otaku culture in Japan. The general understanding within the Japanese critical discourse is that otaku culture crystallized in the late 1970s and early 1980s when anime for a teenage to young adult audience emerged, spearheaded by *Space Battleship Yamato* (1974–75) and *Mobile Suit Gundam* (1979–80).

Although the previous section's enumerations may suggest that anime is just one among many interests in the mix that constitutes

12. *Kaijū* (monster) refers to both the genre of Japanese movies featuring monsters and the creatures themselves, most famously Godzilla. A closely related genre label is that of special effects (tokusatsu) movies and TV shows, which often also feature monsters and/or superheroes.

13. Although there is a strong continuity between Okada's positions in *Otakugaku nyūmon* (1996) and *Otaku wa sude ni shinde iru* (Otaku are already dead) (2008), there is also a difference in relation to the emphasis on who otaku are. Whereas the former work distinguishes otaku from simple fans of anime or manga, as a kind of elite alpha fans, the latter book's approach embraces all fans of the wider otaku sphere of interests from the 1980s up until the early 2000s.

14. However, Yoshimoto also identifies an otaku specific mode of engagement focusing on community and enjoyment (2009: 180), as mentioned in the next section related to the divide in Japanese SF culture which occurred in the late 1970s to early 1980s.

15. The word *moe* is commonly understood to denote the affective reaction of readers, viewers and players to fictional characters or to certain character elements. It has become a key term in the discussions around the shift in the focal interests of otaku culture in the late 1990s (see Azuma, 2009 [2001]; Maejima 2010; Okada 2008; Uno 2018; Yoshimoto 2009) as will be discussed in later sections in more detail. For a discussion of the possible origins of the term, see Morikawa (2003: 31).

otaku culture, it was in fact originally its preferred form. In *Otakugaku nyūmon*, Okada even cites the visual refinedness of otaku in relation to anime viewing as one of their distinguishing features (1996: 10–27). But even more importantly, it is within anime that otaku culture first coalesces into a new recognizable configuration. Furthermore, anime plays a huge role in catalyzing the differentiation of otaku culture from the narrower SF fandom and its spread to a wider public (Yoshimoto 2009; see also Ōtsuka 2004).

In *Otaku no kigen* (The origin of otaku), Yoshimoto offers a detailed reconstruction of the key events and actors that led to the qualitative change in SF fandom and facilitated the emergence of otaku culture. "Imaginary culture" is the unifying theme for Yoshimoto interconnecting SF, *kaijū* or special effects works, manga, the occult and anime. SF fandom originally was a very serious affair which required much reading, often even in foreign languages, and an interest in science. In part influenced by US fan practices, a different and more popular way of enjoying SF emerged. It was motivated by participation, in both senses of the word: stepping into the world of the fantastic and taking part in events. These two ways of SF engagement lived alongside each other in a tenuous relationship, but ultimately it was this latter more popular form of enjoyment that led to the emergence of otaku culture (Yoshimoto 2009: 144–167).[16]

Yoshimoto also explains the role played by anime magazines in creating both the critical discourse needed to normalize the shifting of anime from a children-only form to being enjoyable by teenagers and adults, and a country-wide audience connected by this shared space of information and interaction (2009: 127–136).[17] Ōtsuka also emphasizes the importance of anime magazines as a ground where the first generation of otaku working in various writing and editing roles set the tone for anime criticism (2004: 106). Furthermore, these magazines were key in drawing animators into creating manga, the

16. For an exploration of the connection between participatory fan practices, imaginary culture and the aesthetic principles underpinning otaku culture, see Kacsuk (2016a; 2016b).

17. See also Chapter 4 by Minori Ishida.

most famous example being Hayao Miyazaki's *Nausicaä of the Valley of the Wind* (Ōtsuka 2004: 108).

The DAICON III opening animation

In the late 1970s and early 1980s, the most important convention that would bring a large number of participants from the various interest groups (SF, manga, anime, *kaijū*, etc.) together in Japan was the annual SF convention. In 1981, a group of young enthusiasts from Osaka—including Takami Akai, Hideaki Anno, Toshio Okada, Yasuhiro Takeda and Hiroyuki Yamaga—had the opportunity to host the 20th annual SF convention. It was the third time it was held in the city, thus the event was called DAICON III. The name is a word play on *daikon* radish, and is a portmanteau of the Sino-Japanese reading (on'yomi) of the first character of Osaka (dai) and 'con' from the English word *convention* (a testament to the influence of US SF fandom). The then art students Akai, Anno and Yamaga worked on the convention's opening animation. It was an inspired work produced via dedication rather than a budget—it was famously created on industrial celluloid as opposed to the more expensive and finer material used for animation—and it was not only outstanding as an amateur piece, but also showcased the many interests of what would become otaku culture. The roughly five-and-a-half-minute short piece shows the fighting-filled journey of a small girl who is entrusted with a glass of water by members of the Science Patrol from *Ultraman*, which she successfully delivers to water a dismal-looking radish in the ground. On the way, she is confronted with various *kaijū*, anime and SF-related adversaries, ranging from a *Starship Troopers* mecha through Godzilla to even a *Star Wars* star destroyer, with a host of references to further works sprinkled in for good measure. Upon being watered, the radish turns into a huge radish-shaped spaceship called the DAICON III, which the girl boards as its captain to fly off.

Animec (1978–87) was the flagship magazine where many of the intellectual foundations for anime criticism were being laid down, and it was here that the famous "Is Gundam SF?" debate took place, a portent of the growing divide between SF and anime fans (or fans of literary SF and visual SF) (Yoshimoto 2009: 127–128). It was also around 1980 that the self-evidence of SF literature, manga and anime consumption going together started to break down, in part as a result of the increased supply in works in all of these forms, but also because of a steadily growing audience (2009: 128–129).

Not only does anime play a key role in setting the stage for the fully formed crystallization of otaku culture in the early 1980s, but the first major formulations of what the 'otaku genre' encapsulates also took the form of anime, the first of which was the manifesto-like *DAICON III* convention opening animation (1981) by a group of creators who would later become known as Studio GAINAX (see text box). In 1982, the start of the original broadcast of *Super Dimension Fortress Macross* followed, also created by a very young team, but reaching a far wider audience. This series showcased SF, idol culture, love comedy, mecha, bishōjo and many more elements boys interested in "imaginary culture" were excited about at the time (Yoshimoto 2009: 165–166). The *DAICON IV* opening animation in 1983 was already a self-affirming celebration of the otaku mode of engagement. It featured a short summary remake of the *DAICON III* opening animation, to then welcome back the protagonist as a grown-up woman in a playboy bunny dress fighting and surfing—on Elric's Stormbringer no less—her way through a breathtaking vista of the various interests and stylistic elements that made up otaku culture (including, for example, the highly intricate projectile patterns referred to as "Itano circus" after its animator, Ichirō Itano).[18] This was followed in 1984 by the release of the movies *Nausicaä of the Valley of the Wind*, *Urusei Yatsura 2: Beautiful Dreamer* and *The Super Dimension Fortress Macross: Do You Remember Love?*, which marked the completion of the crystallization of the otaku genre in Yoshimoto's view (2009: 185–187).

Even though the *DAICON III* and *DAICON IV* opening animations were only shown at the corresponding two conventions and later made available on video, the force that would become GAINAX

18. The *DAICON III* opening animation already cites both Western and Japanese works; however, the number of references truly moves to the scale of enumeration in the *DAICON IV* opening animation, to the point of including a panorama-like tableau of characters.

is so central to the formation of otaku culture in a practical, discursive and symbolic sense that Yoshimoto regards them as the most important catalysts (2009: 171). While this premier position in the narrative is no accident, it is not inevitable either. In the last section of this chapter, I will point to potential alternative versions of the history of otaku culture where the centrality of GAINAX is supplanted by other studios.

Defining Anime Booms

One of the most obvious concepts mobilized with regard to the epoch-making status of *EVA* is that of anime booms, or more specifically the very boom it engendered. In order to better interrogate the relationship between epoch-making anime and anime booms, let us first reverse the inquiry into whether all epoch-making anime also give rise to anime booms. *Astro Boy* (1963–66), *Space Battleship Yamato* (1974–75) and *Mobile Suit Gundam* (1979–80) are all considered epoch-making anime. *Astro Boy* was the pioneering work that set the template of limited animation for the whole lineage of TV anime to follow, *Space Battleship Yamato* opened anime up to a teenage and young adult audience (Yoshimoto 2009) and *Mobile Suit Gundam* is commonly understood as inaugurating the Real Robot genre (Uno 2018). Remarkably, two out of three of these anime, *Space Battleship Yamato* and *Mobile Suit Gundam*, are directly linked to the emergence of otaku culture.

But what actually constitutes an anime boom? The animation historian Nobuyuki Tsugata explicitly reflects on the way in which anime boom is a popular expression that has no set definition, and the meaning of which can vary based on the speaker, especially between generations (2005: 180). Nevertheless, the impact of this concept is so strongly felt that he too cannot avoid using it, and thus attempts to provide a working definition. In his view, it is not only a quantitative aspect of having a larger number of anime produced (which in itself would raise important questions regarding what increase would be large enough to constitute a boom), but also a qualitative shift (as hard to pin down as this criterion might be) in the production, distribution and consumption practices of anime (2005: 181). As much as Tsugata tries to reposition the concept as something that can be made sense of within animation research, it is quite telling that the three booms he discusses conform almost completely to the narrative that understands the major turning points within Japanese animation in relation to the development of TV anime and otaku culture. The first anime boom in his interpretation is sparked by the premier of *Astro Boy*, the second anime boom is initiated by *Space Battleship Yamato* and the third is characterized by the emergence of a strong overseas interest, represented by the international success of Hayao Miyazaki's *Princess Mononoke* (1997) (Tsugata 2005: 181–182)—this is the point where Tsugata truly broadens the scope of the discussion of anime booms beyond just TV anime and otaku culture. However, a few pages later, he conforms to the common notion that the third boom is actually spearheaded by *EVA* (2005: 185).

Tsugata's discussion of anime booms shows awareness of the problematic nature of the term, but it also indicates the way in which the concept of anime boom has been intertwined with the lineage of limited animation that finds its most influential manifestation in otaku culture (see Lamarre 2009). Even though Tsugata considers the whole field of Japanese animation, including *Astro Boy* and Miyazaki, he still cannot forego reinserting *EVA* into his discussion if only in a side note.

Uno's lectures at Kyoto Seika University (2018) foreground the importance of anime for otaku culture and the role of otaku as instigators of anime booms even more. Uno cites *Space Battleship Yamato*—instead of *Astro Boy*—as the source of the first anime boom, and he names *Mobile Suit Gundam* the catalyst for the second anime boom, which he explains is easy to miss, since this boom can be seen as a continuation of the one started by *Space Battleship Yamato*. Why then does he highlight *Gundam*? As already mentioned, seemingly objective economic arguments are often underpinned by far softer, for example, aesthetic and genre-related arguments. *Gundam* is central to Uno's argument because it was epoch-making from a genre perspective, as the origin point of Real Robot anime. In this regard, it makes sense to position it as the instigating event of an anime boom. But this positioning itself can also be seen as a telltale sign that epoch-making anime and anime boom are potentially co-constituted concepts. Thus, all the epoch-making anime with which I started this section are, of course, also responsible for anime booms, which renders my initial question of whether all epoch-making anime are also responsible for anime booms tautological.

EVA is positioned by Uno as the source of the third anime boom (2018). Although this might just be a coincidence and would require further substantiation, it is curious that *EVA* seems to occupy a set position in the sequence of anime booms. The common understanding that *EVA* sparked off the third anime boom is apparently so entrenched as to require a narration of anime booms that substantiates its occupation of this position.

Otaku Generations

The idea of otaku generations was introduced by Okada (1996: 37–39, 48–49). In his formulation, each generation has their point of entry or "home position" (a term borrowed from computer terminology) in otaku culture. For first-generation otaku, born in the decade 1955–64, these were special effects series, most notably *Ultraman* and *Kamen Rider*. Anime was the most important entry point for second-generation otaku, born between 1965 and 1974, especially *Space Battleship Yamato* and *Gundam*. The third generation of otaku—born in the Shōwa 50s (1975–84)—have models, *Gunpla* (*Gundam* plastic model kits by Bandai), and video games as their distinguishing generational imprints. And, finally, for the then still children, born from 1985 onwards, this "home position" is/will be video games. Okada is quick to point out that otaku of all generations irrespective of their "home positions" go on to find the related areas and start crossing over and enjoying a variety of formats and genres. Thus, although the entry point for each generation may differ, the consumed media and genres significantly overlap.

Okada's book contains drawn diagrams of typical room interiors for the first three generations of otaku highlighting the various artifacts of interest with small written captions. The third-generation room includes an *EVA* poster. Although the book was published in 1996, this picture anticipates later references to the third otaku generation that often rely on the generational impact of *EVA*.

For example, in *Otaku: Japan's Database Animals* (2009 [2001]), Azuma clearly builds on Okada's idea of otaku generations, but modifies it, regarding the exposure to *EVA* as emblematic of the third generation.

> The first generation centers on those who were born around 1960 and saw *Space Battleship Yamato* . . . and *Mobile Suit Gundam* . . . during their teen years. The second generation is made up of those who were born around 1970 and, during their teens, enjoyed the diversified and matured otaku culture produced by the preceding generation. The third generation consists of those who were born around 1980 and were junior high school students at the time of the *Neon Genesis Evangelion* boom. (Azuma 2009 [2001]: 6–7)

Maejima, who introduces himself as a model third-generation otaku, that is, a dedicated viewer of *EVA* in his teens, provides a version of the generational model that merges Azuma's variation into Okada's, with the first two generations mirroring the latter, but the third being fundamentally affected by *EVA*, voice actors and video games (2010: 52). In both Azuma's and Maejima's accounts, *EVA* clearly moved to the forefront of defining third-generation otaku.

Okada revisits his idea of otaku generations in *Otaku wa sude ni shinde iru* (Otaku are already dead) (2008: 71–81).[19] There, he provides a different angle on what constitutes the main difference between the generations and slightly alters their age range. According to his

19. This part of the book is also available in English translation (Okada 2015 [2008]).

new scheme, first-generation otaku grew up with the TV and were into anime, manga and SF, but did not stand out and just didn't conform to mainstream expectations without much fanfare or backlash. Second-generation otaku, on the other hand, had to bear the brunt of the moral panic following the Miyazaki serial murder case and were consequently most interested in theories about otaku; furthermore, they were the ones who experienced "*EVA* shock" when the series first aired. The third generation of otaku grew up in an environment already saturated with concurrently available media mixes, thus lacking the experience of the evolution of different contents in anime, manga and games. The various elements of a media mix are almost interchangeable for them, with little or no attention paid to the sequence of original, adaptations, etc. Thus, they pay more attention to the impact of a certain work on themselves than to information on creators. In sum, Okada now suggests a development from first-generation hermit hobbyists through the second generation for whom otaku identity posed a central problem to the pure consumers of the third generation.

Okada's new model shifts the defining position of *EVA* back to the second generation and makes *EVA* less central than in Azuma's and Maejima's take, while conforming to the ideas introduced by Azuma in relation to the consumption practices of the third generation, which are the subject of the next section on *sekaikei*. So far, we have seen how closely the concepts of anime boom and otaku generations are related to the significance of *EVA*. With *sekaikei*, the concept most heavily indebted to and animated by *EVA* comes into view.

EVA and *Sekaikei*

In many ways, this chapter could be read as a lengthy footnote to Maejima's book *Sekaikei to wa nani ka: Posuto eva no otakushi* (What Is Sekaikei? A Post-EVA Otaku History, 2010). *Sekaikei* is a genre label that emerged in the late 1990s and continued to enjoy prominence during the 2000s denoting a certain set of works mostly tied to otaku culture. The vagueness of its denotative meaning is precisely why Maejima embarks on the journey to uncover how the term came about and what it connotes.

Today, the most common use of *sekaikei* concerns works that revolve around (1) a (potentially) romantic relationship between a heroine cast in an active (often fighting) role and a passive male protagonist, whose relationship is (2) somehow tied to a much larger conflict that determines the fate of the world or at least that of the protagonists, (3) with major parts of the world or setting remaining unexplained or even unrepresented. This definition, however, is a later development that resulted in part from Azuma's work on the topic (Maejima 2010: 140–148). The fact that the meaning of the term went through such change is a testament to both Azuma's impact on the general discourse around otaku culture and the original vagueness of the term.

Tracing the term *sekaikei* back to its initial appearance, Maejima cites the website *Purunie's Bookmarks*, where it meant "*EVA*-like" in the sense of an intense first-person narrative (2010: 124–127). He is quick to point out that such an equation of *EVA*-ness is not exhaustive, since this aspect becomes prevalent only during the second half of the anime series. In fact, he argues, *EVA* can be seen as having two distinct halves that correspond to the past and future of otaku culture.

According to Maejima's analysis, the first half of *EVA* is first and foremost a well-made anime both regarding the story and the quality of the animation, and, second, it lays the groundwork for (or looking back from the ending, teases its audience with) a possibly huge and complex world setting and backstory, and, finally, it also references many earlier SF, *kaijū* and anime works (2010: 37–39). All this adds up to sensibilities that correspond to Okada's early definition of otaku, namely advanced visual refinedness—the opening at the time was especially pushed regarding the rate of cuts and the amount of visual information all crammed into it—and interest in tracing refe-rences and allusions (2010: 37–39). But the second half of the series departs from the expectations set up initially. First, both the story and the animation become highly experimental in the final two episodes. Second, the focus shifts from the world or setting to the inner self. Third, and most disconcerting of all, instead of affirming otaku dispo-sitions and practices, a self-reflexivity comes to the fore that borders on explicit criticism (see below).

The two halves further correspond to different generations, foci and genre/thematic elements. Whereas the first half exhibits sensibili-ties of the first and second generation of otaku, a focus on "narrative consumption" (Ōtsuka 2010 [1989]) and an interest in SF, *kaijū*, Super Robot and Real Robot works, the second half is geared toward the third generation, built around "database consumption" (Azuma 2009 [2001]) and a focus on the story; as such, it is a forerunner of *sekaikei* and *moe* moving to the fore of otaku culture (Maejima 2010).[20]

In this way, Maejima reiterates and further fleshes out Azuma's arguments. In line with moe becoming the main mode of engagement with otaku creations, and bishōjo characters becoming the emble-matic element of otaku works, a shift occurred in the meaning of otaku.[21] This change in focus coincides with the shift from "narra-tive consumption" to "database consumption" and a corresponding resurgence of interest in the story as opposed to the world or setting. Finally, *EVA* signals the end of anime being the central medium of otaku culture.

As mentioned earlier, anime had been central to the formation of otaku culture. Maejima explicitly references Okada's argument about the highly developed visual refinedness of otaku toward moving images and poses the question why then otaku shift their center of attention to still images (visual novels) and written text (in both light novels and visual novels). According to him, moe as an affective response and the turn toward the inner self in the second half of EVA

20. For a more detailed discussion, see Olga Kopylova's Chapter 8.

21. This is why Okada (2008) as well as other older otaku began to promote a return to the formerly used expression 'mania,' which denotes someone charac-terized by an intense preoccupation with a particular field of interest like anime, manga, special effects series, trains, etc.

both find a better terrain of expression in written text (2010: 62–64). In this way, moe and *sekaikei* stem from a common ground principle, namely, the focus on inner life and emotional states (2010: 112).

EVA appears almost prophetic in its unraveling of animation, heralding the shift toward script. The increasing density of intertitles in episodes 25 and 26 seems to signal the strains in depicting the complexity of inner emotional states. Maejima juxtaposes the otaku anime of the first half of the series with what he refers to as "otaku literature" (*otaku no bungaku*) regarding the second half. Elaborating on this idea helps us to understand the significance of *EVA* for otaku culture on yet another level.

EVA as "Otaku Literature"

In *How to Read Superhero Comics and Why* (2002), Geoff Klock offers a reading of US superhero comics from the second half of the 1980s into the early 2000s through the conceptual framework developed by literary critic Harold Bloom (and to a lesser extent Slavoj Žižek's reading of Lacan). Building on Bloom's ideas about the importance of wrestling with the literary tradition, Klock goes on to identify an important point of saturation and rupture in the US superhero comics tradition:

> Frank Miller's *Batman: The Dark Knight Returns* (1986) and Alan Moore's *Watchmen* (1986) are the first instances of a kind of literature I am going to identify as the revisionary superhero narrative: a superhero text that, in Harold Bloom's words, is a "strong misreading" of its poetic tradition, a comic book whose "meaning" is found in its relationship with another comic book. Although strong work existed in comics before this point—in the works of Will Eisner and Jack Kirby, for example—it is with these titles that, to quote critic Perry Meisel, referring to the blues tradition after swing, "a tradition now [exists] sufficiently dense with precedent to cause the kinds of self-consciousness and anxiety with which we [as students of literature] are familiar." (Klock 2002: 25)

In Klock's interpretation, these two seminal works effected a rupture in the history of US comics—not unlike the one *EVA* produced in relation to otaku culture—which can be seen as "the culmination of the silver age" of comics, and which at the same time is the "the birth of self-consciousness in the superhero narrative" (2002: 3). It would be futile to attempt a detailed Bloomian reading of *EVA* within the space of this chapter, but the impact of *EVA* on both the works that followed[22] and the critical discourse around otaku culture mirrors the interventions enacted by *Batman: The Dark Knight Returns* and *Watchmen*, and can be seen as a similar point of saturation. In this light, the break described by Maejima between the two halves of *EVA* can be re-evaluated as less of a break, but rather a realization of what had been unfolding all along. It is the combined picture of the two halves that represents the point of saturation where otaku culture becomes self-reflexive and wrestles with its own influences.

Just as *Batman: The Dark Knight Returns* and *Watchmen* explicitly thematize the parallels with fascism and the overt violence and sexual innuendo in superhero comics (the latter also tracing the pulp roots of the genre), so too does *EVA* offer a critical look at the sexual and power fantasies coursing through so much of otaku culture, while bringing to the fore the *kaijū* roots at the heart of robot anime.[23] *EVA* brings the Real Robot genre back to its Super Robot and *kaijū* origins by returning to the template of the adversaries (in this case, the Angels, who are also uncannily similar to their *kaijū* forefathers in their otherworldly and perplexing forms) descending on the protagonists' base as opposed to the action playing out in some outer space theater of war (Maejima 2010: 82). Nowhere is this connection made more explicit than in the revelation that the Eva units themselves are created from Angels. Thus, the historical development of a whole lineage of interrelated (sub)genres is captured in the allegory of the *kaijū* body hidden under the surface of the Real Robot exterior. What's more, the gradual unveiling of the connection between the Eva units

22. See Maejima (2010: 56–57).

23. "The giant *kaijū* monsters, heroes, and machines that rose to popularity with mid-1960s *tokusatsu* shows formed the 'soil' from which robot anime would bloom so vibrantly in the 1970s. Robot anime did not develop in a vacuum as an independent, isolated creation of the animation industry" (Hikawa 2013: 12).

24. See Uno (2018) for the significance of the occult in otaku culture; also Yoshimoto (2009).

25. The *DAICON III* opening animation from 1981 was a huge hit, and thanks to the business sense of Okada, its direct video sales to fans greatly contributed to raising the financial resources for the future ventures of the group that would eventually become GAINAX in 1984. Following *DAICON III*, they created various live-action short films, parodies of special effects series like *Ultraman* and *Go Rangers*, under the name DAICON FILM. In 1982, Okada and Yasuhiro Takeda formed the company GENERAL PRODUCTS to deal in custom hobby model kits, T-shirts and other fan-made merchandise. This was seen by many as an attempt to make money off the back of the SF fan culture and led to a certain level of backlash within the fandom (Yoshimoto 2009: 155).

26. See Uno's citing of Shūichirō Sarashina's summary that *sekaikei* is basically the version of *EVA* where Asuka does not reject Shinji (2018: 274).

27. I have not touched on the question of otaku sexuality, which is an import branch of the discussion around the term *otaku*. For more on the topic, see Saitō (2011 [2000]), Ōtsuka (2004), Morikawa (2003) and Galbraith (2015).

and the Angels corresponds to the way in which the two halves of *EVA*, as described by Maejima, are actually linked by the move from the visible exterior trappings to the underlying themes and veins of influence of otaku culture.

Considering that *EVA* was produced by GAINAX, we can see how it reiterates the deep engagement with otaku culture on a meta-level that had been the hallmark of this group of creators from the very beginning. *EVA* is a grand synthesis of the many components of otaku culture from *kaijū* to robot anime, SF and the occult[24] in the vein of the *DAICON III* and *IV* opening animations, and at the same time, it is a critical commentary on otaku culture itself, not unlike the self-reflexivity found in the 1991 part-anime, part-mockumentary *Otaku no video*, which relates the heroic tale of two otaku creating the ultimate otaku business empire (a commentary on GENERAL PRODUCTS[25] and potentially also GAINAX), interspersed with live mock footage of interviews with various types of otaku.

Even though on the surface the ending offered in the feature film *End of Evangelion* might seem to be moving away from the breakdown of animation and the complete focus on Shinji's inner life in the series' finale, the turn toward interiority is not loosened; it becomes even more brutal, in Maejima's view, with Asuka's rejection of Shinji as disgusting (2010: 45–47).[26] Instead of an "extremely otaku-oriented anime," it becomes "otaku literature," and the story of otaku maturing while fighting using a giant robot is replaced with the figure of an otaku masturbating to a bishōjo (2010: 46–47).[27]

Both sides of this last point are closely connected to Ōtsuka's reading of the significance of *EVA* in *"Otaku" no seishinshi: 1980nendairon* (A Mental History of "Otaku": About the 1980s) (2004). As already mentioned in the introduction, Ōtsuka was one of the vocal critics of the series following its original run. Less than 10 years later, he explicitly re-evaluates his stance and aligns his reading of the work to the landmark status it occupies within the Japanese critical discourse. His argument is premised on the lack of rites of passage in modern societies and he relates this to the way youth, and otaku especially, refuse to grow up and to conform to social expectations (2004: 401). In this, Ōtsuka finds a direct connection to "Astro Boy's dilemma" (*Atomu no meidai*). In his book of the same title (2003), Ōtsuka maintains that many developments in post-war manga have been propelled by the inherent tension between the cartoon body and a deeper 'literary' self bestowed on the drawn figure. One aspect of this tension is the inability of cartoon characters to age and grow, and while this is not specific to Japanese manga, Ōtsuka finds it interesting that this trait comes to the fore in a number of Tezuka's protagonists, who are trapped in bodies that are both metaphors for and direct causes of their arrested development, starting with Astro Boy's childlike robot body (2004: 402). He sees many of the defining works in post-war Japanese manga (and anime) as stories of failed attempts at a proper *bildungsroman* (or coming-of-age story) (2004: 402–404). This prevalence of the motif of arrested development in both characters and narratives in post-war Japanese manga, in Ōtsuka's view, is not unrelated to the position Japan occupied vis-à-vis the United States following World War II, most emblematically expressed in the way General Douglas MacArthur had likened the Japanese people to a 12-year-old boy. For Ōtsuka, *EVA* is a significant work because it is the ultimate form of addressing Astro Boy's dilemma. He likens the congratulatory scene at the very end of the anime series to a self-realization seminar[28] and points out that this is the only possible substitute for a rite of passage in late modernity as there are no communities left into which one could enter as an adult. Thus, the series' ending elides Astro Boy's dilemma—neither fulfilling the need for a rite of passage nor postponing it indefinitely—and at the same time, while commenting on it, renders it void (2004: 405–406).

Curiously enough, Ōtsuka reads *End of Evangelion* as an even more radical engagement with Astro Boy's dilemma. The movie's ending

28. Uno makes a direct connection between Ōtsuka's self-realization seminar interpretation and Aum Shinrikyō's focus on changing the self (2018: 259–260). On this note, the Human Instrumentality Project and Shinji's rejection of it could also be read as a critique of Aum Shinrikyō.

turns toward an unflinching affirmation of the unfulfilled *bildungs-roman*. As a result of Shinji trying to choke Asuka, the possibility of identifying with Shinji is negated, and thus the point of identification is moved to Asuka, where it is promptly denied once again (2004: 407–409). For Ōtsuka, this final scene, where the viewers are condemned from the viewpoint of the girl victims, is the first case in otaku culture to address the Miyazaki murders (2004: 410–411).

With its radical formulations of the impossibility of the *bildungs-roman*, *EVA* comes to symbolize the end point of postwar manga and anime history for Ōtsuka. The way it formulates this impossibility is precisely why it cannot be processed within otaku culture, why otaku enthusiastically (re)turn to *Gundam* as if *EVA* had never happened, and why so much of *EVA* merchandise is based on the alternate slice-of-life school setting version of the characters from the series finale (2004: 411).

Consequently, approaching *EVA* as the begining of "otaku literature," that is, a saturation point where otaku culture becomes self-reflexive, not only helps align Maejima's and Ōtsuka's arguments, but also underscores *EVA*'s unique position in the discourse around otaku culture. Even Ōtsuka finds a way to conform to it. A similar transformation can be seen in Uno's writing, but is almost immediately undone by himself, as I will proceed to demonstrate.

Imagining Alternative Versions of the Critical Discourse on Otaku Culture

In *Zero nendai no sōzōryoku* (The Imagination of the Millenial Generation), Uno discussed *EVA* from a point of view that attempts to encompass the development of Japanese popular culture in general, analyzing not just anime and manga, but also television dramas, movies and novels. Furthermore, he tried to create a counter-narrative to Azuma's interpretation, which had become dominant within the critical discourse. One of his key ideas revolved around the change of imagination from the hikikomorism/psychologism of the mid-1990s,[29] represented by *EVA*, to so-called determinationism[30] (*ketsudanshugi*). Hikikomorism was characterized by a fear of hurting others and, as a result, refraining from action (exemplified by Shinji's refusal to pilot his Eva unit), as well as a desire to be nevertheless accepted as is. Determinationism, on the other hand, entailed the realization that even refraining from action is a form of action, and there is no escaping the necessity to act, if one doesn't want to be left behind or killed. This threat is particularly pronounced in the first wave of determinationism works that Uno calls *battle royal* both as a gesture toward the Hobbesian struggle of all versus all, and as a reference to the book *Battle Royal* (1999). In his view, *sekaikei* works are just a belated and debased form of hikikomorism/psychologism. This devaluation of post-*EVA sekaikei* works can be seen as a denigration of the significance of *EVA*, even if the series itself is invoked as the single best representative of hikikomorism/psychologism, and it can arguably make sense from the vantage point of surveying Japanese popular culture in general, as opposed to focusing only on anime and otaku culture.

In comparison, in *Wakai dokusha no tame no sabukaruchāron kōgiroku* (Subculture Theory for Young Readers, Lecture Recordings), Uno concentrates on otaku culture only, and as such yields to the power of the discourse surrounding *EVA*, referring to it as the "final accounts" of the robot anime genre (2018: 195) and positioning it as the landmark work that it is assumed to be. This, however, is only a concession to the power of the critical discourse around *EVA*.

Uno offers a detailed reading of a large number of important robot anime in this book, pointing out at the very start that most of the famous robots after Astro Boy, like Tetsujin 28-gō (or Gigantor), Mazinger Z, Gundam and the Evangelions, are not intelligent beings, but tools (Tetsujin 28-gō is remote-controlled) or vehicles (2018: 140). All are created by a father figure, and after Astro Boy they are all devices of fulfilling the dream of young boys to become men (2018: 199).

29. Hikikomori is the Japanese term for people withdrawing to an extreme degree from face-to-face social interactions (e.g., shutting themselves in).

30. I am following Suan (2018: 233) with this translation, meant to convey the sense of being determined to make a choice and take action.

The robot as vehicle in particular enables the young boy to partake in adult affairs by donning a larger-than-life body. They are further products of industrial mass production (as opposed to the previous quasi-magical and unique super robots like Mazinger Z) starting with *Gundam*, which moves robot anime into full alignment with modern society and thus the problems of teenagers of the time (2018: 199).

Although the first *Gundam* series offered the vista of potential self-realization in a fictional war-torn world, the latter series in the franchise, like *Mobile Suit Zeta Gundam*, provide increasingly grim images of what this self-realization entails, such as going mad, or dying young without ever becoming men, as depicted in *Mobile Suit Gundam: Char's Counterattack* (Uno 2018: 200). In this way, the *Gundam* series signals the limits of the type of masculinity that can be manifested in a militarized industrial society (ibid.). Finally, in the 1990s, *EVA* goes on to destroy the robot anime lineage completely by finding its closure in a "self-realization seminar" (ibid.).

This all seems like a sound line of argument, but Uno himself in the very same book unhinges the underpinnings of his take on *EVA* as the "final accounts" of the robot anime genre. In a latter chapter, he describes in detail how the *Mobile Suit Victory Gundam* series, which already aired in 1993–94 and is thus a precursor to *EVA*, negates all possible positive identification with any of its adult male characters. According to his interpretation, it is an outright declaration of the impossibility of believing in the promise of post-war robot anime about growing up in a fictional space century by getting hold of a giant robot body (2018: 279). He even claims that *EVA* does not go as far as *Victory Gundam* in its demolition of the robot anime lineage. But if this is the case, then Uno's previous statement about *EVA*'s position in the lineage of robot anime does not hold; it turns out to be a concession to the consensus that has come to dominate the critical discourse.

As a quick thought experiment, let's imagine a version of Uno's book in which he does not go along with the common understanding of *EVA*. What if the story of otaku culture were told through a different perspective? One in which *EVA* is no more significant than, for example, *Gunbuster* (1988–89), the hit OVA series from GAINAX that foreshadowed certain elements of *EVA*. The level of detail with which Uno examines the different *Gundam* series stands in sharp contrast to the usual lack of attention afforded to *Gundam* in the publications considered so far. In fact, Uno's discussion of *Gundam* and the role of the creator/director behind the series, Yoshiyuki Tomino, as a pioneer of various themes for which *EVA* is celebrated, provide all the necessary ingredients for a well-formed alternative narrative of otaku culture. This narrative would see a lineage of otaku culture running from Osamu Tezuka in a more tightly coupled fashion[31] via his animation studio Mushi Production leading to the establishment of Sunrise Studio by former members of Mushi Pro in 1972. The emergence of Gunpla would figure as pivotal in the development of custom hobby model sales and the otaku market in general. Finally, in this version, the meaning of otaku culture would probably be more closely aligned with Okada's understanding of otaku as mania (first and second generation otaku), and moe-centered otaku culture might be regarded as a new formation altogether, similar to how otaku culture initially branched off from SF fandom. This potential for different versions of the narrative[32] evinces just how central *EVA* has been within the critical discourse around otaku culture.

Conclusion

EVA's position as an epoch-making anime is often taken for granted, as are the apparently objective arguments in relation to its economic impacts, but I hope to have demonstrated that there are layers upon layers of deeper connections between *EVA*'s position as a landmark work and the way in which otaku culture is addressed in the Japanese critical discourse.

31. See also Yoshimoto (2009).

32. Another possible axis of re-imagining this narrative would revolve around Studio Nue and the *Macross* series (I am grateful to Luca Bruno for pointing this out) and highlight the centrality of idol culture to otaku culture; which is surprisingly very much in line with Uno's assessment of the development of otaku culture following the 2011 Tōhoku earthquake and tsunami, where idol culture moved to the fore in his view. He even points out the uncanny parallels to *Macross* in AKB48's visits to the disaster struck areas (2018: 301–302).

First, *EVA* has left its imprint on a number of concepts and terms that are mobilized whenever its significance is at stake, namely anime booms, otaku generations and *sekaikei*. The series seems to occupy a set position in the enumeration of anime booms as spearheading the third boom. Otaku generations are often conceptualized in a way that one of the generations is defined by the *EVA* shock of the second half of the 1990s. And *sekaikei* is a testament to the power of *EVA*, providing a jumping-off point for both the proliferation and the interpretation of a whole group of related works.

Second, the weight of the consensus around *EVA*'s position forces even previously dissenting voices to incorporate its landmark status into their interpretations. For Ōtsuka, *EVA* has come to symbolize the ultimate engagement with Astro Boy's dilemma, and thus the culmination point of postwar Japanese manga and anime history. On the other hand, Uno, while also espousing *EVA* as the "final accounts" of the robot anime genre, actually provides the blueprint for an alternative retelling of the history of otaku culture, one that would revolve around *Gundam*, which again accentuates the force of the consensus around the centrality of *EVA* in otaku culture.

Third, the position enjoyed by *EVA* can be further substantiated by considering *EVA* as a saturation point where otaku culture becomes self-reflexive and, as Maejima writes, turns into "otaku literature." The impact of *EVA* on the anime industry and otaku culture mirrors the intervention effected by *Batman: The Dark Knight Returns* and *Watchmen* in American superhero comics, as described by Klock.

Furthermore, I also want to draw attention to the fact that, in the present chapter, I perpetuated the very same operations I have been analyzing. While highlighting the way in which *EVA*'s landmark position has been established in the Japanese critical discourse and has become seemingly inseparable from the manner in which otaku culture is understood, I too have added another layer of arguments that work toward further cementing and naturalizing its position as an epoch-making anime.

Finally, I hope that the present discussion has also managed to highlight just how strongly the development of anime and otaku culture are intertwined, from the significance of anime as the focal point for the crystallization of otaku culture to the impact that first generation otaku had on shaping anime criticism as well as the industry itself, with GAINAX being the premier example. Although my focus has been on the Japanese critical discourse around *EVA* and otaku culture, the points of connection between anime and otaku culture go far deeper than the web of concepts and arguments employed within the discussions around these two topics. Indeed, reading the works of Azuma (2009 [2001]), Maejima (2010), Morikawa (2003), Okada (1996), Ōtsuka (2004), Uno (2018) and Yoshimoto (2009) among others on otaku culture provides a wealth of insights into the way so many of the defining creators, major works, genres, formats and audiences of anime, as well as the production, dissemination and consumption practices around anime and its media coverage have all both impacted and have been influenced by otaku culture. Thus, one could say that no serious scholar of anime can neglect to engage with otaku culture, just as no comprehensive work on otaku culture can be written without the necessary foundations in research on anime.

References

Aida, M. (2015). The Construction of Discourses on Otaku: The History of Subcultures from 1983 to 2005 (translation by Thiam Huat Kam). In P. W. Galbraith, T. H. Kam and B.-O. Kamm (eds.), *Debating Otaku in Contemporary Japan: Historical Perspectives and New Horizons* (pp. 105–128). London: Bloomsbury.

Azuma, H. (2009). *Otaku: Japan's Database Animals*. Minneapolis, MN: University of Minnesota Press. (Introduction and translation by J. E. Abel and S. Kono)

Beaty, B. & Woo, B. (2016). *The Greatest Comic Book of All Time: Symbolic Capital and the Field of American Comic Books*. New York: Palgrave.

Becker, H. S. (1982). *Art Worlds*. London: University of California Press.

Bourdieu, P. (1996) [1992]. *The Rules of Art: Genesis and Structure of the Literary Field*. Stanford, CA: Stanford University Press.

Eng, L. (2012). Anime and Manga Fandom as Networked Culture. In M. Ito, D. Okabe and I. Tsuji (eds.), *Fandom Unbound: Otaku Culture in a Connected World* (pp. 158–178). London: Yale University Press.

Galbraith, P. W. (2015). "'Otaku' Research" and Anxiety about Failed Men. In P. W. Galbraith, T. H. Kam and B.-O. Kamm (eds.), *Debating Otaku in Contemporary Japan: Historical Perspectives and New Horizons* (pp. 21–34). London: Bloomsbury.

———, T. H. Kam and B.-O. Kamm (2015). Introduction: "Otaku" Research: Past, Present and Future. In ibid. (eds.), *Debating Otaku in Contemporary Japan: Historical Perspectives and New Horizons* (pp. 1–18). London: Bloomsbury.

Hikawa, R. (ed.) (2013). *Japanese Animation Guide: The History of Robot Anime*. Tokyo: Mori Building Company, Ltd. https://mediag .bunka.go.jp/projects/project/images/JapaneseAnimationGuide.pdf

Itō, G. (2005). *Tezuka izu deddo: Hirakareta manga hyōgenron e*. Tokyo: NTT Publishing.

Ito, M. (2012). Introduction. In M. Ito, D. Okabe and I. Tsuji (eds.), *Fandom Unbound: Otaku Culture in a Connected World* (pp. xi–xxxi). London: Yale University Press.

Kacsuk, Z. (2016a). From "Game-Like Realism" to the "Imagination Oriented Aesthetic": Reconsidering Bourdieu's Contribution to Fan Studies in the Light of Japanese Manga and Otaku Theory. *Kritika Kultura*, 26, 274–292.

———. (2016b). *From Geek to Otaku Culture and Back Again: The Role of Subcultural Clusters in the International Dissemination of Anime-Manga Culture as Seen through Hungarian Producers*. Doctoral dissertation. Kyoto Seika University.

Kamm, B.-O. (2015). Opening the Black Box of the 1989 Otaku Discourse. In P. W. Galbraith, T. H. Kam and B.-O. Kamm (eds.), *Debating Otaku in Contemporary Japan: Historical Perspectives and New Horizons* (pp. 51–70). London: Bloomsbury.

Kikuchi, S. (2015). The Transformation and the Diffusion of "Otaku" Stereotypes and the Establishment of "Akihabara" as a Place-Brand (translated by K. Nishimura and B.-O. Kamm). In P. W. Galbraith, T. H. Kam and B.-O. Kamm (eds.), *Debating Otaku in Contemporary Japan: Historical Perspectives and New Horizons* (pp. 147–161). London: Bloomsbury.

Klock, G. (2002). *How to Read Superhero Comics and Why*. New York: Continuum.

Korzybski, A. (1996) [1933]. *Science and Sanity: An Introduction to Non-Aristotelian Systems and General Semantics*. New York: The International Non-Aristotelian Library Publishing Company.

Lamarre, T. (2009). *The Anime Machine: A Media Theory of Animation*. Minneapolis, MN: University of Minnesota Press.

Leonard, S. (2005). Celebrating Two Decades of Unlawful Progress: Fan Distribution, Proselytization Commons, and the Explosive Growth of Japanese Animation. *UCLA Entertainment Law Review*, 12(2), 189–266.

Maejima, S. (2010). *Sekaikei to wa nani ka: Posuto EVA no otakushi*. Tokyo: Soft Bank Creative.

Malone, P. M. (2010). The Manga Publishing Scene in Europe. In T. Johnson-Woods (ed.), *Manga: An Anthology of Global and Cultural Perspectives* (pp. 315–331). New York: Continuum International.

Morikawa, K. (2003). *Shuto no tanjō: Moeru toshi Akihabara*. Tokyo: Gentosha.

———. (2012) [2003]. Otaku and the City: The Rebirth of Akihabara. In M. Ito, D. Okabe and I. Tsuji (eds.), *Fandom Unbound: Otaku Culture in a Connected World* (pp. 133–157). London: Yale University Press.

Okada, T. (1996). *Otakugaku nyūmon*. Tokyo: Ohta shuppan.

———. (2008). *Otaku wa sude ni shinde iru*. Tokyo: Shinchōsha.

———. (2015) [2008]. The Transition of Otaku and Otaku (translated by B.-O. Kamm, introduction P. W. Galbraith). In P. W. Galbraith, T. H. Kam and B.-O. Kamm (eds.), *Debating Otaku in Contemporary Japan: Historical Perspectives and New Horizons* (pp. 163–177). London: Bloomsbury.

Ōtsuka, E. (2003). *Atomu no meidai: Tezuka Osamu to sengo manga no shudai*. Tokyo: Tokuma shoten.

_____. (2004). *"Otaku" no seishinshi: 1980nendairon*. Tokyo: Kodansha.

_____. (2010) [1989]. World and Variation: The Reproduction and Consumption of Narrative. (Introduction and translated by M. Steinberg). *Mechademia*, 5, 99–116.

Pellitteri, M. (2010). *The Dragon and the Dazzle: Models, Strategies, and Identities of Japanese Imagination: A European Perspective*. Latina: Tunué.

Saitō, T. (2011) [2000]. *Beautiful Fighting Girl*). Minneapolis, MN: University of Minnesota Press. (Translated by J. K. Vincent and D. Lawson, commentary H. Azuma)

Suan, S. (2018). *Anime's Identity: Performativity and Media-Form in Our Moment of Globalization*. Doctoral dissertation. Kyoto Seika University.

Thornton, S. (1996) [1995]. *Club Cultures: Music, Media and Subcultural Capital*. London: Wesleyan University Press, published by University Press of New England.

Tsugata, N. (2005). *Animēshongaku no chikara*. Tokyo: Heibonsha.

Uno, T. (2008). *Zero nendai no sōzōryoku*. Tokyo: Hayakawa Shobō.

_____. (2018). *Wakai dokusha no tame no sabukaruchāron kōgiroku*. Tokyo: Asahi Shimbun Shuppan.

Williams, R. (1979) [1976]. *Keywords: A Vocabulary of Culture and Society*. Glasgow: Fontana/Croom Helm.

_____. (1980) [1961]. *The Long Revolution*. Harmondsworth: Penguin Books.

Yamanaka, T. (2015). Birth of "Otaku": Centering on Discourse Dynamics in *Manga Burikko* (translated by K. Nishimura). In P. W. Galbraith, T. H. Kam and B.-O. Kamm (eds.), *Debating Otaku in Contemporary Japan: Historical Perspectives and New Horizons* (pp. 35–50). London: Bloomsbury.

Yoshimoto, T. (2009). *Otaku no kigen*. Tokyo: NTT shuppan.

8. Manga Production, Anime Consumption

The *Neon Genesis Evangelion* Franchise and its Fandom

Olga Kopylova

The animated TV series *Neon Genesis Evangelion* (*EVA*) is one of the most iconic works in the history of anime. The primary reason is, of course, its cultural impact and commercial success: After its first broadcast in 1995–96, the show became a national phenomenon, whose appeal spread far beyond its initial intended audience. It revitalized the TV anime market and popularized new strategies of anime production, effectively reshaping the industry. Predictably, the series spawned a huge complex network of narrative texts in various media together with an endless flow of merchandise. A quarter of a century later, the *EVA* franchise is very much alive and growing with the latest animated movie—*Evangelion: 3.0+1.0 Thrice Upon a Time*—released on 8 March 2021.

The initial *EVA* boom also coincided with a surge of changes in the so-called otaku market, a site of production, dissemination and consumption of anime, manga, video games and other media (as well as goods and services) that share common aesthetics, narrative tropes and genres, and maintain strong material and conceptual links with one another. At the end of the 20th century, this complex environment generated by cultural industries and dedicated consumers reached another evolutionary stage marked by increasing visibility and popularity of previously marginal subculture in Japan and overseas; the emergence of new media forms such as visual novels;[1] and changes in prevalent modes of fan consumption. Particularly conspicuous was the resurgence of fictional characters as the main object and source of

1. Digital novels with interactive elements and multiple endings. Visual novels are by definition multimodal: images, voice acting and soundtrack are essential parts of the narrative, along with the verbal track.

How to cite this book chapter:
Kopylova, O. 2021. Manga Production, Anime Consumption: The *Neon Genesis Evangelion* Franchise and its Fandom. In: Santiago Iglesias, J. A. and Soler Baena, A. (Eds.). *Anime Studies: Media-Specific Approaches to Neon Genesis Evangelion*. Pp. 247–295 Stockholm: Stockholm University Press. DOI: https://doi.org/10.16993/bbp.i. License: CC-BY 4.0

a fannish affect commonly known as *moe*. The shift in fan interests and practices around 2000 was so radical that it made the anime producer and cultural critic Toshio Okada announce the death of 'authentic' otaku (cited in Maejima 2010: 107). These new developments have been addressed by various cultural critics and researchers, including Gō Itō (2005, with regard to manga), Marc Steinberg (2012, 2015, in relation to strategies of franchise development) and Satoshi Maejima (2010, discussing the concept of *sekai-kei* and its application).[2]

One of the earliest and most influential accounts of this transition belongs to cultural critic and publicist Hiroki Azuma. His landmark monograph *Otaku: Japan's Database Animals* (2009 [first edition 2001]) connects the new trends in the local otaku market and fan practices with the global ideological and cultural changes, namely, the arrival of postmodernity in the second half of the 20th century. While the book covers a number of important issues, from the nature of affect to the role of computer technologies in 21st-century fandom, it constantly comes back to production and consumption of narratives. Following French philosopher Jean-François Lyotard, Azuma associates the postmodern condition with the dissolution of 'grand narratives,' ideological or intellectual frameworks that once served to unite society, imbue socio-political activities with meaning and answer existential questions (2009: 26–29). On the level of subculture, this process is mirrored by the emergence, and decline, of another type of 'grand narratives' described by Azuma's fellow cultural critic Eiji Ōtsuka (2001a, 2001b). Ōtsuka uses the term 'grand narrative' to designate a collection of settings that constitutes a fictional world (or universe) spacious and elaborate enough to host an unlimited number of 'small narratives,' that is, discrete narrative works (the most obvious example would be the *Star Wars* universe conceived by George Lucas). According to Azuma, who combines both Lyotard's and Ōtsuka's definitions

2. Sekaikei: a variety of "works [of popular culture] that were created in the late 1990s–2000s under the influence of *EVA*; that incorporated the highly familiar elements and genre codes of otaku culture such as giant robots, beautiful girl-warriors, or private detectives; and depicted the interiority of young people (mostly male)" (Maejima 2010: 1351, trans. mine). See Chapter 7 by Zoltan Kacsuk for *EVA*'s impact on both otaku-related industries and critical thought.

of the term, during the transition from modernity to postmodernity the void left in place of the 'real "grand narratives"' is partially covered by fictional 'grand narratives.' Operating on the same principle, the latter invite fans to look for a single totality behind discrete stories and pieces of information. With the full arrival of the postmodern, the need for 'grand narratives' of any kind disappears altogether, and the nature of works and franchises that sustain otaku culture changes accordingly. For a new generation of fans, original and derivative works become indistinguishable; interest in consistent and expansive fictional universes gives way to spontaneous play with a 'database,' an intersubjectively constructed and shared virtual archive of units of meaning. Azuma famously calls this new mode of fan engagement 'database consumption.' As the market responds to the demand by database consumers, transmedial representations of carefully crafted fictional worlds (such as Yoshiyuki Tomino's *Gundam* anime) give way to stories, settings and characters fabricated straight out of the 'database.' The latter approach to storytelling and franchise development is exemplified by the *EVA* franchise, which according to Azuma has been produced and consumed as 'an aggregate of information without a narrative [that is, a shared storyworld], which all viewers could empathize with of their own accord and read up convenient narratives' (2009: 38).

Azuma's database model convincingly explains operating mechanisms of both Japanese otaku culture in particular and popular culture in general. At the same time, his postulates are definitely not set in stone. The novelty of the database concept and its allegedly lasting supremacy in Japanese popular culture have been challenged and sometimes dismissed (see Maejima 2010; Ōtsuka 2014; Uno 2008). From the perspective of Western Fan Studies, *Otaku: Japan's Database Animals* provides a number of valuable and astute insights into sensibilities, interests and activities of the global fan community, but is much less convincing when Azuma insists on the correspondence between certain franchise types or modes of fan engagement, and particular periods in socio-cultural history.

This chapter aims to question and rectify certain assumptions in Azuma's theory. The *EVA* franchise serves as a convenient vantage point for this inquiry. First, as a primary example drawn by Azuma himself, *EVA* allows to address his postulates directly. Second, *EVA* can be called one of the weak links in Azuma's chain of argument: he finds all symptoms of a truly postmodern condition in the franchise and its fandom, but does not provide a detailed overview for either. The following discussion attempts to fill this gap in two steps. The first half investigates the *EVA* franchise as a transmedial network of narrative texts with the focus on its content, structure and meaning. It is largely informed by Narratology and Literary Studies, employing instruments for storyworld analysis developed by Jan-Noël Thon and Marie-Laure Ryan, as well as Yūji Yokohama's overview of recurring themes in the *EVA* franchise. The second half of the discussion shifts to the level of consumption as it examines prevalent interests of *EVA* fans and corresponding modes of engagement. This part is informed first and foremost by Western research on fandom, in particular by Henry Jenkins' and Jason Mittell's case studies. This two-partite structure helps illuminate the valid points of Azuma's argument and develop a more comprehensive account of fan activities in Japan and overseas; it also demonstrates that database consumption, an allegedly new and pervasive mode of fan engagement, is in fact a long-lasting, global trend, and one among many others.

Azuma's Theory and the Significance of Franchise Structure

From the perspective of Fandom and Media Studies, Azuma's attempts to provide cultural and psychological background for the emergence of certain franchise types make for an interesting discussion point.

As briefly mentioned above, Azuma expects transmedial franchises launched at the early stages of postmodernity to share a certain set of traits, exemplified by *Gundam*. Such projects develop a single fictional world in a methodical manner, with contents distributed through multiple channels seamlessly blending into a consistent whole. By contrast, constituents of fully postmodern franchises like *EVA* are loosely connected by settings and/or characters only and lack any underlying cohesion. Azuma's claims can be disputed in several ways.

First, the history of entertainment franchises in Japan and overseas defies clear-cut linear succession of commercial, as well as storytelling, strategies. For example, the *Gundam*-like model Azuma associates with the 1980s was described by US media scholar Henry Jenkins as a novel phenomenon of 'transmedia storytelling' that emerged in the early 2000s (2006a: 93–130). Conversely, one of the first world-driven proto-franchises was launched in the United States at the dawn of the 20th century, when L. Frank Baum introduced to the public his *Land of Oz*. Soon afterwards, Edgar Rice Burroughs' *Tarzan of the Apes* (1912) gave start to a sprawling, haphazardly developed and contradictory character-driven franchise (see Freeman 2017 for more on both projects). One hundred years later, Ōtsuka classifies transmedial franchises of the otaku market of today into settings-, world- or character-based, with the addition of projects that employ time loop as a plot device to explain away contradictions (2014: 30). In other words, both world- and character-driven franchises appeared almost simultaneously, long before the arrival of postmodernity, and have lasted well into the 21st century.

Second, challenges of maintaining consistency and continuity in transmedial and transtextual networks are the recurring topic in English-language Fandom and Media Studies, but explanations are usually found in technical and legal circumstances of production (medium specificity, distribution of authorship, licensing practices, etc.). The bulk of related research reveals that such material obstacles and the resulting discrepancies in content are an intrinsic part of franchise development; projects famous for their world-building aspects, such as Lucas' *Star Wars*, just as often fail to establish direct correspondence between the entirety of officially released titles and a single cohesive fictional world (Thon 2015: 37–39; Wolf 2012: 270–271). As testified by fan paratexts, even the *Gundam* franchise has generated several alternate universes over the years (Falldog 2020). It seems, then, that even *relatively* cohesive franchises can be better understood through a conceptual triad offered by Narratology and Media Studies scholar Jan-Noël Thon. To quote Thon at length:

> Instead of assuming that transmedial entertainment franchises generally represent a "single world," then, such an approach allows for a systematic distinction between the local medium-specific storyworlds of single narrative works, the glocal but noncontradictory transmedial (or, in quite a few cases, merely transtextual) storyworlds that may be constructed out of local work-specific storyworlds, and the global and often quite contradictory transmedial storyworld compounds that may, for lack of a better term, be called transmedial universes. (2015: 31–32)

Following this logic, the fictional 'grand narrative' behind *Gundam* anime works is in fact just one of several 'glocal noncontradictory *transtextual* storyworlds' within the vast *transmedial* universe of *Gundam*. What about *EVA*?

It is an established fact that at least two *EVA* works share a storyworld: the TV anime and its direct sequel, the animated feature film *End of Evangelion* (*EoE*, 1997). Furthermore, Yoshiyuki Sadamoto's manga *Neon Genesis Evangelion* (*NGE*, 1993–2014) constitutes a close adaptation of the TV anime. As such, it creates a separate storyworld, which nevertheless provides "the satisfaction of expectations and the answering of questions raised over the course" of the TV series (Abbott 2005: 65–66). Is it possible that other such work constellations exist? Azuma claims that this is not the case, but does not provide any concrete evidence in support. As a matter of fact, he does not mention any narrative works in the franchise apart from the TV anime and animated movie *Neon Genesis Evangelion: Death & Rebirth* (1997). If Azuma's definition of the fictional 'grand narrative' allows for co-existence of several non-contradictory storyworlds within a franchise, then it seems reasonable to look closer into the structure of the *EVA* franchise and determine whether it is really that different from *Gundam*.

Since the primary focus of this study lies on (story)worlds, it borrows a set of analytical tools from Narratology. Thon's terminological apparatus introduced above is used throughout the chapter to describe the overall structure of the *EVA* network and its medium-specific segments. Thon also provides a useful classification of possible relations between work-specific storyworlds, namely a relation of redundancy or expansion (both of which allow to perceive works in question as representing one and the same storyworld), and a relation of modification (which inevitably results in two discrete, albeit overlapping, storyworlds). In order to create a systematic account of modified elements, this study relies on the breakdown of storyworld constituents by narrative and literary scholar Marie-Laure Ryan (2014). The analysis is supplemented by an overview of recurring themes and characters in *EVA* texts. As will be explained later, both themes and characters can determine the overall cohesion of a franchise and, furthermore, imbue it with underlying meaning separate from and independent of Ōtsuka's 'grand narrative.' With central question and methodological approach set down, the last step is to establish the object of analysis. This task requires a brief discussion of its own.

The Breakdown of the *EVA* Franchise: Preliminary Thoughts

As mentioned in the Introduction, the *EVA* franchise has thrived for 25 years. Unsurprisingly, it now contains a large amount of narrative texts in practically every medium associated with the otaku market: from manga series to visual novels to a parody audio drama to arcade games. Covering the entire agglomeration of works is far beyond the scope of this chapter, so a selective approach is required. It should be noted from the beginning that non-contradictory storyworlds that comprise transmedial universes often hold different hierarchical positions. Their status depends on many factors, including the media at play, the work count and authorial presence. For instance, Azuma can insist that *Gundam* sustains a single cohesive storyworld because the franchise is dominated by animated TV series. For almost half a century, TV anime, together with manga, has remained the key medium of the otaku market, only recently joined by video games, light novels and live-action movies (Iida 2012; Joo, Denison & Furukawa 2013). The sheer number of the series and Tomino's direct involvement in their production solidified the supreme position of a corresponding storyworld in the *Gundam* franchise.

The *EVA* franchise also unfolds around the TV anime, which establishes essential settings, introduces all key characters and, together with its direct sequel *EoE*, tells the complete story. Despite this initial similarity, duly noted by Azuma (2009: 36), the storyworld of this core work is clearly not expanded through a serialization in the same medium. What about transmedial development? Fan-generated paratexts often provide valuable insights into franchise topography. The notion of 'canon'[3] widely used by Western fans has been instrumental in describing relevance of work-specific storyworlds and their interrelationships (Fanlore 2020). While canonical status of franchise constituents is always in flux, it is only possible to debate canonicity of a work if its storyworld "could, at least in principle, be comprehended as a noncontradictory expansion of a previously represented storyworld" (Thon 2015: 37). It follows that if the TV anime forms the basis of the *EVA* canon, then any work included in the canon would be automatically assigned to the same storyworld, unless otherwise stated. "Shin-seiki's Tiers of Canonicity" published at the major fan site *The NGE Fan-Geeks Project* suggest the following outline of canonical and semi-canonical works:

1. The anime itself and its scripts and storyboards. The Director's Cuts are the final or official version and take precedence over the On Air version in the event of any theoretical contradiction.

3. Canon is a set of established truths shared by a particular fan community. It is comprised of facts culled from official texts and paratexts, but may also include statements by official producers and indubitable conclusions based on officially released information.

2. Statements made by the show's creators, principally Hideaki Anno.

3. Official supplemental sources such as theatrical programs, Newtype Filmbooks, and Cardass Cards.

4. The Manga (sic!), which is actually its own continuity. At best it can be used to support the anime when they are in explicit agreement; it should never be used to contradict the anime.

5. Statements made by those responsible for adapting Evangelion (sic!) for release outside of Japan. In the English speaking world this would be representatives of A.D. Vision or Manga Entertainment. (Shin-seiki 2020)

It goes without saying that fans outside of the *NGE Fan-Geek* community might have other views on how the *EVA* canon works. Still, this particular paratext seems to support Azuma's conclusion that there is no overarching 'grand narrative' behind the *EVA* franchise. On the other hand, "Tiers of Canonicity" most likely evaluate the entirety of *EVA* works vis-à-vis anime and anime alone, and therefore it is conceivable that a 'grand narrative' on a smaller scale might still exist on the periphery of this transmedial network. After all, it is not unusual for large-scale transmedial franchises to "establish two clearly distinct storyworlds via a high-profile modifying adaptation while still aiming at a further expansion of each of these storyworlds" (Thon 2015: 35). In the otaku market, such expansion is usually carried out via manga, video games or light novels. While official *EVA* producers have generally disregarded purely textual format, the franchise boasts a wide range of narrative-based games, which both adapt and expand on the anime. The preferred structure of the *EVA* games, however, undermines their world-building capacity: most of them involve multiple possible scenarios, as well as random events, generating countless incompatible storyworlds.[4] A game like *Neon Genesis Evangelion 2* is acknowledged as a *source* of valuable canonical information (Shin-seiki 2020), rather than a self-standing alternative to the

4. See Chapter 9 by Selen Çalık Bedir.

anime series. Ultimately, such alternative is found in manga: Authored by the character designer of the first TV series and the subsequent films, Sadamoto's *NGE* is said to generate 'its own continuity,' with a storyworld distinct from, albeit largely overlapping with, the storyworld of the TV anime and *EoE*.

There are currently six officially released *EVA* manga titles apart from *NGE*. If at least some of them established relations of redundancy or expansion with Sadomoto's series as well as works in media other than anime, they could form a new transtextual or transmedial storyworld, that is, a fictional 'grand narrative.' The following sections examine all seven works, including *NGE*, in order to confirm or disprove this proposition.

Part I. *EVA* Manga: Monochrome Drawings, Kaleidoscopic Narratives

The Storyworlds of *EVA* Manga

In recent otaku-oriented franchises, manga series often succeeded successful releases in some other medium (see, e.g., the novel-based *Higurashi When They Cry*, the light novel-based *Full Metal Panic!* and the anime-based *Psycho-Pass*). In each case, the manga series have maintained strong ties to the other franchise constituents. *EVA* is similar on the level of franchise chronology: six officially released manga titles followed either the first anime or animated movies *Rebuild of Evangelion* (2007–present), with *NGE* being the only exception (it is worth mentioning that even though Sadamoto's manga was launched before the TV series, it had been conceived as an adaptation and ended up running for 20 years, long after *EVA* had come to an end). But, contrary to the cases above, the official *EVA* manga have developed in a disorganized manner. The resulting discord is already evident in generic and tonal shifts (see Table 8.1): In addition to the serious, action- and mystery-oriented *NGE*, the manga sector includes a five-volume parody bordering on satire (*The Legend of Piko Piko*

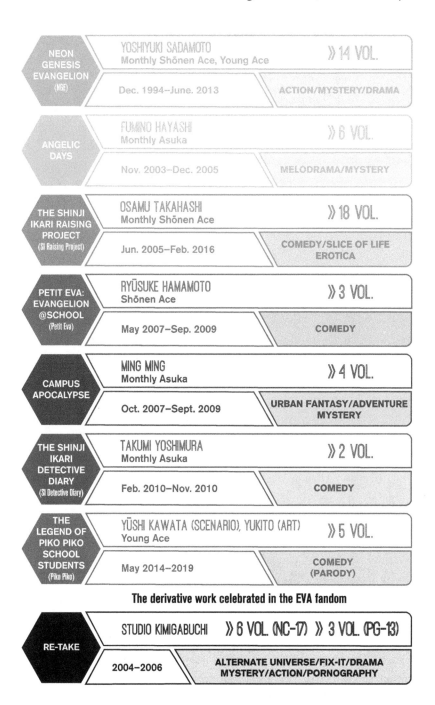

Table 8.1. List of the official *EVA* manga series in chronological order. License: CC BY 4.0.

Middle School Students), a set of four-panel gag comic strips (*Petit Eva: Evangelion@School*) and four titles that cover genres from drama to erotica to urban fantasy (*The Shinji Ikari Raising Project*, *The Shinji Ikari Detective Diary*,[5] *Angelic Days* and *Campus Apocalypse*). With that said, the proliferation of genres by itself (with the exception of parody) should not preclude the existence of a single storyworld behind a range of works. Therefore, this section offers a comparative analysis of storyworld elements as delineated by Ryan (2014: 34–37) in order to define relations between the seven manga titles and the core *EVA* works (i.e., the TV anime and *EoE*) in a systematic fashion (see Table 8.2).

To start with physical and mental events that constitute the fabula of each narrative and organize its storyworld, all of the manga titles do away with the elaborate apocalyptic tale of the anime series and focus instead on school comedy, gags and romantic relationships (the only exception being *Campus Apocalypse*, which brings together supernatural battles, Armageddon and a sinister conspiracy, but still opts for an entirely new 'urban fantasy' setting). The topography, natural laws and props of the respective storyworlds change accordingly.

The easiest to trace are transformations of the Angels and Evas, the iconic entities of the *EVA* universe. In most cases, the Angels maintain their anime design—one of the few recurring motifs across distinct manga titles—but their nature diverges greatly. In *SI Raising Project*, the Angels are no more than manifestations of computer viruses in virtual reality, although from time to time taking familiar shapes. In *Campus Apocalypse*, the Angels are specter-like beings originating from the Life-Tree of Yggdrasil. As they can survive in the outer world only by possessing people, most of them take the form of beautiful men and women (and an occasional cat). In *Angelic Days*, the nature, origin or goal of the Angels remain unexplained (while battles serve mostly to intensify romantic relationships), but their design is again borrowed from the core works. In *Piko Piko*, Angels seem to be the product of collective nostalgia: supernatural creatures who strive to

5. The manga *The Shinji Ikari Detective Diary* (abbr. *SI Detective Diary*) has nothing to do with the game *Detective Evangelion* (Broccoli 2007). A two-chapter manga adaptation of the game by Seijūrō Mizu was serialized in *Monthly Shōnen Ace* (2006–07), but never published in book format, which limits its availability.

Table 8.2. Comparison of storyworld components (after Ryan 2014) in the *EVA* manga vs. the TV anime. License: CC BY 4.0.

	Characters	Species, objects and social institutions	Setting (particular locales & topography)	Natural laws	Social rules & values	Events	Mental events
NEON GENESIS EVANGELION (NGE)	I	I	I	I	I	I	I
ANGELIC DAYS	O	O	O	R	O	R	O
THE SHINJI IKARI RAISING PROJECT (SI Raising Project)	L	R	L	R	R	R	O
PETIT EVA: EVANGELION @SCHOOL (Petit Eva)	R	R	R	R	R	R	R
CAMPUS APOCALYPSE	O	R	R	R	O	R	R
THE SHINJI IKARI DETECTIVE DIARY (SI Detective Diary)	L	R	R	R	R	R	O
THE LEGEND OF PIKO PIKO SCHOOL STUDENTS (Piko Piko)	R	O	R	R	R	R	R

I: ALMOST IDENTICAL   **O: OVERLAPPING TO SOME EXTENT**   **L: LOOSE SEMBLANCE**   **R: RADICAL DEPARTURE**

reverse the flow of time. *SI Detective Diary* does not feature Angels at all, and the Evas are radically transformed, presented as humanoid servants magically summoned from jewellery (an earring, a bracelet, etc.). The only Eva that visually evokes its prototype is Asuka's Dos (Span. two). In *Campus Apocalypse*, Eva is a person's will manifest in the form of a weapon (Asuka's Eva is a whip, Rei's the Spear of Longinus, etc.). In *SI Raising Project*, there are no Evas altogether, only entry plugs used to access the virtual reality. *Piko Piko* and *Angelic Days* both utilize standard *mecha*-like Evas, but *Piko Piko* regularly alters their appearance and function comically. If central entities like Angels and Evas are usually incorporated into the manga storyworlds (albeit in a different form), the localities and props are often erased completely. For instance, GeoFront appears only in *Angelic Days*, while *Campus Apocalypse* and *Piko Piko* feature the NERV Academy and National Middle School of Defence NERV as their primary stage. In *SI Raising Project*, the organization itself is called Artificial Evolution Lab and resides in an ordinary building. In fact, Tokyo-3 transforms into a regular city in all titles where it is mentioned.

Social norms and values get increasingly modified the closer the principal mode approaches parody. At the same time, they are inevitably entwined with characterization. The most obvious example is *Piko Piko*, which, in essence, presents a five-volume chronicle of nonsensical, often hilarious abuse that a couple of reasonable, but disgruntled teenagers (Asuka and Shinji) suffer at the hands of irresponsible and infantile adults (including Misato, Ritsuko, Gendō Ikari and Kaji). Far from protecting the Earth, the primary goal of adults in the *Piko Piko* series is to have as much fun as possible at the expense of their students. The concerns of the children across the titles are also far from stable: Frantic self-searching, traumas and quest for self-acceptance are confined to *NGE*, while other manga series foreground romantic vicissitudes (*SI Raising Project*, *Angelic Days*) or momentary struggles in the face of local crises (*Campus Apocalypse, SI Detective Diary*).

To summarize, all manga titles maintain a relation of modification, rather than expansion or redundancy, with the core *EVA* works. They also all form distinct mutually incongruous storyworlds. This undeniable lack of cohesion within the manga segment of the franchise does not mean, however, that the manga titles in question cannot contribute to the transmedial and transtextual storyworld formation in other ways. After all, the place a narrative takes in a "transmedia [sic] network" (Ruppel 2012) and, one may add, its relevance for the hypothetical 'grand narrative' is determined by several parameters. One is the connections it holds with other franchise constituents, another is its self-sufficiency and completeness. For example, *NGE*, which also adapts the storyworld of the TV anime and *EoE* through modification, manages to supplement and enrich its source, making additions acknowledged by at least some fans as (semi-)canonical. As such, it can potentially contribute to the formation of the 'grand narrative.' Additionally, *NGE* forms a self-standing storyworld, which can be expanded to create a separate canon. It remains to be seen if the same applies to other manga titles.

EVA Manga as Parts of the Transmedial Network

Regarding relations between the manga and works in other media, *SI Raising Project* and *Angelic Days* adapt computer games, *The Shinji Ikari Raising Project* and *Girlfriend of Steel 2nd* respectively. Incidentally, both games employ multiple choice as their main mechanics: Branching dialogues and scenes allow the player to reinforce and break various relationships, learn more about the characters and arrive at different (not always happy) endings. In other words, in terms of gameplay and pleasures offered, both games approximate visual novels. The challenge of adopting a visual novel to a manga is obvious: The game may offer the player half a dozen storylines leading to romance with six different characters (as is the set-up in *SI Raising Project*). Manga adaptations of games have to choose between the bigger story and the individual romance, and thereby they face the risk of alienating a number of their potential readers. In addition, the first game defies a straightforward adaptation, since it introduces several 'parallel worlds' and at one point even addresses its own structure (see Yokohama 2006: 57–58). A manga adaptation of such a multith-read, multilevel narrative could actually try to recreate the metaleptic[6] game on its own terms. And yet, both adaptations chose simplification as their primary strategy. Osamu Takahashi, the artist and writer in charge of *SI Raising Project*, selected the happiest of the game's parallel worlds, the so-called "Campus Ark," limited the range of the protagonist's recurring love interests to three without finalizing any of the potential love stories, and added a moderate amount of heavily altered battles to what otherwise reads as a semi-erotic school comedy. Fumino Hayashi in *Angelic Days*, on the other hand, chose to develop only the romantic Shinji-Asuka plotline and supplement the adapted material with two volumes of original content. In summary, *SI Raising Project* and *Angelic Days* heavily edit their source works, from settings to plotlines to characterization, until it becomes impossible to see them as extensions of the game storyworlds. To reiterate, the same applies to their relations with the core works of the *EVA* franchise.

Despite their lineage as adaptations 'once removed,' both *SI Raising Project* and *Angelic Days* may pass as stand-alone texts. In contradistinction, parodical works like *Piko Piko* and *Petit Eva: Evangelion@ School* cannot be consumed outside of the *EVA* franchise. They require familiarity with the TV anime, *NGE* or *Rebuild of Evangelion*: unless the reader recognizes lore-related facts, patterns of character behavior, trademark phrases, etc., the humour of these parodies falls flat. *SI Detective Diary* can be described in similar terms: its plot and characters are so underdeveloped that it is impossible to process the story

6. Metalepsis happens whenever "the author enters or addresses the fictional world he or she created, and when characters leave their fictional world or address their author and their readers" (Kukkonen 2011: 1). Furthermore, the metalepsis is likely to occur whenever "characters become readers and authors within their own fictional world and produce a secondary fictional world" (ibid.: 8), as happens with Shinji in *SI Raising Project*.

without referencing the 'database' of *EVA*-related information or its primary sources (the core works). All three, however, can be removed from the transmedial network without affecting its legibility. *Campus Apocalypse* is a curious case: despite its equally tenuous connection to the canonical storyworld, it presents an unexpected opportunity to bind all narratives into one continuity through the concept of multiple realities. Despite the bold attempt to validate digressions and contradictions between work-specific storyworlds, *Campus Apocalypse* has not been included in "Shin-seiki's Tiers of Canonicity." All in all, it remains an interesting rift on the *EVA* 'database,' but too much of a digression itself to become an integral part of the franchise.

The subordinate status of the manga titles is best illustrated by gaps, hanging plotlines and contradictions that riddle their narratives. Even the romantic comedy *SI Raising Project* accumulated a remarkable amount of blanks while running: What has the Artificial Evolution Lab been preparing for throughout 18 volumes? What happened to Kaworu, who simply stopped appearing in the middle of the series? Who is Mana Kirishima, beyond a new romantic interest and comic relief? What is the role of SEELE in this continuity? And so on. Some of these questions may be answered by the game, but its material is adopted too selectively (in other words, the game might answer who Kirishima is, but leave obscure all other mysteries and blanks). The same applies to more rounded works like *Campus Apocalypse*, which carefully closes its central plotlines, but leaves much of its idiosyncratic existents and natural laws obscure. Various Angels (in human form) are shown in ominous manner only to vanish quickly. The very mechanism of Kaworu's ultimate sacrifice remains unclear. The fate of Asuka's parents serves as an important plot device, but readers never learn what exactly happened.

This proliferation of blanks resembles the strategy of transmedia storytelling that media scholar Geoffrey Long calls negative capability: Empty spaces are deliberately worked into the narrative in order to spark the audiences' curiosity and imagination (2007: 53, 59), to establish possible vectors for future franchise extensions and, ultimately, to open up the characters and the storyworld for further development (ibid.: 133, 167). Despite formal similarities, however, most of the lacunas discussed here do not have the same functionality. Since each manga work is created as an isolated 'alternate universe' with little to no connection with the main continuity, there is no hope that those blanks will be filled by any existing franchise constituent (of course, a possibility remains that at least some of these texts will be expanded or supplemented in the future). A more productive explanation of gaps and inconsistencies may be gained in view of Marie-Laure Ryan's concept of generic landscapes. As one of the principles that guide the mental reconstruction of textual universes, generic landscapes "predict what will be shown and hidden in a certain type of text, what will be given or denied significance" (1991: 57), and these landscapes are assembled from "the themes and objects characteristic of a certain corpus" (ibid.: 55). One only needs to replace 'genre' with 'franchise' or 'transmedial universe' to see the familiar database principle at work. However, contrary to the 'database,' generic landscapes have the power to determine the relevance of various pieces of information and can thus easily overrun the need for a proper diegetic explanation. Thus, in every setting, SEELE would appear at regular intervals and leave sinister hints; Misato would be the main person in charge of Shinji and his friends and a middle-school teacher, regardless or her actual abilities or qualifications; Gendō Ikari would always be pointedly absent from his son's life, and so on. All of these narrative pieces and characterizations stir the sense of recognition in a regular *EVA* consumer and are accepted more or less smoothly as parts of *EVA*'s generic landscape. *EVA* literacy presumes both awareness of such recurring formulas and high tolerance toward loose ends. This, however, means that most of the narratives can be successfully parsed only by readers already familiar with the core of the network (see Table 8.3).

Table 8.3. Transmedial network of *EVA* narratives (partial) and its topology. License: CC BY 4.0.

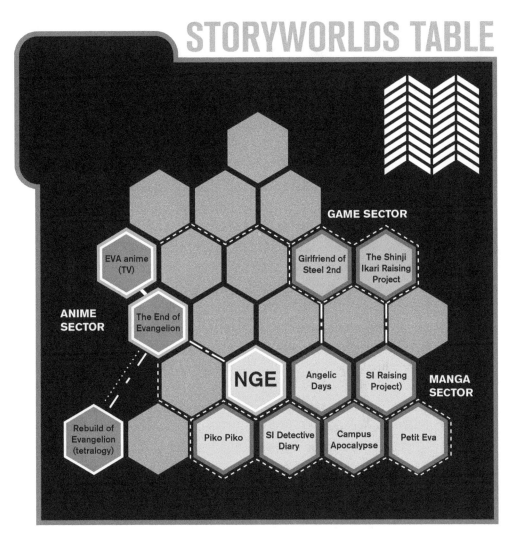

STORYWORLDS TABLE

GAME SECTOR

EVA anime (TV)

Girlfriend of Steel 2nd

The Shinji Ikari Raising Project

ANIME SECTOR

The End of Evangelion

NGE

Angelic Days

SI Raising Project)

MANGA SECTOR

Rebuild of Evangelion (tetralogy)

Piko Piko

SI Detective Diary

Campus Apocalypse

Petit Eva

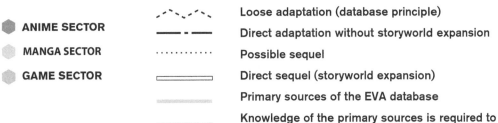

- **ANIME SECTOR**
- **MANGA SECTOR**
- **GAME SECTOR**

Loose adaptation (database principle)

Direct adaptation without storyworld expansion

Possible sequel

Direct sequel (storyworld expansion)

Primary sources of the EVA database

Knowledge of the primary sources is required to adequately understand and interpret the work

As demonstrated above, most of the manga titles utilize plotlines, settings, narrative conventions and characters of the *EVA* franchise (i.e., its 'database') without making any new contributions. To paraphrase, all of them with the exception of *NGE* hold a subsidiary position vis-à-vis the core of the franchise, depending on it in a unidirectional fashion. Even transmedial adaptations included in the list do not lead to the formation of bigger narrative clusters or chains of meaning traversing and connecting multiple texts. In short, the manga sector of the *EVA* network can be visualized as a conglomeration of disconnected texts that form distinct and contradictory storyworlds and share a 'database' instead of a 'grand narrative.'

But it still might be too early to accept Azuma's claims, since they can be challenged from a different angle. In his chronology of changes in thought, commercial production and fannish consumption, Azuma juxtaposes narrative works of the modern period, which project the "real 'grand narratives'"; franchises of the transitional period that replace ideology by elaborate and consistent worlds; and postmodern franchises that supposedly discard either. However, it is entirely conceivable that values, messages or deeper meanings can be integrated into a franchise regardless of its structure. It goes without saying that even design features, characters/creatures, or settings disentangled from a single fictional world have significant cohesive power and thus function as core elements in transmedial universes (Heinze 2015: 88). Furthermore, consistent characterization shapes the intersubjective interpretation of the entire group of texts involved; it may engender a sort of message, as well as thematic unity. Likewise, consecutive adaptations may generate unequivocally interconnected 'families' of texts facilitating and sustaining certain readings, even when the story transforms with each iteration.[7] Azuma's focus on fictional 'grand narratives' as a bridge between modernity and postmodernity makes him disregard all other sources of cohesion or potential for delivering messages in transmedial franchises. The following two sections will

7. See Kopylova (2016) for an extended analysis of such transmedial project.

therefore extend the line of inquiry to examine characters and themes across the *EVA* manga titles.

Characterization in the *EVA* Manga

If characterization is to serve as a vehicle for ideas and messages, it must avoid contradictions and breaches in internal logic. This does not mean, however, that a character should stay fixed throughout a range of narratives: such strategy would work only for 'flat' characters (Forster 1955: 65–82) defined by a single trait or quality. 'Rounded' characters (ibid.) akin to the *EVA* protagonists must react to changing circumstances, but in a consistent and convincing manner. Is this rule maintained in the *EVA* manga?

In *Piko Piko*, Asuka and Shinji behave remarkably out of character (joining forces to beat up Gendō Ikari at the end of the second chapter), but this happens in outlandish settings which amuse rather than surprise. More conspicuous is the tendency in other manga texts to reproduce Shinji and Asuka as recognizable types regardless of their current background. As mentioned above, all manga series, with the exception of *NGE* and *Campus Apocalypse*, transpose the characters into much safer, happier environments and occupy them with trivial problems. For instance, in both *Angelic Days* and *SI Raising Project* Asuka's parents (or her single mother, in the latter case), as well as Shinji's mother Yui, are alive and well. It seems that both children have been raised in happy families. Nevertheless, it is in these two titles that Shinji is at his most vulnerable and indecisive, while Asuka is as fierce, petulant and asocial as ever. *Detective Diary* follows suit, although in this case both Shinji's and Asuka's family circumstances remain unknown. In the absence of any diegetic explanation, such quirks can only be taken as an intrinsic part of the characters' personalities. Needless to say, this is contrary to the initial characterization of Asuka and Shinji in the core *EVA* works, where their drawbacks and weaknesses are firmly grounded in childhood traumas. Prevailing here is the mode of database consumption described by Azuma, where a character is broken down into elements that elicit strong affective reactions in the consumer, and that are then recorded into the database and mechanically reproduced regardless of any particular narrative setting (2009: 42–52). Characters "are imagined not as humans who live one life recounted in one story, but rather as bundles of latent behavioural patterns that can reveal themselves under varying circumstances in various stories" (Azuma 2007: 46; transl. mine).

The other two recurring children, Kaworu and Rei, go through a chain of metamorphoses, sometimes taking the form of character development within the confines of an isolated story (Rei in *Angelic Days*; both in *Campus Apocalypse*). But even basic character settings change noticeably between works. Thus, *Piko Piko* features a coldly aloof, egotistical Rei and an eccentric, but affable Kaworu. In *Angelic Days*, the two are much more down-to-earth, active and involved. In *Campus Apocalypse*, both are forced to negotiate social awkwardness and lack of confidence. It is possible to view such transformations as rearrangements of database elements, but Azuma's theory does not explain at which point the combination associated with a particular existent loses recognizability and effectively turns into another character. Cultural critic Tsunehiro Uno argues that characters can never break free from their originating narratives (2008: 522–546). In Uno's opinion, a character exists only if recognized, acknowledged and shared by a certain community. Each new act of creative consumption entails the reconfirmation of the character and, consequently, of the narrative shared by the community. This act of bonding around a character and its originating narrative, conversely, strengthens the ties within said community. Uno's argument helps to explain how fans can enjoy even radically transformed characters and still keep to the established image, namely, by consuming the gap between the widely shared character image and its novel interpretation. But this leaves unanswered why particular characters remain stable while others change incessantly. One possible explanation is that both endlessly reproduced in-built characteristics (in the cases of Asuka and Shinji) and radical instability of characterization (in the cases of Kaworu[8] and Rei) are parts of *EVA*'s generic landscape. Characterization in the manga sector of the franchise thus functions as an effective means to trigger recognition or generate a sense of play, but it is less expedient in carrying coherent meanings across works.

Thematically Oriented Threads in the *EVA* Manga and the *EVA* Franchise

Even an incohesive group of texts aggregated through a chain of loose adaptations may still be bound by a set of recurring themes and motifs. Such a set is indeed found in both core and peripheral works of the *EVA* franchise. Literary scholar Yūji Yokohama (2006) identifies four major themes in the TV anime, *EoE* and the game *The Shinji Ikari Raising Project*: 'battle' (*sentō*), 'everyday life' (*nichijō*); 'spy drama' (*supai-geki*) and 'Self-Other recognition' (*jita ninshiki*). The template provided by Yokohama is useful for the current analysis, but his wording is rather confusing. 'Everyday life' might be self-evident (involving, for instance, all comical scenes at Misato's place), but 'spy drama' is the term associated with a specific subgenre that has little to do with *EVA*. In Yokohama's discussion, it refers to the entire set of mysteries, secrets and hints strewn across the narrative, as well as the Human Instrumentality Project plotline, which does not involve elaborate espionage. In order to avoid terminological conundrum, then, Yokohama's four terms are modified to 'fighting,' 'everyday life,' 'mystery' and 'Self-Other recognition' (SOR). As demonstrated by Yokohama, these four themes permeate the *EVA* works under discussion in the form of recurring threads. Their interplay directly influences narrative outcomes, as during the final stages of the game (2006: 57–59), or generates polysemic nodes within the narrative.

8. Notably, Kaworu undergoes significant changes even in the core works. One possible line of inquiry into derivative *EVA* works would be to see if Japanese fans had always (re-)constructed Kaworu and Rei as fundamentally unstable entities.

	Chapters	Chapter-thematically oriented sequence correspondence		

NEON GENESIS EVANGELION (NGE)

97

F	37	
EL	16	'SOR' and 'mystery' dominate;
SOR	56	high proportion of 'fighting'
M	50	

ANGELIC DAYS

27

F	2	
R	24	
EL	9	'Relationships'
SOR	8	and 'mystery' dominate
M	15	

THE SHINJI IKARI RAISING PROJECT (SI Raising Project)

120

F	14	
R	56	'Everyday life'
EL	106	and 'relationships' dominate
M	32	

CAMPUS APOCALYPSE

22

F	9	
R	7	
EL	4	'Fighting'
SOR	8	and 'mystery' dominate
M	18	

THE SHINJI IKARI DETECTIVE DIARY (SI Detective Diary)

9

F	4	
R	7	'Relationships'
EL	5	dominate
M	4	

THE LEGEND OF PIKO PIKO SCHOOL STUDENTS (Piko Piko)

66

F	17	
EL	54	'Everyday life'
M	12	dominates

F 》 'fighting' 》 Battles with the Angels; other serious altercations (school fights excluded)
EL 》 'everyday life' 》 School life; daily routine at Misato's place; outdoor activities; festivities
M 》 'mystery' 》 Lore talk; physics and metaphysics of the world explained, Kaworu's insinuations; Seele appearances; data on weapons/creatures; etc
SOR 》 'Self-Other recognition' 》 Soul-searching; identity crises; intergenerational conflicts
R 》 'relationships' 》 Romance; emotional bonding

The same set of thematic threads can be traced across the six manga titles, with the addition of a fifth type, namely, 'relationships' (see Table 8.4). In the TV anime and *NGE*, relationships are part of SOR, but the latter category far exceeds problems in the relationship-building or romance prevalent in the *EVA* manga. SOR is tied to existential crisis, as vividly expressed by Shinji's frantic screaming in *EoE*: "Don't leave me alone! Don't abandon me! Please don't kill me!" SOR becomes quite literally a question of life and death not only for the protagonist, but also for the entire humanity. In contrast, most of the manga titles, with the exception of *Campus Apocalypse* and, to a lesser extent, *Angelic Days*, assume a lighter attitude.

Furthermore, there is an obvious division between the manga works in terms of leading themes: Prevailing in *NGE* is SOR, closely followed by mystery. Mystery is also the key theme in *Campus Apocalypse*, which fits many new terms, concepts, actors and events into its four volumes. *Angelic Days*, *SI Detective Diary* and *SI Raising Project* downplay the fighting and foreground relationships. But *SI Raising Project*'s real emphasis lies on everyday life (although this is difficult to evaluate, because at times it is not easy to distinguish between meaningful interpersonal interactions and gratuitous fan service, that is, details and scenes irrelevant to the story or character development and added with the sole objective of pleasing fans).[9] *Piko Piko* also allots most of its space to everyday life, but eschews relationships altogether.

To summarize, the thematic threads of the core narrative are not shared equally by all manga series. Moreover, the key thread related to SOR is adopted only in a couple of titles. Relationships and everyday life, on the other hand, stand out as the most pervasive themes. Yet, regardless of setting, genre and story, every manga series arrives at the same combination: Shinji and the other children realize the importance of Others, reconfirm their friendships and romantic ties, and decide to move forward ('fight') in their everyday life. Such repetitiveness stands in stark contrast to the anime sector of the *EVA* franchise.

9. For the extended explication of the term 'fan service,' see Lexicon (n.d.).

Table 8.4. Correlation and combinations of thematically oriented sequences in the *EVA* manga. License: CC BY 4.0.

The sense of progress conveyed by the line-up of TV series, *EoE* and *Rebuild of Evangelion* has been noted even by commentators who underscore the introverted impulse in the first anime. For instance, in his 2008 monograph, Uno repeatedly raises the *EVA* anime series as an example of escapism in contradistinction to *EoE*, which he accepts as reconfirming the value of social interaction (2008: 982–1005). Likewise, Maejima positions the TV anime *EVA* as the forbearer of the sekai-kei genre, with its omission of society and persistent introspection, and juxtaposes it with *Rebuild of Evangelion*, which depicts busy social life around Shinji and presents him as more confident and outgoing (2010: 2288–2308). In other words, the protagonist's— and his world's—forward momentum is found not only within separate animated titles, but also across them. In the meantime, each manga resets the characters' progress, so that they are forever stuck in the present (with the possible exception of *Angelic Days*, where the children have to go separate ways at the end). To reiterate, *EVA*'s most ostensible message ("accept yourself—learn to live among the others") is either reinforced (in the animated films) or undermined (in the manga) on the level of network structure, depending on the medium.

EVA Manga as Fanworks?

Apparently, the *EVA* manga constitute a set of disjointed works that correspond to a wide range of equally disjointed storyworlds. Even when borrowing heavily from stories in other media, they do not form a consistent 'grand narrative' or a thematically organized network within the franchise. Instead, each title freely plays with settings and characters, at times leading to bizarre results. Manga characterization is marked by two opposite tendencies: characters' personalities either remain fixed without regard for circumstances and environments, or they change from title to title seemingly at random. Most of the manga are too riddled with gaps and contradictions to be consumed as isolated works, and they stray too far from the canonical settings to serve as effective entry points into the franchise. But they can be easily understood by readers familiar with the core works. Incidentally, the *NGE* is the only manga series that provides new information or new angles on the *EVA* canon. It is also the only valid entry point into the franchise, which allows the reader to immediately master the information needed for efficient consumption of other *EVA* works. The rest of the manga titles offer the pleasures of play and variation instead. All of them rearrange relationships between characters, prioritizing different vectors of friendship and romance; or to use fan slang, each promotes its own set of established and potential pairings. Film scholar Jason Mittell describes such an approach to franchise development as the What If? extension:

> None of [such] extensions reward viewers with trailheads into deeper narrative experiences, flesh out the fictional universe, or relay any seemingly vital story events. Instead, they allow us to spend more time with characters whom we have grown close to over the course of the television serial. (2015: 313)

Mittell also points out that this extension mode has clear precedents "in the realm of fan production and consumption practices" (ibid.: 325). Indeed, almost all aspects of the *EVA* manga line-up discussed so far bring to mind the often-criticized follies of fan fiction: incomplete storyworlds that utilize elements of the *EVA* universe, but do not expand it in meaningful ways; inconsistent characterization; focus on romance, eroticism and comedy to the detriment of plot coherence, etc. If generative principles and organizational logic of a franchise reveal themselves through its narrative-based parts, then the manga sector of the *EVA* franchise corresponds perfectly, and ironically, to Azuma's claim that the anime studios GAINAX and Khara have been developing *EVA* and its franchise as "an aggregate of information without a [grand] narrative," where no fundamental difference between official and fan creativity, 'original' and derivative works exists (2009: 37–38). While this may appear convincing in view of the above, Azuma's line of argument requires closer inspection.

Did GAINAX's *EVA* project really mark a shift in the paradigm of cultural production and consumption? Has database consumption really changed the logic of entertainment? Has it entirely replaced all other paradigms? And how valid are Azuma's claims beyond the narrow segment of the Japanese fan community? The second part of this chapter departs from the *EVA* manga to reintroduce Azuma's line of thought and juxtapose it with general principles that define fandoms and fan activities.

Part II. Engaging *EVA*: Fans and Their Practices

Azuma's Theory and the Early History of the *EVA* Fandom

As pointed out in the Introduction, Azuma repeatedly mentions the *EVA* anime and its franchise as a watershed marking the transition between two modes of cultural production and consumption, which he describes as the inevitable consequence of the advancement of postmodernity in the 1970s and the corresponding decline of Lyotard's 'grand narratives' (Azuma 2009: 26–29). While the early otaku allegedly substituted those ideological frameworks with fictional worlds, the next generation represented by the *EVA* fans was content to play with database elements, their interest in narratives and messages remaining superficial (ibid.: 75–86).

Azuma's understanding of the first generation is partially informed by a series of essays written around 1990, in which Eiji Ōtsuka introduced his model of 'narrative consumption': consumers notice the existence of a 'grand narrative,' or a fictional world, but can access it only fragmentarily, through officially released works and products (Ōtsuka 2001a: 7–40). Once fans' mastery of this fictional universe grows, it becomes a 'story-generating system' for producers and consumers alike (Ōtsuka 2014: 20–29).

Ōtsuka took his point of departure from the contemporary 'hunger' for stories, related to the 'liberation' of narratives "from specific social formations and contexts" that characterized premodern Japan

(2001a: 23–27). Allegedly, in the absence of closed communities and shared narratives, people lose their sense of belonging. Ordinary stories, especially if disconnected from any specific worldview, can no longer satisfy them; thus, the need for a new type of narrative content. Azuma picks up the idea of the world-based franchise as a substitute for the communally shared worldview, and connects it with Lyotard's postmodern condition. However, Azuma's reading of Ōtsuka's model seems reductive when he analogizes fan investment into fictional universes with ideology or religion, something that easily results in prejudiced accounts of fandom as Jenkins has demonstrated (1992: 13). John C. Lyden, scholar in both Film and Religious Studies, seems to follow Ōtsuka's line of thought seamlessly when he writes:

> What can be said about both [religious and fan activities] is that the narratives in question have potentially contributed in some significant way to the formation of communal identity, a set of shared ideas about ultimate meaning and values, and a set of practices that reinforce or express these. (2012: 782)

Shared narratives, including, but not limited to, fictional universes and transtextual or transmedial fiction have cohesive power on a par with mythology, and thus serve as a vehicle for community building. However, contrary to religious doctrine, the content per se is not prescriptive: Values and practices of the group are extraneous to it (which is why fans of the same cult text often split into separate, mutually exclusive groups). Fans' engagement with the content is mostly shaped by a range of desires and motivations other than the need for grand narrative, first and foremost the desire to possess the object of adoration (Fiske 1992: 40), either by means of some material object associated with it[10] or through the accumulation of data. Fans' "epistemophilia," or "pleasure in knowing [and] in exchanging knowledge" (Jenkins 1992: 129), is well-documented in English-language Fandom and Media Studies.

10. For the respective business model, namely character merchandising, see Steinberg (2012).

Forms and formats of information are, of course, subject to change depending on fan community, platform and type of content. With world-driven franchises like *Gundam* or *Star Wars*, the preferred type of knowledge concerns the fictional world (= universe) itself and usually takes the form of an encyclopedia. Fans, correspondingly, develop "the desire . . . to map and master as much as they can know about [fictional] universes, often through the production of charts, maps, and concordances" (Jenkins 2009: web; see also Murray 1997: 84–87).[11] Far from simply cataloguing, they bring in external texts, cross-reference data from various sources to bury gaps, seek diegetic explanations for inconsistencies (Gwenllian-Jones 2004: 91–96; Long 2007; Wolf 2012: 33–64; Maj 2015) and "import knowledge from the real world to fill out incomplete descriptions" (Ryan 2014: 35). Fan activities described by Jenkins, Wolf and others seem perfectly in rhyme with the accounts of the *Gundam* fandom by Azuma and Maejima, who both note the proliferation of printed materials "shrouded in timelines and mechanical data" (Azuma 2009: 34), with fan-produced mooks like *GUNDAM CENTURY* eventually included in the official canon (Maejima 2010: 2511).[12] In other words, the mode of engagement with works of fiction perceived by Azuma as typical of the first otaku generation (2009: 34–37, 54) has been part and parcel of fan communities outside Japan since the emergence of 'Trekkers.'

For Azuma, the new generation of otaku is exemplified by *EVA* fans who "did not really have a concern for the entire world of *Evangelion* [and] focused exclusively on the settings and character designs as objects for excessive interpretation or 'reading up' . . . and for *chara-moe*"[13] (2009: 37). But there are other accounts concerning the early *EVA* fandom. The most direct evidence is given in Hiroshi Daimon's report (1997) which documents the activities of members of the official GAINAX message board SGAINAX during the initial series' run (4 October 1995–27 March 1996).

11. Creators of imaginary worlds have been driven by encyclopedic impulse for centuries. See Wolf (2012).

12. See Maj (2015: 88–89), and Wolf (2012: 45–46) for similar cases in the fandoms of *A Song of Ice and Fire* and *Star Wars*, respectively.

13. Azuma himself does not provide a definition of the term, which is best understood as an intense affection for a character.

According to Daimon, digital fandom emerged immediately. A month after the series' start, the number of posts had already reached such a scale that two new sections were added to the General Discussions: the first one devoted specifically to puzzle-solving and theory-building, the second to *chara-moe*, fan fiction and character-centered discussions (1997: 196). Reportedly, the latter was the most popular, with the character of Rei enjoying a huge following from episode 5 onwards. Despite this overlap with Azuma, Daimon's brief account pictures the fandom in a different way: Apparently, right from the start, computer-savvy viewers were fascinated by the show's numerous puzzles. Theories proliferated. Even though the Angels were eventually demoted to 'monsters of the week,' users' interest in the mysteries of the Human Instrumentality Project and the Second Impact never waned. In addition, *EVA* enthusiasts reached beyond the TV anime to facilitate interpretation: They discovered intertextual links, played their theories against the perceived image of GAINAX as an idiosyncratic producer, tried to factor in complications of the production process and so on (1997: 195–199). Incidentally, the exploratory efforts of the fandom bore some tangible fruit in printed form. Two Japanese-language books published in 1997, *Evangerion kenkyū josetsu* (Kabutogi 1997) and *EVA no tabekata, ajiwaikata* (Evangelion Roppongi Committee 1997), collected all kinds of trivia, guesswork and analyses. Evident here are attempts to decipher and interpret, rather than playing with database elements.

All this factual evidence is corroborated and elaborated by Maejima's treatise on the sekai-kei genre, which positioned the *EVA* anime as a watershed between generations and tastes. Maejima identifies two distinct sides of the *EVA* series (and *EoE*): for the most part, *EVA* constitutes a model case of a text "made by otaku for otaku," while the last two episodes and the subsequent movie redefine it into what Maejima calls "otaku literature" (*otaku no bungaku*). In other words, the target audience for the larger part of the *EVA* anime were the users who engaged in heated discussions in the puzzle-solving section of the SGAINAX message board. These older otaku were genre-savvy, capable of recognizing and following intertextual links, with a keen eye to visual nuances and small details and a detached, even 'cynical,' attitude toward the object of their interest (2010: 383–420). In the last two episodes and *EoE*, *EVA* substituted the mystery-driven narrative with minute exploration of the protagonist's interiority. Correspondingly, the younger otaku shifted their priorities to empathizing with Shinji or admiring the beautiful heroines in a rather unsophisticated, straightforward way (ibid.: 546–561).

Following Azuma, Maejima notes how moe swept over otaku culture in the late 1990s. However, for him, the moe boom and the concurring database consumption both mark the revival of an interest in stories instead of what he calls the "worldview consumption" (2010: 1141–1161). This is not the only point where the critics' arguments part ways. Even though both agree that *EVA* heralded a fundamental change in fans' consumption patterns, for Azuma, this new mode means the dissolution of narratives into isolated units (the database elements), while Maejima underscores the turn toward interiority and self-reflexivity. Furthermore, Maejima regards database consumption as transitory, soon to be replaced by other paradigms, both old and new (ibid.: 1834–1862). Thus, 'narrative consumption' (i.e., consumption of consistent storyworlds) supposedly reappeared in 2004 with the huge success of the *Fate* media franchise (ibid.: 1813–1829) and played a significant part in the development of the equally popular *Suzumiya Haruhi* franchise (ibid.: 1831–1862), which initially seemed to embody Azuma's database model. The *Haruhi* light novels pulled a group of colorful, but stereotypical, characters designed to induce moe response through a series of equally stereotypical situations. The basic premise of the story—the heroine's ability to change reality itself—gave consumers a free hand to create new derivative episodes with their favorite characters. The release of the non-linear anime adaptation in 2006, however, instigated an additional encyclopedic impulse in the old-timers, who found themselves cataloguing information, explaining obscure references and creating guiding paratexts for the newcomers. *Fate* and *Suzumiya Haruhi* are hardly exceptional cases; indeed, making several approaches to the franchise available for the fans is a common practice these days both in Japan and overseas.

EVA Franchise: A Watershed or a Multipurpose Playground?

For all their discrepancies, Azuma's and Maejima's accounts of the *EVA* fandom, or of fandoms in general, are not irreconcilable. Barring the last two episodes, the *EVA* anime series encourages a mode of engagement that is related, but not identical, to the older, encyclopedic one. Azuma emphasizes the gap between the two, while Maejima focuses on similarities. At any rate, different modes of engagement stem less from a generational gap than the operative principle and inner logic of different franchises. Contrary to *Gundam*, *EVA* was delivered to consumers not in the form of a TRPG (tabletop role-playing game) sourcebook, which is Ōtsuka's preferred analogy for narrative consumption (2014: 20–23). Instead, it was a perfect cult text, designed "to be open, to contain gaps, irresolutions, contradictions, which both allow and invite fan productivity" (Fiske 1992: 41). Fans bent on deciphering *EVA*'s endless mysteries, hints and promises were required to scavenge for information in every direction possible. To paraphrase, they had to become what Mittell (2015) calls "forensic." There certainly is an affinity between encyclopedic and forensic fandoms, to the point that they are sometimes difficult to distinguish. Both approaches involve dedicated exploration of fictional universes and the related materials, but the incoming information is utilized differently. While *Gundam* fans catalogued facts or mulled over technical details, *EVA* fans engaged in "excessive interpretation" or "reading up" (Azuma 2009: 37). Exploring a fictional universe and gradually filling its gaps offers a kind of pleasure that is different from playing with possibilities. Therefore, it seems reasonable to draw a line between the two modes.

The forensic mode of engagement has been discussed in connection to non-Japanese cult shows and transmedial franchises such as *Twin Peaks* (1990–91), *Lost* (2004–10) and *The Matrix* (1999–2009). Much of what Mittell and Jenkins have to say about online communities built around *Lost* and *Twin Peaks* coincides with Daimon's and Maejima's accounts of the *EVA* fandom: users' heavy reliance on new technologies, such as VCR and wiki software; the "ludic hypothesizing across . . . gaps in the narrative" (Mittell 2015: 161); the "continued circulation and elaboration of multiple" theories (Jenkins 2006b: 124); or fans' constant awareness of the authorial figures and repeated appeals "to extratextual discourse and intertextual linkages" (ibid.: 119). Similarities do not end with fan activities either: Just like the *EVA* anime, *Twin Peaks* and *Lost* interweave and splice major themes and genres, such as 'rational' and 'supernatural,' Science Fiction and action-adventure, mystery and soap opera (Angelini & Booy 2010: 29; Jenkins 2006b: 126; Mittell 2015: 305–306). In the light of the initial backlash against the *EVA* anime's two last episodes, it is significant that all of the aforementioned projects enjoyed dedicated following, but failed to satisfy forensic fans in the long run (Mittell 2015; Jenkins 2006c; Angelini & Booy 2010: 23). Such an outcome is almost inevitable with shows and franchises that make their regular consumers "presume that there is an answer to be found by drilling down and analyzing" (Mittell 2015: 52) and encourage them to compete both among themselves and with the official producers. It is impossible for the official creative team to outsmart fans' collective intelligence. Fans' interpretations will always be more comprehensive, multifaceted and nuanced (Jenkins 2006c). Furthermore, creators running a popular large-scale project have to constantly balance expectations of actively forensic fans, who want to be properly rewarded for their effort, with the demands of regular audiences, who want the core text to be understandable without extensive, time- and labor-consuming collective work (Jenkins 2006a: 96). As a result, more often than not,

> the pleasure [for forensic fans] is greatest in the middle—once there are enough pieces of information out there to enable multiple competing versions of the story to be placed into circulation and to be debated but before the series starts to close down possibilities. (Jenkins 2006c: web)

Under these conditions, Anno and Studio GAINAX arguably conducted a brilliant maneuver when in the last episodes they radically changed the rules of the game and redefined not only their core text, but also the required mode of engagement (Maejima 2010: 1098–1115). As is evident now, the move paid off despite the initial outrage of the forensic fandom. Not only did the self-reflective quality of the series' finale draw the attention of a wider public, making *EVA* a national phenomenon (ibid.: 351–356, 447–488); it also accommodated the precedence of characters that facilitated the prolonged development of the *EVA* franchise and defined the next generation of otaku.

As already noted, the transformed status of fictional characters in Japanese popular culture has been widely discussed. Azuma contributed to this discourse by connecting character-oriented consumption with the 'database.' Even if database consumption is not as new as suggested, it has certainly gained new significance with the rise of the Internet and the rapid growth of online fan communities. The most prominent manifestation of database consumption is probably the wiki site TV Tropes (active since 2012), which currently hosts thousands of articles covering all manners of cultural tropes, from plot devices to character morality types. The site also demonstrates that database is more than a collection of building blocks: Its elements may serve as beacons that help consumers navigate an increasingly complex mediascape. In other words, database elements may function very much like genres (and, certainly, every genre is itself a database of elements), but with a broader reach. It is also possible to understand database as a form of intertextuality. Either way, it facilitates fans' movement between media and titles, but does not necessarily dictate how to engage with each text. Another important point is the relation between database and characters. Azuma himself contends that the database includes a wide range of narrative elements, including entire plotline templates (2009: 42). Conversely, consumers' focus on characters does not automatically entail database consumption.

Illustrative in this regard are Azuma's and Maejima's different definitions of moe: for Azuma, the term denotes the immediate affective response to specific elements and their combinations, as well as fleeting sentimental reactions to 'small narratives' (2009: 78–86), while Maejima seems to associate with moe the more traditional identification with and empathy toward characters (2010: 1034–1056, 1119–1136). Notably, these variations in consumers' emotional engagement are not unique to Japan. Moreover, quite often, both approaches are applied simultaneously by members of one and the same fandom or even by one and the same person, depending on context. In order to acknowledge this variability, all modes of fan engagement that prioritize characters and their relationships (rather than fictional universes, stories or enigmas) are hereby identified as 'affective.' Considering how central the combination of affective mode with database consumption is for Azuma's argument, one may ask if it only emerged in the 1990s, and whether it has completely displaced the encyclopedic and forensic modes.

As a matter of fact, the affective mode of fan engagement had existed in manga- and anime-related culture long before the arrival of the third otaku generation, even before the new wave of *bishōjo* games[14] in 1996 that would become the main vehicle of male-oriented *moe* narratives in the post-*EVA* period (Maejima 2010: 635–671; see also Sayawaka 2012: 197–198). That mode, however, had been

14. A subgenre of visual novel games that requires the player to foster relationships with a set of beautiful heroines. See Azuma 2009: 75–76.

associated with an isolated part of Japanese fan community, namely "enthusiastic female fans of yaoi and, to a lesser extent, BL manga" (Galbraith 2011: 220) known as *fujoshi* (Jp. rotten girls).[15] Much like Azuma's new otaku, fujoshi allocate most of their attention to characters, consume officially released titles and derivative works with similar vigor and, most importantly, utilize their own 'database' of character types and relationships in pursuit of moe affect (Galbraith 2011: 220–221; S. Azuma 2010: 252–253). These practices have continued since the late 1970s (S. Azuma 2010: 254). Thus, Azuma's failure to acknowledge them appears all the more surprising, even allowing differences between the female fujoshi and male otaku of today.

According to sociologist Sonoko Azuma, otaku engage with single heroines, whereas fujoshi focus on relationships between characters (2010: 253–254). This argument, however, disregards the fact that Hiroki Azuma's 'database' includes not only visual elements, but also character types, "settings [and] stereotypical narrative development" (2009: 42), all of which might shape character relationships and relationships with characters. Conversely, Sonoko Azuma acknowledges that fujoshi do get infatuated with isolated male characters, but have to withhold corresponding fantasies under an unspoken rule (2010: 267). The difference, therefore, lies in the established practices and rules of the community, rather than members' emotional engagement.[16] Following Hiroki Azuma (2009: 94), Sonoko Azuma emphasizes the lack of meaningful social interactions in the male otaku community, as opposed to fujoshi, who are heavily invested in communication (2010: 258). It is indeed possible to juxtapose "exchanges of information" that, according to Hiroki Azuma, constitute the larger part of otaku communication (2009: 93)[17] with so-called *moe* talk (about favorite pairings and scenarios) that "affirms commonality, intensifies intimacy, and accelerates play behaviour" in fujoshi groups (Galbraith 2011: 222–227). Still, the discrepancy between the two communities does not preclude their major common points: database

15. Incidentally, the explosion of bishōjo game genre was closely followed in the 2000s by the boom of *otome* and BL games, which have a similar design, but target female consumers.

16. The male otaku playing a bishōjo game does not necessarily identify with the 'stand-in' protagonist, and the female BL reader need not step back as the onlooker (see Galbraith 2009; Mizoguchi 2008).

17. Azuma himself allows that otaku "form cliques" (2009: 92), "buy and sell derivative works, and discuss their impressions of new works" (ibid.: 94), which implies both social interaction and emotional exchange.

consumption and the priority of affective experiences. In the light of these similarities, it is possible to hypothesize that the changes in the otaku culture of the 1990s resulted from the gradual diffusion of the female mode of engagement in Japanese fandoms. At any rate, as a pinnacle of those changes, *EVA* did not embody radical novelty. Rather, it successfully appropriated a model that had previously remained marginal and, for the most part, unofficial. Moreover, the transition to the affective mode of engagement was neither immediate nor final.

Despite Azuma's claims to the contrary, numerous sources (Daimon 1997; Maejima 2010; Yokohama 2006) testify that, right from the start, the *EVA* fandom employed both forensic and affective modes of engagement. The former was not even abandoned after the series had taken its decisive turn toward the affective, as can be seen from the subsequent publications on *EVA* trivia and mythology. As a matter of fact, forensic aspects of the franchise made their way into the 21st century, first and foremost in the form of the *Rebuild of Evangelion* tetralogy (2007, 2009, 2012, 2021). At a first glance, the three films released so far seem to tell a new version of the same *EVA* story, much in line with the What If? principle implemented in the manga works. But while changing the events and relationships, *Rebuild of Evangelion* openly addresses the mysteries and ambiguities of the *EVA* anime, filling in the gaps that fans have puzzled over for years. Admittedly, for a part of the audience, the storyworld of the new tetralogy has drifted too far away from the storyworld of the TV series to serve as a proper point of reference. However, this ambiguity may generate new discussions and theories, the driving force of forensic fandom. Even more importantly, certain scenes, lines and settings in the new movie heavily imply the possibility of multiple time loops. If this device is indeed introduced diegetically, the entire structure of the *EVA* franchise might change. The core works could get fused into one continuity, forming a single storyworld. Even with the tetralogy almost complete, it is difficult to predict how *EVA* will develop, but the fans continue to elaborate on the loop theory and scour the promotional videos for clues and hints concerning the possible outcome of the new movie series. Forensic fandom lives on.

EVA's Versatile Fandom and Modes of Engagement: A Case Study

The multiplicity of approaches, or the ways in which the fans address official works, is evident not only in their interpretative practices, but also in their creative endeavors. Despite negative stereotypes belittling fan-produced texts as overly relationship- and character-centered, there exist countless examples of fanfiction (the most common form of fan creativity in the West) earnestly invested in world-building and exploration, or in explaining and supplementing the canonical events. When it comes to *EVA*, however, the most illustrative example and the one that connects fans globally is again found in the medium of manga.

The derivative work in question is an adult *dōjinshi* (Jp. fan-made publication) entitled *RE-TAKE*. This six-volume series by the circle Studio Kimigabuchi might be the most widely known fanwork among English- and Russian-speaking fans; in Japan, it was popular enough to warrant the release of a three-volume all-age version (with explicit sex scenes removed or censored)—and, paradoxically, a two-hour live-action adaptation by the adult video maker TMA (2008).[18] What caused such a success? Overseas, at least, *RE-TAKE* is known for its elaborate plot: Instead of drawing a string of loosely connected pornographic scenes involving Shinji and Asuka (as to be expected), Studio Kimigabuchi created a full-fledged sequel to the anime. Taking the final scene of *EoE* as its starting point, *RE-TAKE* leads the characters to an optimistic ending grounded in the events and settings of the source series. Table 8.5 summarizes the relationship between the storyworlds of the *EVA* anime and *RE-TAKE*.

18. The 30-minute all-age cut of TMA's *EVER RE-TAKE* can be found on the Niconico Video site.

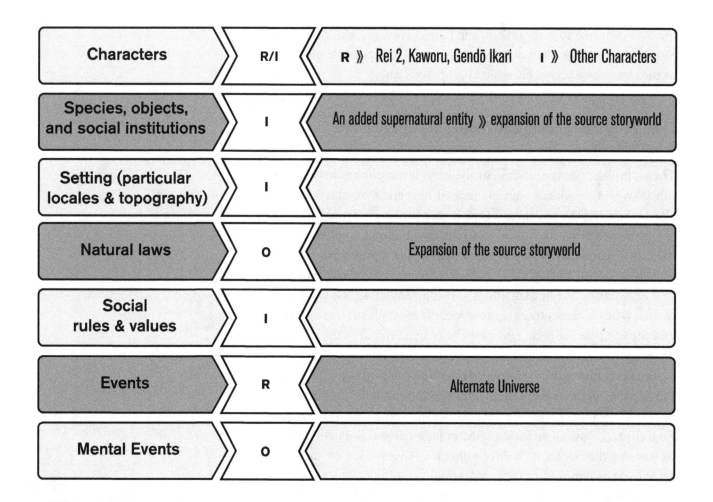

Characters	R/I	R » Rei 2, Kaworu, Gendō Ikari I » Other Characters
Species, objects, and social institutions	I	An added supernatural entity » expansion of the source storyworld
Setting (particular locales & topography)	I	
Natural laws	O	Expansion of the source storyworld
Social rules & values	I	
Events	R	Alternate Universe
Mental Events	O	

RE-TAKE

I: ALMOST IDENTICAL

O: OVERLAPPING TO SOME EXTENT

L: LOOSE SEMBLANCE

R: RADICAL DEPARTURE

Table 8.5. Relationship between the storyworld elements of *RETAKE* and the *EVA* anime. License: CC BY 4.0.

Clearly, there is a significant overlap between the two storyworlds. Changes in natural laws and the list of existents are inevitable because *RE-TAKE* keeps expanding the storyworld. In addition, as a first step in establishing a transmedial continuity, the dōjinshi splices the storyworld of the anime with the storyworld of *NGE*. The most radical, unequivocal departure occurs on the level of events, because *RE-TAKE* does not simply move the plot forward, but utilizes the concept of parallel universes to replay the part of the story that corresponds to the last third of the *EVA* anime. The mental events, defined as "the character's reactions to perceived or actual states of affairs" (Ryan 2014: 36), change accordingly. In terms of characterization, *RE-TAKE* seems to take an approach already observed in the officially released manga works. That is, it attempts to carefully reproduce the mindsets and typical reactions of the leading pair Shinji and Asuka, while Rei 2's and Kaworu's mentalities are reworked to fit the needs of the story. However, there is no consensus among fans as to whether the latter two are completely out of character or can be read as plausible interpretations of Kaworu and Rei in the TV series and *NGE*.

As for the major *EVA* themes analyzed in the first part of the article, *RE-TAKE* includes all of them, with emphasis on fighting, mystery and relationships. Particularly important is its ambition to imitate the cryptic narration style of the TV series, on the one hand, and to provide a non-contradictory explanation for the unfolding events, on the other. As a result, the dōjinshi simultaneously provokes and satisfies the forensic impulse in readers. Furthermore, it delivers an emotionally gratifying denouement lacking in the source series. Considering all of the above, *RE-TAKE* looks like a model instalment in the franchise developed under the principles of continuity and consistency, where all works correspond to a single non-contradictory storyworld. At the same time, as a fanwork, it is tied to moe sensibility and database consumption. The former reveals itself in gratuitous sex scenes found in the original six-volume edition of the dōjinshi. The latter is reproduced quite literally in battle scenes that remix and repurpose Sadamoto's artwork.[19] Following the same logic of database consumption, *RE-TAKE* has spawned a small franchise of its own. In addition to the aforementioned adult video adaptation, a soundtrack CD was released in 2006 and, in 2017, Studio Kimigabuchi launched a sequel series *RE-TAKE Kai* (once again in the form of adult dōjinshi), which builds the new *EVA* movies into the continuity.

RE-TAKE is therefore a fanwork shaped by all three modes of engagement: the affective mode determines its focus on characters and their relationships; the forensic mode drives it to cover gaps and resolve puzzles left by the TV series, but also supply its own enigmas; and the encyclopedic mode makes it anticipate, perhaps even surpass, the *Rebuild of Evangelion* movies by developing a cosmology capable of uniting all Shinji- and Asuka-focused *EVA* texts, official or not, within one continuity. In a never-ending cycle of consuming and producing meanings, *EVA* fans across nations took different approaches to the text. The affective mode of engagement obviously prevailed: Shinji x Asuka shippers[20] enjoyed the story (as well as the juicy scenes), while Rei supporters rejected it for character mistreatment. But the most interesting response so far has been a 5,000-word essay by a forensic Russian fan, who addresses every contradiction, loose end and enigma in *RE-TAKE* (Red Priest Rezo 2007). For this person, the dōjinshi's main achievement lies in the interpretive framework (the parallel world theory) it offers—in other words, Red Priest Rezo recognizes and appreciates its hermeneutic value. Certainly, this telling reaction comes from outside of Japanese otaku community. However, it is a direct response to something that the Japanese otaku community created and promoted. The official segment of *EVA* manga might conform to the logic of database consumption, and yet its unofficial counterparts might suddenly evoke other models and modes of fan engagement, as they strive to answer the needs that the official works have left unsatisfied.

19. For an analysis of several such scenes by a disgruntled fan, see https://imgur.com/a/bU86w#0

20. Fans who support and promote a particular romantic relationship.

Conclusion: From Fan Studies to Media Studies

Azuma's database model has helped explain a major tendency in the contemporary consumption of popular culture, throwing light on a significant component of fandom life within and without Japan—the 'database.' Most researchers readily accept Azuma's theory, especially the parts concerning practical application of the 'database' by fans. But as demonstrated above, Azuma's understanding of otaku culture in particular and fan culture in general is limited: He broke a heterogeneous fan community with a set of multifarious practices and motivations into several 'clear-cut' segments, which he then lined up and matched with particular stages of Japanese socio-cultural history. Thus, encyclopedic and forensic modes of engagement (which Azuma conflates into one) are associated with the transitional stage between modernity and postmodernity; affective mode of engagement and 'database consumption' are understood as both signs and consequences of postmodernity that finally revealed itself in the 1990s.

However, when considering various accounts of fan activities in Japan and elsewhere, it becomes obvious that reading strategies and rules of meaning-production do not replace each other neatly and linearly—rather, they co-exist in different proportions and with varying degrees of visibility at any time, in every fandom. Needless to say, fans can read, dissect and repurpose a certain text in radically different ways even when it does not invite them to do so, and even small fandoms often divide into segments according to "desirable and undesirable ways of relating to cultural objects, desirable and undesirable strategies of interpretation and styles of consumption" (Jenkins 1992: 16). At the same time, all modes of engagement have much in common, and the principles governing fandom communities remain more or less the same, including interconnectedness of research, communication and creativity (Jenkins 1992, 2006b; Toton 2008), knowledge functioning as the main currency within the "cultural economy of fandom" (Fiske 1992: 42; Jenkins 2006b: 125), and the "dual interpretive stance" that combines "a sense of proximity and possession . . . with a sense of ironic distance" (Jenkins 1992: 65–67). It is this common ground that allows a franchise, indeed, a single work, official or fan-produced, to support and encourage multiple responses, affects and interpretations.

The *EVA* anime was, in fact, a text designed from the start to support and encourage several modes of engagement, and the *EVA* franchise inherited the approach. As stated before, the official *EVA* manga works follow the principles of affective database consumption, while new animated features call forth the forensic, or even encyclopedic, impulse. To enjoy *EVA* as a transmedial franchise, the consumer does needs not only "multimodal literacy" (Delwiche 2017: 1055–1063), but also the ability to switch between different modes of engagement. This last point is important not only when considering *EVA* specifically or fandom in general—it has rather important implications for Anime Studies, in particular for their new, media-oriented strand concerned with how highly segmented, serialized, transmedially engaged and open-ended anime texts "work within local and global media environments" (Berndt 2018: 7), which include various discrete and overlapping (rather than homogenized) consumer groups and their tastes and practices. That is not to say that more conservative research informed by Literary and Film Theory, as well as Cultural Studies, cannot benefit from paying more attention to the aforementioned media environments. As demonstrated by numerous inquiries into franchises and their discrete constituents, the juxtaposition between texts designed for interpretation, or 'reading,' and texts meant to instigate affective responses, material consumption or fan exchange (Berndt 2019: 472) is rather moot. Reading a TV anime, however, would mean taking into account its intended audience and anticipated responses, its transmedial links and potential vectors of expansion—in other words, the modes of engagement the text most readily lends itself to. From this point of view, too, it seems unreasonable to discard various demands, values and approaches that characterize Japanese fan culture in favor of one single model, no matter how prominent it is. This very variety warrants the range and complexity of transmedial franchise development within and without Japan. One expects that acknowledging it should produce a rather similar effect on academic inquiries into anime, as well as other media involved with the contemporary otaku market and popular culture in general.

References

Abbott, H. P. (2005). Closure. In D. Herman, M. Jahn and M.-L. Ryan (eds.), *Routledge Encyclopedia of Narrative Theory* (pp. 65–66). New York: Routledge.

Angelini, S. & Booy, M. (2010). Members Only: Cult TV from Margins to Mainstream. In S. Abbott (ed.), *The Cult TV Book* (pp. 19–27). London: I.B. Tauris.

Azuma, H. (2007). *Gēmuteki riarizmu no tanjō: Dōbutsuka suru posutomodan 2*. Tokyo: Kodansha.

_____. (2009). *Otaku: Japan's Database Animals*. Minneapolis, MN: University of Minnesota Press. (Introduction and translation by J. E. Abel and S. Kono)

Azuma, S. (2010). Mōsō no kyōdōtai: "Yaoi" komyuniti ni okeru ren'ai kōdo no kinō. *Shisō chizu*, 5, 249–274.

Berndt, J. (2018). Anime in Academia: Representative Object, Media Form, and Japanese Studies. *Arts*, 7(4), 56. Retrieved from: DOI: https://doi.org/10.3390/arts7040056

_____. (2019). *Interpreting Anime* by Christopher Bolton (review). *The Journal of Japanese Studies*, 45(2), 471–475.

Daimon, H. (1997). Nifuti sābu dokyumento/saibāsupēsujō no EVA. In T. Igarashi (ed.), *Evangerion kairaku gensoku* (pp. 194–200). Tokyo: Daisan Shokan.

Delwiche, A. (2017). Still Searching for the Unicorn: Transmedia Storytelling and the Audience Question. In B. W. L. Derhy Kurtz and M. Bourdaa (eds.), *The Rise of Transtexts: Challenges and Opportunities* (pp. 33–48). New York: Routledge. Kindle.

Evangelion Roppongi Committee. (1997). *EVA no tabekata, ajiwaikata*. Tokyo: Daisan shokan.

Falldog (2020). Falldog's Guide to Gundam Canon and Timelines. *Otaku Revolution*. Retrieved from: https://otakurevolution.com/content /falldogs-guide-to-gundam-canon-and-timelines

Fanlore (2020). Canon. Retrieved from: https://fanlore.org/wiki/Canon

Fiske, J. (1992). The Cultural Economy of Fandom. In L. A. Lewis (ed.), *The Adoring Audience: Fan Culture and Popular Media* (pp. 30–49). London: Routledge.

Forster, E. M. (1955). *Aspects of the Novel*. New York: Hartcourt.

Freeman, M. (2017). *Historicising Transmedia Storytelling: Early Twentieth-Century Transmedia Story Worlds*. New York: Routledge.

Galbraith, P. W. (2011). Fujoshi: Fantasy Play and Transgressive Intimacy among "Rotten Girls" in Contemporary Japan. *Signs: Journal of Women in Culture and Society*, 37(1), 211–232.

_____. (2009). Moe: Exploring Virtual Potential in Post-Millennial Japan. *Electronic Journal of Contemporary Japanese Studies* [no vol. number], 343–365.

Gwenllian-Jones, S. (2004). Virtual Reality and Cult Television. In S. Gwenllian-Jones and R. E. Pearson (eds.), *Cult Television* (pp. 83–98). Minneapolis, MN: University of Minnesota Press.

Heinze, R. (2015). "This Makes No Sense at All": Heterarchy in Fictional Universes. *Storyworlds: A Journal of Narrative Studies*, 7(2), 76–91.

Iida, I. (2012). *Besutoserā raitonoberu no shikumi: Kyarakutā shōsetsu no kyōsō senryaku*. Tokyo: Seidosha.

Itō, G. (2005). *Tezuka izu deddo: Hirakareta manga hyōgenron e*. Tokyo: NTT.

Jenkins, H. (1992). *Textual Poachers: Television Fans and Participatory Culture*. London: Routledge.

_____. (2006a). *Convergence Culture: When Old and New Media Collide*. New York: New York University Press.

_____. (2006b). *Fans, Bloggers, and Gamers: Exploring Participatory Culture*. New York: New York University Press.

_____. (2006c). Getting Lost. In *Confessions of an Aca-Fan: The Official Weblog of Henry Jenkins*. 24 August. Retrieved from: http://henryjenkins.org/blog/2006/08/getting_lost.html

_____. (2009). Revenge of the Origami Unicorn: The Remaining Four Principles of Transmedia Storytelling. In *Confessions of an Aca-Fan: The Official Weblog of Henry Jenkins*. 12 December. Retrieved from: http://henryjenkins.org/blog/2009/12/revenge_of_the_origami_unicorn.html

Joo, W., Denison, R. & Furukawa, H. (2013). "Manga Movies Project Report 1: Transmedia Japanese Franchising." Report for UK Arts and Humanities Research Council Research Project "Manga Movies: Contemporary Japanese Cinema, Media Franchising and Adaptation." Retrieved from: https://www.academia.edu/3693690/Manga_Movies _Project_Report_1_-_Transmedia_Japanese_Franchising

Kabutogi, R. (1997). *Evangerion kenkyū josetsu*. Tokyo: KK Bestsellers.

Kopylova, O. (2016). *Media Mix as Adaptation: With Maeda Mahiro's* Gankutsuō *as an Example*. Doctoral Thesis. Kyoto Seika University. Retrieved from: https://johokan.kyoto-seika.ac.jp/uploads/2016_dr /2016_dr_thesis_01.pdf

_____. (2018). Media mikkusu to monogatari: kyokō sekai no mondai. *Naratibu Media Kenkyū*, 7, 155–192.

Kukkonen, K. (2011). Metalepsis in Popular Culture: An Introduction. In K. Kukkonen and S. Klimek (eds.), *Metalepsis in Popular Culture* (pp. 1–21). Berlin: de Gruyter.

Lexicon (n.d.). Fan Service. *Anime News Network*. Retrieved from: https://www.animenewsnetwork.com/encyclopedia/lexicon.php?id=54

Long, G. A. (2007). *Transmedia Storytelling: Business, Aesthetics and Production at the Jim Henson Company*. MS Thesis. Massachusetts Institute of Technology. Retrieved from: https://www.researchgate.net /publication/38004738_Transmedia_storytelling_business_aesthetics _and_production_at_the_Jim_Henson_Company

Lyden, J. C. (2012). Whose Film Is It, Anyway? Canonicity and Authority in Star Wars Fandom. *Journal of the American Academy of Religion*, 80(3), 775–786.

Maejima, S. (2010). *Sekai-kei to wa nani ka: Posuto EVA no otakushi.* Tokyo: Soft Bank Creative. Kindle.

Maj, K. M. (2015). Transmedial World-Building in Fictional Narratives. *IMAGE. Journal of Interdisciplinary Image Science, 22,* 83–96.

Mittell, J. (2015). *Complex TV: The Poetics of Contemporary Television Storytelling.* New York: New York University Press.

Mizoguchi, A. (2008). *Reading and Living Yaoi: Male–Male Fantasy Narratives as Women's Sexual Subculture in Japan.* Doctoral Thesis. University of Rochester.

Murray, J. (1997). *Hamlet on the Holodeck.* Cambridge, Massachusetts: The MIT Press.

Ōtsuka, E. (2001a). Monogatari shōhiron nōto: 1. Sekai to shukō: monogatari no fukusei to shōhi. In *Teihon Monogatari shōhiron* (pp. 7–20). Tokyo: Kadokawa. (Translated by M. Steinberg, 2010). *Mechademia, 5,* 99–116)

_____. (2001b). Monogatari shōhiron nōto: 2. Monogatari shōhiron no kiso to sono senryaku. In *Teihon Monogatari shōhiron* (pp. 21–54). Tokyo: Kadokawa.

_____. (2014). *Mediamikkusu-ka suru Nihon.* Tokyo: Eastpress.

Red Priest Rezo. (2007). RE-TAKE Analysis. *Living FLCL.* Retrieved from: http://www.project5555.com/p1/retake/Re-Take_analysis.doc

Ruppel, M. N. (2012). *Visualizing Transmedia Networks: Links, Paths and Peripheries.* PhD Thesis. University of Maryland.

Ryan, M.-L. (1991). *Possible Worlds, Artificial Intelligence, and Narrative Theory.* Bloomington, IN: Indiana University Press.

_____. (2014). Story/Worlds/Media: Tuning the Instruments of a Media-Conscious Narratology. In M.-L. Ryan and J.-N. Thon (eds.), *Storyworlds across Media: Toward a Media-Conscious Narratology* (pp. 25–49). Lincoln, NE: University of Nebraska Press.

Sayawaka. (2012). *Boku-tachi no gēmu-shi.* Tokyo: Seikaisha Shinsho.

Shin-seiki. (2020). Theory and Analysis: What Is Canon? *The NGE Fan-Geeks Project.* Retrieved from: https://wiki.evageeks.org/Theory_and_Analysis:What_Is_Canon%3F

Steinberg, M. (2012). *Anime's Media Mix: Franchising Toys and Characters in Japan*. Minneapolis, MN: Minnesota University Press.

_____. (2015). *Naze Nihon wa "mediamikkusu-suru kuni" na no ka?* Tokyo: Kadokawa. Kindle. (Translated by Y. Nakagawa, edited by E. Ōtsuka)

Thon, J.-N. (2015). Converging Worlds: From Transmedial Storyworlds to Transmedial Universes. *Storyworlds: A Journal of Narrative Studies*, 7(2), 21–53.

Toton, S. (2008). Cataloging Knowledge: Gender, Generative Fandom, and the Battlestar Wiki. *Flow Journal*, 7 (17 January). Retrieved from: https://www.flowjournal.org/2008/01/cataloging-knowledge-gender-generative-fandom-and-the-battlestar-wiki/

Uno, T. (2008). *Zeronendai no sōzōryoku*. Tokyo: Hayakawa Publishing. Kindle.

Wolf, M. J. P. (2012). *Building Imaginary Worlds: The Theory and History of Subcreation*. New York: Routledge.

Yokohama, Y. (2006). Shinseiki Evangerion ni okeru monogatari sekai no kōsei: Media mikkusu sakuhinron no kanōsei. *Nihon bungaku*, 55(1), 51–60.

9. Combinatory Play and Infinite Replay
Underdefined Causality in the *Neon Genesis Evangelion* Anime Series and Games

Selen Çalık Bedir

The *Neon Genesis Evangelion* (*EVA*) anime series has attracted a great deal of attention, first and foremost with its finale. The 26th episode significantly thwarted viewers' expectations, with the protagonist failing to become the legend promised by the opening song of the series and the animation itself struggling to maintain its identity in a jumble of barely moving lines and drawings. Interestingly, with this twist at the end, *EVA* has also laid bare the presence of a narrative engagement model that does not acknowledge the centrality of endings. Despite the frustration that the series' finale must have triggered in some, the original fate of the characters did not stop the viewers from imagining them in alternative scenarios, just as it did not stop the official creators revisiting and *replaying* the same scenario.

In the scope of this chapter, it is argued that this particular 'game-like' narrative engagement (which is built on replays) is reinforced by the *EVA* video games. The contemporary media environment is marked by an intensity of exchange that takes place not only among media, but also between objects and subjects, forming an extended web of circulation involving producers, consumers and critics alike. This situation requires one to consider *a multitude in relation*, even when the aim is to focus on the analysis of one specific medium or an individual work. Since 1996, a wide variety of *EVA* games has been released, ranging from Visual Novels to Dating Sims, Fighting games to Role-playing games, digital Mahjong to card games and so on. Instead of offering a comprehensive historical account, this chapter focuses on a small selection of video games to paint a clear picture

How to cite this book chapter:
Çalık Bedir, S. 2021. Combinatory Play and Infinite Replay: Underdefined Causality in the *Neon Genesis Evangelion* Anime Series and Games. In: Santiago Iglesias, J. A. and Soler Baena, A. (Eds.). *Anime Studies: Media-Specific Approaches to Neon Genesis Evangelion*. Pp. 297–326 Stockholm: Stockholm University Press. DOI: https://doi.org /10.16993/bbp.j. License: CC-BY 4.0

of their peculiar interrelation with the narrative of the anime series. In doing so, the author attempts to develop a framework (which takes medium-specificities into account without necessarily prioritizing them) in order to address media relations in franchises such as *EVA* and to locate the centrality of a specific medium (if there is any), which comes forward as the anime series in *EVA*'s case.

In the scope of this chapter, 'gamelikeness' as a concept is derived from Hiroki Azuma's writings on the consumption of narratives in the postmodern age, and the medium-specificity of video games is explored in reference to Game Studies. In order to compare and contrast gaming experience with the experience of engaging with narratives, the author borrows Brian Upton's concept of 'play,' defined as "free movement within a system of constraints" (2015: 15). Upton applies this concept to narrative and ludic engagement alike, noting that narrative play takes place in the mind as an interpretive and anticipatory process. Revising Upton's theory in the light of Azuma's, this chapter suggests considering narrative *replay* as 'combinatory play,' which is defined here as "free combination of narrative elements allowed by a suspension of causal constraints." Finally, as the video games' relationship with the anime series is discussed in connection with the weakening of causality in contemporary narratives and with serialization, this particular study can be categorized under Media Studies with a narratological bent.

Azuma brought together narrative media with games to discuss the significant change in audience engagement with popular narratives in Japan, a trend which seemed to have emerged with *EVA* itself. Employing the concept of 'play' to lay a solid ground for comparison and including the medium-specificity of games in this discussion yield even more insight into audience engagement in general. Taking these steps centers the discussion around *dominant* patterns of causality management. These patterns are dominant, but not absolute, as they are constantly contested and prone to change in relation to the constant interaction between media. The following discussion posits that, in this case, within the *EVA* franchise, the anime series is not only the start, but also the reference point in setting the model for causality management, according to which certain medium-specific features of the *EVA* games seem to be set aside.

Severing Characters from their Contexts

In *Otaku: Japan's Database Animals*, Hiroki Azuma attracts attention to a rupture in audience engagement with narratives, which he demonstrates by comparing the wants and needs of *Gundam*[1] and *EVA* fans.

> [N]umerous fans of *Gundam* desired the completion and close examination of a singular *Gundam* world. That is to say, in their case they preserved the current passion for a fictitious grand narrative. However, even during the peak of the craze, the fans of *Evangelion* who appeared in the mid-1990s—especially those of the younger generation (the third generation of otaku)—did not really have a concern for the entire world of *Evangelion*. Instead, they focused exclusively on the settings and character designs as objects for excessive interpretation or 'reading up' (exemplified in derivative works), and for *chara-moe*. (2009: 37)

In Azuma's account, *EVA* fans stood apart from earlier diehard consumers with their disinterest toward the totality of the narrative they were consuming, or toward how the characters, their world and whatever should happen in that world (the main events of the plot) were particularly interwoven. The real source of attraction for them was any sort of *EVA*-related data that they could enjoy separately or in relation to other characters in different diegetic contexts.

Azuma relates this consumption tendency to Jean-François Lyotard's theories on the postmodern condition, especially to the disappearance of grand narratives. To put it briefly, along with postmodernity (which came to full bloom, according to Azuma, with the collapse of communism in 1989), widely accepted social ideals

1. One of the biggest media franchises from Japan, which started off with the *mecha* (giant robot) anime series *Mobile Suit Gundam* (created by Yoshiyuki Tomino, released between 1979 and 1980).

that organized human life turned untenable. As a result, storyworlds seemed to be less and less guided by organizing principles as well, gradually leading to a disintegration of the once very closely knitted characters, setting and plot. In tandem with the advancing information storage and sharing technologies, especially with the widespread use of the Internet, both producers and consumers have grown familiar with massive sets of elements that compose narratives and gain meaning as they are combined. The perception of each work as a particular combination of such compatible 'database elements' has granted narrative consumption a gamelike quality as well, in the sense that it has enabled everyone to replay a finalized plot if they choose to, by taking the characters out of their diegetic contexts and building them new ones with an alternative set of pieces.

The possibility of taking characters out of their diegetic contexts may seem like a stark contrast between the mindsets producing contemporary popular narratives and works of realist literature where characters' fates are sealed by authors. However, it can be claimed that the birth of the circumstances loosening up this character-context connection (resulting in character mobility) goes back to the 19th century and manifests in a certain sense in realist narratives first. In *The Future of the Image*, Jacques Rancière points out that the proliferation of information, which reveals itself with the widening use of printing technologies and culture (2007: 16), finds its reflection in realist novels as a confusion of causal connections (2007: 121). These novels revolve around anything and everything that can happen in real life, and picture the mundane details of daily life alongside the phenomena that cripple human mind and agency in their gravity (i.e., traumatic events, such as war). In this manner, first of all, realism paves the way for combining narrative elements which are unlikely to come together. However, at the same time, it becomes particularly challenging for the reader to untangle the connections between them, hence to pinpoint the exact causes and to anticipate the exact outcomes of actions in the depicted storyworlds. Be that as it may, the grand narratives still functional back in the 19th century set some limitations to hold the characters in check in realist literature. In *Oliver Twist*, for example, despite the fact that Charles Dickens gives the protagonist's name to his novel, the socio-economical status of Oliver becomes the most impactful factor defining how his fate unravels, as well as the most significant limitation which can be overcome only through meticulously interrelated chance encounters. This particular, uniquely woven contextual fabric makes Oliver who he is, and it is through Oliver that one can understand the figurative mold which gives him this shape.

At first glance, the *EVA* anime series seems to preserve the character-context connection when it puts an unexpected end to the journey of the characters as the context collapses literally in an apocalyptic scenario. The chaos that reigns in their world correlates with the characters' psychological as well as physical condition, making it impossible for them to take a stable position or form. However, perhaps as it is signaled by the fact that apocalyptic incidents are not unprecedented in the *EVA* universe (the story takes place 15 years after a cataclysm after all), the ending does not prove to be a point of termination. While the collapse of the diegetic context results in the disintegration of characters, characters' clear-cut depictions (which allow them to be recognized via any of their most dominant characteristics in any context) and the centrality of their emotions in the narrative (which occupies the attention that would otherwise fall on the other elements surrounding the character) prove enough to summon them back to life. As a result, it can be said that characters overshadow the context and emerge as the orbital axis of causality, making it possible to break down and reconstruct the chains of action and outcome in whichever way necessary to present attractive characters in an affect-inducing manner. Used to the wildest combinations of narrative elements already, both creators and audience engage with *EVA* in a gamelike manner, reimagining characters in different contexts regardless of whether or not it was the original intention of the director Hideaki Anno in the first place.

Character-Driven *EVA* Games

How about the *EVA* games? How are they aligned with the anime series that displays the above described gamelikeness? What kind of audience engagement do they offer? And how does this reflect back on the audience engagement with the anime?

As a wide variety of *EVA* games has appeared since 1996,[2] it is in fact quite difficult to make sweeping statements while addressing the above questions. Luckily, an earlier study on the relation of video games and another popular anime-manga series, *NARUTO*, provides an excellent starting point. Studying four *NARUTO* video games in detail, Martin Roth demonstrates the inapplicability of Azuma's theory to video games, particularly with regard to the formation of characters. Roth states that game characters should be considered "beyond their appearance and names, little more than empty shells that can be filled with content or functionality as demanded" (2013: 251). In Azuma's understanding, the characters of gamelike narratives feed on a huge database of distinguishable features. The video games discussed by Roth maintain the looks of the *NARUTO* characters, which produces a direct visual connection between the games, the manga and the anime series. However, it might be said that the characters in the discussed games are pretty much hollowed-out versions of the original characters. Roth explains that particularly in fighting games, for programming reasons and for balancing up the experience of playing with one character instead of another, the behaviors assigned to characters largely overlap in a fashion that erodes characters' particularities beyond their looks. Moreover, gamers may be allowed to challenge friendly characters on the battlefield or to form unlikely alliances with sworn enemies, despite how unimaginable it would be to see such actions performed in the original plots.

2. Over 30 titles according to the Computer Entertainment Rating Organization (CERO) website.

With a selection of titles featuring battle modes at the very least, Roth also demonstrates that video games *do not* have to tell stories. This fact, though apparent, is necessary to underline especially in cases where the experience of playing games is compared to audience engagement with narratives. The term 'narrative' can be taken as the semiotic representation of a world, populated by characters and displaying change over time, as well as a sense of causality.[3] In this sense, it is possible to talk about narrativity in video games as well, despite the once popular divide between this particular medium and narrative media. At the beginning of the 2000s, certain scholars (self-labeled as the ludologists) reacted to the tendency they spotted in narratological analyses to reduce video games to just another storytelling medium, and advocated centralizing the distinguishing features of the medium instead. The ensuing ludology-narratology debate settled over time with the emergence of more nuanced approaches underlining the potential of the medium to tell stories, while recognizing the primacy of its interactivity.[4]

NARUTO games intersect with the anime and manga on several occasions as they allow players to control and interact with a long list of characters from the entirety of the series. But as Roth demonstrates, some of these games (especially of the fighting genre) and some modes offered within separate games mainly aim to engage players in a cyclical interactive experience: to explore the range of possible actions enabled by the game system, pick the most advantageous ones to perform and carry on doing so based on the output produced by the system. The fights themselves may not reveal extra data about the storyworld or make a significant contribution to story progress; rather than that, they prioritize the practice of honing gaming skills crucial to the in-game progress. The pleasure taken from such games has a direct connection with the quick display of control skills, and playing *NARUTO* games makes a distinct contribution to the engagement with the whole media franchise thanks to this particular experience it offers. Beyond the looks of the characters, the game establishes its

3. For a detailed definition, see Ryan (2003: para. 1).

4. For a detailed account, see Simons (2007).

relationship with the original story via cutscenes (video clips) interspersed between fights. However, these cutscenes are not necessarily presented in temporal or causal connections with the fights either. After dealing the last punch in the ring, a character can appear in a completely different setting engaged in a completely different action. These examples reveal clearly that narrative coherence is not among the primary objectives for such games.

These observations by Roth can also be applied to *Neon Genesis: Battle Orchestra*. *Battle Orchestra* is a fighting game that comes with a rumble mode enabling up to four different Evas (the mecha controlled by the main characters of the series) or Angels to attack each other without necessarily abiding by the 'facts' set straight by the series. But among the rest of the *EVA* games there is a significant number of narrative-oriented and character-driven titles. The prime examples of these would be Visual Novels (such as *Girlfriend of Steel* *1* and *2*) and Raising simulations (*Ayanami with Asuka Raising Project*, *Shinji Ikari Raising Project*, etc.) that centralize the engagement with the characters from the series and excite *EVA* fans, especially with the opportunity to form a direct connection with exactly *who these characters appear to be in the series*. Azuma defines visual novels as "multistory, multiending novels . . . that can be 'read' on the computer screen with images and sounds" (2009: 75). Raising simulations, on the other hand, put players in a more active position which requires observing a high number of interrelated variables and overseeing characters' growth by carefully balancing their use of limited resources (i.e., time that can be spent on certain actions). To generalize, the common goal of these more character-centered *EVA* games becomes traversing the game and observing the characters in different contexts as a result of players' well or poorly made decisions. While control skills are largely swapped with instances of clicking, the physical performance of the players is replaced with their capacity of perseverance for the love of discovery. However, interestingly, despite the fact that this is precisely the structure that inspires Azuma to develop his theory of narrative consumption revolving around the primacy of the character, we can find a sort of 'characterlessness' in these games as well.

For example, an online event guide describes one of the possible routes for character development in *Ayanami with Asuka Raising Project* in the following fashion:[5]

> Conditions:
> Sensitivity is above 200
> Fatigue is higher than morality
> Comments:
>
> Have you ever wondered what Rei [Ayanami] would be like with Asuka's personality? Well, get this state and you can find out! You'll know when you've gotten this when Rei poses, her head held high and a confident smirk on her face. She'll occasionally disobey poor San'i and go off and do her own thing (despite the schedule) but she's still kind at heart. I believe there's an event where she runs away from home and comes back when San'i is angsting while it's raining heavily, but I'm not too sure how to trigger it. (GrunGast82 2004)

In order to describe the consequences of reaching the above-listed conditions, the author of the guide suggests that we imagine how Rei would look if she had the personality of Asuka. In other words, the author invites us to imagine a familiar character acting completely out of character, saying things another character would say with the expressions commonly seen on that other character's face. Although this may sound like a total erasure of character, it may also be considered the proof of *how a character can be reduced to her most defining parts*. In this case, Rei's appearance (minus her usual facial expressions) is chosen from the sum of her character traits established through the series. Moreover, the same event guide also reveals that choosing to engage with Asuka in the same game basically presents the same outcomes if the gamer is to follow the same instructions.[6] This being the case, it is only the visuals that should convince us that Asuka (instead of Rei) is the one we are engaging with.

5. The following quote employs informal use of English. Grammar mistakes are left unedited on purpose.

6. Final note of the guide's author reads: "All the above also apply to Asuka, except Asuka's normal state (low social skill) can be described as 'Grumpy,' while her normal state (high social skill) is the Asuka we all know and love."

It is safe to assume that playing the same game with a second character would not be that challenging or enjoyable for a person who is interested in mastering simulations in general. Mastering this particular simulation means reaching favorable states by closely observing the interrelation between variables such as sensitivity and fatigue levels and making decisions accordingly. The second run of the same game, on the other hand, should be rewarding rather for those who aim to see precisely such variations of Asuka (available combinations). The very first sentence of the excerpt above finds its target audience right away: this game is right for those who have wondered what Rei would be like with Asuka's personality.

Causal Connections in Story Generating Games: The Case of *Neon Genesis Evangelion 2*

Among the *EVA* games, another title that stands out is *Neon Genesis Evangelion 2*. *NGE2* is a very complex dating simulation (which requires a skillful management of resources to win the non-playable characters' affection) interspersed with (real-time) combat. During combat, the controls grow more challenging than simple clicking, and players need to pay attention to timing while developing their strategy. Consequently, the branching of the story is not solely decided by the choices of the gamers, but also by the results of the battles and the additional points collected throughout the game. In comparison to the Raising simulations discussed above, there is a higher number of conditions to meet in *NGE2*. But this complexity comes with its own advantages.

NGE2 bases its reward system on the discovery of alternative scenarios circling around familiar characters, spiced up with the opportunity of forming romantic relationships with them. First of all, the PlayStation Portable (PSP) version of the game released by Bandai in 2006, *Neon Genesis Evangelion 2: Tsukurareshi Sekai—Another*

Cases, contains extra scenarios, as well as revisions of those presented two years earlier in the PlayStation 2 version. Second, both versions of the game reveal some information allegedly sanctioned by Anno himself; the canonicity of the so-called 'Classified Information Files' is debated, but intriguing in any case. Third, according to a statement of *NGE2*'s system project manager, the team wanted to incorporate Anno's view of *EVA* into the game, reflected by the fact that the system itself was named Anno AI.[7] Lastly, the same press release reports Anno himself saying that while he is not planning to make a sequel to *EVA*, he would like to see the audience produce their own *EVA* story via this game (Dengeki Online, 2003). This statement alone shows how *NGE2* is supposed to connect us directly with the series by functioning as a call to write one's own *EVA* story with the data *from the series*, but also echoes the narrative consumption style that leads the audience to imagine what else could have been.

NGE2 and the *EVA* series are purposefully connected in the manner described above. However, it doesn't mean that these differing media take the audience through the same process. The diversity among games (from games with a clear goal to those with no winning states, games that require the use of certain materials as opposed to those that don't, games of chance, make-believe, sports, etc.) makes it quite challenging to come up with a simple and inclusive definition. By taking a comparative look at the available definitions and listing the most common traits, Katie Salen and Eric Zimmerman propose the understanding of game as "a system in which players engage in artificial conflict, defined by rules, that results in a quantifiable outcome" (2004: 80). While this is a good definition, as games can also tell stories, counterposing them to narrative media is one other step to delineate the limits of the medium further. One of the big names in Game Studies to discuss medium-specificities, Espen J. Aarseth, starts his seminal work *Cybertext* with an attempt to exemplify the main feature setting narrative engagement apart from play.

7. It is even recommended to imagine the thoughts of the director when playing the game the second time (Dengeki Online, 30 October 2003).

> A reader, however strongly engaged in the unfolding of a narrative, is powerless. Like a spectator at a soccer game, he may speculate, conjecture, extrapolate, even shout abuse, but he is not a player . . . He cannot have the player's pleasure of influence: "Let's see what happens when I do *this*." The reader's pleasure is the pleasure of the voyeur. Safe, but impotent. (1997: 4; emphasis in the original)

At first glance, the focus in Aarseth's comparison seems to fall on the passivity of the readers who show only a trivial physical effort to witness story development, but cannot influence the course of action. However, there is one more point of equal importance. 'The player's pleasure of influence' seems to depend on *the system's ability to produce the outcome of the action that players initiate.* Following the footsteps of Aarseth, Gonzalo Frasca presents traditional narratives as the exact counterpart of simulations and underlines the fact that games enable objects to react to the input provided by the gamer by modeling their behaviors:

> Traditional media are representational, not simulational. They excel at producing both descriptions of traits and sequences of events (narrative). A photograph of a plane will tell us information about its shape and color, but it will not fly or crash when manipulated. A flight simulator or a simple toy plane are not only signs, but machines that generate signs according to rules that model some of the behaviors of a real plane. (2003: 223–224)

As these quotes attest, first of all, both Aarseth and Frasca seem to consider the game players' freedom to explore in-game possibilities and the control they have over (characters') actions as the prominent features of ludic engagement. However, as discussed earlier, the consumption of gamelike narratives gives a considerably more active role to the audience. The consumption model presented by Azuma goes beyond an individual's comprehension of 'descriptions of traits and sequences of events'; it allows and encourages the audience to go through several reiterations of the same story and to modify it if desired. Therefore, in the comparison between games and gamelike narratives, the following fact underlined in both of the above quotes plays a more decisive role: games can *simulate* the outcome of an action (falling within the range of actions enabled by the game system) that the gamer prefers to perform. The outcomes of the gamer's 'non-trivial efforts' (which may go beyond decision making, and involve skills of problem solving, coordination, etc. depending on the game) are calculated according to a certain set of rules that regulate possibilities in the gameworld (modeling). These outcomes may or may not display narrative value.

At this point, let us turn to another unofficial online guide, this time for the extended *NGE2* for PSP, to have a better understanding of how the *NGE2* games work.[8]

– SCENARIO 02: Shinji Ikari –

TITLE: "I like this world, though"
MAIN TARGET: Get along with every other character and beat the EVA Series.
CHARACTER SKILLS: Work (10), Knowledge (10), Self Defense (02) and Synchro (10)
CHARACTER STATS: A.T.: 42 / IMP: 90
SLEEPING TIME: From 01 a.m. to 07 a.m.

In this Scenario, Shinji must try to get along with every other character (except PenPen), so he can feel more comfortable with his life in Neo Tokyo-3. Shinji must raise his relationship values with everyone at +700, and everyone must feel for him the same high relationship values. This is quite tough to achieve, especially without the help of any special item like "Unbreakable Heart."

Once you reach +700 values with someone who also feels +700 values for Shinji, a scene will activate in which Shinji and the character share an intimate (and usually fun) event that develops their friendship. These events will only appear when you enter at the required place for each character:

Misato's apartment (before 4 p.m.): Misato, Asuka and Kaji.
School (studying time): Hikari, Kensuke and Gendou.

8. The following quote employs informal use of English. Grammar mistakes are left unedited on purpose.

Convenience Store: Hyuga (7–11 p.m.) and Touji (3–9 p.m.).
NERV: Fuyutsuki, Maya, Aoba, Kaworu, Rei and Ritsuko.

[Jumping to instructions on battle]

The order of the battles is random (except the first against Sachiel), and they can get quite tough depending on your ability, stats, and the help that you get from other Pilots. I recommend you to do a lot of training with other Pilots. Not only it will raise your Synchro, but also will enhance your relationship.

You will know that the EVA Series are about to attack when the DefCon has all turned red but still no Angel attacks. Once you enter NERV, you will watch many scenes. Misato (or your favourite NERV Personnel person) will come to rescue you, and then your Self Defense will be important to survive. (If you happen to die here, reload your game: it's a random event, actually, although the higher Self Defense, the higher probabilities that both you and the Misato will survive.) After this, the battle against the EVA Series will begin. Defeat them to watch the ending.

Note that if any character dies for any reason during this Scenario, you will not be able to get the best ending. (Pler 2008)

This lengthy excerpt proves very helpful for demonstrating how the game system generates a multiplicity of *EVA* stories based on gamers' non-trivial effort, as well as elucidating the causal connections that the game relies upon. First of all, both *NGE2*s make it possible to test out the consequences of a wide variety of actions. In this particular scenario found in the *NGE2* for PSP, as Shinji needs to raise his relationship values, the player may decide to have him engage in a conversation, or smile at or even kiss other characters at a given time. This freedom of action is way more emphasized if we consider that the scenario above is only one of the 18 scenarios found in the game.

However, as in any other game, only certain actions are possible in this version of *NGE2* and only some of these actions are desirable, granted that the aim is opening alternative routes for plot development and completing the game. In the given scenario, while it is up to the player to decide what Shinji will do, the character's actions will have to fall within the range set by the game system and should earn him over 700 relationship points for successful completion. These points can be collected by performing one's own selection among a variety of actions which are assigned numerical values, hence are swappable in terms of their long-term, cumulative consequences. But the guidebook also reveals that some actions have direct consequences on whether and how the game will progress. For instance, although it is possible to reach an ending despite casualties, in order to get the good ending one needs to keep every character alive in this particular scenario. Then, if the goal is first to progress and then to discover all the routes for plot development and endings, staying within certain parameters will be the only way to reach that goal. In other words, the general outlines of the narrative and the consequences of narrative significance (breaking points in the fates of characters and their inter-relations) are largely predefined.

That being said, randomness does not stay entirely out of the picture either. In the given scenario, in order to reach the listed conse-quences, one should meticulously follow the guidebook and collect points as advised. Nevertheless, whether Shinji will live to see the final battle depends on a randomized event. In fact, as Greg Costikyan states, randomness plays a bunch of significant roles in games: "it adds drama, it breaks symmetry, it provides simulation value, and it can be used to foster strategy through statistical analysis" (2013: 86). However, as Costikyan immediately adds, incorporating the random is also pretty risky, for "in excess, it imbalances games, it can foster a sense that success is a consequence of luck rather than excellent play, and it can produce frustration when a streak of bad luck affects a player" (ibid.). While adding variation to gameplay (thus individu-alizing it), as well as reinforcing the element of surprise, randomiza-tion reduces the non-trivial effort of the player to an act of chance.

Therefore, game designers usually aim to strike a good balance in randomization, and harness the sources of uncertainty.

With randomness involved in its 18 scenarios, *NGE2* for PSP presents a wide variety of possible actions and invites gamers to explore alternative routes for plot development again and again for long hours. However, while relying further on randomization can increase replayability even more, both *NGE2*s opt for keeping it at a certain level. In addition to the warnings by Costikyan, in the case that randomization is maximized in games such as the *NGE2*s, it is inevitable that asymmetries will arise between the stories to emerge. Due to chance factor, some stories might end simply too early, before any significant change is observed in the state of characters or suddenly after a long and unrepeatable gaming session. Instead, in the *NGE2*s, causal connections are built in advance to ensure that these sessions can produce meaningful *EVA* stories with equal dramatic impact to that of the series. Seen from a different angle, the guidebook reveals not only the possibilities enabled by the *NGE2* systems, but also the certainties it rests upon. In the given scenario, most obviously, if the players manage to keep Shinji alive with over 700 points, it is certain that the game system will reward them with the promised ending. Then, it is only through this emphasis on causality and by assuring the birth of certain consequences that the *NGE2*s emerge as storytelling games.

Narrative Play vs. Narrative Replay, or Anticipatory vs. Combinatory Play

The fact that gamers play an active role as they engage with an interactive medium is mentioned quite often as a specific aspect in research on games. However, it would be misleading to think of narrative engagement as an entirely passive activity. In fact, Brian Upton suggests that engagement with both narratives and games should be considered an experience of play, which he defines as "free movement within a system of constraints" (2015: 15). From this point of view, the activity of interpreting what is happening in a story and anticipating what will happen next becomes the counterpart of gamers' activity that is both limited and enabled by rules. Play in general requires players to map out the potential field of action, but while gamers face the consequences of the actions they choose, readers or cinema goers have their guesses tested out as the story unfolds. In this sense, narrative play becomes an active mental exercise. However, as discussed in the very beginning, gamelike narratives encourage if not necessitate the audience to give a more concrete form to their mental experience by producing alternative stories in the form of derivative works.

In realist literature, although trivial things and events occupy the stage along with grave occurrences, the causal axis for plot development stays very clear. The consequences of actions are supposed to be defined to a great extent by the rigid grand narratives of the 19th century, while unlikely developments are meticulously woven into the story as wild twists of fate. With the waning of grand narratives, the possibility of turning readers' mental activity into an autonomous re-creation process has gradually gained visibility. The liberation and materialization of audience experience emerged as an option, thanks to, first of all, the media environment. The increasing accessibility and consumption of narratives enabled the audience to identify the most common elements and patterns in different works. As a result, it became possible to think of new narratives as variations of the already present ones. With every 'new' version of a familiar story, with every new connection between actions and their consequences, it becomes clearer that everything, no matter how unexpected, is potentially explainable. This being the case, everything becomes possible in any given storyworld. Some narratives embrace this possibility and display a blatant lack of causal organization. As the audience's understanding of the field of possible actions grows vague, even when the ending of a story is revealed at its very beginning, the route that will lead to that end remains a mystery. The use of familiar narrative elements is crucial for the process of anticipation, but not entirely enlightening either.

Even though the use of standardized characters, settings and events seems to narrow down the number of the narratives that can be produced, what they can form together is practically endless as there are no guiding principles determining how they should be combined. In worlds where not only wild coincidences but even contradictions are justifiable (as branching timelines and alternate realities), chaos evolves into infinite adventures, provided that characters are distinguishable enough in any context. Then, the discovery of each particular combination of characters, settings and events becomes an object of audience interest, whereas the connections between them seem temporary from the start and re-built whenever necessary. Instead of asking 'what should happen in this world?' (according to rules that regulate causality) and meticulously meshing unlikely coincidences with the fabric of narrative, it is possible to start from a desirable consequence and loosely pave the way up until that point, skipping steps if desired, knowing that anything can be forced into the gaps left in the process.

Equipped with such a view on narratives, the audience might be interested in building their own set of connections at will as well. If a character is attractive enough, the audience can build an alternative scenario with that character, embarking on new adventures that are not present in the original work or even clearly conflicting with what is depicted officially. This vicious cycle guarantees infinite twists to an audience satiated with stories and provides the space as well as the incentive for the creation of new, surprising stories. Then, the weakening of causal order and its deliberate undermining in gamelike narratives enable the audience to simulate alternative routes for plot development themselves. In this way, they also initiate a form of serialization that differs from the traditional type which takes the shape of prequels and sequels. They encourage everyone to *replay* the same story and produce alternative versions as derivative works, through abandoning the attempt to establish and abide by causal connections, combining whatever they want to keep from the original work with other narratives of their picking. This form of narrative replay can be named 'combinatory play,' that is, free combination of narrative elements allowed by a suspension of causal constraints (as opposed to Upton's interpretive or anticipatory play, which takes place entirely in the mind of the audience).

Combinatory Play across the *EVA* Games

Pursuing alternative directions for plot development in narrative play becomes an end in itself and brings the experience of engaging with narratives one step closer to the experience of playing games. In the absence of guiding principles concerning the consequences of actions, along with the unraveling of connections between characters and contexts, everything seems equally possible in any storyworld and complete rewrites become valid forms of serialization. Gamelikeness ensues in that these narratives allow the audience to take control of characters' actions in the alternative stories of their own making. However, this type of engagement differs from playing games in that the audience can also control *the outcomes* of actions. This results in the possibility of producing alternative stories starting from their end. In other words, rather than asking what would happen in a particular world, one can fill in the background of any desirable situation. Instead of delineating characters' capacity of action under certain circumstances, the production of gamelike narratives depends on a level of recognizability in character design that is also transferable to the parts that constitute a character. This allows characters to preserve the core of their identity in any context and do whatever they like.

The previously cited online guide of *NGE2* for PSP demonstrates how both versions of the game differ from gamelike narratives precisely in these respects. The *NGE2*s allow players to observe what would be possible in the *EVA* world, based on the way in which this world is modeled (i.e., organized by a relatively simplified set of rules) in each case. Moreover, as they are intended to be story generators, the *NGE2*s fix causal relations to a great extent and minimize randomness to ensure that noteworthy events can be meaningfully aligned in every complete play. Although the wide variety of system-enabled actions makes it highly unlikely for different people to play the games in the exact same way, performing certain actions and reaching certain states (as a result of carrying out sets of actions that may vary in themselves) will produce the same consequences for all. The *NGE2s* provide players with alternative stories of emotional impact, precisely by setting the range of what in-game objects can do, and by predetermining causal relations to an extent through assigning direct consequences to some actions and states. But surprisingly, taken as a series, the *EVA* games offer an experience bearing an unexpected similarity to that offered by gamelike narratives.

Considering the fact that there is a wide variety of *EVA* games, it is difficult to approach them as a set. The *EVA* games differ in genre and in the ways they connect with the anime series. *Detective Evangelion*, for example, is an Adventure game which surprisingly turns Shinji Ikari into an investigator of some murders that do not exist in the anime series. However, despite the variations, a common trait that cuts across the *EVA* games is worthy of notice: almost each of them borrows a certain set of elements from the anime. Not only do we see familiar characters appearing in familiar settings (sometimes in the company of newly introduced faces), we also see these characters once again grappling with the same traumatic events from the series. In the Raising simulations (such as the *Ayanami with Asuka Raising Project*), the attacks of the Angels are still a part of the characters' otherwise ordinary lives. Those who play these Raising sims are responsible for characters' clothing, as well as their battle training. In *Detective Evangelion* as well, despite the fact that the game scenario blatantly digresses from the *EVA* anime series, we see that the protagonist is still fighting Angels as he tries to solve murders.

As discussed previously, games don't have to tell stories or maintain consistency when they tell stories, just as in the *NARUTO* games discussed by Roth in detail. But the *EVA* games obsessively relate to the same story, by featuring the same characters, settings and main events from the anime series. Even *Evangelion New Theatrical Edition: 3nd Impact*, which is a Rhythm game that requires players to trace the beat of a song or sound clip, goes directly back to the series with each correct move and reveals familiar images or video clips. Moreover, at certain levels, the game switches to monologues from the series instead of music, which transforms the experience into an information hunt ('Which parts am I going to see? Will there be anything new?' being the concerns) instead of an ordinary music game simply employing the *EVA* soundtrack. The games, therefore, seem to engineer an audience engagement that is most enjoyable in reference to the anime series.

This referential loop is actually established by the anime itself. At its end, the anime series reveals flickers of alternative directions for plot development, which spiral into rewrites in the shape of animated movies and other works. Despite the high number of overall *EVA* titles, rather than the addition of new story arcs, the official franchise expands via alternatives of the same story. This cyclical serialization produces a very small pool of *EVA*-related elements to rely upon in the creation of new works, and the surprise value in these works does not come from what will be combined as much as it comes from *how* the same elements will be combined. The *EVA* games take part in the same practice, as specific narrative elements are interwoven in each game especially around the fight with Angels. This step shapes the engagement with the games to a noteworthy extent.

If "traditional narrative media lack the 'feature' of allowing modifications to the stories," as Frasca states (2003: 227), gamelike narratives trigger the materialization of alternatives in the next work to follow. Pursuing alternative stories in games such as the *NGE2s*, on the other hand, is a requirement rather than a mere possibility according to Frasca. However, interestingly, although it is possible *within the same game* to picture different paths for plot development, these games tend to go back to the same iconic *EVA* battles one after another to retrace or reimagine the relationships between a selection of the same characters *in separate works*.

While it is always an option to use the same mechanics or modeling in serializing games, which is not only cost-effective, but also preferable for establishing a particular style, these games keep changing both elements and explode the possibilities of interaction with the same series across time and different genres. The *EVA* games do not rely on downloadable content (DLC) to prolong consumer engagement either. Through DLCs, new objects or environments can be introduced in installments without changing the mechanics or the rule system of a game. However, instead of capitalizing on this strategy, the *EVA* games seem to connect over a specific set of narrative elements as the games keep increasing in number. (Bandai-Namco's *Tales of Zestria* JRPG series has an Evangelion DLC pack that comes with a costume set though.)

Even when the gameplay centralizes gamers' non-trivial efforts or the aspect of randomization, connecting with the anime series by featuring the same characters and events creates the expectancy as to what the gamer will do in order to see another version of the same story. To the extent that this concern gets pronounced, the experience with the whole franchise appears narrative-oriented and emerges as a rewriting process. Moreover, the endless reiteration puts story-generating games such as the *NGE2s* in a specifically paradoxical position. Although they enable hours of replay in themselves, this quality seems limited in comparison to the inexhaustible potential of rewriting the same story forever.

The *EVA* games, in sequence, build an obsessive connection with the anime series by featuring its main characters and events over and over. In this respect, the *EVA* franchise treats games like narratives, as if they needed serialization to introduce alternative ways for plot development. *EVA* games like the *NGE2s* flaunt the medium-specific capacity to simulate the outcomes of possible actions, but this capacity

gets absorbed by serialization: games that function as story generators seem to rewrite the same story one after the other. The causal
infrastructure (that these games build in order to enable the process
of creating alternatives) seems like an alternative to infinite others in
the first place, and each game seems to herald the coming of the next
one already. In this light, setting medium-specificity aside, instigating
combinatory play becomes the common point across the video games
and the anime series. Regardless of their genres, these games instigate
an active discovery of a new set of connections between the same
characters and events once again.

Final Remarks and Future Directions

In literary realism, although chance encounters are not uncommon
and in fact quite influential on how actions and consequently characters' fates will unravel, the diegetic context (encompassing physical
surroundings as well as socio-economical circumstances) is given an
undeniable and unequalled weight in shaping causal connections. To
put it differently, while chains of actions and consequences are mostly
organized as the context dictates, unlikely yet often observed occurrences are meticulously justified by chance. The resulting configuration (of what happens when and where) draws a unique fate for the
characters, pinning them down at a certain position and making them
who they are.

Gamelike narratives, on the other hand, start from the premise
that everything is justifiable on the condition that characters are well-
defined. This type of narrative severs the character-context connection
and annuls their interdependence. As characters are attributed recognizable traits from the start, there is no need for them to be defined
by a particular context, and conversely, they don't need to function as
an anchoring pin for a contextual fabric that could otherwise unravel.

Gamelike narratives leave causal connections underdefined on
purpose, in order to allow characters to roam outside their original

contexts, outside any zones of restriction. Such narratives encourage the audience to engage in a specific type of 'combinatory play,' which can be defined as the free combination of narrative elements allowed by a suspension of causal constraints. As long as there are well-defined characters in a narrative, one can always select a set of favorites and imagine them in new diegetic contexts. Moreover, it becomes possible to completely rewrite these characters' actions, for their scope is not predefined by causal necessity. Gamelike narratives, then, not only unlock the potential of endless serialization, but also (more remarkably) enable the creation of endless alternatives, worlds of infinite possibilities where the exact same action can produce different consequences. *EVA* is a great example of the latter tendency.

Gamelike narratives seem to get closer to games by allowing for a quest for alternatives via downplaying causality. However, in the case of video games, the range of possible actions is necessarily predetermined to differing extents, so that the system can calculate and present the consequences of a variety of in-game actions and encounters. Standing out among the *EVA* games as the ultimate story generators, the *NGE2s* rely on specifically pronounced causal connections (which is not a requirement for all types of games).

NGE2 for PSP offers quite a variety of in-game actions and a high replay value, given that it consists of 18 different scenarios with multiple endings. However, performing actions randomly is not enough to successfully traverse all the courses for plot development and reach the desired endings. In both versions of *NGE2*, at certain times, characters must be led to do certain things in a certain sequence. Using Jesper Juul's terminology, the *NGE2s* come with a great deal of such predetermined 'progression structures,' so that the alternative stories to emerge from play sessions are all rewarding, striking narrative experiences. (Juul sets 'games of emergence' apart from 'games of progression' on the grounds that the former introduce a bunch of rules which loosely define the range of what is possible in a game, while the latter require players to follow specific to-do-lists to successfully cover a game. Nonetheless, progression structures can be observed in games of emergence as well, especially in the shape of specific quests or objectives.) At other times, even when the gamer is entirely free to make a pick within a field of possible actions, these actions must still yield enough points to stay within a certain range for progress. Provided that at least one of their aims is to present stories on a par with the anime, the creators of the *EVA* games need to make sure that there will be significant events with sufficient dramatic impact on the way in which the stories progress.

Of course, not every game needs to centralize the role of narrative in the particular experience it offers. Despite the fact that there is a narrative potential in video games, it is not the goal of each to construct a narrative-driven experience. Through a cross-media analysis of *NARUTO*, Roth settles down to prove "how software-based video-game adaptations go beyond textual media in that they can facilitate a wide range of ways to play with and without narrative elements by combining franchise elements in ways unique to the medium" (2013: 244). *NARUTO* games feature familiar faces from the manga and the anime, along with a selection of settings and events from the series. However, Roth underlines that in a game, narrative coherence may be only of secondary importance or not sought after at all. The action and fighting games examined by Roth do not necessarily make significant contributions to the anime or manga storylines. In fact, they even discard some of the unique features of the characters, for their priority falls on creating a balanced environment of challenge, where gamers test their control skills. Nevertheless, be it limited to visual similarities or a strong adherence to plot, any connection with the series presents an extra source of fun for those who are familiar with the original narrative.

Similarly, the *EVA* games differ in genre and offer players novelties in gameplay as well as in the ways they connect with the anime series. Some of these games present the opportunity to play out the exact same scenario as the anime series. Some allow players to carry out new actions with the original set of characters. A final group of games introduce entirely new characters to mingle with the rest. Nevertheless, all of these games present clear connections with the anime series, specifically by featuring a number of the original set of characters along with certain recurring events. Even games like *Detective Evangelion*, which introduce striking divergences from the anime series in terms of plot, include not only the characters, but also their traumatic battle with the Angels. Furthermore, in some instances, this strong linkage between the games and the series goes beyond genre-specific concerns as well. In the Rhythm game, *3nd Impact*, on top of the cutscenes being a narrative reward, at times the music is exchanged for the characters' dialogue lines from the anime series. The sense of rhythm is thus severed from music, and control skills are employed to open up the same story once again.

The *EVA* games are most rewarding to fans of the anime series, as they allow for detailed comparisons. But more interestingly, as they take up the same elements obsessively and tend to reimagine a selection of the same happenings with the same characters, each of these games seems like an installment of a never-ending rewriting process. As a result, despite the fact that games are alternative producing systems in themselves, each new game seems to be an alternative to the previously released games as well as those that will probably follow. Instead of going exclusively in a medium-specific direction, the cumulation of the *EVA* games seems to gain a gamelike quality, supporting a specific consumer engagement.

Games certainly do not need to offer narrative experiences. Even when they feature characters whose stories are told across different media, they can centralize gamers' control skills and minimize narrative information. Their priority falls on incorporating the gamers' will and simulating the consequences of the actions they choose to perform. However, if combinatory play is defined as the free combination of narrative elements allowed by a suspension of causal constraints, it can be said that the *EVA* games as a series display a gamelikeness by featuring the same characters obsessively in combination with the same traumatic events from the series and by assigning new consequences to the same actions over a multitude of games. In this way, not only do they form a bridge with the anime series as they leave the control of the characters' actions to the gamers, but also lead the audience familiar with the anime series or the games to ask certain questions. The concern of the gamers goes beyond what they can perform in the *EVA* universe by stepping in the shoes of these characters, which may be seen as the medium-specific charm of games. The question instead becomes, 'How else will I be relating these characters through my actions?' This transformation reveals a narrative overtone in the player's engagement with the games and turns the experience into a form of story production (which is enabled by the games, but supervised by the consumers themselves). Individual gaming sessions thus get connected to the totality of the games and the anime series regardless of genre and (non-)narrative orientation.

This chapter aimed to expose how the *EVA* games are aligned with the anime series in terms of gamelikeness, and looked at the audience engagement with both media from the perspective of this alignment. In Azuma's writings, gamelikeness emerges as a point of similarity between games and narrative media, providing new ground for discussing the latter in a new light. This chapter dissected the concept of gamelikeness to underline that the similarity observed between narratives across contemporary media (i.e., the common drive toward the exploration of alternatives in narrative production and consumption) is founded on a downplay of causality, which sets narrative media once again in contrast to games. Yet again, as this discussion of the *EVA* games revealed, suspending medium-specific affordances is also an option, especially to set a particular tone in a media franchise. The *EVA* games seem to support a certain manner of audience engagement that is established by the anime series in the first place. The obsessive rewriting allowed by the extreme downplay of causality in the anime series finds its reflection in the serialization of the games, as an outward explosion of alternatives over a multitude of alternative generating systems. All in all, this discussion underlined not only the need to consider the medium-specificity of anime and games in relation to each other, but also the centrality of the anime series within the *EVA* franchise. What remains to be discussed, through comprehensive comparisons between similar franchises from all around the world, is to what extent the *EVA* franchise should be considered exceptional and to what extent representational of a contemporary media tendency.

References

Primary sources

3rd Impact: Grasshopper Manufacture. 2011. *Evangelion Shin Gekijōban— Saundo Inpakuto*. PlayStation Portable. Japanese version.

Ayanami with Asuka Raising Project: Broccoli and Gainax. 2002. *Shinseiki Evangelion: Ayanami Ikusei Keikaku with Asuka Hokan Keikaku*. PlayStation 2. Japanese version.

Detective Evangelion: Broccoli. 2007. *Meitantei Evangelion*. PlayStation 2. Japanese version.

NGE2: Bandai. 2004. *Shinseiki Evangelion 2*. PlayStation 2. Japanese version.

NGE 2 for PSP: Bandai. 2006. *Shinseiki Evangelion 2: Tsukurareshi Sekai—Another Cases*. PlayStation Portable. Japanese version.

Secondary sources

Aarseth, E. (1997). *Cybertext: Perspectives on Ergodic Literature*. Baltimore, MD and London: The Johns Hopkins University Press.

Azuma, H. (2009). *Otaku: Japan's Database Animals*. Minneapolis, Minnesota: University of Minnesota Press. (Introduction and translation by J. E. Abel and S. Kono)

Computer Entertainment Rating Organization (CERO) website. Retrieved from: http://www.cero.biz

Costikyan, G. (2013). *Uncertainty in Games*. Cambridge, Massachusetts: MIT Press.

Dengeki Online (2003). *Evangerion 2 kansei kinen!* Anno kantoku to Shibamura shi ga akasu Eva 2 no sekai (30 October). Retrieved from: https://dengekionline.com/data/news/2003/10/30/da06e64083185f76 d1da5f5417d7a811.html

Frasca, G. (2003). Simulation versus Narrative: Introduction to Ludology. In M. J. P. Wolf and B. Perron (eds.), *The Video Game Theory Reader* (pp. 231–235). New York and London: Routledge.

GrunGast82. (2004). *Shinseiki Evangelion: Ayanami Ikusei Keikaku with Asuka Hokan Keikaku*—Condition/Event Guide. Retrieved from: https://gamefaqs.gamespot.com/ps2/917346-shinseiki-evangelion -ayanami-ikusei-keikaku-with-asuka-hokan/faqs/32256

Pler, L. (2008). *Neon Genesis Evangelion: Tsukurareshi Sekai—Another Cases*—FAQ/Walkthrough. Retrieved from: https://gamefaqs.gamespot .com/psp/930008-neon-genesis-evangelion-tsukurareshi-sekai-another -cases/faqs/45735

Rancière, J. (2007). *The Future of the Image*. London: Verso. (Translated by G. Elliott)

Roth, M. (2013). Playing "Naruto": Between Metanarrative Characters, Unit Operations, and Objects. In J. Berndt and B. Kümmerling-Meibauer (eds.), *Manga's Cultural Crossroads* (pp. 243–258). New York: Routledge.

Ryan, M.-L. (2003). On Defining Narrative Media. *Image [&] Narrative*, 6. Retrieved from: http://www.imageandnarrative.be/inarchive/medium theory/marielaureryan.htm

Salen, K. & Zimmerman, E. (2004). *Rules of Play: Game Design Fundamentals*. Cambridge, Massachusetts: The MIT Press.

Simons, J. (2007). Narrative, Games, and Theory. *Game Studies: The International Journal of Computer Game Research*, 7(1). Retrieved from: http://gamestudies.org/0701070I/articles/simons

Upton, B. (2015). *The Aesthetics of Play*. Cambridge, Massachusetts: The MIT Press.

10. Creating Happy Endings

Yaoi Fanworks as Audience Response to Kaworu and Shinji's Relationship

Jessica Bauwens-Sugimoto

Shinji Ikari is the undisputed protagonist of the *Neon Genesis Evangelion* (*EVA*) franchise, and Kaworu Nagisa has a short but pivotal role in Shinji's story. But many fans were left unsatisfied with the ending of the series, including *fujoshi*.

Fujoshi, or 'rotten girls,' is a self-depreciating term for mostly female fans who interpret and rewrite relationships between male characters as romantic and sexual, within a fan-created genre called yaoi (the analogous commercial genre with original stories is called BL, short for boys love) (Galbraith 2011: 212). This type of fan stories is what Henry Jenkins calls "textual poaching" (1992): Fans will pilfer the elements they like from their favorite stories, and combine and rewrite them to their own satisfaction, not just as a solitary pastime, but often as a way to connect to other fans and find a community of like-minded people (see Bauwens-Sugimoto 2014). Jenkins and others active in English-language scholarship like Joanna Russ (1985) and Constance Penley (1997) discussed the equivalent and mostly English-language genre of slash, where fans recombine relationships between male characters, particularly characters poached from Science Fiction works like Kirk/Spock (K/S) from the TV series *Star Trek*, one of the earliest popular pairings. The term slash, derived from the "/" sign placed between capital letters, is the English-language equivalent of yaoi.

Inside and outside of Japan, for more than a decade now, a large amount of research on yaoi and BL has been conducted. Many academic inquiries focus on these genres as a whole, and as the field grows, so

How to cite this book chapter:
Bauwens-Sugimoto, J. 2021. Creating Happy Endings: Yaoi Fanworks as Audience Response to Kaworu and Shinji's Relationship. In: Santiago Iglesias, J. A. and Soler Baena, A. (Eds.). *Anime Studies: Media-Specific Approaches to Neon Genesis Evangelion*. Pp. 327–352 Stockholm: Stockholm University Press. DOI: https://doi.org/10.16993/bbp.k. License: CC-BY 4.0

do subgenres like BL featuring Arab princes (see Nagaike 2009). Some researchers investigate the activities of yaoi fans in particular locations, such as the Philippines (see Fermin 2013), but few yet have analyzed yaoi fanworks based on just one canon series, or one franchise, usually a work of popular fiction used as a source text for characters to form romantic and sexual connections in the fanwork. Yet, by doing so, it is possible to illuminate how one particular subset of fans, which is mostly female, resolve their issues with the ending of *EVA*. This chapter foregrounds the relationship between the *EVA* characters Kaworu and Shinji, called *Kawoshin*. The contraction Kawoshin is used as both shorthand for the couple in speech and a tag by many yaoi fans within their works, but also in discourse about the pairing on and offline. Kaworu's name is listed before Shinji's because most fujoshi see him as the more dominant character in their relationship, as will be detailed later.

Kawoshin fans devotedly explore the characters' relationship through their fanworks and create an endless variety of 'What if?' stories, whether in peer-produced *dōjinshi*, the prevalent type of fanwork in Japan and mostly available in printed form, traded between fans at specialized amateur markets, or online fanfiction, which is the most common type of fanwork globally (especially in English). Left wanting after Shinji killed Kaworu (in episode 24), Japanese and foreign yaoi fans have created vast amounts of Kawoshin stories and art for more than two decades. At present, the Kawoshin pairing is regarded as a classic, or *ōdō* (lit. way of the king) where *EVA* is concerned. The fan stories build on the relationship of the two characters within the 'canon,' that is to say, the texts they reference stretch from the initial TV anime series and the subsequent films, and to interviews with the director Hideaki Anno and his collaborators about the series, as well as about their interpersonal relationships. Within Anno's original series, the relationship is unstable and hazily defined, but it already transcends homosociality because of Kaworu's transgression of normative male (and human) boundaries, and precisely this tension, or the resolution of it, is a starting point for many fan stories.

As several chapters in this volume demonstrate, *EVA* is of endless fascination to fans, critics, scholars and those active in the anime industry because of its openness to interpretation and speculation. This chapter uses a digital ethnographic approach tailored to specific websites where fans are active (based on Herring 2004). It delves into the large amount of Kawoshin fan narratives currently available online, both novels and manga, to find out if and how yaoi fans engage with the issues that have been prevalent in general fan criticism as well as academic discourse on *EVA*, such as the deconstruction of the mecha genre or posthumanism.

The first part of this chapter looks at the way in which the characters interact in the initial TV, or canon, series and how fans' interpretation of these interactions vary wildly. The second part is a first and somewhat rough attempt at analyzing the most common tropes in popular Japanese and English language yaoi fan stories focusing on Kawoshin, as well as the related online discourse. The third part summarizes the methodological hurdles encountered along the way, which are caused by the fact that each fan site and community has its own culture and characteristics.

Looking for Kawoshin in Text and Subtext

Yaoi fans extract 'proof' of a relationship between two male characters from within the narrative of the original or source work and between its lines. Yet, depending on perspective and desire to believe, this proof can be obvious or completely fabricated.

Many yaoi fanworks rewrite male characters who have been present in popular series from the initial episodes as a romantic couple. These include Naruto and Sasuke from *NARUTO*, Erin and Levi from *Attack on Titan*, Sebastian and Ciel from *Black Butler*, and Sherlock Holmes and Dr. Watson to name a non-anime example with a much longer history. Kawoshin is an exceptional pairing for yaoi standards since Kaworu appears very late in the series, in episode 24 of 26. The time he spends with Shinji is a turning point in Shinji's life, eventually ending with Kaworu's demise, when he magnanimously sacrifices his immortality so that humanity may live, and dies by Shinji's hand, or the hand of the Eva unit operated by Shinji. There is an alternative ending in the Q theatrical release (*Evangelion: 3.0 You Can (Not) Redo*, 2012), in which Kaworu dies in a different way, but again self-sacrificially.

Whether before Kaworu's death he and Shinji were ever in a romantic and sexual relationship is like most things in *EVA* open to interpretation. The series itself, and in particular some works in the rest of the franchise, do suggest that there is more to the Kawoshin relationship than mere admiration, friendship, platonic love and finally betrayal and enmity. And this is what activates fannish imagination. But there are hurdles to the pairing of the two characters. One would be that Shinji is only 14, mid-puberty, which poses a risk for some fans, as in a number of jurisdictions it would be illegal to depict him in homosexual and/or graphically sexual situations. Thus, pictorial depictions are often off limits, and in some cases even written ones. Another is that Kaworu is the 17th Angel, immortal yet not indestructible. It is never clear if his notions of love, whether platonic or romantic, align with what humans consider to be love. As a character who has the power to destroy all of humanity but chooses to desist, his power is that of a god, and what he felt for Shinji may have been deeper than something a human can feel, yet still not necessarily sexual or romantic in nature. It is this openness to interpretation, the leaving open of many possibilities, that invites fans' imaginations to expand on Anno's story, allowing fans to make it their own stories too.

Many *EVA* fanworks are not yaoi. They feature other couples, most notably heterosexual romance between Shinji and Rei or Asuka, a potential love triangle which is supplied right from the start. In the series, Shinji and Kaworu get close extremely fast due to Kaworu's attitude, which differs fundamentally from those of the female characters in whom Shinji expresses sexual interest: Kaworu reads Shinji like an open book and without hesitation discloses his insights into all of Shinji's insecurities, which embarrasses and confuses Shinji. Kaworu's lack of conventional physical boundaries only furthers Shinji's bewilderment, indicated by his blushing in many of his interactions with Kaworu.

When fans write Kawoshin, many interpret Shinji as more feminine relative to Kaworu, as is customary in yaoi as well as BL stories, where one character is usually coded as more masculine and called the *seme* (lit. attacker, top), while his paramour is the *uke* (lit. receiver, bottom). In *Seibo Evangelion* (*Holy Mother Evangelion*), an entire volume analyzing *EVA* and one of the earliest to do so, author and feminist SF critic Mari Kotani, also considered an expert on fandom, yaoi, feminism and the techno-gothic, discussed Kaworu as a queer (or *hentai*, i.e., 'perverse') character with both male and female characteristics, and remarks that Kaworu is a character purposefully made for "a special subset of fans from all over the country" (my translation, 1997: 90). She clarifies that she is talking about yaoi fans, of which there are now many more not just all over the country, but all over the world, and goes on to give a brief history of the yaoi genre (ibid.: 91) and how it relates to feminist critique, citing her 1994 book *Joseijō muishiki (*technogynosis*): Josei SF ron josetsu* (Unconscious Femininity, Technogynosis: An Introduction to Women's SF). For this book, she won the 15th *Nihon SF Taishō* (Japan SF Grand Prize), and she was one of the first critics to discuss yaoi from a feminist perspective.

Kaworu himself describes Adam as the mother of all Angels, which, as the first and last of his kind, makes him his own mother. What further feminizes Kaworu is that he is non-human, a dangerous creature akin to a monster, a "female who can wreck the infinite" (Kristeva 1982: 157), and therefore abject. In one of the most confusing scenes in the series, Kaworu calls the crucified Lilith, mother of all humans, Adam, causing more gender blurring.

Some fans new to Kawoshin yaoi do wonder why Shinji is always drawn as an uke, and one fan on a scanlation site offers this explanation in the English comment section of an originally Japanese-language dōjin work, scanlated into English:

> It's because Shinji throughout canon is almost always the passive/dependent party. He lives for the approval of others, and rarely ever initiates things on his own . . . With Shinji as the bottom, you get to fill him up with the love, care and support he so desperately wants. (Squinut 2017)

Another fan responded to the comment, calling it insightful enough to want to frame it and put it on their wall, and others expressed agreement with the idea of filling Shinji up with love, which is what they want to see in fanworks as they were denied this by the source work.

Fans have been justifying their yaoi reading of Kawoshin by reference to authorial intention, but director Anno did not set out to explicitly depict the two characters as a romantic couple. This distinction is important in view of the controversy surrounding the new English subtitles of the 2019 Netflix adaptation. Anno supervised the translation and had the translator work as closely to the Japanese original as possible. Controversy arose when the Japanese word *suki*, used by Kaworu and directed at Shinji in episode 24, was translated as "like" rather than "love," the way it had been in earlier localizations. The ADV film 2003 localization (for DVD) translated the line *suki-tte koto sa* as "It means I love you"; however, the 1998 VHS ADV also translated it as "It means I like you."

Some fans heavily invested in the Kawoshin relationship insisted that anything less than explicit representation within the source work equals the erasure of real sexual minorities, and they launched a vicious and unwarranted attack on official translator Daniel M. Kanemitsu on social media. The word *suki* is in general translated as "like," whereas it takes a *daisuki* (lit. big like) to be translated as "love." The distinction can be murky and vague. Even when the distinction between "love" and "like" is clearly based on context, the characters' earlier interactions in the text, the depiction of their inner thoughts, their background and more, *suki* and *daisuki* can still be "like" or "love" without carrying the nuance of romantic or sexual attraction. Given that Shinji and Kaworu have only three episodes to become close (episodes 24–26), and Kaworu comes on strong by very directly communicating his thoughts to Shinji, a like can still be interpreted as romantic: he may indeed mean love, but this is never clear, a common trait of interpersonal issues between the characters in *EVA*.

Among fans, not confined to yaoi, Shinji is widely regarded as an avatar for Anno since he voiced as much himself in a short essay included in the first volume of the 1995 *EVA* manga series, and while Kaworu does not necessarily have or need an avatar in the flesh, some fan and business insider sources (GAINAX 2008: 54–55) point out that part of Kaworu's character design, whether good looks or personality, is based on anime director Kunihiko Ikuhara, known for several seasons of *Sailor Moon* (1992–96) and *Revolutionary Girl Utena* (1997), and one of the people within the same industry whom Anno looks up to. When Ikuhara was interviewed in an article for the GAINAX volume *All about Nagisa Kaworu a Child of The EVANGELION*, subtitled "The magic of 'You are fine just the way you are'" (2008: 54–55), he said that one of Kaworu's other pivotal lines directed at Shinji, the famous "You are deserving of good-will"[1] (translated as "You are deserving of love" in the 2003 ADV DVD), is something that he once may have said to Anno. In turn, Anno has stated that Ikuhara is someone whom he admires, and someone who encouraged his work as an anime creator.

Apart from Ikuhara being projected onto Kaworu, Shinji is habitually discussed within fandom as a stand-in for Anno, an avatar to work through his own psychological issues, which include depression. In this regard, fans refer to the fact that character designer Yoshiyuki Sadamoto had convinced Anno to use a male instead of a female protagonist (1999: n.p.), and that he sketched Shinji like the titular character of *Nadia—The Secret of Blue Water* (1990–93), only with short hair.

---

1. Original Japanese: *kōi ni atai suru yo*.

Putting staff relations aside, Anno himself was clearly aware of yaoi fandom when he voiced that Kaworu is an idealized version of Shinji, in other words, everything Shinji aspires to, which meant for fans that their relationship could easily be rewritten as Shinji being in love with Kaworu. Anno made his comment in an interview in the first issue of *Bessatsu JUNE* (vol. 1, September 1996, n.p.), a companion publication to the oldest specialized magazine for *shōnen'ai* (lit. boys love, in disuse for contemporary BL stories) and *tanbi* (narratives focusing on male beauty, often but not always adolescent), *JUN/ JUNE* (1978–2012). *JUNE* magazine was a precursor of commercial BL and an offshoot from general girls' manga magazines, which were the first to publish shōnen'ai narratives. The magazine editors' motivation to interview Anno, who was not a BL anime director, rested on the knowledge that, at the time, Kawoshin was the hottest new pairing among Japanese fujoshi.

Kawoshin Fanworks, an Analysis

Kawoshin fans read and write stories about the couple not necessarily because they wish the source work would be different, but because through watching *EVA* they developed love for the characters, and this love translates into a desire for the characters to meet fates other than death—many and varied fates, often light-hearted, but sometimes as dark or darker than the source material itself. Looking at what fans do with Kaworu and Shinji in these stories and how they interpret and rewrite the source material, I aim to give some insight into a part of *EVA* and SF anime fandom that is skewed heavily toward the female.

Researching Fan Sites with Varying Amounts of Legality and Regulation

The main method used for this chapter is similar to the one used by my co-author and I in 2012 (published in 2013) when analyzing long fan narratives (up to half a million words) based on the anime and manga hit series *NARUTO*, written in English by male fans (Bauwens-Sugimoto & Renka 2013). Since it was impossible to analyze all stories on fanfiction.net—where I also examine Kawoshin stories this time around—and we were interested in not just the content of the stories, but also the interaction between fan authors and their readers, we narrowed our sample by looking at fan author/reader engagement, and limited our analysis to the top 10 stories, where author/reader engagement was highest (based on the number of comments per chapter). Because of its flexibility, we then used CMDA (Computer Mediated Discourse Analysis) as an approach to research online comments and interaction, or computer-mediated communication (based on Herring 2004) and to look for the most common tropes in the fanworks (the text), and the most common themes apparent in author/reader interaction (the metatext), which I also use this time. On a limited scale such as for this chapter, CDMA requires no specialized software (both times Google documents and spreadsheets were used) and similar to grounded theory, the findings emerge from the data, with tentative hypotheses starting to form from there. For this chapter, I looked at three different websites (ifanfiction.net, Pixiv and one unnamed site with pirated translations of dōjinshi) where fan-created content is posted and readers can comment. On the scanlation site, I examined the comments where there was a clear disconnect between the text, that is, the scanlated dōjinshi, and the metatext, that is, the comments by fans who often directly addressed the artists of these dōjinshi, but who never got a response as the artists had not authorized the uploading of their works on the website. All data for this chapter were gathered between 30 May and 13 July 2019. The considered fanworks and creator/reader interaction were all posted publicly online, though some of them without authorization by the fan author, in which case I will not name the site.

Given time and space restraints, the scope of this chapter is limited to works that are (also) known outside of Japan, and it is further limited to the major languages the Japanese Kawoshin fan narratives known overseas have been translated into. Where the work discussed is originally Japanese, I will mention which languages are readily available in scanlation, to capture the borderless nature of the fan discussion about the work in question.

A study should be verifiable and data gathered easy to interpret, but research into fanworks has to cope with very limited verifiable quantitative data and with materials that are published, traded and sold within a shadow economy in a legal gray zone (see McLelland 2018). Dōjinshi sold in Japan have a limited amount of copies, and fanworks published online may disappear suddenly, at the whim of the author or an administrator of the website.

Kawoshin Fanworks on fanfiction.net and Pixiv

Fanfiction.net, established in 1998, is the largest, and oldest, multilingual all-genre fansite on the Internet (mostly English, but boasting a total of over 40 language options) and also the one we used in 2013 when sourcing *NARUTO* fan narratives (Bauwens-Sugimoto & Renka 2013). Pixiv is an online fanwork archive that went live in 2007. Originally geared toward Japanese users, it hosts mostly drawn content (illustration and manga), as well as some written works, mainly fan novellas and novels. As its popularity outside of Japan grew, so did the diversity of its artists; to date, it has over 20 million users. I am looking at these two sites together and separate from the scanlation site discussed below because fanfiction.net is based in the United States, and given the 'fair use' doctrine in US copyright legislation, its content is legal. The fan content on Pixiv is not technically legal in accordance with Japanese law, but in a legal gray zone usually left undisturbed by copyright holders. Both sites have a certain amount of regulations to which submissions need to adhere and contributors upload only content they created. Scanlation sites, on the other hand, feature mostly pirated content uploaded without permission.

Fanfiction.net's terms of service forbid the uploading of stories that are extremely sexual or violent in nature, which limits the extent to which fans can depict sexual encounters in their stories. By virtue of being written and not (porno)graphic in nature, Kawoshin stories on fanfiction.net are tamer than the illustrations, manga and fan novels posted on Pixiv and much tamer than the explicit dōjinshi hosted on scanlation sites.

Fanfiction.net has multiple sections divided by the media format of the original work on which fan stories are based, like books, TV, films, video games, musicals and more, and in its large Anime/Manga section, *EVA* to date has 8,500 stories, a modest amount compared to juggernauts in the same section like *NARUTO* (418,000) and *Inuyasha* (119,000), but still making the top 40 within its category. Fanfiction.net has a more user- and researcher-friendly interface than Pixiv, and allows the use of filters when searching for stories. With the genre filter 'romance' and the character A and character B filters for Kaworu N. and Shinji I., the site brings up 167 stories. A small margin of error is expected as some fan authors may use a tag mistakenly. Further narrowing it down, of these, 129 are written in English, of which nine are over 20,000 words long, with two longer than 100,000 words, all published between 2012 and 2017. The limited time span during which fans wrote such long stories is puzzling since *EVA* was distributed overseas more than a decade earlier, and the earliest *EVA* fanwork in English was published on the site in 1999. None of the stories created before 2012 that has a focus on the Kawoshin pairing is longer than a short story.

Given space constraints, I limited my analysis to the three longest stories as they demonstrate a more than casual dedication to the Kawoshin pairing by the author and the readers following them and giving feedback. All three deal with many of the complex issues present in the original work and may be inaccessible to those who haven't watched *EVA*. They were all written by the same author, Laryna6, between July 2012 and October 2014. Other long Kawoshin stories by different authors all have under 10 reviews, which shows a lack of engagement by the Kawoshin fans on the site with the stories, as well as the fan authors and their readers, and this limits insights to be gained from examining them. Laryna6's oldest story, *Book of Revels*, is an impressive 226,304 words long, divided into 46 chapters (93 reviews); the next, *This Alien Shore*, 132,118 words (52 reviews) is somewhat less popular with readers, and the newest, *Babylon*, 89,048 words (119 reviews) is not set in the *EVA* universe, but uses all the same characters. The stories' interpretation of the Kawoshin relationship, the reader reviews and the author's response to them form the basis for my analysis.

The first thing the author does in *Book of Revels* is to tell readers the story is a slashfic. The term slash (see above) is still used for written fanworks featuring romance between male characters, while some fans use slash and yaoi interchangeably or will stick to yaoi for fanwork based on Japanese productions and slash for others.

The author Laryna6 engages with comments on the story by writing short author's notes at the start or end of each chapter. She is well-versed in obscure *EVA* details from all versions. She sets her story in an alternative universe where Kaworu is initially called by his Angel name Tabris. He takes control of SEELE and turns it into an organization that defends the Lilim, which takes caring about Shinji to another level. When Shinji and Kaworu first sleep together, their physical union is described as a merging rather than intercourse, and until the very last chapter, merging is how they make love, distinguishing the author's interpretation significantly from the other works examined for this chapter. There is a comical note about the way the author sees Kawoshin in chapter 24, and her use of the word uke here means she is aware of yaoi, making the designation of her story as slash intentional:

There's a joke about "What happens when you put two ukes in a boat? They fix the boat." Or in this case work together to fix the planet.

The comments on the story are universally praising. The author's next story, *This Alien Shore*, takes inspiration from the various *EVA* manga series; it is a complicated, nuanced story where Kaworu comes over as needier than Shinji, and many readers comment that the story was so good it made them cry. The last story, *Babylon*, is set in an alternative universe in Victorian times, where Gendō and almost the entire cast of *EVA* participate in Satanic rites. Kaworu, again called Tabris, is a demon that keeps Shinji, who has cat ears, as a sex slave. In spite of the outlandish setting that does have some similarities with the dōjinshi examined in the next section (cat ears are a common trope and characteristic of uke characters), the story has a serious tone. The author explains controversial aspects of the story, like Shinji's age (chapter 4), as follows:

> Note that in this time period in England, it was legal for a boy to marry . . . at fourteen, which is why Tabris set that as the minimum age at which someone could sell their soul . . .

I would have liked to examine a larger variety of Kawoshin stories on fanfiction.net, but surprisingly the longest ones with the most author/reader engagement all have the same author. Also surprising is that she did not follow the yaoi convention of designating one character as uke and the other as seme, and apart from her story *Babylon*, Kaworu was not written as more dominant than Shinji. Given the high amount of reader engagement with her stories, my tentative conclusion is that the audience on fanfiction.net does not necessarily require this yaoi convention to enjoy Kawoshin stories. Now that *EVA* is going through a renaissance thanks to the recent Netflix adaptation, the number of stories fans share on this site will hopefully increase.

Coming then to Pixiv, on 13 July 2019, the site hosted 7,998 illustrations and manga (746 of those rated adult) and 2,530 novellas and novels (overwhelmingly in Japanese) with the tag 'kawoshin.' The site allows users to sort both categories by new/old, and is limited to the illustration and manga category, general or rated adult (R-18). Premium users who pay a monthly fee of 450 Japanese yen can further sort by popularity, but for the purpose of this study, I will only discuss those that are public, similar to Noppe (2013), and visible to all non-paying users.

The oldest Kawoshin fanworks were uploaded in 2007, soon after the site went live, while the newest is from 11 July 2019 at the time of this writing. Users who are signed in can like and bookmark artist submissions, and get updates on serialized stories, manga as well as novels.

The level of skill of the artists in the illustration and manga categories varies, but most artists take great care to present their works as professionally as possible, with clean lines, often adding color and visual effects. Some are mere sketches, and many show both Kaworu and Shinji in romantic and sometimes sexual settings. A common theme is redrawing scenes from the first TV series in a way that focuses on the Kawoshin pairing, like replacing Rei with Kaworu in the famous scene where Shinji and Rei merge into each other, an alternative way of intercourse also described in one of the popular stories on fanfiction.net.

There are numerous stories in the illustration and manga as well as the novel categories that resurrect Kaworu or put the characters in alternative settings without Eva units or Angels, for example, turning them into normal high-school students. This is a common way for fans to rewrite favorite characters from SF, fantasy or action stories in which the characters' lives are in peril. Mundane settings are a manifestation of fans' desire for beloved characters to be safe and happy. There are numerous fan artists who focus exclusively on the Kawoshin pairing and who have gained thousands of likes on their works and a following of hundreds of users.

In some illustrations, Shinji is wearing women's apparel (sun dresses, ball gowns, bikinis, lingerie, bloomers, maid costumes and cat ears) or is depicted as a girl with short hair. A small minority of stories features him as being pregnant with Kaworu's child. This does not come as a surprise in a fandom context, and the same is true for the manga dōjin works on the scanlation site discussed below.

In contrast to English-language fanwork archives, written stories on the Japanese-language site Pixiv are a minority, but not rare. The length of them varies, with some having only around a thousand characters, and many others tens of thousands of characters, the same length or longer as commercially available novels. Instead of leaving comments, fans can click a heart button, which functions like a like button on the SNS Facebook.

Kawoshin Fanworks on Dōjinshi Scanlation Sites

Scanlations are fan-made translations of manga and dōjinshi (subtitles on pirated anime episodes are called fansubs, fan-made voiceovers are fandubs). Many of these works are manga that have not been officially localized in many countries, and a number of scanlation sites employ an honor code: translators vow to take down their scanlation once a work is licensed in the language featured on the site.

Fan-made parody dōjinshi,[2] however, have a very low chance of ever being localized, as they are neither legal nor official from inception, and in Japan, too, their creators operate in what is regarded as a gray zone, but again, technically illegal. Many publishers turn a blind eye on the trade in fanworks as a lively fan culture supports the manga industry at large, and because they can scout for new talent at dōjinshi direct sales events. Dōjinshi artists are understandably worried about losing control of the distribution of their works and never agreed to having them uploaded online publicly. Because of this, studying and especially quoting these works and the websites that uploaded them presents a moral dilemma for the researcher. But these works are important for the impact they have on the global Kawoshin fandom and cannot not be ignored when examining the proliferation of common tropes for the pairing, like Kaworu taking care of Shinji like a parent and a lover rolled into one, or Shinji's personal weaknesses being rewritten as feminine, often in a positive rather than derogatory way. Foreign fans are grateful to these scanlation sites for

2. In Japanese usage, the word parody does not refer to a funny, mocking reinterpretation of an original work, but merely means not original; the fanwork can be parody in the English-usage meaning of the word, but isn't necessarily.

providing access to works otherwise only available in Japanese and on the Japanese fan market. In addition to not naming the site to which these works are uploaded, I will not mention artist or circle names and obfuscate the titles by renaming the works, somehow similar to but different from the original. The commenters on these sites all use pseudonyms, which I will keep as these are also public and submitted voluntarily.

As mentioned above, stories available here rely entirely on the whim of fan translators as well as the dōjinshi to which they have access. Technically a pirate site, the artists whose content is uploaded do not have the legal clout required to protest and have their works taken down. The works discussed tend to be of the same generation as those on Pixiv and fanfiction.net, mainly from the 2000s to the late 2010s. I use the number of translation languages, as well as the number of comments each dōjinshi has, as a very rough measure of their popularity, and then discuss the most common tropes in these popular works in more detail.

On the most popular global, but mainly English, site I searched for Kawoshin works tagged as "Kaworu Nagisa x Shinji Ikari." There are 109 works to the date of writing, not all of them different, as some works are available in the original Japanese,[3] English, Korean, Chinese, Spanish and Russian. A total of 78 results are in English, 14 in Japanese, 10 in Korean, three in Chinese, two in Spanish and one in Russian. The site has yaoi dōjinshi in more languages, but not for the Kawoshin pairing.

Among these 109 works, it is difficult to gauge for popularity as the site doesn't have any filters that allow sorting for this purpose. It does have a comment section, and checking the amount of comments as well as what readers say gives some idea of the popularity. I read all 78 works and looked at how lively the reader interaction in the comments was, when picking the examples discussed here.

The first dōjinshi scanlation I chose is *Fooling around in the Bath* (title altered), which was uploaded to the site in 2017 (date of creation

3. These scans are called 'raws' and are meant for fans who don't want to wait for a translation.

unknown) in three languages. The site has a page with the original Japanese raws (not translated, this page has seven comments in English by fans who enjoyed the pictorial content of the scans without fully understanding the story) and the English (14 comments in English) and Korean scanlations (12 comments in Korean). Bath stories form a small but fairly popular subgenre among Kawoshin stories on both the scanlation site and Pixiv, which is to be expected as Kaworu and Shinji get closer in the first TV anime series while having a bath together in a communal bath house, or *sentō*, complete with a picture of Mount Fuji on the wall. This is a scene in which Shinji tells Kaworu he has to go to bed, to which Kaworu immediately responds, "With me?" Shinji reacts flustered, and they do not end up in the same bed, but many fans like to imagine they did and create their own stories accordingly. On the scanned cover of *Fooling around in the Bath*, Shinji is featured alone in contrast to the vast majority of Kawoshin *dōjinshi* that have a cover with both characters. Shinji is covered in foam and has a yellow rubber duck bath toy between his legs. From the first page, Kaworu and Shinji are not in a *sentō*, but the average Japanese bathtub in an apartment, with Shinji sitting in front of Kaworu, leaning into his chest. They engage in frottage and anal sex, with graphic depictions of both, and there is no mention of any of the life-and-death situations or philosophical issues otherwise so prevalent in *EVA*.

In the comments, readers interpret Shinji being the receptive partner during anal sex as getting "filled with love," and contrast the original story, expressing their delight that nobody dies. On the cover of another *dōjinshi* entitled *Bath Lovey-Dovey Time*, rated R-18, Kaworu and Shinji are both featured, with a rubber duck, and in the same position as they are in *Fooling around in the Bath*. This scanlation is only available in English, with 15 comments; it was also uploaded to the site in 2017, but originally published in 2014 (date printed on the back cover). In contrast to the first where there is only the bath scene, this one features other young *EVA* characters, albeit in a light-hearted fashion and without scenes or dialogue referring to battle, violence and potential death.

As mentioned previously, many fans enjoy the idea of Shinji getting his needs fulfilled and filling him with love. In most dōjinshi, the shape of 'love' used to fill Shinji up is Kaworu's penis and sperm. One popular story, with 31 comments in English, gives Shinji three Kaworus in a foursome where only Shinji is the uke, filled by the Kaworu from the first TV series, the Q version (2012) and Sadamoto's manga series (1995-2014). To readers unfamiliar with yaoi and BL, the equation of love with sex might seem unrealistic, naïve, dangerous and even comical, but yaoi, and to a somewhat lesser extent its commercial cousin BL, hardly ever presents realistic scenarios, and its fans rarely assume that it does. What is depicted is an ideal, a fantasy of perfect intimacy, where romantic love and sexual intercourse are synonymous.

There are more bath scenes in stories that don't feature a bath or a rubber duck prominently on the cover. In *Hubris*, published in 2013 and uploaded to the site in 2014 (in English and Korean), Shinji is self-conscious about what he said to Kaworu, and while he battles inner turmoil, he ends up fainting in the bath. There are 20 comments on the English version (22 on the Korean), including many requests for a sequel as there is a masturbation scene in the story, but no full intercourse, no metaphorically getting filled with love and thus no closure. Another story uploaded in 2014 and with several bath scenes is *My Secret Hole Condition*, which does depict full intercourse and wins wild praise from fans in the comments for a dash of comedy in the panel where Kaworu calls his penis his Lance of Longinus, which he fully intends to insert into Shinji's "central dogma." Comedy through parody plays an important role in these fanworks to defuse the gravity of the conclusion of the original series. In some stories, Shinji displays confusion about his sexual orientation and is still attracted to Rei and Asuka, but since only Kaworu enthusiastically likes him back, he invariably surrenders to his attraction to Kaworu. Another common trope is that, as a non-human (tagged as *jin-gai*, other than human, lit. outside of human, a tag also used on Pixiv), Kaworu displays an unabashed attitude toward physical pleasure, frequently encouraging Shinji to engage in it too, by calling it natural for humans, the children of the Lilim. Using persuasive lines like "This is just a part of human physiology, it can easily be dealt with" would sound like a predator grooming a younger boy in a more realistic genre, but among the 109 Kawoshin scanlations on the site, there wasn't a single one which drew the dynamic as clearly abusive.

While variations can be found in many Kawoshin works, the above-cited line is from the dōjinshi *Take Me Up to the Moon* (2015). This story also includes a bath scene and an inside joke where "thermal expansion" is used as a metaphor for an erection. Like the fanworks on Pixiv, some dōjinshi completely divorce the characters from the series' setting, placing them in mundane or school settings with no mention of the *EVA* universe at all, but about nine in ten do not, which allows for canon references. There are some works with allusions to the bad end the couple have in the series, but these tend to be vague. To quote one example, Kaworu tries to persuade Shinji to sleep over after they have already had intercourse, and Shinji declines, saying, "There's always tomorrow." Kaworu smiles, and Shinji reconsiders, staying over after all. This can be read as Shinji merely being unable to resist Kaworu's charm, but it adds a layer of pathos for fans of the series, aware that in the series Kawoshin have no future and will not have a happily-ever-after (*No Title*, R-18, 2010, English scanlation uploaded to the site in 2016).

Among the works on the site, there was just one that ends according to canon, *Overbeam* (2013, uploaded to the site in 2015). After Kaworu and Shinji have intercourse, Shinji is called to his Eva unit, and Kaworu is identified as the humanoid Angel he has to, and does, destroy. The dōjinshi contains three fully black pages after Kaworu is gone, depicting Shinji's emotional state, as well as expressing the fan artist's reaction to *EVA*'s devastating end. The artist is also active on Pixiv, where the work has only two wordless comments, yet 1,841 people to date have liked it, and over 78,000 have viewed it. In contrast, on the scanlation site, there are 34 comments in English, many of which express admiration and gratitude to the artist, although she may never see these comments. The scanlation site has no view number, but as with all sites, most readers and viewers will read without ever leaving a comment, and the amount of people who have read the manga on the scanlation site is without a doubt by several digits higher than the amount of comments.

Discussion

This chapter is an attempt to analyze the many ways in which Kawoshin fans rewrite the characters, and the way in which readers of these fanworks react to them. The amount of engagement within *EVA* fan communities concerning these fanworks can tell us much about to what extent and in what ways fans are invested in the source text, the characters within the source narrative and the characters themselves, taken out of their narrative setting even if not completely divorced from it. Unsurprisingly, most fans prefer fanworks in which both Shinji and Kaworu are alive, as well as works in which they are relatively healthy and happy. Many works have a light-hearted tone and can be categorized as 'slice of life' stories, where the terrifying occurrences of the original work are glossed over or omitted.

During my analysis, I found that I could not easily apply the exact same method to all three websites equally and had to adapt parameters accordingly. Like Nele Noppe, who examined the websites DeviantART and Pixiv for her work on transcultural fannish interactions, I found Pixiv the least accessible. As Noppe points out, getting reliable data from Pixiv as a researcher is a challenging endeavor (2013: 150), and among the three sites I looked at I found it the least useful to draw any kind of conclusion about tropes and trends in the way fans create and consume Kawoshin stories. There is no option to filter fanworks by popularity. Many stories have little to no comments and see very few reader interactions, posing a problem because these interactions form the brunt of my useable, collected data. Noppe noticed the same, while also pointing out that the comments on Pixiv don't necessarily say anything about the popularity of a work. While Pixiv is unfortunately resistant to effective data gathering and thus challenging when undertaking fandom research, the site does feel welcoming to fan creators and their audiences. The site also features its own fandom dictionary, with a treasure trove of details on popular characters and pairings, and has more features that make it attractive for the average user.

Another method considered but abandoned was going through all the catalogues of the annual Comic Market since the airing of *EVA*. Yukari Fujimoto employed this method when looking at *NARUTO* yaoi fandom (2013: 173, 181–187). The Comic Market is held twice a year in Tokyo, and it is the largest dōjinshi direct sales event in the world. Its catalogue would yield clues to how many fan clubs, or 'circles,' have sold Kawoshin dōjinshi, but it would be incomplete and inconclusive given that certain circles are cryptic about the kinds of works they will sell, and not all dōjinshi are sold at the Comic Market. Morever, it would yield only quantitative data and virtually nothing qualitative, little about the content of the stories and nothing about buyers'/readers' reactions and interaction with the fan artist/ author and each other.

Given the limited scope of the websites researched, as well as the difficulties when trying to gather data on Pixiv and to a lesser extent on fanfiction.net, further research is required. A follow-up study of the most prevalent tropes that is statistically valid can be conducted within a generous time frame at the Yoshihiro Yonezawa Memorial Library in Tokyo, with access to all the Kawoshin dōjinshi in their collection. But such a follow-up study can only illuminate how fan artists and authors redraw and rewrite the pairing, and it would not include reactions from fans to these stories and thus be qualitatively different from this chapter.

Fan creators often use their stories as attempts to create a happy ending for Kawoshin, and popular dōjinshi show that, barring exceptions, Kaworu, as the more dominant character in the pairing, is also the more nurturing, guiding and supporting, meeting the emotional needs of Shinji, who at age 14 still needs his parents, but who has a cold father in Gendō and a mother who is long dead.

It is possible to interpret Kaworu's feelings for Shinji, including his eventual self-sacrifice, as motherly. And yet, this does not form any obstacle for writing Kawoshin in a romantic and sexual way, not realistically, but as idealized romance. The tenderness and care with which Kaworu approaches Shinji, bolstering his lacking self-esteem, and the two then falling in love, especially within a narrative created by mostly female artists for a mostly female audience, is in line with what Radway discussed first in 1983: that female romance readers look for nurturing qualities in the fantasy object of the male hero, qualities that are very much like those of a mother, but packaged as a good looking man, which fits yaoi as a subgenre of romance fiction for a mainly female audience. Shinji is usually the uke in fan narratives, and as the main character, easy for fans to identify with or project onto. Shiori Shimomura's yaoi survey showed that more than three times as many readers identify with the uke than with the seme (2006: 164), and the Hanamura Henshūbu guidebook on how to write successful BL stories recommends making the point-of-view character the uke (2004: 104). However, as mentioned above when discussing works on fanfiction. net, readers there don't require the yaoi conventions of seme and uke to enjoy Kawoshin stories. Kaworu can be nurturing as a lover without necessarily being dominant.

On the scanlation site, where the fans cannot directly interact with the author and don't know the identity of the site's contributors of pirated content, fans engage with one another and have conversations in the comments, most of them full of praise for the Kawoshin work on the same page. These conversations are what Patrick Galbraith (2015) called "moe chat." He conducted fieldwork between 2006 and 2007 in Japan, with Japanese fans, and the moe talk on which he focuses is fans discussing yaoi face to face, which he distinguished from moe chat, that is, online talk on websites (2015: 157–158). Moe means to burn (with passion), which in the case of yaoi fans, signifies affective behavior toward an imagined male/male couple (ibid.: 156). Galbraith observed fans shrieking and clapping and expressing their excitement in other ways during moe talk (ibid.: 159). In my study, something similar was apparent in the comments section of the technically illegal scanlation site, where fans expressed their affection not just in text conversation like on the more regulated fanfiction.net, but with images or animated gifs of fiery flames and nosebleeds, the latter being a manga and anime convention signifying acute arousal. Below are some examples of comments that function as moe chat, expressing readers' love for the pairing and the way in which fan artists and authors rewrite and redraw their relationship, but often also the original work:

oh god I feel like crying, I did not come here for the feels man, all I wanted was some good fornication ;A; (Usagina, 2014)

OH MY FREAKIGN (sic) GOSH, FULL COLOR R-18 KAWOSHIN DJ. WHAT A TIME TO BE ALIVE (suomynonA, 2014)

Son of a bitch, how could you. The first Kaworu/Shinji I've read in how many years and this depressing shit of a doujinshi made all the depressing shitty feelings that come with reading/watching the depressing shit of a masterpiece that is Evangelion come rushing back like a motherfucker. Fuck my life. Ugh, brilliant. (minisoysquares, 2015)

> Aw I thought they were gonna fuck on the piano (catmerchant, 2016)
>
> Reply from Maria (2016): It happened in another DJ and that was a wonderful thing XD
>
> My heart . . . So much moe! (Moe Mami, 2017)

It is very rare for a comment on any of the sites to be negative. Fans focus on their common likes, using sexually tinted language they may not be able to frequently use offline, and expressions people outside of the Kawoshin fandom may not understand.

This chapter shows that, by and large, yaoi fan creators as well as fan audiences tend to avoid a head-on engagement with the life-or-death situations in which the *EVA* canon places their favorite characters, but some artists do go there, writing long romantic Kawoshin narratives in which they, and the readers, still have to brace for the worst in spite of being in their more comfortable, escapist fandom space. For as difficult to understand as *EVA* is, part of its legacy is giving the global fujoshi fandom a pairing that has brought female fans together and allowed them to turn Kawoshin into something that within their world has become a pairing many are familiar with, love and will continue to write stories about with the encouragement and support of likeminded fans.

Lastly, anime fandom and in particular SF anime fandom is still regarded as a nerdy, mostly masculine, pursuit, and from my own experience working in academic circles the field of Anime and Animation Studies is also male-dominated and does not reflect the diversity of the audience nor what moves audiences. Works that are now considered mainstream and classics in the genre, like *EVA*, have a demonstrably large number of female fans who engage passionately with the source material. Anime Studies from a feminist perspective is as yet an insufficiently explored area of research, and this chapter is a small contribution to a body of research that will hopefully continue to grow.

References

Bauwens-Sugimoto, J. (2014). Manga Studies #3: On BL Manga Research in Japanese. comicsforum.org, n.p. Retrieved from: https://comicsforum .org/2014/07/29/manga-studies-3-on-bl-manga-research-in-japanese-by -jessica-bauwens-sugimoto/

_____ & N. Renka. (2013). Fanboys and Naruto Epics: Exploring New Ground in Fanfiction Studies. In J. Berndt and B. Kümmerling-Meibauer (eds.), *Manga's Cultural Crossroads* (pp. 192–208). New York: Routledge.

Fermin, T. (2013). Appropriating Yaoi and Boys Love in the Philippines: Conflict, Resistance and Imaginations through and beyond Japan. *EJCJS*, n.p. Retrieved from: http://www.japanesestudies.org.uk/ejcjs /vol13/iss3/fermin.html

Fujimoto, Y. (2013). Women in NARUTO, Women Reading NARUTO. In J. Berndt and B. Kümmerling-Meibauer (eds.), *Manga's Cultural Crossroads* (pp. 172–191). New York: Routledge.

GAINAX. (2008). *All about Nagisa Kaworu a Child of The EVANGELION*. Tokyo: Kadokawa.

Galbraith, P. W. (2011). Fujoshi: Fantasy Play and Transgressive Intimacy among "Rotten Girls" in Contemporary Japan. *Signs*, 37(1), 211–232.

_____. (2015). *Moe* Talk, Affective Communication among Female Fans of Yaoi in Japan. In M. McLelland et al. (eds.), *Boys Love Manga and beyond, History, Culture, and Community in Japan* (pp. 153–168). Jackson, MS: University of Mississippi.

Hanamura henshūbu (2004). *Bōizu rabu shōsetsu—moe no tsutaekata*. Tokyo: Hakusensha.

Herring, S. C. (2004). Computer-Mediated Discourse Analysis: An Approach to Researching Online Behavior. In S. A. Barab, R. Kling and J. H. Gray (eds.), *Designing for Virtual Communities in the Service of Learning* (pp. 338–376). Cambridge: Cambridge University Press.

Jenkins, H. (1992). *Textual Poachers*. New York: Routledge.

Kotani, M. (1997). *Seibo Evangerion*. Tokyo: Magajin House.

Kristeva, J. (1982). *Powers of Horror: An Essay on Abjection*. New York: Columbia University Press. (Translated by L. S. Roudiez)

McLelland, M. (2018). Managing Manga Studies in the Convergent Classroom. In A. Freedman and T. Slade (eds.), *Introducing Japanese Popular Culture* (pp. 93–104). London and New York: Routledge.

Nagaike, K. (2009). Elegant Caucasians, Amorous Arabs, and Invisible Others: Signs and Images of Foreigners in Japanese BL Manga. *Intersections: Gender and Sexuality in Asia and the Pacific*, Issue 20, April, n.p. Retrieved from: http://intersections.anu.edu.au/issue20/nagaike.htm

Noppe, N. (2013). Social Networking Services as Platforms for Transcultural Fannish Interactions, DeviantART and Pixiv. In J. Berndt and B. Kümmerling-Meibauer (eds.), *Manga's Cultural Crossroads* (pp. 143–208). New York: Routledge.

Penley, C. (1997). *NASA/Trek: Popular Science and Sex in America*. New York: Verso.

Radway, J. A. 1983. Women Read the Romance: The Interaction of Text and Context. *Feminist Studies*, 9(1), 53–78.

Russ, J. (1985). *Magic Mommas, Trembling Sisters, Puritans and Perverts*. New York: Crossing Press.

Sadamoto, Y. (1999). *Der Mond: The Art of Neon Genesis Evangelion Deluxe Edition*. Tokyo: Kadokawa.

Shimomura, S. (2006). Josei muke nijisōsaku ni mirareru jiko hyōgen. *Josei gaku nenpō*, 27, 153–175.

Plot Summary of *Neon Genesis Evangelion* and Analysis of Character Interrelations

Tatiana Lameiro-González

Summary

First broadcasted in 1995, *Neon Genesis Evangelion* is set 20 years in the future from its release (2015). The events of the series take place in a post-apocalyptic world caused by the Second Impact, a global cataclysm responsible for the annihilation of almost half the human population. The Second impact took place in September 2000 as a result of a 'Contact Experiment' during the Katsuragi expedition to the South Pole—led by Misato Katsuragi's father—to research and experiment with Adam, also known as the First Angel.

Angels are enigmatic entities, descendants of Adam, one of the two Seeds of Life that collide on Earth. While they are said to have a genome that is 99.89 percent identical to that of humans, their appearances do not seem to follow any pattern, and there is no shared shape or physical traits among them: An Angel's size can range widely, ranging from microscopic beings to gigantic creatures. To kill an Angel, the core (usually a red sphere) must be destroyed. In *Neon Genesis Evangelion*, 15 different angels are depicted as Adam's progeny (Sachiel, Shamshel, Ramiel, Gaghiel, Israfel, Sandalphon, Matariel, Sahaquiel, Ireul, Leliel, Bardiel, Zeruel, Arael, Armisael and the human-shaped vessel Tabris, also known as Kaworu Nagisa). The second Seed of Life and Adam's counterpart, Lilith, is sometimes considered as the second Angel, and it is the progenitor of the human race (also known as Lilin). Although the Angels' origin is unknown, their eventual arrival was predicted in the Dead Sea Manuscripts possessed by SEELE, a secret worldwide society shrouded in mystery.

How to cite this book chapter:
Lameiro-González, T. 2021. Plot Summary of *Neon Genesis Evangelion* and Analysis of Character Interrelations. In: Santiago Iglesias, J. A. and Soler Baena, A. (Eds.). *Anime Studies: Media-Specific Approaches to Neon Genesis Evangelion*. Pp. 353–363 Stockholm: Stockholm University Press. DOI: https://doi.org/10.16993/bbp.l. License: CC-BY 4.0

Following the catastrophic events of the Second Impact, the United Nations commissions the defence of humanity against Angels to NERV, a paramilitary private organization commanded by Gendō Ikari, an enigmatic scientist and father to the main character, Shinji Ikari. Established out of the research organization GEHIRN, throughout the series, NERV becomes increasingly autonomous in its decision making under Commander Ikari's direction. NERV central headquarters is located in the Geo-Front (under the city of Tokyo 3), where they are in charge of research, maintenance and deployment of large humanoid biomechanical combat units, also known as Eva. Exclusively piloted by teenagers, Evas can be equipped with specific tools to fight against the Angels, and despite their biological basis, they are usually protected by thick layers of armor, giving them a robotic look. In order to defeat Angels, Evas share some unique traits with their enemies, such as the AT Field, an almost impenetrable force-field barrier capable of rendering conventional weapons useless.

In *Neon Genesis Evangelion*, there are two main and intertwined plots: on the one hand, a lighter and more conventional approach to the genre, revolving around melee combat strategies for fighting against the Angels; on the other, an underlying narrative focused on the mental and emotional state of the characters, wounded by deep personal trauma, which is increased by their ongoing exposure to Evas. As the series progresses, the fight between Evas and Angels becomes secondary to the subjective perspective of the protagonists, whose search for their own identities is increasingly foregrounded.

As the episodes elapse, some mysteries regarding the different characters and the obscure organizations involved are eventually revealed: NERV—whose primary role was to defend humanity from the Angels—seems to be undermined by its parent organization SEELE, which appears to seek the triggering of the Third Impact, a key event for the culmination of the Human Instrumentality Project. This mysterious plan aims to release human beings from their physical bodies and merge them into a large primordial liquid mass. As a result of this project, human beings would lose their individuality and form a unique existence made up of all their souls. For SEELE, the Human Instrumentality Project is meant to answer humanity's distressing evolution—where pain, frustration and negative feelings prevail—by means of a reinforced collective existence.

Showing the dramatic events taking place in the external world, the film *The End of Evangelion* depicts the forces of SEELE and NERV as engaged in a battle, resulting in the eventual execution of the Human Instrumentality Project and the eventual destruction of life on earth. However, the final two episodes (25 and 26) of the TV series show a different point of view, presenting Shinji's introspective journey. Shinji's psyche is depicted as an empty stage filled with his thoughts and fears. Some previously unknown secrets from the past and details of the characters' lives are revealed, but they are presented in cryptic and complex ways. Ultimately, Shinji seems to come to terms with his own persona, and the series ends with him surrounded by all his friends and family, after he decides that he wants to be himself and continue living in the world. Taken together, the denouement of the series does not explicitly provide a single conclusive ending, but is left open with multiple possible meanings.

Main Characters

Eva unit pilots

Shinji Ikari

Shinji Ikari is a 14-year-old boy, Evangelion Unit-01 pilot, and protagonist of the series. Also known as the Third Child, Shinji was chosen by NERV to drive the Eva-01 and fight against the Angels, consequently reuniting with his father—Commander Gendō Ikari—after having been

© khara, inc.

apart from him for 11 years. A number of dangerous situations as pilot triggers his frustration and forces him to face his fears, while pushing him to accept himself and ultimately allowing for personal growth.

Shinji's character is defined by his past traumas—the death of his mother, bioengineer Yui Ikari, and being abandoned by his father—showing behavioral disorders and existential doubt. He is usually portrayed as a sensitive, fragile and confused child. Despite being the hero in the series, his traits differ deeply from those of the hero archetype. Due to his low self-esteem, his lonely, introverted personality and his vulnerability, Shinji often seeks approval and love from the adults around him. Shinji's longing for closeness with others produces various points of conflict for him, addressed in the series as the Hedgehog's Dilemma. On the one hand, personal contact brings him distress and uneasiness, causing him suffering. On the other, the more he stays away from relationships, the more he feels the anguish and pain of loneliness.

Rei Ayanami

© khara, inc.

Rei is a 14-year-old girl and is known as the First Child. Chosen by Gendō Ikari to pilot Eva-00, at the beginning of the series her background is mostly unknown, with no information about her origins, childhood or family. Rei is a distant and unaccessible person, introverted, quiet and enigmatic; sometimes unable to express her own feelings or understand other people's emotions. Throughout the series, Rei feels pushed to question her own existence and to define her identity. As a fellow pilot of the Eva units, Rei quickly catches Shinji's attention, ultimately establishing a relationship of empathy and mutual affection.

Asuka Langley Sohryu

© khara, inc.

Asuka is a 14-year-old girl of German-Japanese-American origin and the Second Child, the pilot of the Eva-02. She has a strong personality and a rebellious temper, but she also craves social approval. She possesses remarkable intelligence, but despite her obvious childish overtones, she constantly struggles to be considered by others as an adult, often in an attempt to get away from her troubled past. Her self-confidence and competitive attitude are presented as reflections of her superiority complex, occassionally making her violent and offensive toward others. In some senses, Asuka is the emotional opposite of Shinji, even though they both share an unhappy childhood.

Asuka tries to justify her own existence as the result of her lack of maternal recognition (her mother goes insane, ignores her daughter and eventually commits suicide). Although she hides her feelings to avoid being hurt, Asuka's cold and hostile behavior toward others eventually changes. She shares a twisted love/hate relationship with Shinji. While they seem to feel attracted to each other, both end up shutting out their mutual feelings. Moreover, Asuka sometimes replies to Shinji with contempt and abuse, or teases him by pointing to her sexuality.

Tōji Suzuhara

Tōji is one of Shinji's classmates. Despite their initial disagreements, they end up becoming good friends, learning to respect each other. As the story unfolds, Tōji is revealed to be the Fourth Child, chosen to drive Eva-03. However, his unit ends up being possessed by an Angel on the test run, and he is gravely injured after his Eva is torn apart by unit-01. Despite his overall joyful disposition, Tōji has a protective temperament, revealed early on, when he attacks Shinji, blaming him for his younger sister's critical injuries from one of the Angel attacks. Tōji is generally presented as a strong-tempered boy with a spirited character, rough around the edges, but a kind, honest and loyal friend.

© khara, inc.

Kaworu Nagisa

Kaworu is a 15-year-old boy, first presented in episode 24, and designated as the Fifth Child by SEELE, in order to replace Asuka. Kaworu immediately shows an open and honest personality, quickly gaining Shinji's trust and admiration, who ultimately finds in him the ideal companion. However, as events unfold, Kaworu is revealed to

© khara, inc.

be Tabris, the 17th Angel. Chased by Shinji on board the Eva-01, Kaworu is killed by his friend in Terminal Dogma before he tries to unleash the Third Impact.

NERV staff

Commander Gendō Ikari

© khara, inc.

Also known as Gendō Rokubungi, Gendō Ikari (48 years old) is NERV's supreme commander and director of Project E. In his youth, he married Yui Ikari, taking on her family name, and fathered Shinji. However, after Yui's death, he entirely devoted himself to his research, abandoning Shinji and erasing any paternal feelings. Gendō is mostly driven by his personal ambition and remarkable qualities as a scientist. Moreover, he stands out as a cold, calculating and almost inhuman person, placing the young pilots in danger's way without remorse. As NERV's Commander, he poses as someone obsessive, severe and quite authoritarian.

His life's goal initially appears to be to avoid the Third Impact—and thus the end of human life—by destroying the Angels. However, it is later revealed that his true aim is the completion of the Human Instrumentality Project, following the directives of the secret society SEELE, but under his own scenario, presumably to reunite with Yui.

Major Misato Katsuragi

© khara, inc.

Misato is a NERV officer in charge of the Tactical Operations branch, responsible for making battle plans and coordinating the Eva units in combat. In the absence of Commander Ikari, Misato is responsible for the military operations against the Angels. She is a smart, hard-working and independent woman, skilled in combat tactics. She usually displays an overall cheerful disposition, but becomes very serious during battle plans. Upon Shinji's arrival at NERV, she acts as the boy's guardian and mentor. Moreover, once Asuka arrives in Japan, the three of them live in Misato's apartment.

Misato suffered the consequences of the Second Impact in her childhood. Her father was the chief scientist of the expedition to Antarctica, and she was at the site when the catastrophe took place, ultimately being saved by her father and becoming the sole survivor of the expedition. After dealing with her heavy injuries and serious personal trauma, she joins NERV determined to destroy the Angels and avoid the Third Impact.

Misato is friends with NERV's chief scientist Ritsuko Akagi and Ryōji Kaji, sharing an intense physical and emotional relationship with the latter. Her bond with Shinji goes beyond her duty as guardian, including support and mutual protection. Ultimately, both Shinji and Misato share social problems, but they deal with them through different mechanisms.

Dr. Ritsuko Akagi

Ritsuko is NERV's chief scientist, in charge of the Technological branch. She is also responsible for the Evangelion units research project and the supercomputer Magi System. This supercomputer was created by Ritsuko's mother, Dr. Naoko Akagi, and consists of three advanced organic computers, featuring three different aspects of her creator's personality—woman, scientist and mother. Although Ritsuko is an incredibly talented scientist, her career is mostly defined by the life choices and innovations developed by her mother. This situation ultimately drives Ritsuko into an existential crisis, struggling to define her own identity and showing contradictory feelings toward her mother, admiring her as a scientist and a scholar, but despising her as a mother. Moreover, Ritsuko is in a romantic relationship with Gendō—despite his apparent lack of interest—who was himself also involved with her mother.

© khara, inc.

Ritsuko has been friends with Misato and Kaji since the time they spent together in college. Through the series, their friendship becomes strained due to ethical differences and Ritsuko's involvement in the Human Instrumentality Project. In fact, Ritsuko—together with

Gendō Ikari and Kōzō Fuyutsuki—knows the real nature of the Eva units and the Human Instrumentality Project.

Ryōji Kaji

© khara, inc.

Kaji is a triple agent working as a NERV observer, SEELE's operative and a spy for the Japanese government. Former boyfriend of Misato in college, they resume their romantic relationship upon his arrival to Japan. Among other tasks, he is responsible for delivering Adam's embryo, recovered from Antarctica, to Gendō Ikari.

Kaji is a mysterious character, ultimately driven by his personal quest for truth. He is an independent, calm and seductive man. Moreover, he often acts as a fatherly character toward Shinji, showing him a friendly side. Kaji's righteous and honorable nature is repeatedly proven before he meets his end.

Kōzō Fuyutsuki

© khara, inc.

Dr. Fuyutsuki (58 years old) is a scientific advisor, NERV's Vice-Commander and Gendō Ikari's most trusted associate. He is a former Kyoto University professor, and there he met Yui Ikari, who made an impression on him as a promising young scientist. After the Second Impact, he joined the official research expedition led by the United Nations to the South Pole, in an attempt to find out the truth hidden behind the catastrophe and SEELE's secret purpose. Dr. Fuyutsuki is invested in supporting the Human Instrumentality Project, but he shows a calm and hard-working nature under Gendō's command.

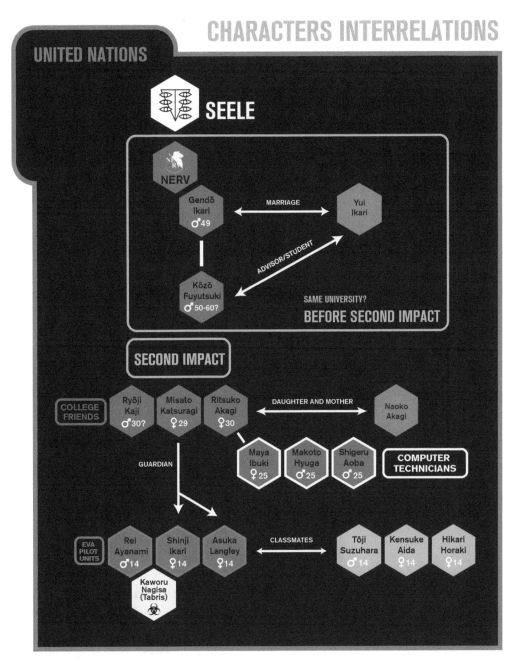

Table of character's interrelations. License: CC BY 4.0.

Anime

Neon Genesis Evangelion (in this volume abbreviated to *EVA*) is an anime featuring 26 episodes, first broadcasted between October 1995 and March 1996. Created by Studio GAINAX and directed by Hideaki Anno, the production also involved Yoshiyuki Sadamoto's work on character design, and Yoh Yoshinari and Hiroyuki Imaishi on the design and animation departments.

Death & Rebirth is the first movie of the franchise, premiering in Japan in March 1997, and summarizing the main events that took place in the first 24 episodes of the series. A second film entitled *The End of Evangelion* debuted in July 1997, showing the events taking place in the real world during Shinji's introspective journey in episodes 25 and 26 of the original series. Finally, *Revival of Evangelion* merges both films into a single one. It was first shown in March 1998. Including some short additional scenes, it is a remastered edition improving sound and video quality.

Years later, a new tetralogy called *Rebuild of Evangelion* was announced, produced by Studio Khara in partnership with GAINAX. The international titles of the four movies are *Evangelion: 1.0 You Are (Not) Alone* (2007), *Evangelion: 2.0 You Can (Not) Advance* (2009), *Evangelion: 3.0 You Can (Not) Redo* (2012) and *Evangelion: 3.0+1.0 Thrice Upon a Time* (2021). Presenting alternative events from those of the initial *Neon Genesis Evangelion* series and films, the *Rebuild of Evangelion* tetralogy is usually considered a reboot of the original series rather than a remake.

Manga

Closely following most of the events and characters presented in the original anime series, Yoshiyuki Sadamoto's manga adaptation *Neon Genesis Evangelion* (NGE) was published by Kadokawa Shoten in *Shōnen Ace* magazine (from December 1994 to 2008) and *Young Ace* magazine (from July 2009 and June 2013), with some breaks in between, and eventually collected into 14 volumes.

Nonetheless, there are other manga titles which expand *EVA*'s world-setting and characters. *Neon Genesis Evangelion: Angelic Days*, by Fumino Hayashi, was published in *Monthly Asuka* from November 2003 to December 2005 (collected in six volumes). Osamu Takahashi adapted the namesake video-game into the manga series *Shinji Ikari Raising Project*, published by *Monthly Shōnen Ace* from June 2005 to February 2016, later collected in 18 volumes. Between May 2007 and September 2009, *Petit Eva: Evangelion@School* by Ryūsuke Hamamoto was serialized in the *Shōnen Ace* magazine. Also starting in 2007 (in October and running to September 2009), *Neon Genesis Evangelion: Campus Apocalypse* by Ming Ming was serialized in the *Young Ace* magazine, with a different look for the characters and events and situations apart from the original series.

Between February 2010 and November 2010, *Monthly Asuka* published a new comedy series entitled *The Shinji Ikari Detective Diary*. Depicting a similarly parodic sense of humor, *Neon Genesis Evangelion: The Legend of the Piko Piko Middle School Students* by Yūshi Kawata and Yukito was published in *Young Ace* from 2014 to 2009 (later collected in five volumes).

About the Editors and the Contributors

José Andrés Santiago Iglesias (University of Vigo), editor

Dr. José Andrés Santiago Iglesias is a visual artist, postdoctoral researcher and lecturer at the Fine Arts Faculty (Universidade de Vigo, Spain) focused on expanded-field Comics, Manga and Anime Studies. He graduated with honors (valedictorian award) in 2004, and defended his PhD thesis in 2010 (Universidade de Vigo) addressing manga from a contemporary art perspective; the book edition entitled *Manga: Del cuadro flotante a la viñeta japonesa* was published by Comanegra in 2010. Since 2005, he has worked as a full-time member at the dx5 digital & graphic art research group (Universidade de Vigo), specializing in contemporary expanded-field graphics. Within this research group, he is currently leading a Ministry-funded research project entitled *Estudios Transdisciplinares sobre Cómic* (ETC) [*Transdisciplinary Comics Studies*]. He is a founding member of the ACDCómic [Spanish Association of Critics and Researchers of Comics] since its inception in 2012. He is a former fellow of the Japan Foundation's Japanese Studies Program (2012) and invited researcher at the Graduate School of Manga (Kyoto Seika University, Japan, 2014–16). He also holds more than 70 group and solo exhibitions in galleries, museums and art contests, in both Spain and the international art scene. www.jsantiago.es

Ana Soler Baena (University of Vigo), editor

Dr. Ana Soler Baena is a visual artist, researcher and professor at the Fine Arts Faculty (Universidade de Vigo, Spain) since 2000. She holds a Degree in Design and Engraving, and a PhD in Fine Arts from the University of Seville. Throughout her artistic and research career, she has been involved with many international art institutions, such as the Kyoto City University of Art (Japan), the National Chiayi University (Taiwan), the Toronto York University (Canada), the École supérieure des arts decoratifs in Strasbourg (France), the Kupferstichkabinett Museum at Basel (Germany), the Heriot-Watt University College of Art at Edinburgh (United Kingdom) and the Scuola Internacionale di Gráfica d'Arte di Florencia (Italy), among others. Her artwork has been featured in many solo and group exhibitions, and can be found in private collections, as well as in public institutions and museums. She has also been granted numerous awards and distinctions, such as the National Printing Award at Calcografía Nacional (2001), Honorary Mention at the Liège Biennale, Fenosa International Grant (Kyoto), Academia de España (Rome), La filature (Ottawa), Fundació Pilar i Joan Miró (Mallorca), 10th National Engraving Award at the Museum of Contemporary Spanish Engraving (Marbella), First Prize at the IV International Iberoamerican Biennale (Cáceres), Lumen-Ex Digital Art Prize (Cáceres), 10th Seoul International Biennial of Engraving (Korea) and the First Prize Generación 2001 (Madrid), among many others. www.anasoler.es

Jaqueline Berndt (Stockholm University)

Dr. Jaqueline Berndt is presently Professor in Japanese Language and Culture at Stockholm University. From 1991 to 2016, she worked at Japanese universities, teaching courses on visual culture and popular arts in Japanese as well as English; eventually, she became Professor of Comics Theory at the Graduate School of Manga, Kyoto Seika University. Holding a first degree in Japanese Studies (1987) and a PhD in Aesthetics/Art Theory from Humboldt University Berlin (1991), her research has been informed by media aesthetics and focuses on manga as graphic narratives, anime and modern Japanese art. https://jberndt.net

Ida Kirkegaard (Stockholm University)

Ida Kirkegaard is a PhD candidate in Japanese Language and Culture at the department of Asian, Middle Eastern and Turkish Studies, Stockholm University. She holds an MA in Visual Culture and a BA in Japanese Studies from the University of Copenhagen. Her PhD research focuses on stillness, repetition and conventionality in TV anime, and she is particularly interested in the use of bank footage in the works of Kunihiko Ikuhara.

Heike Hoffer (The Ohio State University)

Heike Hoffer is a PhD candidate in musicology at The Ohio State University. Her doctoral thesis examines the relationship between Western classical music and anime in terms of the cultural landscape of modern Japan. Before starting her PhD, Heike spent five years teaching full-time in the Department of Music at the University of Texas Pan American (now the University of Texas Rio Grande Valley). Today, Heike lives in Tokyo, where she is conducting research and playing the oboe in various local ensembles.

Minori Ishida (Niigata University)

Dr. Ishida Minori is Professor at Niigata University and Co-director of the Archive Center for Anime Studies at Niigata University. Her research field is visual and audio cultures focusing on voice and gender in anime. She published *Hisoyaka na kyōiku: Yaoi-Boys Love zenshi* [*Secret Education: Prehistory of Yaoi and Boys Love*], which received the Abe Prize from Niigata University in 2009. Her English-language articles include 'Deviating Voices: Representation of Female Characters and Feminist Readings in 1990s Anime' (in *Image: Journal of Interdisciplinary Image Science*, 29) and "Sounds and Sighs: 'Voice Porn' for Women" (in *Shōjo across Media*, Palgrave, 2019).

Stevie Suan (Hosei University)

Dr. Stevie Suan is an Associate Professor at the Department of Global and Interdisciplinary Studies at Hosei University in Tokyo, Japan. His main area of expertise is in anime aesthetics, which he explores through conceptualizing the dynamics of different performance modes. In his recent work, he aims to develop anime research at the intersection of Media Studies, Asian Studies and Performance Studies. This is the topic of his book, *Anime's Identity: Performativity and Form beyond Japan* (University of Minnesota Press, 2021), which utilizes performance/performativity theory and media theory to approach issues of area studies (Japan Studies and Asian Studies), using anime as a prime example of the shifting currents of cultural production in our moment of globalization.

Manuel Hernández-Pérez (University of Salford)

Dr. Manuel Hernández-Pérez is Lecturer in Digital Media at the University of Salford, Manchester. From 2013 to 2020, he was Lecturer in Digital Design at the University of Hull (United Kingdom), where he led the UG program in Game & Entertainment Design (2015–18). He finished his PhD in Information Science and Communications at the University of Murcia (Spain) in 2013. He published *Manga, Anime and Videogames: Japanese Cross-Media Narrative* (PUZ, 2017) and coordinated *Japanese Media Cultures in Japan and Abroad: Transnational Consumption of Manga, Anime, and Media-Mixes* (MDPI, 2019). He is interested in transmedia narratology and cognitive approaches to Media Studies.

Zoltan Kacsuk (Stuttgart Media University)

Dr. Zoltan Kacsuk holds a doctoral degree in Manga Studies from Kyoto Seika University. He is currently a postdoctoral researcher at the Japanese Visual Media Graph project, Institute for Applied Artificial Intelligence, Stuttgart Media University.

Olga Kopylova (Tohoku University)

Dr. Olga Kopylova received a BA in translation (Japanese, English) at Irkutsk State Linguistic University and defended her PhD thesis on media mix and adaptations at the Graduate School of Manga Studies at Kyoto Seika University in 2016. She is currently employed as a translator and lecturer at Tohoku University Graduate School of Arts and Letters. Her research interests include comparative Media Studies, Fandom Studies, Adaptation Studies and Narratology of popular media texts. Furthermore, she regularly engages with Japanese manga as a reader, researcher and official translator (collaborating with Russian publisher Istari Comics).

Selen Çalık Bedir (Beykoz University)

Dr. Selen Çalık Bedir is an Assistant Professor at Beykoz University's Animation Department. She received her BA in English Language and Literature from Boğaziçi University (2008) and her MA in Comparative Literature from İstanbul Bilgi University (2010) in Turkey. From 2012 to 2017, she studied in Japan on a MEXT grant. After spending one year as a research student at Kyoto University (2012–13), she entered the PhD program in Manga Studies at Kyoto Seika University. She completed her PhD in 2017 with a thesis entitled *'Playing' Anime: A Comparative Media-Theoretical Approach to Anime as a Specific Medium*.

Jessica Bauwens-Sugimoto (Ryukoku University)

Dr. Jessica Bauwens-Sugimoto is Associate Professor at Ryukoku University, Kyoto, where she teaches at the Faculty of International

Studies, Department of Intercultural Communication, Arts & Media. She holds several MAs (Japanese Studies, Anthropology, Sociology) and a PhD in Humanities from Osaka University. Originally from Belgium, she currently teaches mainly Film Studies and Comics Studies, and her research interests are Cultural Studies, particularly applied to sequential art, film, fashion and gender.

Tatiana Lameiro-González (University of Vigo)

Tatiana Lameiro-González is a designer, visual artist and researcher. She is also a lecturer at the Fine Arts Faculty (Universidade de Vigo, Spain). She holds a degree in Fine Arts and a master's degree in Advertising Art Direction and Teaching, specialized in Art and Drawing. As a qualified professional with a broad experience in design and photography, her research focuses on the conceptualization of graphic and publishing design, photographic images and the boundaries between art and design. She is currently working as a researcher and Art Director at the dx5 digital & graphic art research group (Universidade de Vigo), specializing in expanded field contemporary graphic art.

Index

CPSIA information can be obtained
at www.ICGtesting.com
Printed in the USA
BVHW010259220322
632075BV00012B/254

9 789176 351673